JUSTICE IN LYON

Klaus Barbie and France's First Trial for Crimes against Humanity

The trial of former SS lieutenant and Gestapo chief Klaus Barbie was France's first trial for crimes against humanity. Known as the "Butcher of Lyon" during the Nazi occupation of that city from 1942 to 1944, Barbie tortured, deported, and murdered thousands of Jews and Resistance fighters. Following a lengthy investigation and the overcoming of numerous legal and other obstacles, the trial began in 1987 and attracted global attention.

Justice in Lyon is the first comprehensive history of the Barbie trial, including the investigation leading up to it, the legal background to the case, and the hurdles the prosecution had to clear in order to bring Barbie to justice. Richard J. Golsan examines the strategies used by the defence, the prosecution, and the lawyers who represented Barbie's many victims at the trial. The book draws from press coverage, articles, and books about Barbie and the trial published at the time, as well as recently released archival sources and the personal archives of lawyers at the trial.

Making the case that, despite the views of its many critics, the Barbie trial was a success in legal, historical, and pedagogical terms, *Justice in Lyon* details how the trial has had a positive impact on French and international law governing crimes against humanity.

RICHARD J. GOLSAN is a University Distinguished Professor of French at Texas A&M University.

Justice in Lyon

*Klaus Barbie and France's First Trial
for Crimes against Humanity*

RICHARD J. GOLSAN

UNIVERSITY OF TORONTO PRESS
Toronto Buffalo London

© University of Toronto Press 2022
Toronto Buffalo London
utorontopress.com
Printed in the U.S.A.

ISBN 978-1-4875-0644-5 (cloth)   ISBN 978-1-4875-3417-2 (EPUB)
ISBN 978-1-4875-4559-8 (paper)   ISBN 978-1-4875-3416-5 (PDF)

Library and Archives Canada Cataloguing in Publication

Title: Justice in Lyon : Klaus Barbie and France's first trial for crimes against
    humanity / Richard J. Golsan.
Names: Golsan, Richard Joseph, 1952– author.
Description: Includes bibliographical references and index.
Identifiers: Canadiana (print) 20210383933 | Canadiana (ebook) 20210383968 |
    ISBN 9781487506445 (cloth) | ISBN 9781487545598 (paper) |
    ISBN 9781487534172 (EPUB) | ISBN 9781487534165 (PDF)
Subjects: LCSH: Barbie, Klaus, 1913–1991 –Trials, litigation, etc. |
    LCSH: War crime trials – France – Lyon. | LCSH: War crimes
    investigation – France – Lyon. | LCSH: Crimes against humanity –
    France – Lyon. | LCSH: Holocaust, Jewish (1939–1945) – France. |
    LCSH: World War, 1939–1945 – Social aspects – France – Lyon.
Classification: LCC KJV133.B37 G65 2022 | DDC 341.6/90268445823–dc23

We wish to acknowledge the land on which the University of Toronto Press
operates. This land is the traditional territory of the Wendat, the Anishnaabeg,
the Haudenosaunee, the Métis, and the Mississaugas of the Credit First Nation.

University of Toronto Press acknowledges the financial support of the
Government of Canada, the Canada Council for the Arts, and the Ontario Arts
Council, an agency of the Government of Ontario, for its publishing activities.

Canada Council   Conseil des Arts
for the Arts   du Canada

ONTARIO ARTS COUNCIL
CONSEIL DES ARTS DE L'ONTARIO

an Ontario government agency
un organisme du gouvernement de l'Ontario

Funded by the   Financé par le
Government   gouvernement
of Canada   du Canada

Canadä

For Nancy,
For our granddaughter, Elouise Ines "Lou" Golsan,
For family and friends
With love and gratitude.

Contents

Illustrations   ix

Acknowledgments   xi

Introduction   3

1   Klaus Barbie: Nazi "Idealist"   29

2   The Historical Judicial Backdrop: From Nuremberg to the 1980 Cologne Trial of Kurt Lischka, Herbert Hagen, and Ernst Heinrichson   51

3   The Investigation: War Crimes, Crimes against Humanity, and the Long Road to Compromise   79

4   The Barbie Trial Begins: Opening Rituals and the Departure of the Accused   111

5   The Witnesses   140

6   The Civil Parties and Prosecution Make Their Case   181

7   Barbie's Defence Takes Centre Stage   211

Conclusion   237

Chronology   257

A Note on the Sources   263

Notes   267

Bibliography   293

Index   301

Illustrations

The palais de justice in Lyon, France 2
Klaus Barbie's cell in Montluc Prison   28
The Izieu telegram   78
President André Cerdini and his two associate judges or
    "assessors"   110
The Resistance survivor and trial witness Lise Lesèvre   142
The Jewish survivor and trial witness Simone
    Kadosche-Lagrange   143
Serge Klarsfeld in 2016   182
Pierre Truche   183
Jacques Vergès in 1989   210
A memorial marking the location of the "Baraque aux juifs"
    in the courtyard of Montluc Prison   236

Acknowledgments

This book has been more than four years in the making. During that time, I have benefitted enormously from the help and support of colleagues, friends, and family. I would like to thank them here. First, I wish to thank Serge Klarsfeld for generously sharing with me his archives of the trial, consisting primarily of the extensive documentation developed by the investigating magistrate Christian Riss during the lengthy *instruction* or investigation of the case. Klarsfeld was also generous with his time, answering my questions about the case with patience and clarity. I would also like to thank Alain Lévy, who generously met with me in Paris in summer 2016 to discuss Klaus Barbie, the Barbie trial, and the subsequent trials of French collaborators also on charges of crimes against humanity. Both Klarsfeld and Lévy were civil parties lawyers during the Barbie trial.

I am grateful as well to the several institutions who have supported my research over the years and generously provided funding for the publication of this book. At Texas A&M University, I wish to thank Andrew Natsios and the Scowcroft Institute in the Bush School of Government and Public Service. I would also like Stefanie Harris and the Department of International Studies as well as and the France/TAMU Institute (*centre d'excellence*).

I also wish to recognize and thank several institutions that have made the research and writing of this book possible. First, a semester leave sponsored by the Glasscock Center for Humanities Research at Texas A&M in Spring 2020 allowed me to focus exclusively on writing the manuscript. The United States Holocaust Memorial Museum generously made available to me the entire written transcript of the Barbie trial. I also made several fruitful research trips to the *Archives du Rhône* in Lyon. Visiting and exploring that beautiful city is rich compensation for studying and writing about the terrible crimes committed there by Klaus Barbie and his colleagues during the "Dark Years" of World War II.

I also wish to thank dear friends and colleagues who at various points were instrumental in bringing this book to fruition. Annette Lévy-Willard, a journalist at *Libération* and expert on France's trials for crimes against humanity, offered timely insights and introduced me to Serge Klarsfeld. Henry Rousso and Lynn Higgins read multiple drafts of the manuscript and offered continuous and much-needed criticism and encouragement. Without them, this book would not have seen the light of day. Pascal Bruckner also read the manuscript, sharing valuable insights with me as well.

As I began researching the Barbie trial, I was invited to speak about it by colleagues and Yale University and the University of Chichester in the UK. I wish to thank Maurice Samuels and Alice Kaplan at Yale and Hugo Frey and Andrew Smith at Chichester for their generosity and warm welcome. I enjoyed both visits immensely.

While researching *Justice in Lyon* I was fortunate to have a wonderful undergraduate assistant, Emily Scott. Emily did a masterful job of preparing a detailed table of contents of the files Serge Klarsfeld shared with me. Emily's outline proved invaluable during the writing of the manuscript. I also wish to thank Baile Dobson and Ede Hilton-Lowe for preparing the final manuscript for submission.

There are many other colleagues and friends on both sides of the Atlantic whose knowledge, intellectual curiosity, and generosity have been inspirational to me. I would like to mention them here. In France, these include Marc and Sylvie Dambre, Stéphane Audouin-Rouzeau, Hélène Dumas, Nicholas Werth, Jean-Jacques Fleury, Ludi Boeken, and Pat and Hervé Picton. In the UK Chris and Joan Flood have been wonderful friends for decades. In this country, I would especially like to thank Susan Suleiman, Phil Watts, Leah Hewitt, Mary Jean Green, Lex McMillan, Van and Mary Kelly, Alfred Reid, and Tom and Inès Hilde. In Bryan-College Station, Terry Anderson, Rose Eder, Larry Reynolds, Susan Egenolf, Nathan Bracher, Brian Harley, Stefanie Harris, Melanie Hawthorne, Sarah Misemer, and Bob Shandley have shared their ideas and generous friendship for many years. While I was writing this book during the height of the COVID-19 pandemic, playing tennis and learning from expert coaches and friends kept me going, so I would like to thank Jamie and Jacy Smith and Alberto Bautista for their excellence and patience.

Three anonymous readers of the manuscript of this book in draft form offered tremendous suggestions for improvement, for which I am deeply grateful. Stephen Shapiro at University of Toronto Press has been a wonderful and patient editor, keeping me on track and encouraging me all along the way.

Finally, I want to thank my family: Nancy, James and Julie, Jody, Ashley and Lou, Maryanne, Katie, and Sonia, and last but not least Jawad, Ruthie, and Rocko. They are constant inspirations.

JUSTICE IN LYON

Klaus Barbie and France's First Trial for
Crimes against Humanity

The palais de justice in Lyon, France. Photograph by Richard Golsan

Introduction

Shortly after midnight on Saturday, 4 July 1987, in the Lyon Assize Court where former SS lieutenant Klaus Barbie was on trial for crimes against humanity dating from World War II and the German Occupation of France, the bailiff rose and ordered those present in the courtroom to be seated. The trial that was about to conclude was France's first trial for crimes against humanity. The assembled crowd of several hundred, including lawyers for the defence and prosecution, court recorders, security officers, witnesses, victims and their relatives, French and foreign journalists, and spectators from Lyon and around the world quickly resumed their places in the massive, makeshift courtroom. Outside, on the steps of the *Palais de Justice*, an imposing, Corinthian-columned building on the banks of the Saône River, a large crowd of spectators awaiting the verdict fell silent. Back inside, a small bell announcing the return of the judges and jury began to ring. The bailiff then stated simply, "la cour!" – "the court!" All present rose in unison as the judge – the *président* of the Assize court in the French judicial system – his two assistant judges, or "assessors," and nine jurors entered the courtroom. Sorj Chalandon, a reporter for the Parisian newspaper *Libération*, wrote that whether it was due to the artificial lighting or the "suffocating heat" of the courtroom, the faces of the judges and jury shared the "pallor of enormous fatigue."[1]

The president of the Assize court, André Cerdini, an avuncular man who had calmly guided the trial through eight weeks of occasionally contentious and even tumultuous proceedings, ordered the accused brought into the courtroom. For a fifth and final time, a small visibly aged Klaus Barbie, in need of a haircut and wearing an ill-fitting black suit and tie, was escorted into the packed courtroom by his guards. As Barbie's handcuffs were being removed, he nodded at his defence counsel seated in front of him and exchanged a few words with the translator next to him. President Cerdini then asked "defendant Klaus Barbie" to stand for the judgment and sentence to be read. Barbie adjusted his tie, rose, and buttoned his suit jacket, his face impassive.

Following French judicial procedure, Cerdini read out the verdict of the jury. The latter had been asked to respond to 340 questions pertaining to specific charges against Barbie and one question concerning the possibility of extenuating circumstances in favour of the accused. On all counts, Cerdini announced to the accused and to the hushed courtroom, Barbie had been found guilty by "a majority of eight votes at least" out of the twelve votes cast. (In the Assize system, the three judges deliberate and vote with the jury. See chapter four here.) Citing the appropriate French and international statutes applicable to Barbie's crimes, as well as those statutes in the French Criminal Code pertaining to punishment for these crimes, Cerdini then briefly described the three major crimes against humanity of which Barbie had been found guilty. The first crime was organizing the arrest and deportation of some eighty-four Jewish refugees at the headquarters of the *Union Générale des Israélites de France* (UGIF) on the Rue Sainte-Catherine, a tiny Lyon backstreet, on 9 February 1943. The second was the arrest and deportation of forty-three Jewish children, aged six to fourteen, and six adult teachers and other personnel from a Jewish school in the hamlet of Izieu near Lyon on 6 April 1944 (one child and one adult worker at the school escaped deportation). The third crime against humanity was the deportation on 11 August 1944 of several hundred Jews and Resistance fighters by train to concentration and death camps to the East. The train was the last deportation train to leave German-occupied Lyon during the war.

At 12:40 a.m., Cerdini concluded his statement by informing Barbie that he was sentenced to life in prison. Cerdini added that in accordance with French law, Barbie had five days to file an appeal. Cerdini then thanked and dismissed the jury and announced the criminal trial concluded, to be followed immediately by the civil trial. Quite spontaneously, loud applause and cheers broke out in the courtroom, interrupted repeatedly by Cerdini's calls for silence and "a little dignity." Through it all Klaus Barbie remained impassive, his eyes cast down in front of him for the most part. At one point he stifled a yawn, clearly one of fatigue rather than boredom.

Instead of attending Barbie's civil trial,[3] which he left to his defence co-counsel, Barbie's lawyer, Jacques Vergès, exited the courtroom to make a statement to the assembled crowd and press from the top steps of the *Palais de Justice*. This Vergès did against the strong advice of journalists and others, who were well aware of the crowd's animosity towards the lawyer and his client. Tempers were high following the verdict, exacerbated by the extraordinary heat that continued well past midnight in Lyon that night. As Vergès addressed the press and assembled crowd, cameramen, journalists taking notes or holding microphones to record the defence lawyer's words, and even security forces were jostled violently. Initially undeterred, Vergès announced the conviction and sentence of Barbie. Then, referring to Barbie's Nazi predecessors and superiors tried at Nuremberg and elsewhere, many of whose criminal responsibility exceeded Barbie's own but who received lighter sentences than he, Vergès concluded ironically: "Clearly, we are surpassing our masters in these matters."

Insults and threats from the crowd grew louder. Obscene gestures were aimed in Vergès's direction. As the crowd violence increased, Vergès was spat upon and spattered with eggs, punches were thrown, and security forces began to use their nightsticks. The danger increasing, Vergès was hurried back inside the *Palais de Justice*, to depart later by a different exit. As Sorj Chalandon wrote, Vergès finally had his *lynchage*, or "lynching." Chalandon added: "a real one, an ugly one" (149). This, Chalandon noted, was exactly what Vergès had claimed the Barbie trial to be all along. Following Vergès's departure, the crowd finally began to disperse. Chalandon wrote that laughter now replaced the anger that shortly before had "tightened the throats" of those who had waited outside for the verdict.

The Barbie trial, an historic event that had garnered national and international attention for months, was over. Justice, it appeared, had been served, not only for the accused but for dozens of his victims. Many of these victims had waited forty years and more to confront their tormentor in a court of law. Four years of judicial investigations and conflicting court decisions had passed since Barbie's arrest in Bolivia and expulsion to France in February 1983, and two months of courtroom deliberations and testimony had resulted in the conviction of the man most in France knew as the "Butcher of Lyon." Barbie had earned the label for the wartime torture, imprisonment, murder, and/or deportation of thousands of Resistance fighters and Jews alike in Lyon and in the surrounding region. With Barbie's conviction, what the renowned medieval historian Emmanuel Leroy-Ladurie had predicted after Barbie's arrest and expulsion would be an "enormous national psychodrama, a psychoanalytic cure at a national level"[4] – if that had in fact occurred – was concluded. In early July 1987, the summer vacation season in France was just getting underway. Barbie, his crimes, and his trial now seemed – happily, at least for some – a successfully concluded case, a thing of the past.[5]

Justice in Lyon: Klaus Barbie and France's First Trial for Crimes against Humanity is a history of the 1987 trial of Klaus Barbie in Lyon, France's first and most historic trial for crimes against humanity. In addition to an exploration of the proceedings themselves, this book examines the lengthy, four-year-long investigation leading up to the trial as well as earlier trials in France and elsewhere that together form the Barbie trial's judicial "backdrop." Finally, *Justice in Lyon* examines the Barbie trial's subsequent impact on France's legal and judicial reckoning with its troubled recent history and the legacies of Nazism and France's wartime collaboration with Hitler. In the wake of Nuremberg, the trial of Adolph Eichmann in Jerusalem in 1961, and the 1963–5 trial of former Auschwitz guards in Frankfurt, the Barbie trial stands out as one of the great historical trials of former Nazis, reflecting the post-war world's efforts to come to terms with Nazism's horrific and unprecedented crimes.

In France, the Barbie trial constitutes what Pierre Nora has labelled *un lieu de mémoire*, a crucial "place of memory" in the French national psyche. Indeed, the Barbie trial marked a major turning point when, for most French and certainly for French media, the nation's focus on the so-called Dark Years of the Nazi occupation shifted away from the history of Resistance heroes and their martyrdom to the memory of the Jewish victims, Hitler's Final Solution, and Vichy France's complicity in that crime. Before the trial began, Barbie was most widely recognized as the Nazi responsible for the death of France's greatest Resistance hero, Jean Moulin, whose remains are interred in the *Panthéon* in Paris, along with other French national heroes. By the end of the trial, Barbie's role in the Holocaust, and especially his role in the arrest and deportation of the children of Izieu had assumed centre stage.[6] Despite claims to the contrary, also in the limelight in the courtroom and after the conclusion of the trial was the role played by Barbie's French accomplices and collaborators. Indeed, had the Barbie trial not taken place, two subsequent trials of the Frenchmen Paul Touvier and Maurice Papon, also tried on charges of crimes against humanity for complicity in the Holocaust, would likely not have occurred. Having tried and convicted a Nazi in a French courtroom for crimes against humanity, it would have appeared hypocritical in the extreme for the French judicial system *not* to try Frenchmen who were complicit in similar crimes during the Occupation. In fact, the crimes of Touvier, Papon, and other Frenchmen involved in the Nazi Final Solution of the Jewish Question were well-known by some at the time of the Barbie trial. Several civil parties lawyers referred to them directly in the Lyon courtroom. The civil parties lawyer Alain Lévy went so far as to call for the prosecution of these Frenchmen following Barbie's anticipated conviction in his *plaidoirie* or closing argument before the court.[7]

***

Why write a book about the Barbie trial now, more than thirty years after its conclusion? First, and most importantly, no comprehensive history of the Barbie trial has been written in any language to date. This makes the Barbie trial unique among all the great historical trials of Nazis. There are dozens and dozens of books on the Nuremberg and Eichmann trials, and new books on these trials appear in English as well as other languages on a regular basis. Important books in English have also appeared recently on other trials of Nazis, from the Auschwitz trials to the trial of John Demjanyuk, a small fry by comparison with Klaus Barbie. Indeed, even the subsequent trials for crimes against humanity in France of French collaborators with the Nazis Paul Touvier and Maurice Papon, "sequels," as noted to the Barbie trial, have had more coverage in book form certainly in English than the Barbie trial.[8]

In part at least, the absence of a history of the Barbie trial can be attributed to the lack of public access to the trial archives and to the video recording of the trial. Inspired by the example of the Eichmann trial, the filming of the Barbie trial was ordered by the minister of justice at the time, Robert Badinter. In ordering the filming of the trial Badinter also mandated that the film not be viewed by the public for thirty years. But in summer 2017, this lack of access to archival materials related to the Barbie trial changed dramatically. In accordance with French law and at the behest of president Emmanuel Macron, the court records of the trial, held at the *Archives du Rhône* in Lyon, were opened to researchers for the first time. (As a rule, trial records of criminal cases in France are kept in the local archives where these crimes took place.) Additionally, in summer 2017, the *Mémorial de la Shoah* in Paris received permission as part of an exhibit on the Barbie trial to make available to spectators who wished to see the video recording of the entire courtroom proceedings. (Seventy hours of trial footage had previously been shown on French television in 2000, and twenty hours were made available on DVDs by *Arte Editions* in 2011 – see A Note on the Sources here). Following the closure of the exhibit, the *Mémorial de la Shoah* continued to make the film available to scholars in the video research centre at the *Mémorial.*

In researching and writing *Justice in Lyon* I have benefited from these two newly available resources. I have profited as well from access to two additional sources related to the trial and the four-year-long *instruction* or investigation that preceded it carried out by the young investigating magistrate Christian Riss. The first of these additional sources is the complete transcript of the trial recorded by court stenographers. That transcript can be found in the archives of the United States Holocaust Memorial Museum in Washington, DC. Because to a significant degree there is a *performative* dimension to any trial, and certainly to historic trials like the Barbie trial, it is helpful to view the film of the proceedings in concert with reading the transcript. The former allows the observer to get a sense of the impact and effectiveness of witness testimony as well as interventions and statements by lawyers, prosecutors, etc. The latter generally allows for the verification of what was said in court and gives a better sense of the structure of the arguments and intellectual sources of the arguments made. Given that French lawyers and magistrates, certainly in the Barbie trial, were well versed in France's humanistic culture, often citing iconic writers and philosophers in making their arguments – Albert Camus, André Gide, and the moral philosopher Vladimir Janké-lévitch were favourites – reading the transcript allows one to better appreciate the intellectual roots as well as the artistry of their pleas.

The second source consists of the dossiers of the *instruction* or investigation of the case carried out by investigating magistrate Riss very generously made available to me by the famous Nazi hunter, historian, and lawyer Serge Klarsfeld. Klarsfeld served as one of the principal civil parties lawyers at the trial, representing the children of Izieu deported to their deaths at Auschwitz. Indeed, without Serge Klarsfeld and his German-born wife, Beate, there would have been no 1987 trial of Klaus Barbie for crimes against humanity. The role of the Klarsfelds in the years leading up to that trial and Serge Klarsfeld's role during the trial itself will be discussed in the following pages. As one might imagine, the documents in Klarsfeld's files provided the author with a privileged "behind-the-scenes" perspective on what would emerge later in court. For example, numerous interviews with the accused and "confrontations" with his victims in the presence of magistrate Riss as well as lawyers for the defence and prosecution afford a harrowing, indeed terrifying, glimpse of the extraordinary criminality of the accused and of Nazism itself. Both would be revealed even more shockingly in the Lyon courtroom.

A second and related reason for writing a comprehensive history of the Barbie trial now is the fact that of the works about the Barbie case appearing over the past thirty-five years, many if not most focus primarily on Klaus Barbie the man and not on his trial.[9] Some of these works centre on Barbie, the SS killer in Lyon, as well as the historic circumstances of his crimes in occupied France. Others concentrate on Barbie, the post-war American intelligence agent in occupied Germany, or the friend of South American, and specifically Bolivian, dictators. Some focus on all of the above. In virtually all these works, however, the trial itself is treated as little more than the logical culmination point of Barbie's trajectory. Moreover, in many instances, Barbie's conviction is dismissed as a foregone conclusion, or worse. In *An Uncertain Hour* the American journalist Ted Morgan harshly described the trial as "a necessary travesty" because, from the outset, there was "an enormous presumption of guilt."[10] In all these works, the *real story* of Klaus Barbie, so to speak, plays out elsewhere, outside the courtroom. As a recent example of this phenomenon, Peter Hammerschmidt's *Klaus Barbie: Nom de Code: Adler* is a richly documented account of Barbie's post-war work for the CIA in Europe and in South America, where Barbie, his wife, and two children arrived in 1951. It also details Barbie's links to the Federal Republic of Germany's intelligence services and to South American dictators. Hammerschmidt's book devotes only six of three hundred pages to Barbie's trial.

Why the narrow focus on Barbie the individual and his long history of criminal activities and intelligence work, to the exclusion of his historic 1987 trial in Lyon? One fairly obvious explanation is that, at least since the Eichmann trial and Hannah Arendt's controversial and influential account of the accused as an exemplar of the "banality of evil" in *Eichmann in Jerusalem*, Nazi killers and the kind of evil they represent have been a subject of scholarly as well as general interest and even fascination. Indeed, given this reality it should not be surprising that there have been many more post-war trials of ex-Nazis than of Japanese war criminals, for example. And while Barbie was no Eichmann either in terms of his role and function in the Nazi hierarchy or in terms of the performance he gave (or more accurately, did not give) in court, for many he *did* represent some form of evil incarnate, if not the same form represented by Eichmann. Barbie's victims, and even his wartime collaborators, characterized him as a "jackal," a "sadist," in short, a demonically inhuman creature. In his closing statement before the court, Vergès described his client as "tailor-" or "custom-made devil" (Chalandon 147). As such, Barbie was a source of extraordinary repulsion and also fascination. Indeed, when Barbie announced his refusal to attend the trial after the third day, courtroom audiences thinned out considerably, and many French observers and foreign journalists left the trial and Lyon, not to return.

Another source of Barbie's sinister "appeal" was his Cold War work for American intelligence and later for brutal right-wing dictators in Bolivia. These connections, in fact, are crucial components of Marcel Ophuls's 1989 Academy Award–winning film *Hôtel Terminus: The Life and Times of Klaus Barbie*, as they are of other books and documentary films. Barbie's work for the American Central Intelligence Corps (CIC) between 1947 and 1951 has stoked interest as well as controversy. When Barbie's work for the CIC became public knowledge in the early 1980s, the US State Department commissioned a report by federal prosecutor Allan Ryan, which, when issued, included a recommendation by Ryan that the US government apologize to the French for shielding Barbie from them when he worked for the CIC. That apology was later made. [11]

Finally, for some critics, Barbie the man overshadowed his trial because in that trial he was a symbol of, or scapegoat for, something larger still: Western democratic governments that expediently used criminal sorts like Barbie for "democratic purposes," only to cast them aside and leave them exposed to prosecution when they were no longer useful. In Kevin Macdonald's 2007 film about Barbie, *Mon meilleur ennemi*, following documentary footage of Barbie's conviction in Lyon, former US congresswoman Elizabeth Holtzman cites the example of Barbie to denounce America's practice of hiring extremists and not "democrats" for covert political ends. If the ends justify the means, if one can use Nazi war criminals for "democratic" purposes, Holtzman asks, then "Where do you draw the line, ever?" The British journalist and historian Neal Ascherson, who co-authored a book on Klaus Barbie,[12] echoes Holtzman's views in Macdonald's film. He voices his disgust for "the modern world," in which states hire the likes of Barbie, only to disavow them when they are no longer useful. For Ascherson, Barbie's conviction bespoke hypocrisy rather than justice.

In addition to the fact that interest in Klaus Barbie the Nazi, the American intelligence operative, and *eminence grise* of South American dictators dwarfs interest in his 1987 trial in many books, articles, and documentaries about the former Nazi, there is another reason to write a comprehensive history of the trial at present. Most scholarly and popular works that *do* focus on the Barbie trial all too often miscast or mischaracterize the trial and/or dismiss it as a failure in accordance with preconceived ideas and biases. These negative assessments of the trial have proven persistent, continuing into the new century.[13] Moreover, even before the proceedings in Lyon got underway, many critics dismissed the very idea of a trial of Klaus Barbie as too risky, or as a propaganda exercise, or as not worth the effort for a variety of reasons. Some of these views have proven tenacious as well. Among the more dubious, or what the reporter Pierre Mérindol described as "vulgar,"[14] of the latter was the argument born of fear that Barbie and his lawyers would put the Resistance itself on trial, thereby destroying what amounted to a sacred national myth. Rumour had it that Barbie had arrived from South America with "suitcases of incriminating archives" against the Resistance.[15] When revealed in court, these imaginary documents would compromise the good name of France's wartime Resistance, its "Army of the Night," once and for all. Indeed, Vergès had stoked such fears almost from the moment of Barbie's 1983 arrest. In the media he had himself brought false accusations against living members of the Resistance for betraying their fellows to Barbie during the war. Vergès was eventually sued by the former *résistants* in question for libel. He was found guilty very shortly before the trial began.[16]

Another reason given not to hold the Barbie trial at all was that it "cost too much money" and that that money could better be spent elsewhere. On the other hand, some dismissed the trial as of no real interest, certainly for the majority of French at the time. For example, in a strangely conceived *procès/roman* or "trial/novel" appearing in 1987 entitled *Monsieur Barbie n'a rien à dire* ("Mister Barbie Has Nothing to Say"), Bertrand Poirot-Delpech argued that the French people were more interested in the French Open tennis tournament occurring in late May and early June than they were in the trial in Lyon. The latter was simply less entertaining. When it came to "Noah" (Yannick Noah, France's great tennis champion at the time) versus "Shoah," or the Holocaust, at the heart of the trial in Lyon, Delpech wrote, the former easily carried the day.[17]

Other arguments given against holding the trial were more overtly political. These were predictable, especially given the historical backdrop of Barbie's arrest as well as the political context surrounding the trial itself. Barbie's arrest and expulsion from Bolivia had been engineered in part by Régis Debray, a leftist intellectual and revolutionary who had fought alongside Che Guevara in South America. Later, Debray became an influential advisor to president François Mitterrand. In exchange for expelling Barbie, the newly elected leftist Bolivian government had been handsomely rewarded by the French government. While some, including Vergès, criticized the mercenary nature of the transaction in court, others, especially Mitterrand's critics on the right, dismissed the trial of Klaus Barbie in advance as essentially a political ploy. They argued that the trial constituted a dubious spectacle staged to allow Mitterrand and the Socialists to claim their share of the mantle of the Resistance, long the exclusive domain of the Gaullists and the French Communist Party. Along the same lines, four years after the conclusion of the trial, in the provocatively titled book-length interview *Le salaud lumineux* ("The Luminous Bastard"), Vergès also maintained that the Barbie trial was essentially political. Except that for Vergès, in foregrounding the sufferings of Jews during the Holocaust, the Barbie trial had also been a sop to France's Jewish vote, also engineered by Mitterrand and his cronies.[18]

If the views of many of the French right were harshly dismissive of the trial before it began, for the extreme right the trial of Klaus Barbie was much worse in the abstract and in the reality of the trial's aftermath as well. In probably the most repugnant, not to say toxic, essay about the Barbie trial appearing shortly after its conclusion, André Chelain's *Le procès Barbie, ou la Shoah-Business à Lyon* (The Barbie Trial, or Shoah Business in Lyon) offered a sweeping denunciation of the Barbie trial. It was, Chelain wrote, just one more example of "Shoah Business," the exploitation of the Holocaust by Jews for their own benefit, financial and otherwise. Moreover, like Nuremberg, the Barbie trial was also a distasteful display of the "justice of the victors," where the accused had "no chance" of receiving justice. Barbie, Chelain maintained, was just a sickly old man – a view echoed by many of the trial's more moralistic critics – and the victim of a judicial and media "lynching." Chelain also claimed that Barbie in fact knew nothing about the fate of those he deported, a crucial point if he were to be convicted of crimes against humanity.

As for the witnesses for the prosecution, they were hardly believable, or pulled out of a Pandora's box at the last minute. Their testimony, Chelain argued, was "surrealistic" and worse. In the case of some Jewish victims, Chelain argued, echoing Hannah Arendt's controversial claim in *Eichmann in Jerusalem*, their deportation was the fault of other Jews, not Barbie.[19] As for Resistance witnesses like Mario Blardonne, who testified that he had seen one of Barbie's police dogs mount one of his female torture victims, Chelain speculated that Blardonne must have read a lot of pornographic literature. He concluded, "This gentleman (Blardonne) does not seem to be of Italian origin for nothing."[20]

If all of this were not problematic enough in Chelain's view, much of the crucial material evidence used by the prosecution was no more reliable than the witnesses' testimony. It was artificial, ginned up by the prosecution and civil parties lawyers, with the complicity of the archives of the *Mémorial de la Shoah* in Paris.[21]

Chelain revealed his true colours as a Holocaust denier, or what the French call a "negationist" in referring to the "bigger lies" that lay behind the "obfuscations" of the Lyon trial. These, he believed, needed to be exposed rather than covered up. The lies in question included the "myth" of the gas chambers, the six million Jewish dead, etc. Chelain cited approvingly an earlier French Holocaust denier, Maurice Bardèche, who had written in *Nuremberg ou la terre promise* (1950) (Nuremberg, or the Promised Land) that the Allies had their own reasons to propagate and maintain the lie of the Holocaust. They needed to cover up their own horrific crimes, specifically the aerial bombardment of Germany that destroyed entire cities and killed hundreds of thousands of innocent civilians.

By its very nature and inspiration *Le procès Barbie, ou la Shoah Business à Lyon* would not attract a large (or historically literate) audience. More to the point, it would not be worth discussing in detail here, were it not for the fact that the trial of Klaus Barbie occurred, as noted, against the backdrop of the resurgence of Holocaust denialism in France in the late 1970s and 1980s. Indeed, many saw the Barbie trial as a prophylactic measure against that dangerous trend. The publication of the then obscure French literature professor Robert Faurisson's "negationist" tracts in the pages of *Le monde* in the late 1970s was still fresh in the minds of many. The controversy surrounding Faurisson had sucked in distinguished historians like Pierre Vidal-Naquet and the American activist Noam Chomsky, who took diametrically opposed positions on the publication of Holocaust denial materials. (To the consternation of many, Chomsky defended Faurisson in the name of "free speech.") Moreover, along with the renewal of the historical revisionism of this sort, the extreme right had received new life in France in the 1980s in the growth and visibility of Jean-Marie Le Pen's National Front. In fact, the two phenomena made common cause when Le Pen provocatively declared in September 1987, a few months after the conclusion of the Barbie trial, that the gas chambers were a "minor detail in the history of World War II."[22] Certainly those in the Lyon Assize Court in May, June, and July 1987 were aware that in dealing with Nazism, Nazi crimes, and the Holocaust in trying Klaus Barbie, they were not dealing with the past alone but with issues that were very much *de l'actualité* – "of the present." Indeed, as the proceedings got underway at the *Palais de Justice* in Lyon protesters, including neo-Nazis, Holocaust deniers, and other right-wing extremists, demanded Barbie's release as they marched in the streets outside. It is worth noting that in France today the extreme right, anti-Semitism, and negationism have hardly disappeared. Indeed, where the French far right is concerned, they are resurgent. At least arguably, this makes recalling the Barbie trial and the historical and political circumstances surrounding it all the more relevant in the present.

As opposed to André Chelain's ideologically driven screed, the more substantive of the critical assessments of the Barbie trial written or voiced after its conclusion focused on the structure of an Assize court trial or on two crucial legal decisions which profoundly affected, and for some critics fatally compromised, the trial from or near its outset. Outside France, and in particular in the Anglophone world, where the structure and nature of criminal proceedings are so different,[23] it is not surprising that in assessing the Barbie trial the vagaries, if not the outright failings, of French criminal law and procedures came into play in criticisms made. For example, in the UK, the aforementioned Neal Ascherson was interviewed on the BBC radio program *Meridian* on 18 July 1987 about the BBC television dramatization of the trial that aired in the UK shortly after the trial's conclusion in France. In the interview Ascherson did express his disappointment with the BBC performance. But rather than criticize the British production and actors, Ascherson blamed the French Assize court system instead.[24] He explained that, unlike the adversarial trial system in which crucial testimony occurs in the courtroom itself and where lawyers duel with each other across the courtroom, in the French system that testimony is given during the *instruction* or investigation of the case (often in so-called confrontations between witnesses and the accused). Moreover, once the trial begins, opposing counsel do not face off and debate one another in the Assize courtroom, as this is not permitted by procedural rules. As a result, a French Assize trial, Ascherson maintained, is given to "oratory" and "ego contests" by the lawyers rather than to dramatic revelations and confrontations. Admittedly, there was no dramatic episode in the Barbie trial comparable to the moment in the 1995 murder trial of former American football star O.J. Simpson, when Simpson tried on a glove found near the crime scene and it appeared not to fit. For many, including jury members, this confirmed Simpson's innocence.

For Ascherson, the Barbie trial itself was sadly just "a play within a play," as in Shakespeare's *Hamlet.* The real action occurred "offstage." It transpired not in the Lyon courtroom but in the corridors of the *Palais de Justice* or on the steps outside. During the Barbie trial, as noted, large crowds gathered regularly outside the *Palais de Justice.* Vergès in particular was fond of pleading his case there. Moreover, in a "symbolic trial" such as the Barbie trial, the real drama, Ascherson maintained, played out in the heads of the spectators and the French people themselves. Under these circumstances, it was impossible for a television reenactment, so deliberately faithful to "the original," so to speak, to provide real drama for its viewers.

As for the two legal decisions that for some critics fatally compromised the Barbie trial, the first decision was taken before the 1987 Assize court trial began, while the second was made shortly after the trial got underway. In December 1985, under pressure from groups representing Resistance members and their families, the French Court of Cassation – France's supreme court – opted to modify the definition of crimes against humanity under French law, allowing *some crimes* against members of the French Resistance to figure among the crimes against humanity with which Klaus Barbie was charged. Moreover, the court maintained, crimes against humanity under French law could *only* be committed on behalf of a "regime practicing a politics of ideological hegemony." The decision caused consternation, controversy, and even outrage at the time. Later, during the trial itself, it had the effect of creating tensions and disagreements among the civil parties lawyers, some representing Barbie's Jewish victims and others representing his Resistance victims. Vergès and Barbie's defence team tried to exploit these tensions and disagreements to disrupt the trial. As president Cerdini and prosecutor Pierre Truche well understood, if Vergès was successful in exploiting these divisions, the trial itself could implode.[25]

Then, on 13 May 1987, the third day of the Assize court trial in Lyon, apparently at the behest of Vergès (who slipped the accused a note shortly before he spoke), Barbie announced that he would no longer attend his own trial. The reason he gave was that the trial was illegal because he had been illegally expelled from Bolivia. In the Assize court system, the accused has the right not to attend his trial, although the presiding judge or president of the court on his or her own initiative can force the accused to be present. In the moment, Barbie's announcement created a storm of protest among civil parties lawyers. After a recess, during which he consulted with his assistant judges or assessors, president Cerdini allowed Barbie to absent himself except when witnesses who had not confronted Barbie during the pre-trial investigation testified.[26] When those witnesses testified, the accused would be required to return to the courtroom. In subsequent sessions of the trial, president Cerdini opened the proceedings by verifying with Barbie's guards that their captive had refused to appear in court that day. Cerdini then ordered that the accused be kept apprised of what transpired in the courtroom in his absence. As a consequence, trial hearings most often began with a monotonous ritual that belied the drama of the courtroom testimony and exchanges that often followed.

Among those critics who argued that the December 1985 Court of Cassation decision to include Resistance fighters as victims of crimes against humanity essentially doomed the Barbie trial in historic as well as symbolic terms, Guyora Binder offered the most thorough and thoughtful analysis in an essay appearing in the *Yale Law Review* in 1989. In his essay Binder stated first that limiting crimes against humanity committed against Resistance fighters to a regime practising a "politics of ideological hegemony," i.e. Nazi Germany and, implicitly at least, *not* France, meant that the Barbie trial would inevitably foreground "French humanity by contrast with Nazi inhumanity."[27] Moreover, given the law's insistence on "ideological hegemony," the prosecution was obliged to focus exclusively on Nazi *ideology* as opposed to the entire complex of factors that actually led to the Holocaust and the participation of figures like Barbie in it. In so doing, according to Binder, the prosecution attributed greater consistency and coherence to Nazi thought than "may be appropriate" (1344).[28]

The most egregious consequence of the 1985 decision for Binder, however, was that in casting Jews and Resistance fighters alike as victims and martyrs of Barbie's crimes against humanity, it obliged the prosecution in the courtroom to stress the fundamental *innocence* of *all the victims* over the guilt of the accused. In so doing, according to Binder, it cast "the millions as martyrs." Consequently, the Holocaust was presented as "a vast sacrifice that would finally redeem the world from violence." The Barbie trial itself became its "dramatic reenactment, in which the dead died, not in vain, but for our moral instruction." Ultimately, the symbolism of the Barbie trial "was more sacrificial than judicial" (1346). Binder concluded: "From a Christian perspective, this use of the dead as a sacrificial symbol may be legitimate; but Jews should greet this redemption of irredeemable suffering with ambivalence" (1346).[29] In *One, by One, by One*, published three years after the trial's conclusion, the American journalist and writer Judith Miller also argued that the Barbie trial was essentially a failure, but for a different reason. In Miller's view this was a direct consequence of president Cerdini's decision on day three of the trial to allow the accused to absent himself from the courtroom. Consequently the ends of justice could not be and were not served. Miller argued that even though Cerdini was acting in accordance with French law in allowing Barbie to leave his own trial, he had committed an egregious error: "By removing himself Barbie made sure that Frenchmen would not be able to search his eyes for hatred for Jews (he said that he had none). They would not be able to watch the men and women he had tortured and humiliated confront him with their survival. They would not be able to look for any sign of revulsion about the crimes he had committed so long ago or for any sense of remorse."[30] Miller concluded hyperbolically: "It was almost as if Barbie had never been brought back from Bolivia, as if he were being tried in absentia, as he had been in 1952 and 1954" (119).[31]

A final work harshly critical of the Barbie trial and its lessons and outcomes especially worthy of discussion here is Alain Finkielkraut's essay *La mémoire vaine* (*Remembering in Vain*), published in France in 1989. An influential work on both sides of the Atlantic, *La mémoire vaine* has shaped perceptions of the trial in many quarters, even among lawyers who participated in the trial.[32] Indeed, any positive assessment of the Barbie trial as the present study proposes to offer must take Finkielkraut's criticism into account.

Like Guyora Binder, in *La mémoire vaine* Finkielkraut lamented the December 1985 Court of Cassation decision to allow Resistance fighters to be included among Barbie's crimes against humanity. But he did so for different reasons than Binder. In Finkielkraut's view there was something "paradoxical" in seeing the same Resistance fighters who had earlier demanded the status of combatants and *not victims* now demand to be included in the latter category (20).

But Finkielkraut's criticisms of the Barbie trial also went well beyond the negative impact of the 1985 ruling. First, Finkielkraut lamented the fact that the Barbie trial occurred in France rather than before an international tribunal. Quoting Hannah Arendt, he observed that "the very monstrousness of the event [the Holocaust] is minimized before a tribunal that represents one nation only."[33] Then Finkielkraut maintained much more problematically that despite Barbie's conviction, Vergès had succeeded in making Barbie's trial a "mockery" of the Nuremberg trials rather than an "exemplary continuation" of them. According to Finkielkraut, Vergès accomplished this by making Nazi crimes seem unexceptional, nothing out of the ordinary (26). Vergès and his defence co-counsel argued in effect that Barbie and Nazism's crimes were in the final analysis no worse than French crimes committed during the Algerian war or American crimes in Vietnam or Israeli crimes against Palestinians. And while for the West Hitler's crimes against the Jews constituted the epitome of political and moral evil, for the rest of the world they were considered a matter of concern only for white people, whose "narcissistic lamentations" were reserved exclusively for their own kind. In the end, the Holocaust was merely a "family quarrel" at which the rest of the world simply laughed (32–3).[34]

In *La mémoire vaine* Finkielkraut did not claim that Vergès and his defence co-counsel attempted or succeeded in sending the message that the Holocaust never occurred. He did argue, however, that Vergès was successful in using the Lyon courtroom to diminish Nazi crimes to the point of insignificance from a global perspective. Thus, rather than serve as a prophylactic against the rising tide of negationism in France, the Barbie trial ironically reinforced a historical vision that helped sustain it. Equally importantly, in putting the Third World victims of colonialism past and present on a par with the victims of the Holocaust, Vergès and his co-counsel helped launch a phenomenon that would prove particularly significant in France into the 1990s and into the new century. This was the idea that most, if not all, victims of genocides and political crimes around the world, past and present, were equally deserving of being remembered, even celebrated, and somehow compensated for their suffering. Henceforth, they would legitimately vie for recognition and public attention. Once this idea took hold in the French mindset, it would have a remarkable impact on future public debates especially in the 1990s and early 2000s, not only about the Nazi and Vichy regimes, and their crimes against Jews, but also on historical debates about the crimes of communism, French colonialism, and France's role in the slave trade. These issues will be discussed in the conclusion here.

Have negative perceptions of the Barbie trial, certainly influenced by criticisms made of it at the time, persisted into the new century? The answer is a qualified "yes" in the sense that, while some scholarly appreciations of the trial have focused on what the proceedings accomplished,[35] recent assessments by prominent and influential public intellectuals in France have remained strikingly negative. For example, in 2001, as part of a broader discussion of recent international and historical trials and especially the International Criminal Tribunal for the former Yugoslavia, the imminent French/Bulgarian philosopher Tzvetan Todorov returned to the Barbie trial to make a stunning claim. In the end, Todorov wrote, "Whatever the intentions of the public authorities who organized the trial, the trial's lesson was: the torturers were German, the victims French."[36]

Strikingly similar to one of Guyora Binder's conclusions about the "lessons" of the Barbie trial cited earlier, the problem here is that, given what occurred in the Assize court in Lyon, Todorov's claim is inaccurate. Moreover, as part of a broader critique of more recent "political trials," such as the International Criminal Tribunal for the former Yugoslavia, which Todorov vigorously opposed, it points to two final issues that have plagued the memory of the Barbie trial up to the present.

First, in lumping the Barbie trial in with other historic trials of recent memory (and earlier ones as well) and those that involved contemporary actors, Todorov underscores a common prejudice against all such trials. They are fundamentally just "political trials," which inevitably impose some form of "victor's justice," or a form of justice that serves only the political aims of those currently in power. In her classic work *Legalism*, dealing in part with the Nuremberg trials, Judith Shklar criticizes this perspective. Shklar points out that the dismissive label "political trials" obscures real differences in *the political agendas and aims* being served. The latter are by no means necessarily negative if they are democratic and pluralistic in nature. But despite such valid distinctions, there is still, at least arguably, a public stigma attached to any trial labelled a "political trial."[37]

A second issue concerns the question of context: historical, legal, and otherwise. This issue is raised not only by Todorov's harsh assessment of the Barbie trial as part of a more general critique of what he perceived to be modern political trials but also by earlier criticisms and condemnations of the trial discussed here. For example, in *Remembering in Vain*, Alain Finkielkraut also placed the Barbie trial in a restrictive and arguably misleading legal context in considering what it did or did not accomplish *solely* as a successor to Nuremberg. In legal terms, this was inadequate. Like the Eichmann trial in Jerusalem twenty-six years earlier, the Barbie trial was also a *national* trial dealing with French rather than international law. Moreover, to account for the full legal context of the Barbie trial, one needs also to situate it in relation to post-war French and German trials of other Nazi criminals, including especially Barbie's Nazi and SS superiors in Occupied France.

***

As virtually all the criticisms of the Barbie trial discussed here suggest, what has most crucially been missing to date in understanding and assessing the Barbie trial is a close examination of the subtleties and complexities of *what actually transpired* in the Lyon courtroom in spring and summer 1987. Who were the witnesses, and what did their testimony reveal, or fail to reveal? Which testimonies were effective, which ones less so, and why? Which testimonies helped prove the case against Barbie, and which ones, inadvertently or not, posed difficulties to the prosecution? There were, after all, more than one hundred witnesses at the Barbie trial, often with very different stories to tell.

In addition, what strategies were adopted by the state prosecution, the defence, and the nearly forty civil parties lawyers present at the trial? How did the different interests of all these lawyers shape their courtroom strategies, and how did their own philosophical and historical perspectives shape their courtroom discourses? Given the structure of a French Assize court, how did president Cerdini's management of the case shape the outcome of the trial? His role, after all, was crucial. It included leading the questioning of the witnesses, taking important and often necessarily hurried decisions (like allowing Klaus Barbie to absent himself from his trial), managing the enormous courtroom crowd and extraordinary media attention, and handling the outbursts and disruptions brought about by civil parties and defence lawyers as well as some of the witnesses themselves.

Finally, what *did* the trial on charges of crimes against humanity of Klaus Barbie in Lyon in summer 1987 accomplish? Was the trial more than a mere spectacle, a "play within a play," as Neal Ascherson described it, or a "necessary travesty" whose verdict was a foregone conclusion, a propaganda exercise in the service of the political powers that be?

As its title suggests, *Justice in Lyon* argues that despite its many critics at the time and since, the Barbie trial was a success. It *did* serve justice, in that Klaus Barbie was prosecuted fairly, and his defence was given every latitude (too much latitude, for critics) to make the case for his innocence, or at least his lack of responsibility for the crimes against humanity with which he was charged. In different ways, the Barbie trial also served history to the extent that through all the distractions a clearer understanding of Barbie's and Nazism's world view and the nature and specificity of their crimes emerged. In this, the trial served a pedagogical function as well. Moreover, as the film recording and transcript of the trial reveal, the proceedings in Lyon hardly consisted of lawyers, judges, jurists, expert witnesses, and victims "going through the motions" or engaging only in "oratory" or "ego contests" (although there were some, if not plenty, of both) before arriving at an inevitable outcome. Testimony and courtroom debate were often highly dramatic, stressful, and even, on occasion, gut wrenching for spectators and participants alike. After her emotional testimony on 9 June, the Resistance heroine and concentration camp survivor Geneviève de Gaulle-Anthonioz had to be hospitalized briefly for observation due to stress and exhaustion. And if for critics of the trial, like Judith Miller, Barbie's absence marred and even undermined the proceedings, for others, as noted, it proved beneficial to them in symbolic terms. According to the civil parties lawyer Alain Lévy, Barbie's absence and the spectacle of the empty box of the accused actually heightened rather than diminished the impact of the testimony of victims.[38]

In her outstanding book *Transformative Justice: Israeli Identity on Trial*, Leora Bilsky argues that historical trials of the magnitude of the Eichmann and Barbie trials do much more than simply expose the facts of the case and arrive at a verdict. They offer what Bilsky calls "competing historical narratives" linked to "divergent forms of reconciliation" that clash with one another and highlight the larger issues at stake. In her discussion of the Eichmann trial, for example, Bilsky notes that the first "historical narrative" that sought to establish the trial's meaning and significance was crafted by Gideon Hausner, the state prosecutor at the trial. Two years later, that narrative was contested by Hannah Arendt, whose highly controversial *Eichmann in Jerusalem* rejected Hausner's narrative (which was also the version championed by Israeli prime minister David Ben Gurion). Essentially, according to Bilsky, Hausner's account of Eichmann's crimes was situated within the narrative of the age-old persecution of the Jewish people, from the Egyptian Pharaohs on. Arendt's view, on the other hand, attributed these crimes to the destructiveness of the modern totalitarian state, of which Hitler's Third Reich was a prime example. In this context, the Nazis' "physical extermination of the Jews" was not just another manifestation of the universal history of anti-Semitism, but rather a "crime against humanity, perpetrated on the body of the Jewish people."[39] More than fifty years after the Eichmann trial's conclusion, Hausner's and Arendt's competing historical narratives still inform and shape the majority of discussions of the proceedings in Jerusalem.

In *Transformative Justice*, Bilsky notes in passing that, unlike the Eichmann trial, during which Gideon Hausner "retained a monopoly over the trial's [historical] narrative" until Arendt's subsequent challenge to it, control of the historical narrative of the Barbie trial was complicated from the outset by the presence of the exceptionally large contingent of civil parties lawyers. As noted, each of the latter had their own historical narrative, with reference to their clients' experiences, with different points of emphasis, perspective, etc. And, of course, Bilsky's observation does not include whatever historical narrative the defence chose to generate on Barbie's behalf.

Given the explicitly national focus of her book (Israel), Bilsky does not discuss the Barbie trial in detail, nor does she analyse the competing historical narratives that defined it and ultimately determined its outcome. But to understand the proceedings in Lyon in 1987, and how and why they ultimately accomplished their aims and achieved a just outcome, these competing historical narratives need nevertheless to be identified and analysed. Moreover, they need to be assessed not merely in terms of their impact on the court – and the jury – but also in terms of the historical, political, moral, and even aesthetic perspectives that inspired and shaped them.

If Barbie were to be convicted, and hopefully justly so, the historical narrative that needed to "win out," so to speak, would be primarily that of the prosecution, articulated by chief prosecutor Pierre Truche. Truche's narrative in his summation was complicated from the outset by a number of factors. First, it had to navigate through and ultimately harmonize with the many and occasionally divergent and digressive voices of the civil parties lawyers. Second, it had to make a compelling case against the accused within the arguably restrictive framework of the 1985 Court of Cassation decision and *its* definition of crimes against humanity.[40] Third, it had to counter in advance the fireworks that would surely come from Vergès and the defence. In all this, Truche succeeded admirably. He did so not by haranguing the judges and jury but by speaking to them calmly and appealing to their *bon sens*, or "good sense," their ability to think for themselves. The chief prosecutor's demeanour before the court, his dignified modesty contrasted with the excitability and high-flown rhetoric of the defence and several of the civil parties. In essence, Truche was arguing from a position of a classical French humanism, whose spokespersons from Montaigne on had shaped French self-perceptions for centuries. He was not wrong in believing that the jury would both recognize and identify with the historical and cultural vision and values he was championing and act in accordance with the dictates of that tradition.

The historical (and cultural) narrative articulated by Vergès and his co-counsel, the Algerian lawyer Nabil Bouaita and the Congolese lawyer Jean-Martin Mbemba, was altogether different. As Alain Finkielkraut rightly observed, that narrative was radical, not to say revolutionary, in its implications. It called into question the specificity and uniqueness of Nazism and Nazi crimes in a way that repeatedly and justifiably shocked the court. Moreover, it was unconstrained by any of the limitations imposed on Truche's narrative by his role as chief prosecutor speaking on behalf of the French people and republic and in collaboration with civil parties lawyers.

Vergès and his co-counsel took full advantage of this freedom. As Finkielkraut's analysis suggests, Barbie's defence lawyers articulated a globalized vision of oppression and violence where the perpetrators were not (only) Nazis but civilized Europeans and their allies, and where the real victims were people of colour belonging to the Third World and not other Europeans, that is, Jews. Accordingly, Barbie was no different from any other white, European oppressor or killer. The accused was simply a scapegoat for France's and the white world's guilty conscience. Given Vergès's disdain for and even hatred of French and European institutions, it is not surprising that he saw the Assize court itself as part of that oppressive state apparatus and often acted accordingly in the courtroom. In fact, in numerous works written before and after the trial, Vergès articulated his idea of the *procès de rupture*, the "trial by rupture." Although in its basic configuration Vergès's "trial by rupture" resembles the *tu quo que* or "you did it, too" defence, it goes well beyond that. Its ultimate aim is to turn the trial in question against the court and the state whose interests it supposedly serves by transforming the defendant, even a brutal Nazi like Klaus Barbie, into a righteous political enemy of an oppressive state. The ultimate intent of a "trial by rupture" is to discredit and even overturn that oppressive state. In essence, by its very nature it is a *revolutionary* act, certainly as Vergès conceived it. Throughout the Barbie trial, Vergès and his defence co-counsel relentlessly deployed a number of strategies to transform the proceedings along these lines. These strategies included orchestrating Barbie's abrupt departure on the trial's third day, among other disruptions. Although alien in its vision to the perspectives of most of those present in the Lyon courtroom, and in all likelihood to the judges and jury, as Finkielkraut surmised, it nevertheless posed a formidable challenge for the court to overcome and convict Klaus Barbie.

Writing a history of the 1987 trial of Klaus Barbie in Lyon poses a number of challenges that, for example, writing a history of the 1961 trial of Adolph Eichmann in Jerusalem does not. First, there was not *one trial* of Klaus Barbie, as was the case with Eichmann, there were *three trials* of the Gestapo lieutenant, culminating in the 1987 trial. Barbie was tried in absentia and convicted of war crimes and sentenced to death by two French military tribunals in 1952 and 1954. To prosecute Barbie in

1987 for crimes against humanity, during the *instruction* or investigation of the case investigating magistrate Riss had to make sure that the crimes against humanity of which Barbie would be judged were not the war crimes for which he was convicted and sentenced to death in 1952 and 1954. Otherwise, the 1987 trial would be a case of double jeopardy. As will be discussed especially in chapter four here, one of Vergès's defence strategies was to argue precisely that, that in his 1987 trial Barbie was, in effect, being tried for the same crimes twice.

Second, whereas the criminal statutes governing the Nuremberg IMT trial as well as the Eichmann trial were not modified during the leadup to the trials themselves, as noted long after the *instruction* or investigation of Barbie's case was underway, French law defining crimes against humanity was radically altered by the Court of Cassation in December 1985. As a result, the investigation itself, carried out over almost four years, had to be re-done to include Resistance plaintiffs before the trial itself could occur. For some, this decision hamstrung the prosecution and made it impossible for the trial itself to succeed.[41] As it was, French law dealing with crimes against humanity was already vexed from its initial incorporation in French law in 1964. In December of *that* year, the French National Assembly made crimes against humanity imprescriptible, or not subject to a statute of limitations, but it offered *no definition* of what such crimes were. It relied instead on the definition used at Nuremberg.

As if these factors were not vexing enough, there was also the complicating reality that the trial of Klaus Barbie for crimes against humanity, if it could overcome the daunting issues it faced, would in all likelihood occur more than forty years after Klaus Barbie had terrorized Occupied Lyon and committed his many crimes. In judicial terms, this meant that the vast majority of French and international post-war prosecutions of Nazi war criminals had long since concluded. Indeed, even Barbie's immediate superiors in the Paris Gestapo had been tried and convicted in Cologne, West Germany, in 1980 (see chapter two here). As the Klarsfeld documents mentioned above reveal, this judicial legacy made its presence felt in the criminal investigation of Barbie and clearly informed the prosecution as it prepared its case. Moreover, in the French press and French media coverage in the years between Barbie's arrest and his 1987 trial, the historic nature of the trial naturally raised comparisons with the great historic trials of Nazis in the past (the Eichmann trial in particular) as well as France's post-war Purge trials occurring in the 1940s and lasting into the 1950s.

A second consequence of the 1987 trial occurring forty years and more after Barbie's tenure in Occupied Lyon was that, historically, other very significant traumas on a national level had occurred in the intervening years. Most notably in France, this meant the bloody and tragic consequences of decolonization and especially the terrible events associated with the Algerian war, the "war without a name." Because France had inadequately dealt with its own crimes in Algeria, Vergès and his team exploited that fact repeatedly in the Lyon Assize court room, which they considered to be a perfect soapbox from which they could denounce French hypocrisy as they saw it in trying Barbie.

Finally, the forty intervening years between Barbie's crimes and his trial also meant that Klaus Barbie, now a tired and sickly old man, had become essentially a caricature or an enigma of sorts to most French. For the French, it should be recalled, the experience of Nazi brutality was either a distant memory if they were old enough to have experienced it at all or an historic trauma from a time before they were born. Moreover, in the intervening years, Barbie had led multiple "afterlives," as an American intelligence agent, a wealthy South American businessman, and an advisor and more to South American right-wing dictators and strongmen. While these "afterlives" had been covered often in spectacular and lurid detail in articles and books published on both sides of the Atlantic, Barbie's motivations in wartime Lyon, his psychology, and the kind of evil he represented had not. To put the matter simply, the question remained as to who Klaus Barbie was and how the Nazi ideology he embraced helped to shape the brutal killer he was in Occupied Lyon. Had Barbie repented at all for his horrific wartime actions?

In organizing the chapters in *Justice in Lyon*, these considerations have been taken into account. Specifically, the first three chapters of the book deal with the extraordinary legal and historical "backdrop" of the 1987 trial for crimes against humanity. The final four chapters dissect the proceedings in the Lyon courtroom, focusing on witness testimony and the strategies of the defence and prosecution. The conclusion examines the Barbie trial's own "afterlife," its legacies in the 1990s and beyond.

In chapter one, "Klaus Barbie: Nazi 'Idealist,'" the subject is Klaus Barbie himself, the individual and Nazi who served in Lyon from 1942 to 1944. This chapter does *not* offer a biography of Barbie from his childhood to his embrace of Nazism as a young man, nor does it chronicle Barbie's post-war rocambolesque life.[42] There are already numerous books devoted to this topic, as well as films like *Hôtel Terminus* (1988) and *Mon meilleur ennemi* (2007). Rather, through an examination of interviews with Barbie's victims over time, Barbie's own shifting accounts of himself, examinations of the reports of court psychologists, questioning of Barbie during the long investigation leading up to and during the 1987 trial itself, chapter one argues that through it all Barbie was and remained a

"Nazi idealist." He never changed. It was a matter of "character," Barbie himself observed, and he would remain faithful to his self-perception as a committed Nazi throughout his life. Because the characterization "Nazi idealist" seems like an oxymoron in and of itself, chapter one also explores how the Nazis conceived of themselves as "idealists," and what that commitment meant to them.

Chapter two, "The Historical Judicial Backdrop: From Nuremberg to the 1980 Cologne Trial of Kurt Lischka, Herbert Hagen, and Ernst Heinrichson," deals with the legal and judicial backdrop to the Barbie trial. It examines earlier historic trials of Nazi criminals from Nuremberg to the trials of Barbie's SS superiors who served with him in France: Karl Oberg, Helmut Knochen, Kurt Lischka, Herbert Hagen, and Kurt Heinrichson. As noted, the Nuremberg and the Eichmann trials served as points of reference for lawyers, journalists, and others before and during the 1987 trial. As Barbie's criminal dossier reveals, the accused himself frequently referred to Eichmann and his 1961 trial in an effort to exonerate himself during the investigation of his case. As for the later trials of Knochen, Lischka, and Heinrichson in Cologne in 1980, these served as valuable reference points for investigating magistrate Riss and prosecution lawyers as they prepared the case against Barbie.

Chapter three, "The Investigation: War Crimes, Crimes against Humanity, and the Long Road to Compromise" focuses on the four-year-long investigation of the Barbie case and the legal decisions – especially the December 1985 Court of Cassation decision that incorporated some crimes against the Resistance into the charges of crimes against humanity – that shaped the 1987 trial. It also looks at the earlier 1952 and 1954 trials by Lyon military tribunals of Klaus Barbie, both of which convicted him of war crimes and sentenced him to death in absentia. (By the time these trials took place, Barbie was already safely in South America.) Because the definition of crimes against humanity under French law was a fraught topic in the lead-up to and during the 1987 Court of Assize trial itself, the vote by the French National Assembly to incorporate statutes related to these crimes in French law in 1964 and the debates that surrounded that vote are examined here as well.

Chapter four, "The Barbie Trial Begins: Opening Rituals and the Departure of the Accused," examines the first "stage" or "phase" of the Barbie trial, including the events of the days leading up to the opening of the trial and concluding with Klaus Barbie's dramatic announcement that he would no longer appear in court during the third day of hearings. As one might expect of a trial of the historical (and political) magnitude of the Barbie trial, for days preceding its opening, the city of Lyon as well as the surrounding area were alive with protests, commemorations, as well as pre-trial predictions and arguments made by lawyers involved in the case. All of this was covered in the national and international press. Once the trial got underway, the first three days' events included the interrogation of the accused by president Cerdini concerning Barbie's wartime and post-war itinerary, his personal life and beliefs, as well as initial skirmishes between civil parties lawyers, chief prosecutor Pierre Truche, and lead defence counsel. The implications of these skirmishes are discussed here. Finally, Barbie's abrupt decision to quit the trial on the third day changed the tenor of the proceedings entirely and offered the first true test of the president and prosecution to keep the trial on track to a successful outcome.

Chapter five, "The Witnesses," examines the testimony of the most impactful of the one hundred–odd witnesses who testified at the Barbie trial. These include civil parties witnesses (in most cases Barbie's victims) who had attached themselves to the prosecution and were also represented by their lawyers at the trial; expert witnesses, including historians, jurists, psychologists, and others; so-called witnesses of general interest called to provide context and clarification for the trial; and, finally, witnesses called by the defence. In historical trials from the Eichmann trial on, the witnesses and especially the victims of Nazi perpetrators have had a crucial role to play. They were to bring the past and the crimes committed by the accused back to life and make those crimes *present and real* in the minds and hearts of the court and jury. In the Barbie trial, this was especially difficult, given that more than forty years had passed since Klaus Barbie's brutal sojourn in Lyon. Moreover, the responsibilities of the victims and witnesses also included, indirectly, validating in human if not legal terms the problematic re-definition of crimes against humanity handed down in 1985 by the Court of Cassation. As will be argued here, this they accomplished. It is worth stressing that some critics who have argued that the Barbie trial was essentially a failure (Finkielkraut, Miller, and Binder, among others) have tended to downplay the value of that testimony or ignore its efficacy in a trial in which it in fact proved crucial.

Chapters six and seven, "The Civil Parties and Prosecution Make Their Case" and "Barbie's Defence Takes Centre Stage" focus, respectively, on the closing statements or arguments of the civil parties lawyers, the *réquisitoire or* summation of chief prosecutor Truche, and the closing statements of Vergès and his co-defence counsel. Given the extraordinary number of civil parties lawyers who addressed the court (thirty-nine), it was crucial for the coherence of the prosecution for these lawyers to maintain a "united front." This would not be easy, given the different experiences and perspectives of their clients and the fact that there were important differences of opinion among these lawyers as to what crimes against humanity were, or should be. As will be argued here, with some disagreements as well as the eruption of a troubling incident concerning divergent views of the rights of the defence to plead as it wished, unity among the civil parties lawyers was generally maintained. The arguments made by Truche in his summation and by Vergès and his defence co-counsel have been briefly summarized above.

The conclusion of *Justice in Lyon* explores the legal and historical legacies of the Barbie trial extending into the 1990s and beyond. It examines the 1994 trial of Vichy militia member Paul Touvier and the 1997–8 trial of Vichy bureaucrat Maurice Papon, with an eye to the legal and historical impact of the Barbie trial on both. It also briefly considers some of the consequences of the "competition of victims" alluded to earlier and engendered by the Barbie trial. These include subsequent debates in France over the troubled legacies of colonialism, the 1997 *Black Book of Communism* debate, and the controversy in the early 2000s over the so-called Memorial Laws, which attempted to extend the stigma of crimes against humanity to other dark episodes in France's past. And although the Barbie trial deliberately avoided the case of Jean Moulin and divisions and betrayals in France's wartime Resistance against the Nazis that Barbie and Vergès sought to exploit, these divisions did erupt in spectacular fashion during the so-called Aubrac Affair of 1997. The Aubrac Affair will be discussed here as well. Finally, the Barbie trial's impact on international criminal law will be briefly examined here. While critics in France, especially at the time of the Touvier trial, underscored problems created by legal decisions made in the context of the Barbie trial, more recently scholars of international law have stressed positive impacts of the Barbie trial on that jurisprudence. Here as well, the Barbie trial has proven largely, if not entirely, successful.

Klaus Barbie. When brought back from Bolivia in February 1983, Barbie was symbolically imprisoned in Montluc Prison, where he kept most of his wartime captives before being transferred to Saint-Joseph Prison, where he remained for the rest of his life. In Montluc Prison, where this photograph was taken, the commemorative photo of Barbie can be found on the wall of the cell where he was kept. Photograph by Richard Golsan

Chapter One

Klaus Barbie: Nazi "Idealist"

Who was Klaus Barbie, and what motivated him to commit the crimes he did in wartime Lyon and the surrounding area? Like earlier trials of former Nazis, from Nuremberg to the Eichmann trial, these questions were central both to Barbie's trial and to the four-year-long investigation leading up to it. Indeed, ever since Barbie had been discovered and identified in Bolivia, they inspired a flood of newspaper articles, books, interviews with the accused, his victims and associates, and later documentary films like Marcel Ophuls's *Hôtel Terminus* and Kevin MacDonald's *Mon meilleur ennemi.*

Unfortunately, in all these trials, the assessments of the accused offered by witnesses, lawyers, psychologists, critics, and observers are all-too-often simplistic, prejudiced, misplaced, or misinformed. Or they prove to be so highly controversial that the actual subject being analysed is lost from view or wrongly assigned extraordinary qualities he does not possess in the first place. In the case of Klaus Barbie, his obstinate refusal to appear in court unless ordered to do so, and his stone-faced impassiveness, sardonic smiles, and brief or evasive answers to many, if not most, questions posed to him when present, only augmented the problem. In hindsight, it is perhaps the most straightforward solution to dismiss Barbie as a *salopard,* a "total bastard," as two *partie civile* lawyers described him in 2018, and then move on. But this straightforward assessment was certainly not the attitude that dominated in Lyon and in the international press at the time. One need only watch the film of the opening session of the trial to grasp the anticipation, tension, and in some cases, the sense of dread that suddenly gripped the large, packed-to-overflowing courtroom when Barbie was led in.

This chapter will argue that in order to understand Klaus Barbie the man, the motivations for his criminal actions and his behaviour in court, it is most helpful to consider his commitment to Nazism, what that commitment meant to him, and in light of recent studies, what that ideology meant to its most devoted adherents, like the former SS lieutenant. Indeed, Barbie possessed a "Nazi conscience," and he was, as Robert Taylor, the man who hired him to work for American intelligence in 1947 affirmed, a "Nazi idealist." In one of the more striking scenes in *Hôtel Terminus*, Taylor is confronted with his earlier, immediate post-war characterization of Barbie and asked what he thinks of it now. A clearly embarrassed Taylor admits that he does not know. But this does not mean Taylor was wrong in his earlier assessment of the man he hired. Nor does characterizing Barbie as a Nazi idealist mean that this epithet takes into account *every aspect* of Barbie's character or resolves all the contradictions that emerge in the testimony of witnesses at the trial or in the recollections of individuals who encountered or knew Barbie under different circumstances in a variety of locations over many years. These contradictions stand as they are. At best, they may nuance one's understanding of the former Nazi, but they should not distract from the fact that throughout his life, Klaus Barbie was *committed* and single-minded. Kevin MacDonald's film *Mon meilleur ennemi* opens with documentary footage of Barbie's return journey to France and a stop-over in French Guyana, where he was arrested by French police following his expulsion from Bolivia. On board the plane, a Bolivian reporter asks a very disheveled, old, and tired Barbie if he has any regrets in his life. Barbie pauses, and then responds that, in the end, there were certainly errors, but no regrets. By way of explaining himself, he adds, "all men must follow a line, no?" When asked if this means a "line of conduct," Barbie responds in the affirmative. Then he states in response to a follow-up question, "It's a question of character." In Barbie's case, that character was deeply imbued with Nazi beliefs and attitudes which remained with him all his life.

To understand Barbie's "Nazi conscience," his Nazi "idealism," and why it failed to emerge clearly, or at best in piecemeal fashion during his trial, it is first helpful to review the varied and contradictory assessments by witnesses, victims, colleagues, and others that emerge from these sources and have been gathered over many years. Then it is important to recall that efforts made by courts and tribunals to understand the Nazis they were prosecuting, from leaders of the regime, like Hermann Goering, to major players like Adolph Eichmann, down to "foot soldiers" like Klaus Barbie, relied heavily on clinical assessments of the accused made by psychologists, psychoanalysts, and other medical professionals. Unfortunately, all too often these assessments started from the assumption that the Nazi criminals under investigation were pathological individuals, psychologically abnormal in one way or another. In more specific terms, Joel Dimsdale observes of the attitudes of psychologists working at Nuremberg that they considered the Nazi leaders to be "beasts, monsters, wholly other" (Dimsdale 1–2). This, of course, often skewed their findings, as did the long-held and prevalent opinion shared by many if not most people in the Western democracies before and after the war. This belief was that Nazism itself was fundamentally aberrant in psychosexual terms, indeed that all Nazis, starting with Hitler himself, were perverts and deviants and that this explained their politics.

Part One: Witnesses, Victims, Associates, and Others on the Barbie They Knew (or Thought They Knew)

As one might expect, for those who knew or encountered Klaus Barbie frequently or only briefly, their impression of the man most often depended on the individual's background and the historical context or circumstances under which they met Barbie. To German neighbours, like Johann Otten, who recalls Barbie as a child in *Hôtel Terminus*, he was a friendly young fellow who suffered at the hands of an alcoholic father. Otten, like his neighbours, called Barbie "Sonny." To some of his school classmates, including former Wehrmacht major Peter Minn, also interviewed in *Hôtel Terminus*, Barbie was gregarious and a "natural-born leader." A positive opinion of Barbie was shared as well by some of Barbie's SS colleagues who also appear in Ophuls's film. Wolfgang Gustmann, for example, calls Barbie a "fantastic guy," and takes the occasion to affirm to Ophuls that without the SS, the Soviets would have made it to the English Channel by the end of World War II.

To his SS superiors, Barbie was an excellent and committed officer, as official reports about him read by president Cerdini at the outset of his trial make clear.[2] These reports, the translations into French of which are held in the archive of the trial in Lyon, stress that Barbie was "joyous, a lover of truth and comradery," that his service was "disciplined and irreproachable" and that his "will and personal firmness (*dureté*) were very marked." The report also states that Barbie's "judgment was clear" and his conduct "irreproachable."

Nevertheless, even with such excellent ratings, Barbie rose somewhat slowly through the ranks of the Gestapo and SS. Despite his supposed exemplarity as an SS officer, Barbie was promoted to the rank of captain only after he left wartime Lyon and was recovering in German hospitals from wounds he received before leaving France.[3] The delay in promotion does nevertheless suggest possible reservations about Barbie on the part of his immediate superiors. During the war, Barbie was asked by these superiors to explain why he was not having more children, in keeping with his SS and Nazi commitment. And, as a former colleague, Kurt Abendroth testified in 1964, during the war he was obliged to substitute for Barbie in Lyon while the latter was being treated for venereal disease in hospital. Perhaps Barbie's morals were an obstacle to his promotion. In Lyon, Barbie was known to frequent the *Lapin Blanc*, "Lyon's most risqué night club, where the girls were pretty and available, and often useful sources of information" (Linklater et al. 97). While apparently indulging his sexual appetites with some of the women there, Barbie also maintained a long-term relationship with a woman called Thédy, who "was a secretary at Gestapo Headquarters and who would often be present at interrogation sessions, sometimes actually sitting on Barbie's lap as his victims were tortured" (Linklater et al. 97).

To many of his victims in Lyon, and even some of his colleagues there, Barbie was purely and simply demonic, a monster and/or a sadist. Among the epithets applied to Barbie by his victims who testified at his trial were "jackal" (André Courvoisier, 5 June, Hearing 18) and "wild animal." In *Hôtel Terminus*, one of those tortured by Barbie, the Resistance hero Raymond Aubrac, observes that Barbie took particular pleasure in inflicting pain. According to Lise Lesèvre, another Resistance member tortured repeatedly by Barbie and his men, Barbie seemed more interested in inflicting pain to get answers than he was in the answers he got. Simone Kadosche, arrested along with her mother and father near the end of the Occupation and tortured by Barbie in front of her parents, was struck by Barbie's capacity to fly into a violent rage after appearing so gentle and soft-spoken when first encountered.

Among Barbie's colleagues in Lyon, Ferdinand Palk, interrogated in Germany in August 1964, expressed admiration for Barbie as a "desperado" (*tête brulée*) and as the real "motor" of the Gestapo in Lyon. But Palk also described some of Barbie's actions against Nazism's enemies in disturbing, not to say appalling, terms. According to Palk, Barbie had taken wounded Resistance fighters from a hospital in Bourg and then had them killed on the way back to Lyon. He characterized Barbie as "sadistic" because he liked to physically torture his prisoners and then brag about his actions to his colleagues later. (K: P1/93–7) The aforementioned Kurt Abendroth shared Palk's assessment that Barbie was a sadist, which he believed "brought discredit to the Gestapo office in Lyon." In his 1964 testimony, Abendroth describes the following episode to back up his claim: "Toward the end of September 1943, a high-ranking French officer, probably a colonel, was arrested for supposed acts of resistance. As he refused to talk, he was 'bathed.'[4] After a second 'bath,' he would probably have become more talkative [but] the avowals given did not satisfy Barbie, so he ordered a third 'bath.' The elderly gentleman was apparently shot after that" (K: P1/ 152–8). Abendroth also claimed that, after the war, in 1948, Barbie betrayed colleagues to the French and Germans in order to protect himself.

While working for the American Counter Intelligence Corps (CIC) from 1947 to 1951, Barbie was perceived differently. One of his superiors, Eugene Kolb, affirms in Ophuls's film that Barbie was a real "professional" and that he doubted Barbie tortured anyone because "he didn't have to." In Kevin MacDonald's 2007 documentary on Barbie, *Mon meilleur ennemi*, another CIC superior, Earl Browning, expresses the view that despite evidence to the contrary, Barbie was "not a sadist." As already noted, for CIC agent Robert Taylor, Barbie was a "Nazi idealist" above all else.

In South America, opinions of Barbie varied as much as they did in Europe. These opinions reflected as well the nature of the experience or experiences one had had with the former Gestapo chief. The head of the German-Peruvian Chamber of Commerce, Johannes Schneider-Merck, who had been swindled by Barbie and his colleagues in dubious currency-trading transactions, describes in *Hôtel Terminus* a social occasion in which in an angry outburst Barbie revealed that he remained a fanatical Nazi loyalist, stating, "No one insults the *fuehrer* in my presence." Schneider-Merck adds that Barbie was "absolutely anti-Semitic" and a "crook." In both *Hôtel Terminus* and *Mon meilleur ennemi*, a Bolivian neighbour of Barbie's states that Barbie treated him abominably while he believed him to be a Jew. Barbie changed his tune, however, and invited him to be a friend, once he found out the neighbour was not Jewish. A peasant gardener who worked for Barbie near La Paz testifies that Barbie was a *seigneur* but not of "God's people." The gardener adds, however, that "only God" should judge him.

In *Mon meilleur ennemi*, leftist activists who fought against the right-wing regimes in Bolivia that Barbie served testify to his brutality. Yolanda Caldéron, a syndicalist activist, is moved to tears as she describes the back pain she still experiences from when Barbie kicked her during her imprisonment by Bolivian authorities. The journalist Mirna Murillo describes similar treatment at Barbie's hands in both *Mon meilleur ennemi* and *Hôtel Terminus*, although she is able to keep her composure during both interviews. Finally, in *Mon meilleur ennemi*, Barbie's daughter, Ute Messner, is interviewed, apparently after the conclusion of the trial. For Messner, Barbie was always "gentle," "sweet," and "kind." She also wonders who labelled her father the "Butcher of Lyon" and adds sardonically that the butchers of Lyon are angry about this. "Being a butcher is an honourable profession, isn't it?" she asks her interviewer. In a document contained in files in the archives in Lyon, Ute Messner's husband describes his father-in-law in similarly positive terms (AR:4544W7, B-8).

Many biographical accounts of Barbie that have appeared to date provide further insights into Barbie's psychological impulses, his prejudices, animosities, and indeed visceral hatreds, but these also do not add up to a coherent account of Barbie's core beliefs and motivations. For example, there is no doubt that a number of factors from his childhood and youth had a bearing on the man and ruthless SS officer he would become, although as his British biographer Neal Ascherson observes, Barbie was by no means "destined" to become what he became. The fact that Barbie was a bastard (his parents were married only after his birth) in all likelihood left its mark. More concretely, Barbie, like his mother, was physically abused by Barbie's alcoholic father, who, in addition to his alcoholism, suffered throughout his life from a war wound in the neck he received during four years of frontline fighting during World War I. Because he was the schoolmaster's son, Barbie was, as he later wrote, his father's "exemplary victim," intended to serve as an example for the other boys. According to Peter Hammerschmitt in his recent biography of Barbie, the effect of Barbie's mistreatment at the hands of his father not only contributed to a "loss of confidence in paternal authority" but also to a "passionate longing for a charismatic political leader" (Hammerschmidt 28). Interviewed in *Mon meilleur ennemi*, Neal Ascherson says that Barbie suffered as a boy from "a lack of self-esteem" and that he "wanted to matter." Ascherson also states that, in his view, Barbie was no more anti-Semitic than "the people in his background," that in Trier, where Barbie grew up, there was a substantial Jewish population with which he undoubtedly had contact. Ascherson also expresses the view that Barbie learned interrogation techniques, i.e. torture, as "a kind of trade."

At about the same time, Barbie's political outlook, and more specifically his "visceral hatred" of the French, began to take shape when French troops occupied the Rhineland following Germany's failure to make reparations payments. This hatred would remain with him throughout his life. In Lyon, he readily expressed a passionate dislike of the French to his subordinates on numerous occasions. The French had, after all, wounded his father and destroyed his life (not to mention made domestic life in his family miserable). In Bolivia in the 1970s, Barbie lamented to a friend that he felt the French were "pursuing him everywhere" when his son decided to marry a French woman. In his memoirs and elsewhere, Barbie described most of his French collaborators in Lyons in positive terms, indeed as "idealists." But this was precisely because they had embraced the Nazi cause and betrayed the French one (Wilson 188).

The experience of the French occupation of the Rhine shaped Barbie's political outlook, or, more accurately, his political "mythology," in other ways as well. He greatly admired those Germans who resisted the French and came to admire political resistance in general, which he considered deeply heroic. One of the more perverse consequences of this attitude is that Barbie admired and indeed identified with his most famous victim, Jean Moulin. In "A Gestapo Memoir," Barbie devotes some thirty pages to his capture of Moulin's betrayer, René Hardy, or "Didot" (who, he claims, became a lifelong friend) and the arrests at Caluire of Resistance leaders, including Moulin, in June 1943. Barbie then describes Moulin, and his prison encounters with him, in glowing terms. Moulin was "a very strong man, a very intelligent man" (qtd. in Wilson 254), who, Barbie believed, would have changed French history, had he survived the war. He was "impressed" by Moulin, upon meeting him, "probably because he looked a lot like me, physically. Also, he was calm and firm in his manner, like me" (qtd. in Wilson 166). Photos of the two men from the period in question hardly reveal the resemblance. Moreover, it is reasonable to assume that Barbie's admiration and identification with Moulin accounts for his denial in the "Gestapo Memoir" and elsewhere that he tortured Moulin, a claim belied by witnesses at the time.[5] According to Barbie, his exchanges with Moulin were cordial, not to say fraternal, born of mutual respect. Indeed, Alvaro de Castro, Barbie's friend and bodyguard, states in *Mon meilleur ennemi* that many years after the war, while visiting Paris as head of Transmaratima Boliviana shipping line, Barbie visited Moulin's grave at the Panthéon in Paris and placed an expensive bunch of flowers on it.

What is one to make of these often widely divergent descriptions of Klaus Barbie? Was Barbie demonic, a "monster," and what does that mean, exactly? Was Barbie anti-Semitic, in what ways, and to what degree? Was he a sadist, or merely a consummate "professional" in interrogation techniques? How does one reconcile Barbie's brutality and rages with his "gentleness" and "kindness"? What is one to make of the Bolivian peasant's apparently paradoxical assessment that Barbie was a *seigneur* but not a "man of God"? Is there a way to assemble the disparate descriptions recorded here into a coherent and integrated picture of the accused that makes sense of his behaviour over time? Other than confirming Barbie's exalted sense of self, his egotism, what does his sense of fraternity, of being on a par with Jean Moulin say about his supposed hatred of the French? If his admiration for idealistic resisters like Moulin outweighed his distaste for the French, does that mean it also outweighed all other virtues, including loyalty to Nazism itself? If that is the case, then Ferdinand Palk's assessment of Barbie as essentially a *tête brûlée*, a desperado, seems all the more apposite – but still only a partial assessment, in light of other takes on Barbie's character.

If, as did most of those victims who were tortured or otherwise abused by Barbie, one sees him – understandably – as something inhuman, a "monster," a demonic being, one runs a different risk of misunderstanding him, while also of unintentionally enhancing him in the eyes of others. In a 1964 conversation with Joachim Fest, Hannah Arendt warned in challenging popular views of Nazis (and Adolph Eichmann in particular) that "if you demonize someone, not only do you make him more interesting, you also secretly ascribe to him a depth that other people do not have."[6] In the lead-up to the Lyon trial, and certainly in the extraordinary and intense media and public anticipation of and reaction to the trial at the outset, this was certainly the case with Barbie. It is instructive to recall along these lines that when Barbie absented himself from the courtroom after the trial's third day, attendance in the courtroom fell precipitously and then climbed again when Barbie was forced to reappear.

Hannah Arendt's own prescription for Nazi evil as it manifested itself in Adolph Eichmann and described in detail in *Eichmann in Jerusalem* is also of little help in solving the Barbie riddle either. In his brutality and certainly in his obviously sadistic behaviour on occasion, Barbie was no "desk killer" like Eichmann, who destroyed his victims with orders given at a distance. In his taciturn behaviour in court, Barbie was also not the voluble and seemingly "thoughtless" person Arendt thought she observed in Eichmann, a man who could only speak in clichés and platitudes and could only follow what Arendt describes as Nazi "language rules," built on euphemisms and other forms of linguistic misdirection. Nor, if one accepts the views of one of Arendt's recent critics, Bettina Stangneth, was Barbie the consummate actor Eichmann was in Jerusalem, who fooled Arendt into elaborating her striking but ultimately wrong-headed hypothesis about Eichmann and the "banality of evil." Barbie's "performance" and certainly the *coups de théâtre* or dramatic moments he performed were limited essentially to his comings and goings and then his dramatic use of French in making his final statement before the court. In that statement, Barbie affirmed: "I did not order the round-up at Izieu. I fought the Resistance with extreme force, but I offer my respect to them here. But that was war, and the war is over." Whether a performance or not, it failed to impress the judges and jury, as it did not conform to historical realities, nor, to all appearances, did it truthfully reflect Barbie's real sentiments in wartime Lyon. Certainly, the many Resistance fighters tortured and physically broken for life at his hand would disagree that Klaus Barbie showed them any respect at all.

Part Two: Psychoanalysing the Accused from the Nuremberg Defendants to Klaus Barbie

As stated above, the Barbie trial was by no means the first historic trial of a former Nazi or Nazis in which understanding the motives of the accused, and indeed discovering what compulsion or psychological aberration or illness had led them to commit their crimes, proved central to the prosecution's case. Revealing the motives of these men, prosecutors believed, could prove helpful to the court in making its judgment, while also serving as a warning for the future to the community that spawned them or, in the case of the Barbie trial, the national community that suffered their crimes. As a result, at Nuremberg and in other historic trials, specialists – psychologists, psychiatrists, and psychoanalysts – were brought in during the investigation of the case to interview the accused. In some of the trials in question – including the Barbie trial – these specialists also testified in court as to their findings and conclusions.

Historically speaking, this approach was not surprising, in light of the fact that long before the post-war trials got underway, Nazism itself was widely understood as an unprecedented and profoundly aberrant phenomenon by its opponents and victims. As the exemplary Nazi, Hitler was – and continues to be – the subject of intense and sustained psychological interest and speculation.[7] Historians, biographers, psychologists, and others have repeatedly sought to discover the dark motives that drove the man and to ascertain how such an obvious failure and "nobody," to quote Berthold Brecht, could succeed in galvanizing an entire people in the way that Hitler did (qtd. in Dean 106). Or, as Thomas Mann would have it in his famous 1939 essay "Brother Hitler," just because Hitler was a "catastrophe," that was "no reason why we should not find him interesting, as a character and an event."

In *The Fragility of Empathy after the Holocaust*, Carolyn Dean notes that in their efforts to expose the well springs of Nazi psychology, psychologists and others have most often linked Hitler – and fascists more broadly – to latent and implicitly criminal homosexual drives. In the 1950s, the British psychoanalyst characterized these drives in terms of the "psychological condition of the homosexual" (Dean 107). In Hitler's case, they were supposedly manifested not only in his eagerness to enjoy the company of known homosexuals like Otto Strasser, but in unnatural feelings he supposedly felt for his Hitler Youth. These were, as Walter Langer wrote in a 1943 report prepared for the OSS, pedophilic and more akin to "the feelings of a woman than a man" (Dean 113). In most, if not all, of these efforts to psychoanalyse Hitler, Dean writes, the aim was to "degrade or mock" his charisma and suggest that he and the movement he created were shams, that he was "a fraud" (Dean 112).

Efforts to link Nazis and Nazism to homosexuality or to sexual aberrance or perversion did not of course end with the post-war period. During the late 1960s, 1970s, and even into the 1980s, during the so-called *mode rétro* in France and Europe,[9] sexual perversions – homosexuality, pedophilia, and sadism – were linked to Nazism in any number of films and novels, often evoking the latter's dangerous "seductions." These included, most notably, works like Luchino Visconti's *The Damned*, Lina Wertmuller's *The Night Porter*, Louis Malle's *Lacombe Lucien*, and novels like Michel Tournier's brilliant work *The Ogre*, whose portrait of a pedophile-turned-Nazi remains as troubling today as it did upon publication in 1970. In 1981, the historian Pascal Ory lamented the pervasiveness of the phenomena as well as its purported message in an essay entitled "Comme de l'an quarante: dix ans du 'rétro Satanas" ("Just as in the year 1940: Ten Years of 'Retro-satanas'").[10]

Regardless of what form of psychosis or pathology, sexual or otherwise, from which the Nazi criminals were presumed to suffer, there was another problem the clinical approach revealed at these trials: the tests and examinations given to these criminals confirmed, shockingly, that in most cases, these men were essentially "normal." At Nuremberg, as Harald Welzer recounts in *Les Exécuteurs*, when Douglas Kelley, the first psychologist appointed by the tribunal, sent Rorschach test results of the Nazi leaders being tried to ten international specialists for analysis, none of the specialists responded with their assessments, excusing themselves for a variety of reasons. One of the solicited experts, Molly Harrower, explained thirty years later that the reason the experts did not respond was that all were aware of public expectations that they would discover among the accused a "common personality structure that was particularly frightful."[11] In fact, none of the experts drew that conclusion from the Rorschach tests and therefore chose simply not to report their findings or make public their conclusions. Regardless, in his final report, Kelley was forced to conclude that "not only are such individuals not ill, or of a particular personality type, but also that we could encounter them today in any other country in the world" (Welzer 11).

As Welzer also reports, any number of subsequent surveys and profiles done of Nazi executioners over subsequent years also confirmed their disturbing "normalcy." In 1980, a team of pyschologists concluded on the basis of clinical tests administered to former SS members confirmed that fully 90 per cent of officers and men would have passed the psychological tests administered by the US Army as well as the Kansas City Police Department (Welzer12). A few years earlier, another psychologist, Barry

Ritzler, reviewed the sixteen Rorschach tests administered at Nuremberg and concluded that the accused had only one trait in common: they shared a very limited capacity for empathy (Welzer 13).

As part of the pre-trial *instruction* or investigation of Klaus Barbie's case, investigating magistrate Riss assigned a team of three psychologists and psychoanalysts – Jacques Védrinne, Didier Weber, and Daniel Gonin – to conduct interviews and administer a variety of psychological tests to the accused. The team interviewed Barbie on twelve occasions over the span of a year. Perhaps as a means of demonstrating that he was their "equal," when responding to the psychologists' questions, they reported, Barbie spoke in French, although he did, on occasion, have recourse to a dictionary.

The report the psychologists submitted is interesting in a number of ways.[12] After beginning with a brief disclaimer, stating that the analysis of Barbie required a certain "suppression of the imagination" on their part in order to put aside the repugnant ideology the accused embraced and that had caused their ancestors to suffer, the psychologists report on their findings. First, they quote a number of biographical details and personal observations Barbie made about his background and family and about the war itself. Barbie stressed that his ancestors were French Huguenots who were forced to flee France to avoid persecution. (Was this another reason for hating the French?) Barbie also stated that he admired his father for his service during the Great War but that he was closer to his mother. At one point, Barbie lamented the death of his son, who died tragically in a hang-gliding accident in 1982, with his parents watching. (According to Vergès, Barbie administered mouth-to-mouth resuscitation to his son, even though he knew he was dead, so that his wife would not know immediately that her son was dead.[13]) When Barbie turned to World War II itself, his observations were frankly apocalyptic. The war, Barbie stated, was "a war of night, a dirty war, not clean." He added, "the war was psychologically beyond the possibility of man," and that it was "difficult for everyone to show self-control every day."

Before drawing more theoretical conclusions about the accused in their report, the psychologists sum up the results of cognitive and intelligence tests they submitted to him. Barbie's IQ test confirmed that his intelligence was "above normal," especially in terms of his verbal skills. As to his ability to "perform mental calculations," he had difficulty remembering a large number of variables. When asked to organize images, Barbie had no difficulty if they could be organized chronologically, but if an element of "humor or surprise" was introduced, he had great difficulty with the test. For this and other shortcomings, the psychologists report, Barbie felt the need to justify himself.

In terms of general conclusions, the psychologists revert to a rather technical jargon to affirm, first, that Barbie was incapable of "interiorizing, of registering a personal movement or its affects addressed to him." In other words, apparently, Barbie lacked empathy. Moreover, he was concerned, indeed apparently obsessed, with presenting himself in the best light to others, as well as to himself. Anything that might reveal a personal flaw, or failing, Barbie blamed on external factors.

Not surprisingly, Barbie's need for control, even as to the meaning of the words he spoke to others, was completely dominant. Faced with a particular reality, he is quoted as saying, "I am capable of concentrating exclusively on it." This meant blocking "any interference having to do with thought or sentiment." As a result, according to the psychologists, Barbie is "never confronted with anything but his own imaginary constructions which can never vary or evolve over time." He is "immune to all alterity." And, the psychologists add, in the only directly political observation they make about Barbie, Nazi ideology worked very well for him because it served as an "external re-enforcement" of his internal "defenses." In terms of observations concerning Barbie's emotional responses during the interviews, the psychologists state that the only time Barbie showed emotion to them, the one time he was at a loss for words, was in attempting to discuss the death of his brother. Mentally handicapped, Barbie's younger brother, Kurt, died the same year as Barbie's father, in 1933. "Better that he died," the neighbour Johan Otten observes in *Hôtel Terminus*.

In their conclusion, the psychologists write that Barbie is not in an *état de démence*, not in "a demented state," as defined in Article 64 of the penal code, and therefore he is eligible to stand trial.

On the third day of the trial, 13 May, the three experts were called to testify in court. [14] All three affirmed that Barbie was competent to stand trial under French law and more or less amplified what they had written in their report to the investigating magistrate. Jacques Védrinne stated that Barbie suffered from no "mental malady" but then stated that Barbie sought repeatedly to project the best image of himself possible, that that image was white-washed (*aseptisée*), and that above all Barbie wanted to appear "normal." The accused, Védrinne affirmed, also sought to appear "cultivated" and "sensitive." He was prone to "moralizing." In concluding his testimony, Védrinne stated that Barbie's manner of speaking never varied during the interviews and that it was evidence of a "frozen system of thought" that allowed for no flexibility whatsoever. When his turn to testify came, Didier Weber confirmed what his colleague had stated and that tests administered to Barbie revealed no "psychiatric syndrome or problem." However, Weber added, more striking than the test results themselves was Barbie's extraordinary ability to manipulate others, including the expert administering the tests.

When his turn to testify came, Daniel Gonin, a Freudian psychoanalyst as well as a psychiatrist, broke stride with his colleagues and launched into a lengthy discussion that hardly confirmed Barbie's normality and even seemed to suggest that the accused was in fact psychologically unfit to stand trial. Gonin spoke at great length about Barbie's obsessive *anal-ité*, or anal fixation, expressed in the defendant's repeated references in interviews to his chronic constipation. According to Gonin, this was evidence that Barbie was essentially stuck in what Freud referred to as the "anal phase" of human development. Characteristic of this phase are a fixation on order, a pronounced parsimony, and a notable wilfulness or stubbornness, all characteristics, Gonin affirmed, easily observed in the defendant. Extending his analysis, Gonin went on to stress that Barbie was also locked in what he described as the *stade sadique anal*, the "sado-anal phase." In this phase, Gonin testified, sadism manifested itself in the "bi-polar" desire to destroy its object while simultaneously preserving it, in order to be able to destroy again. This, Gonin concluded, was precisely the game a cat plays with a mouse, and, presumably, the game Barbie played with his victims.

Pedantic and overly jargon-ridden in its delivery, Gonin's testimony, as the film of the trial reveals, hardly proved compelling or convincing to the court or, one might guess, to the spectators in attendance. Indeed, sensing his moment, Vergès's responded to Gonin's remarks by asking him sarcastically if a "good purgative" might not cure Barbie of his anal fixations and therefore of his murderous impulses. Moreover, in accordance with the analysis Gonin had provided, Vergès also suggested that others, and not just confirmed Nazis, might reveal entirely similar impulses. Might they therefore not be dangerous, psychologically abnormal individuals as well? Citing Molière's choice of names for his characters in *Le malade imaginaire*, Vergès inquired of Gonin if, in keeping with his analysis of Barbie, perhaps the great dramatist himself might not also be locked in an anal and pre-fascist phase? Summing up Gonin's testimony, Vergès observed ironically, if not disdainfully, "So that's why he [Barbie] is guilty!"

As if to confirm the inadequacy (not to say the failure) of the three psychological expert witnesses' efforts to convey to the court a satisfactory understanding of who Klaus Barbie was and what motivated him to commit his crimes, a month after their testimony, chief prosecutor Pierre Truche decided to address the issue directly with the accused. On 5 June (Hearing 18), Barbie was brought back to the courtroom to face witnesses and victims he had not encountered during the *instruction*.

(As noted, president Cerdini had ruled that these were the only circumstances under which Barbie would be forced to return to court, other than his final statement and sentencing.) During the testimonies of these victims, the accused remained coldly detached, refusing to respond to them or comment on what they were saying. The last witness to testify was André Courvoisier. During his testimony, Courvoisier, a Resistance fighter who had been deported by Barbie, turned to face Barbie and asked him directly if he recognized him. Barbie offered a rare sardonic smile while shaking his head "no." Immediately after Courvoisier's testimony, chief prosecutor Truche rose to address the accused. He told Barbie that he wished to speak to him of "another Barbie," the Klaus Barbie of 1933. At that time a young man of twenty, Truche recalled, although already a Nazi, Barbie had written movingly of the recent deaths of his brother and father. Moreover, as a volunteer in Catholic relief services, Barbie had worked with poor indigents and had expressed sympathy for the affronts to their human dignity they suffered daily. How had this young man of twenty, Truche asked Barbie, a man of "normal reactions," become a fanatical and brutal SS member, now on trial for crimes against humanity in the Lyon Assize court? "What happened in your life between 1934 and 1937?" Truche enquired. Then, reminding Barbie that at some point in the future, his grandchildren, or their children, looking into their own past, would want to know what Barbie had to say in response to this question, Truche informed Barbie that his answer was nothing less than "the key to your life, and the key to this trial." After a pause, Barbie spoke up, reminding Truche that he had been illegally extradited, "kidnapped" as he put it, from Bolivia, and that he was therefore "juridically absent" from the trial. Because he was waiting to see the outcome of his challenge to his illegal extradition, he could not answer Truche's question. In a rare moment in which his emotions seemed to get the best of him, Truche responded: "I pity you for living in this fiction, and you know it."

While Pierre Truche's final response to Barbie's obstinate silence was rhetorically powerful in the moment, his questioning of the accused, coupled with the psychologists' and especially Gonin's complicated and largely unpersuasive assessments of him, serve to underscore one apparent failing of the Lyon trial. Despite the best efforts of judges, prosecutors, and witnesses to make him discuss them, Barbie never revealed who he was and what his deepest motivations were. In this, the Barbie trial resembled other historical trials of Nazis, all of which, arguably, were largely unsuccessful in this part of their pedagogical mission.[15]

At this stage, the question arises as to *why*, precisely, Barbie and his defence team wished to obscure his inner feelings and the motivations for his crimes. In earlier trials of Nazis, beginning with Nuremberg, similar efforts at obfuscation had occurred, especially among Barbie's SS colleagues. In *Croire et Détruire: Les intellectuels dans la machine de guerre SS*, Christian Ingrao devotes a chapter to the strategies of defence – and obfuscation – shared by many SS war criminals as they confronted Allied courts after the war. To be sure, some of these defences presented by SS members were clearly ludicrous, even to the judges. A good example is Franz Six's claim that the main function of his *Einsatzcommando* during the invasion of the Soviet Union was to reopen churches rather than round up Jews to exterminate them. Other defences, however, were more subtle and, at least at first blush, arguably credible. Some relied on holes in the prosecution's knowledge, due to a lack of documentary evidence and other lacunae. Others included partial confessions of guilt by the accused carefully crafted to fail to measure up to the standard of culpability required by the law under which the accused was being tried. In this category, Ingrao cites the case of Walter Blume at Nuremberg. Blume admitted to carrying out killings but denied any "exterminating impulse'" required by the law.

Other SS members followed similar strategies of confessing their crimes but then deployed the "only following orders" defence by insisting that, unlike the top echelons of the SS, they were not aware that in implementing the Final Solution they were sending the Jews to their deaths. This was the strategy Werner Best recommended to his SS colleagues tried belatedly in the 1960s. Of course, the higher ups in question – Adolph Eichmann, Reinhard Heydrich, etc. – were already dead by the time of these trials, so they could be blamed all the more easily. In the investigation of Barbie's case, the accused also appeared to follow this strategy. In fact, during the investigation Barbie repeatedly invoked Eichmann's responsibility as part of an effort to deny any knowledge of the ultimate fate of the Jews he deported.

By the time of the Lyon trial – and even during the *instruction* of the case – any effort on Barbie's part to deny knowledge of the fate of Jews deported stood on very shaky ground. Already in the 1970s, when Barbie was discovered living in Bolivia, to prompt German investigators to reopen their case against him, Serge and Beate Klarsfeld had already located witnesses who provided clear evidence that he was very much aware of the terrible fate of those he deported.[16] So the question remains: why his obstinate silence on this question, and more broadly, why not open up to the court, as Truche had pleaded, and reveal something of the sensitive, "normal" human being he had been before giving himself over entirely to Nazism? This might, if fact, have secured some degree of sympathy from the court.[17]

There were several reasons. First, as part of Barbie's defence strategy, Vergès was intent on turning Barbie's trial into a "trial by rupture," in which, as noted, the court and the French nation would, in effect, "replace" the accused in the box. It was important, in accordance with this strategy, that Barbie and his crimes remain shadowy, ill-defined in the eyes of the court and jury. That way, at least in theory, he could serve as a kind of "everyman" and could be presented ultimately as the (innocent) victim of an oppressive system.[18] Barbie certainly played along with this aspect of his lawyer's strategy. At the outset of the trial, during the rehearsal of his CV, he readily responded to purely factual questions about his life and career posed by president Cerdini. But he drew the line when asked what Nazism and anti-Semitism consisted of and his feelings about both. When queried during the second audience by president Cerdini about National Socialist principles to which he personally adhered, as well as his attitude towards those the Nazis persecuted, Barbie declined to answer, explaining that his answer would take too long. When Cerdini returned to these issues at the outset of the next audience, Barbie again demurred, responding this time that all that went back forty years and implying that the subject was no longer relevant. When Cerdini insisted, Barbie stated that he had no hatred for minorities and that he did not "know the word 'hatred.'" In Bolivia, he explained, there was no racial prejudice: Jews, Arabs, Europeans, and Bolivians all worked together without animosity. On the subject of Nazism and its racialist animosities, Barbie refused to speak (13 May, Audience 3).

In *Le salaud lumineux*, a series of conversations with Jean-Louis Remilleux published a few years after the trial concluded, Vergès offered another reason for Barbie's refusal to participate in the trial to the extent of expressing his views and beliefs: pride. According to Vergès, during their many pre- and post-trial conversations in prison, Barbie candidly discussed his views about the war, expressing criticisms and reservations and admitting that even he was shocked by "this or that occurrence." When asked by Vergès why he did not express these reservations in court, presumably because they might have helped his case, Barbie responded: "*Maître* I am confiding in you because you esteem me, even if we did not share the same views during the war. You don't disdain me. [But] don't count on me to humiliate myself by repeating these things to the victors who refuse to understand me anyway" (Remilleux 286). For Vergès, at least, this refusal to humiliate himself was proof that Barbie was "a respectable man."

But there was at least arguably a more deep-seated reason for Barbie's obstinate refusal to reveal himself or discuss his motives during the trial, and that leads back to his understanding of the "line" he followed throughout his life, the "question of character" he referred to in his conversation with the Bolivian journalist during his flight back to France. This was the Nazi "ethics," or code of conduct, Barbie embraced as he had come to understand that code and live it. In responding to president Cerdini's query as to what he thought Nazism was, Barbie's response was that the answer would take "too long." This was so not just because Nazism as he understood it was too complex to sum up briefly. It was also Barbie's way of stating that neither president Cerdini, nor the court, nor the huge audience gathered could truly *understand* Nazism, the obligations it imposed, and the sense of superiority – the *true* superiority, in Barbie's eyes – it conferred on its adherents.

Part Three: Klaus Barbie and Nazi Idealism

In what ways can Klaus Barbie be considered a Nazi "idealist," and in what ways did his early experiences as a Nazi SS and Gestapo officer shape his outlook and even his brutality?[19] Truche was not wrong in insisting to Barbie – and to the court – that the "key" to Barbie's life could be found in the three years between 1933 and 1936 when a previously "sensitive" and religious youth had been transformed into a hardened SS and Gestapo officer. During that time, Truche reminded Barbie, he had attended the SD School at Bernau, where ideological indoctrination was the very heart of the training. During that time as well, Barbie had trained with the Berlin police. On night patrols, Barbie had frequented the milieus of prostitution where, according to Peter Hammerschmitt, "he had used extreme physical violence, and this experience excited him because it made him experience the intoxication of power" (33). In all likelihood, it taught Barbie more than that. As so much of the witness testimony at the trial as well as other accounts discussed earlier here suggest, it removed any scruples Barbie might have felt about torturing and abusing *women* in particular. In fact, many of the most horrendous accounts of Barbie's brutality were by women who experienced it directly or by witnesses who saw Barbie physically abuse and humiliate women in front of them (see chapter five here).

But at the heart of Barbie's beliefs and the motivations for his actions was his embrace of Nazi ideology as best he understood it. To begin with, in explaining his brutality in Occupied Lyon, Barbie certainly had personal reasons for hating the French, but hatred of the French also constituted a core belief in Nazi thinking.[20] Second, Barbie's absolute belief in his own superiority, so evident in, among many other instances, his profoundly presumptuous comparison of himself to Jean Moulin[21] certainly derived in part from the Nazi belief in the "absolute inequality between the races"[22] (Welzer 35) and in Nazi superiority. This belief, in turn, coupled with the notion that the struggle between the races was one to the death, meant that the obligation of each Nazi was to protect the Nazi race and to assure its survival. On more than one occasion, Barbie justified his crimes in Lyon in stating that German soldiers were being threatened and killed and that he would do anything necessary to protect them. These claims were not made simply to justify his actions; he clearly believed in this – for him – essentially sacred mission of protecting his fellow Germans.

One could attribute Barbie's refusal to explain himself in court, and his lack of an apology to his victims in his final statement there, to personal pride. But that reticence was also due to the fact that, as a true Nazi, Barbie believed in the *absolute morality* of his actions.[23] For the Nazis, morality was entirely race dependent, and Barbie, along with the likes of Heinrich Himmler and many other Nazi and SS before him, was secure in his own *righteousness*, his own *decency*,[24] up to the end (Welzer 35). Moreover, because morality was a function of race, and since according to Nazi ideology the races were hermetically sealed off from each other, Barbie felt no compunction to explain or justify his own morality, his moral positions, in court. In his view, those present would not have been understood anyway. Besides, to the degree that Barbie had absorbed Nazi ideas concerning the function of the law, a court such as the Lyon Assize would, for any number of reasons, have no standing, no legitimacy in his eyes.[25]

Given the nature of Nazi "morality," it is not surprising that, as reported above, psychologists like Barry Ritzler, examining the Rorschach tests of the Nuremberg defendants long after the fact, determined that the one trait they shared was a marked "lack of empathy." In his conversations with Barbie in South America in the 1970s and 1980s, Robert Wilson detected a similar lack of empathy, indeed a frightening detachment on Barbie's part, when he discussed his wartime crimes. After Barbie described killing two twelve-year-old boys who had thrown bombs into a café in Lyon and killed German troops there, Wilson observed that it "was astonishing how he could make the grotesque so plain and ordinary" (56). In describing his (imagined) fraternal encounter with Moulin, Barbie, Wilson states, discusses it like the two men were "characters in an Errol Flynn movie" (51). The war itself, Wilson adds, was "glory" and "romance," it was "exotic." Indeed, in his Gestapo memoir, Barbie refers to his brutal work in Lyon as "the Game." It is hard to imagine anyone *not* possessed of a Nazi sensibility being able to describe Barbie's actions in Lyon in similar terms. And it is important to remember that Barbie's description of his wartime actions as "the Game" occurred long after his crimes were committed. In other words, Barbie remained, as the psychologists who examined him testified in Lyon, "frozen" in his system of thinking, incapable of seeing the world from any perspective but his own point of view, one which, as the psychologists also suggested, was re-enforced by his Nazi beliefs, Nazi ideology itself.

In *Hôtel Terminus*, when Johannes Schneider-Merck laughingly alludes to Barbie's outburst "No one insults the Fuehrer in my presence," his tone and laughter suggest that he finds Barbie's attitude ridiculous, not to say ludicrous, so long after the war was over. But this response is to ignore a key component of Nazism that Barbie apparently also embraced, and that is absolute loyalty to Hitler *in perpetuity*. Hitler, after all, had "revealed the laws of History and of nature, so to obey him amounted to obeying the dictates of the [German] race itself that is, obeying all that which is the purest and most authentic in oneself" (Chapoutot 236).[26] Moreover, as Chapoutot's analysis confirms, Nazism's adherents understood full well that, despite its reliance at the outset on the person of Hitler, the Nazi utopia they sought to establish would not be "built in a day," so to speak. It would take hundreds, perhaps thousands, of years to bring to fruition; hence the idea of the "Thousand Year Reich." All the evidence accumulated in the biographies of Barbie written to date confirms that he never wavered in his Nazism and that he proudly announced that fidelity to acquaintances in South America. If Robert Taylor's epithet "Nazi idealist" is valid, Barbie clearly did not try to hide his beliefs to his American handlers in the CIC either.

More than that, Barbie also remained firm in the Nazi belief that hopes for the realization of a Nazi utopia did not end with Germany's defeat in 1945. In *The Nazi Legacy*, Magnus Linklater points out that the July 1980 coup that brought general Garcia-Meza to power in Bolivia, which Barbie helped engineer, was not intended to lead to just another right-wing dictatorship. The coup, for which Barbie had recruited European neo-fascists (the core of the so-called fiancés of death) and secured state-of-the-art weapons, was also undertaken to establish a "Fourth Reich" in the Andes. In that Andean Fourth Reich, Barbie would not be simply a loyal servant but the *eminence grise* of the regime itself. That regime, financed by cocaine money and initially supported by the CIA, collapsed when the regime's role in exporting cocaine to the United States became public knowledge and the United States withdrew its support.[27]

Barbie's role in the 1980 Bolivian coup (as well as his earlier involvements with right-wing Bolivian dictators throughout the 1970s), confirms his belief in and fidelity to Nazi ideals, as well as a willingness to apply these ideals in the post-war world. This being the case, how did he interpret events in the present? In an interview with Robert Wilson and Tom Ardies recorded in Bolivia, Barbie makes a number of observations about global politics at the time. In some ways seemingly paradoxical, these observations nevertheless confirm that his basic Nazi outlook had not changed. As might be expected, Barbie expresses his disdain for Nuremberg and, in his view, its hypocritical prosecution of "German generals" for "making war" (here, presumably, Barbie is referring to Nazi leaders being prosecuted for "crimes against peace"). Did not Anthony Eden in the Suez crisis, the French in Algeria, and the Americans in Vietnam "make war" as well, something that Nuremberg supposedly forbade (237)? Then, in discussing the case of William Calley, the American lieutenant tried for the My Lai massacre, Barbie stresses that he was a "war hero" (Wilson 109) and totally justified in his actions. Calley's "crime" reflects his ferocious will to protect his fellow Americans, just as Barbie had done in slaughtering those in France who killed German troops. In the interview with Wilson and Ardies, Barbie states (in fractured English): "I understand Lieutenant Calley very good. I understand for what reason they have deemed the liberty for him ... He has seen what I have seen 10 times or 100 times in this war [World War II]. German soldiers murdered. And Mr. Calley, Lieutenant Calley, has seen. I know. I have read he has seen these people, four or five or six American soldiers killed and their heads cut off" (231).

In turning to the Palestinian–Israel conflict, Barbie's views initially seem surprising, until his remarks make it clear that they are in keeping with Nazism's insistence on the protection of the race. Although he doesn't express support for the Jewish state – and despite the fact that it *is* the Jewish state – Barbie offers historical comparisons that justify Israel's right to put down Palestinian "Resistance." He had himself put down French Resistance in Lyon, and so, he asserts, "The Israeli people must defend [themselves]." Then he adds – clearly approvingly – "The commander from Israel imitated the SS commander ... He has defended his country, he meets resistance in an occupied country, he defends his Zionist dignity" (237).

The discussion of Israel, of course, raises a final point, and that is the nature and persistence of Barbie's anti-Semitism over time. Despite his innumerable wartime crimes against the Jews (and subsequent indicators of his anti-Semitism in South America, as described), is there any legitimacy to Barbie's own statements before the court in Lyon that he did "not know the word 'hatred'"? Were his claims to have lived peaceably in Bolivia where there is "no difference between Bolivians, Jews, Arabs, French, Germans and Americans" legitimate?

To be sure, to deny his own anti-Semitism, or evade any discussion of it in court, would be consistent with Barbie's overall defence strategy of denying his crimes against Jews. This was evident in the claim made in his final statement before the court that he did not deport the Jewish children of Izieu. But, given the weight of evidence that was presented in the trial, this claim was clearly without merit. And if Barbie embraced Nazism as fervently as he did, and remained faithful to it throughout his life, as shown, it stands to reason that his anti-Semitism was deep-seated and *permanent*.

So, then, how does one explain Barbie's recognition of Israel's right to put down Palestinian resistance and his clear admiration for the Israeli officer who acted as an SS officer would have and defended "Zionist dignity"? One possible explanation lies in a 1967 essay by Vladimir Jankélévitch under the seemingly paradoxical title "Anti-Semitism is not a Racism." In justifying his title, Jankélévitch stresses, first, that anti-Semitism is a hatred born of envy, whereas other racisms are born of disdain. (135). Moreover, as opposed to other objects of racist hatred, the Jew closely resembles the racist in physical terms[28] and for this reason cannot be simply dismissed as wholly "other" and so is all the more easily "disdained." This "difference in resemblance," as Jankélévitch describes it, is then perceived as a form of "defiance, of irreverence." But at the same time, the resemblance remains and therefore the recognition of the other in oneself. In consequence Jankélévitch writes provocatively, anti-Semitism must also be an "amorous hatred" (141) to the extent that one loves oneself.

To be sure, the subtleties of Jankélévitch's analysis may well not have applied to a figure like Klaus Barbie, whose own education was limited essentially to a high school degree and who was arguably fundamentally intellectually limited,[29] or just "passably intelligent," according to Erna Paris (36). But there is one detail of Barbie's life that makes it possible that Jankélévitch's distinctive description of anti-Semitism might apply to him, after all. According to most accounts, when Klaus Barbie was fleeing with his family along the Rat Line from Europe to South America in 1951, in choosing the alias he would use in his identity papers, he chose the name Klaus Altmann. As Barbie's biographers point out, the name "Altmann," not a common name in Germany, had belonged to Rabbi Adolph Altmann, the chief rabbi of Trier. With the rise of the Nazis, Altmann fled Germany to Amsterdam, where he was deported to his death at Auschwitz. Barbie was well aware of his existence and, according to Magnus Linklater, for the people of Trier it was "not possible" that Barbie did not choose the name deliberately as "a savage parting jest against history" (23–4) following Nazi Germany's defeat and destruction at the end of the war.

Jankélévitch's analysis of anti-Semitism, however, would offer another explanation for Barbie's choice of the name "Altmann" that is both more complex and more sinister. It would reflect Barbie's own sense of the "similarity in difference" of the Jew and explain thereby why he could alternate between a certain perverse admiration for Israelis as resembling the SS (and Barbie along with them) and a need to lash out at the "defiance" and "irreverence" their very existence seemed to project. These powerful emotions would explain Barbie's violent outbursts against his Jewish victims and his willingness to deport so many to their deaths. In the end, however, attempting to understand the deepest personal well-springs of Barbie's anti-Semitism (if indeed there were any) beyond his commitment to Nazism must remain a matter of speculation.[30]

To conclude: what loose ends, what elements in Barbie's behaviour, what moments from his past remain unaccounted for here? To return to Truche's questions to Barbie on 5 June 1987, what had become of the young man who had spoken movingly of the deaths of his father and brother and more crucially, perhaps, had discussed his charitable feelings towards, and efforts on behalf of, indigents he hardly knew? In other words, what had happened to Klaus Barbie's capacity for empathy? A straightforward answer is that it had been snuffed out entirely by Barbie's Nazi and SS training, which emphasized toughness and emotional detachment while murderously suppressing the enemy. But it is also true that Barbie's itinerary and early experiences in life mirror those of many of his brutal SS superiors, described in works like Ingrao's *Believe and Destroy: Intellectuals in the SS War Machine* and Michael Wildt's *An Uncompromising Generation: The Nazi Leadership of the Reich Main Security Office.*[31] Like these men, Nazi fanaticism derived from a number of factors and frustrations. Like them, Barbie was too young to be a participant in World War I, experiencing it instead on the home front. Like them as well, Barbie experienced the trauma of the war indirectly through the devastating effects of his father's painful war wound and alcoholism and their impact on his family. Moreover, as noted, Barbie shared with his SS and SD superiors the dislocations of post–World War I Germany, and the presence of foreign troops to be resisted at all costs marked him deeply as well. In addition, certainly, the unprecedented ferocity of World War II itself, the "war of night," in which Barbie proved to be such an enthusiastic participant, played a part. Finally, the absolute cold bloodedness of Nazi policies in occupied territories could also certainly explain or cover for Barbie's own sadistic impulses and actions that shocked even some of his SS colleagues in Lyon.

But to the end, Barbie was also capable, as the psychologists reported, of being overwhelmed by emotion when attempting to tell them about the death of his brother. As his daughter, Ute, reported, he was an affectionate and tender father (and grandfather) and never wavered in that. During the trial, as he was being questioned about his life and career by president Cerdini, Barbie visibly choked up when acknowledging his son's death in the hang-gliding accident. To all appearances, whatever Barbie's capacity for feelings for others, perhaps sympathy or empathy for their sufferings, had been reduced to encompass only the immediate circle of his family members. In this, at least, Klaus Barbie remained human.

Chapter Two

The Historical Judicial Backdrop: From Nuremberg to the 1980 Cologne Trial of Kurt Lischka, Herbert Hagen, and Ernst Heinrichson

Although the trial of Klaus Barbie was unprecedented in that it was the first French trial involving charges of crimes against humanity, it nevertheless formed part of a continuum that included earlier trials of prominent Nazis and their French collaborators. During the lead-up to the Barbie trial, as well as subsequently, these earlier trials served frequently as reference points and points of comparison that helped reporters and critics, as well as lawyers and judges, sort out the issues at stake in the Lyon courtroom. Comparisons with earlier trials of Nazis also influenced judgments on the ultimate success or failure of the Lyon proceedings and the lessons to be drawn from Barbie's conviction.

Foremost among the trials referenced were the 1945–6 International Military Tribunal (IMT) at Nuremberg of Nazi leaders, including Hermann Goering, Julius Streicher, Karl Doenitz, and nineteen others, and the 1961 trial in Jerusalem of Adolph Eichmann. Comparisons with these trials in the contemporary press as well as in subsequent analyses were frequent and certainly not surprising, given the magnitude and visibility of the proceedings in Lyon. In the courtroom itself, lawyers for the defence and prosecution referenced the IMT and the Eichmann trial in making legal and historical points and, on occasion, in framing their own arguments and rhetoric.

At the same time, however, there were other, less visible or memorable trials of former Nazis that did not draw the attention of the media or of subsequent commentators on the trial but that nevertheless shed light on the Barbie trial or crucial aspects of it that have been overlooked. The trials of Barbie's SS superiors in France provided legal and historical context for Barbie's actions and crimes. Documents from these trials were helpful to lawyers, judges, and magistrates involved in the case and in fact formed part of Barbie's criminal dossier. For example, legal documents, including indictments and records of interrogations of the accused from the 1980 Cologne trial of Kurt Lischka, Herbert Hagen, and Ernst Heinrichson, were requested from the West German government by investigating magistrate Christian Riss. These documents were translated into French by official court translators and made available to lawyers for the defence and prosecution.

This chapter examines these earlier trials and considers the ways in which comparisons with them proved helpful, or detrimental, in contextualizing and understanding the historical, legal, and moral issues at stake in Lyon in 1987.

The Nuremberg, Eichmann, and Auschwitz Trials

In retrospect, the attention devoted to the Nuremberg and Eichmann trials in discussions and assessments of the Barbie trial seems misplaced, to the extent that the accused in the earlier trials were major figures in the Nazi hierarchy and of much greater historical significance in the history of World War II than Klaus Barbie. Barbie, after all, held the relatively modest rank of lieutenant in the SS while serving in Lyon, and unlike the Nuremberg defendants and Eichmann, Barbie's criminal activities were limited to that city and the surrounding region. Indeed, as noted in the introduction here, in the lead-up to the 1987 trial, some in France expressed the view that Barbie was unworthy of a trial of the historical magnitude that his trial would necessarily assume. The former wife of Jean Moulin, for example, suggested that Barbie deserved nothing better than simply to be shot for his crimes and then forgotten.[1]

Nevertheless, the Barbie trial *was* in fact a successor to or legacy of the International Military Tribunal at Nuremberg in that, until subsequently modified by the Court of Cassation in 1985, the definition of crimes against humanity used in drawing up the initial indictment of Barbie was essentially the definition used by the IMT. Especially for critics of the Barbie trial, Nuremberg was much more than that. Comparisons with the 1945–6 Nuremberg tribunal afforded these critics, first, the opportunity to underscore perceived shortcomings and failings of the proceedings in Lyon. Just another example of "victor's justice" for some, for others the Barbie trial besmirched the legal and historical legacies of Nuremberg. Indeed, as noted, for Alain Finkielkraut, the Barbie trial was ultimately a "mockery" of the earlier trial. Rather than underscore the horrific and unprecedented nature of Nazi crimes, as had Nuremberg, the Barbie trial foregrounded what Finkielkraut called the "spectacular collusion of the representatives of the Third World [Barbie's defence counsel] with a Nazi torturer" (26).

In *Remembering in Vain,* Finkielkraut went on to emphasize other ways in which the Barbie trial compared unfavourably with Nuremberg, even while criticizing the latter. For example, the fact that the IMT yoked the charge of crimes against humanity to the crime of aggressive war, or "crimes against peace," meant that victims of Nazism's crimes against humanity committed before the war began were not classified or prosecuted as such. As Finkielkraut observed, victims of "the anti-Jewish decrees [in Germany] made before the war were excluded from the case for the prosecution," even though they constituted, in his view at least, the victims of "the first stage of the Final Solution" (55).

At stake for the framers of the laws applied at Nuremberg was the protection of the principle of national sovereignty, specifically that each nation has the right to apply its own laws internally, with no external interference. This protection served the interests of the accusing nations as well. But for Finkielkraut, tying crimes against humanity to Germany's war of aggression had the effect of "watering down" the core idea of what crimes against humanity actually *were.* In Finkielkraut's view, crimes against humanity "transcended" such practical, but arguably no longer morally valid, principles as national sovereignty so thoroughly abused by Nazi Germany.

At least implicitly, the Court of Cassation's 1985 decision linking crimes against humanity to a "regime practicing a politics of ideological hegemony" did undo the Nuremberg shortcoming just described, to the extent that there was no restriction linking crimes against humanity to acts of aggressive war in French law. However, according to Finkielkraut, the Court of Cassation "blurred even further the definition of crimes against humanity [than had Nuremberg]" by including some Resistance fighters among the victims of Barbie's crimes against humanity. This was done, Finkielkraut argued, out of a newly predominant sense or "feeling" of sympathy in the West for *all* those who suffer, a sympathy "that has enabled us to mobilize ourselves without preliminary selection, for all the victims of inhumanity" (56). As a result, "today we feel free enough to denounce all crimes without drawing distinctions about their origin or finality" (56). In Finkielkraut's view, this could and did ultimately serve Vergès and his legal team's disruptive aims and strategies.

In *The Memory of Judgment,* the American legal scholar Lawrence Douglas echoed Finkielkraut's views, although Douglas articulated these views in different terms. For Douglas, the 1985 definition of crimes against humanity handed down by the Court of Cassation also freed these crimes from Nuremberg's "restrictive judicial moor" in no longer linking them explicitly to a war of aggression, but rather to a particular state. Following Finkielkraut once again, Douglas also believed that in including

Resistance members as victims of crimes against humanity, it blurred that definition. In Douglas's colourful language, this had the result of "enfolding" all atrocities into crimes against humanity's "bloated domain" (196). But as Douglas pointed out, the Court of Cassation's definition of crimes against humanity was consistent with earlier French legal thinking on the subject articulated precisely at Nuremberg. There, the French deputy prosecutor Charles Dubost had dissented from the notion that crimes against humanity needed to be tied to aggressive war, or "crimes against peace." According to Douglas, Dubost posited that "the international component of crimes against humanity was satisfied not by the connection to aggressive war, but because the agent of such crimes was a state" (194). In this sense, in making its decision in 1985, the Court of Cassation actually remained closer to minority French opinion in these matters at Nuremberg than to the actual Nuremberg precedent.

Finally, the Nuremberg precedent served as a means of appreciating another change or modification made in French law as a result of the 1985 Court of Cassation decision. According to Guyora Binder, the London Agreement had deemed "the execution of combatants to be a crime against humanity" only if it involved an animus towards these combatants' origins and beliefs. But, Binder explained, the Court of Cassation decision expanded the class of potential victims of crimes against humanity to include any combatant "opposing" the persecution of *others* because of their origins and beliefs. In strictly human terms, if not in legal ones, the 1985 decision marked a positive step beyond the Nuremberg precedent.

There is one further comparison between the Barbie trial and the IMT that should be mentioned which critics did not discuss. This concerns the matter of restricting the possibility of committing crimes against humanity to agents of a particular nation or regime. In the revised 1985 definition of crimes against humanity applied in Lyon in 1987, the clause concerning "regimes practicing a policy of ideological hegemony" prevented French crimes in Algeria, American crimes in Vietnam, and similar crimes by other democracies from being included, as these regimes by definition did not practise a politics of "ideological hegemony." At Nuremberg, yoking crimes against humanity to a war of aggression had the same effect. It meant that Soviet crimes, such as the slaughter of Polish elites at Katyn, or American and Allied carpet bombing of German cities and civilian populations could not be incriminated in accordance with the laws applied at Nuremberg. Both nations were the victims of aggression in the war and not the aggressors. But then, as Judith Shklar argued in *Legalism*, while comparisons between the prosecuting nations and Nazi Germany in terms of *conventional warfare* might be justified

(Robert Jackson appeared to have thought so on witnessing the destruction in the city of Nuremberg) there were acts which only the Nazis, "and no one else, had performed. These acts, in fact, were Nazism" (164).

Unlike the IMT in Nuremberg, the 1961 trial of Adolph Eichmann in Israel was not an international tribunal. Rather, it was a national trial involving domestic criminal law. Moreover, only one man was on trial in Jerusalem, as opposed to the twenty-two accused in the dock at Nuremberg. For these reasons, the Eichmann trial more closely resembled the Barbie trial than did Nuremberg.

There were more substantive reasons to compare the two national trials as well. First, the two accused were powerful national symbols at the time of their respective trials. Eichmann was the so-called architect of the Final Solution of the Jewish Question, which concerned *all Jews*. He was tried in the newly established Jewish state still seeking to establish a national identity that included the victims of the Holocaust as well as those who had been in Palestine long before the war. For his part, Barbie, the legendary "Butcher of Lyon," was the epitome and embodiment of the cruel Nazi oppressor in wartime France who martyred hundreds if not thousands of French Resistance fighters. But he was *also* responsible for the deaths of thousands of Jews, and his trial was the first in France to focus explicitly on the Holocaust and those responsible for it. As such, as noted, the Barbie trial marked a crucial stage in a "coming to consciousness" of France's role in the Nazi Final Solution, in addition to offering a public and national forum to expose and reflect on the martyrdom of France's Resistance victims.

Additionally, the circumstances of the South American "arrests" of both Eichmann and Barbie were highly controversial before, during, and even after their respective trials were over. Both actions were denounced by their critics as illegal, clear violations of international law. The kidnapping of Eichmann from Argentina proved to be an international diplomatic incident involving Israel and Argentina, stirring a global debate that reached the floor of the United Nations. In Barbie's case, the issue was different, but controversial nonetheless. While the newly leftist Bolivian government was eager to get the increasingly visible and unrecalcitrant former Nazi off Bolivian soil, many internationally decried the fact that that government had been "paid off" by the French government under Mitterrand to expel Barbie. In fact, Bolivia was rewarded handsomely for its cooperation. Peter Hammerschmidt cites a CIA document that states that the Mitterrand government proposed fifty tons of arms to the Bolivian government for Barbie, to be distributed to leftist militias supporting the new government in power. When the trial got underway in Lyon, the defence pointed out to the court that the accused was in the process of appealing his "illegal extradition" from Bolivia to France to the Bolivian Supreme Court. Hammerschmidt points out, however, that under Bolivian law, the sitting government had the authority to expel individuals, but only the Bolivian Supreme Court could extradite them. Hence Barbie's appeal (282). When Barbie abruptly left the Lyon Assize court on the third day of the trial, his stated reason was that he had been brought to France illegally and that he was therefore "juridically absent" from his trial.

Third, the Eichmann and Barbie trials were connected by another concern, the question of applying the death penalty to the accused, should that individual be convicted. In both countries, capital punishment was outlawed, but in Israel an exception was made for Eichmann, given the unprecedented magnitude of his crimes. In France, during the investigation of Barbie's case, some proposed following Israel's example in making an exception for Barbie. But in France, the question was somewhat more fraught politically, given that one of the signature accomplishments of the Mitterrand government and its justice minister, Robert Badinter, was the elimination of capital punishment in France in October 1981. Still, in a national poll taken in February 1983, 56 per cent of French were in favour of restoring the death penalty exclusively for Barbie. In the end, however, French authorities declined to make an exception in the former Nazi's case.

From the standpoint of the nature of the arguments made in the Lyon Assize court, there is another interesting comparison between the two trials as well. In her book *Transformative Justice*, Leora Bilsky notes that, as opposed to Hannah Arendt, who wished to make the Nazi Holocaust an outgrowth of modern totalitarianism, the Israeli prosecutor Gideon Hausner sought to make it the continuation and outcome of an age-old and *universal* anti-Semitism that continued into the present. In the Barbie trial, it was Vergès and his co-counsel, ironically, who offered a comparable global and "timeless" perspective on Barbie's crimes by submerging them (and all Nazi crimes, implicitly) in a universalizing narrative of the centuries-old violence and oppressiveness of Europe and the white man. In both the Jerusalem and Lyon courtrooms, these arguments led away from the specificity of the Holocaust and crimes committed in implementing its aims, and arguably at least – and certainly inadvertently in Hausner's case – thereby blurred the historical specificity (not to say uniqueness) of the crimes committed by the accused.

Finally, given the legendary status of the Eichmann trial for many French – justice minister Robert Badinter, for one, had actually attended the historic trial in Jerusalem[2] – it is not surprising that echoes of the

Jerusalem trial could be heard in statements and claims made by lawyers for the prosecution and defence.

Invoking the memory – and memorable rhetoric – of the Jerusalem courtroom, civil parties lawyer Alain Jakubovicz chose to begin his final statement before the court by stating that "through my voice, six million victims are attempting to speak to you." (This was, of course, an exaggeration, given the limited number of civil parties Jakubovitz represented.) For many of those present in the Lyon courtroom, Jakubovitz's choice of phrasing certainly recalled Hausner's opening statement in the House of the Jewish People in Jerusalem in which he claimed to be the spokesperson "for the six million accusers who stood with him but who no longer had voices."[3]

In his defence of Barbie, Vergès also referred to the Eichmann trial in challenging the legitimacy of a key piece of evidence used in Lyon: the telex in which Barbie reported the arrest and deportation of the Jewish children of Izieu. That same document, Vergès claimed, was dismissed as evidence in Jerusalem because, for the Israeli court, it could not be adequately authenticated.

In a 19 December 1983 interrogation by investigating magistrate Riss, the accused himself invoked the Eichmann trial record in an effort to deny personal responsibility for the round-up of Jews at the offices of the UGIF in February 1943. Pressed on the matter by Riss, Barbie stated unequivocally: "I'd like, once and for all, to place into evidence certain points [*sic*] for which I am indicted, and these deal with Jewish affairs. It is recorded in the minutes of the Eichmann trial that all actions concerning Jews were centralized through Berlin at Office IV. It was called at the time 'Office IV Eichmann'" (K: P1/ 83–7). So all such actions in the occupied territories against the Jews were undertaken on orders coming from Berlin, via Paris. Which is to say, not on Barbie's initiative. The trial eventually confirmed that this claim was false.

Later, during the same interrogation, Barbie referred to the Eichmann trial again. Barbie was confronted with the testimony of Raymond Geissmann, the director of the UGIF in Lyon in 1943–4, who confirmed that he had overheard Barbie state to his victims: "Shot or deported, it's the same thing."[4] For all intents and purposes, this proved that Barbie was aware of the ultimate fate of those he sent to the camps. Barbie's response was that this phrase was "placed in the mouths" of many SS members tried after the war, and that "a comparable expression" appeared in a memoir of the Eichmann trial written by an "Israeli Captain Less."[5]

In what ways do these comparisons between the Barbie trial and the Nuremberg and Eichmann trials, some explicitly made and others gleaned from issues and controversies that arose in the press and else-where, clarify legal, historical, and moral issues at stake in Lyon in 1987?

In legal terms, concerns about the blurring or "bloating" of the concept of crimes against humanity in moving from Nuremberg to the Barbie prosecution were legitimate. In fact, within the French context, they would re-emerge later, and occasionally dramatically, especially in relation to the 1990s prosecutions of the *milicien* Paul Touvier and Vichy bureaucrat Maurice Papon.

But on another level, the tendency of commentators and critics of the Barbie trial to focus almost exclusively on damage done to the concept and clarity of crimes against humanity in moving from Nuremberg to the Barbie trial overlooked crucial lessons of Nuremberg that a national trial like the Barbie trial would perhaps necessarily obscure. Specifically, these concerned international law and international cooperation in bringing what are now often described as "rogue states" like Nazi Germany to justice.

In the Annual Address given to the New York Bar Association in January 1947, the chief prosecutor at the International Military Tribunal and associate justice of the US Supreme Court, Robert H. Jackson, discussed what he considered to be the major accomplishments of the IMT as well as its lessons for future international tribunals. Of the many topics Jackson addressed, *none* concerned the definition or meaning of crimes against humanity. Rather, they concerned such issues as the IMT's legacies in the evolution of international law. They also addressed what Jackson described as the "function" of the court and the discussions among the prosecuting nations pertaining to matters such as rules of evidence and what kind of evidence was ultimately used in court. Jackson also addressed the question of whether or not cross-examination of the witnesses would be allowed at Nuremberg, whether the accused would be permitted to testify on their own behalf, and subsequently what impact these testimonies had on the court and the public. Finally, Jackson discussed the lessons that could be derived from these testimonies.

For Jackson, the most important legacy of Nuremberg were the precedents it set for international cooperation and international law. He stressed that "the Nuremberg undertaking afford[ed] lawyers an actual working experiment in the comparison of laws."[6] And in its outcome and judgments, the IMT also demonstrated "the extent to which four nations, despite the different systems of jurisprudence were able to agree on issues at stake." As a result, the judgment stood as something of a "landmark in international cooperation and understanding."[7]

Some of the other issues Jackson addressed were more germane to the Barbie trial. In discussing the "function" of the Nuremberg Tribunal,

Jackson addressed the absolute necessity of the latter's independence, not specifically in terms of individual prosecutors responding to state directives, but to the degree to which the court was able to avoid being seen as an "organ" of a state whose primary function was to protect state power or that state's people. At Nuremberg, after much discussion among the prosecuting nations, the decision was made that the tribunal should be entirely independent of *any* state or national influence or purpose.[8] This was essential to protect its legitimacy in the eyes of world opinion. In the Barbie trial and in the French Assize court system itself, by contrast, this is not the case, as the court is an arm of the state to the extent that its function is to protect the French republic and people. It was precisely this linkage between the French state and the Lyon Assize court that Vergès repeatedly denounced in an effort to sway the judges and especially the jury to his client's advantage.

Another issue discussed by Robert Jackson which was relevant to the Barbie trial was the testimony of key defendants. In his address, Jackson mentioned specifically the testimony of Hermann Goering. In its defiance and "cynical wit," Goering's testimony won the "applause of the galleries and the admiration of shallow sympathizers" (149). But Goering's testimony also underscored the fact that his "guilt was unique in its enormity" and his "conviction inevitable." And, Jackson concluded, that testimony should instruct "the American people" (and presumably those of other democracies) as to what the early symptoms of totalitarianism are and "serve as a reminder that totalitarianism itself can only be stopped in its early stages" (149).

In absenting himself from the Lyon courtroom and, when present, refusing to discuss Nazism or answer anything but factual, largely biographical, questions by the president and chief prosecutor, Barbie deprived the Lyon court of precisely the crucial information and insights that could justify his conviction. Moreover, his testimony certainly did not provide the kind of lesson and warning Goering's testimony provided to the Nuremberg court. If Barbie revealed anything, it was that he shared Goering's disdain for the court as well and the idea of justice it represented.

In refusing to testify in any substantive sense, Barbie also made the prosecution's case that much harder, both in explaining his motives and offering evidence of his own numerous and horrific crimes. For those critics who used the Nuremberg comparison to diminish the Lyon Assize court's accomplishment in successfully prosecuting and convicting Barbie, Goering's volubility as opposed to Barbie's silence underscored the fact that in important ways the Lyon prosecution had to overcome obstacles that the Nuremberg IMT did not face.

If comparisons between the Nuremberg and Barbie trials proved illuminating in some instances and less so in others, comparisons between the Eichmann and Barbie trials also offer mixed results. For example, the civil parties lawyer Alain Jacubowicz's variation on Gideon Hausner's famous statement to the effect that he spoke for six million Jewish ghosts who could not speak for themselves seems to have represented a good faith effort to inscribe Barbie's crimes in the enormity of the Holocaust. At the same time, however, it appeared to place the crimes perpetuated by the two accused, Eichmann and Barbie, on the same level, and this simply was not accurate. Moreover, raising such issues as suspending the ban on capital punishment for Barbie as had been done for Eichmann during the lead-up to the trial may have enjoyed a brief national popularity, but it also tended to anticipate the outcome of the trial. This justified claims by some who, like the American journalist Ted Morgan, described the trial as a "necessary travesty."

In the meantime, other interesting connections were missed or not emphasized. Perhaps most notably, the Barbie trial resembled the Eichmann trial in the sheer *power* and importance of witness testimony. This dimension of the Barbie trial also distanced the Lyon proceedings from the IMT, which eschewed witness testimony in favour of documentary evidence. Indeed, after the Barbie trial was over, several individuals who had been involved as participants in the Lyon trial remarked that the most memorable aspect of the entire proceedings was the testimony of many witnesses, especially women witnesses. If, for many, the Eichmann trial is most memorable for the testimony of figures like the distraught writer and Holocaust survivor K Zetnik, who collapsed in the courtroom following his testimony, and the Jewish Resistance hero Abba Kovner, among the most remarkable moments in the Barbie trial occurred with the testimonies of Barbie's female Jewish and Resistance victims. These included the testimonies of Simone Kadosche-Lagrange, Lise Lesèvre, and the aforementioned Geneviève de Gaulle-Anthonioz, Charles de Gaulle's niece. To the degree that the Barbie trial is memorable – and perhaps most memorable – for these testimonies, it marks an important episode in what Annette Wieviorka has labelled the "era of the witness," inaugurated years before in the courtroom in Jerusalem in 1961.

Another and perhaps final point of comparison between the Eichmann and Barbie trials concerns what might be described as the respective linguistic advantages and disadvantages of the accused. Critics have noted that in the Eichmann trial, even in testifying in German, Eichmann was at a relative linguistic and indeed cultural disadvantage before his judges, as his pedestrian and cliché-ridden German did not measure up to the elegant and refined language skills of his judges, all of whom were highly educated German Jews. In the Lyon courtroom, Barbie's power of silence, his deliberate use of German throughout most of the proceedings such that judges, jury, lawyers, and audience members had to wait patiently for translators to render it into French, and then his deliberate – and stunning – use of French before the court in making his final statement, all made Barbie more the "master of the game," than Eichmann. And without question Barbie used this advantage effectively. If Barbie's linguistic manipulations did not help his case in the end, they certainly served as distractions to the court and prosecution in their effort to keep the trial focused on the task at hand. At least one of Barbie's SS superiors in France, Helmut Knochen, tried the same tactic to distract the court in his 1954 trial in Paris for war crimes, ultimately to no avail.[9]

Before turning to French and German trials that were more directly linked to the Lyon trial, it is instructive to consider briefly another postwar trial that has been overlooked by critics of the Barbie trial. This is the 1963–5 trial in Frankfurt of SS officials and guards serving at Auschwitz on charges of murder. In her book *Beyond Justice*, Rebecca Wittmann notes that for a number of reasons, until the early 1990s the Auschwitz trial was largely forgotten by the public or conflated with the later Nuremberg trials (NMT) that lasted until 1949. This may explain why it was not alluded to in commentaries on the Barbie trial. Nevertheless, the Auschwitz trial was noteworthy in that in some ways it foreshadowed the Lyon trial and in fact underscored legal successes that the prosecution of Barbie accomplished that the German trial did not.

Like the Barbie trial in Lyon more than twenty years later, the Auschwitz trial was the "largest, most public, and most important" trial of Nazi criminals to be carried out in accordance with domestic, national law (Wittmann 3). And like the Barbie (and Eichmann) trial, it was a trial of truly national significance. It was intended, as chief prosecutor Fritz Bauer stated in a news conference shortly before the trial opened, to show "Germans and the world" that "a new Germany, a new democracy" were "necessary." This must be a democracy, he continued, where the "dignity of everyone is guaranteed." The accused, Wittmann notes, were "guards and functionaries of the lowest rung of the Nazi hierarchy" (6), many of whom were torturers and "sadists," – as was Klaus Barbie by most accounts. Due to the sheer horror of their crimes, described in lurid detail in the Frankfurt courtroom, the Auschwitz personnel on trial inspired "sensational, attention-grabbing news" that "most Germans could not ignore" (6).

There were other parallels with the Auschwitz trials as well. According to Hannah Arendt, all but one of the defendants at the Auschwitz trial displayed a remarkable arrogance and "open contempt for court," insulting witnesses, demanding that prosecuting attorneys apologize, and occasionally glaring at members of the audience who gasped on hearing the details of what witness-victims had undergone.[10] The American playwright Arthur Miller, who reported on the trial for the *New York Times* also observed that "none of the accused has suggested he may have done something wrong: there is no sign of remorse."[11] Moreover, regardless of the complete implausibility of their claims, most of the accused at Frankfurt stated that they had no knowledge of the brutal crimes that had occurred under their noses at Auschwitz. As an exasperated Judge Hans Hofmeyer later stated, "I have yet to meet anyone who did anything at Auschwitz. The commandant was not there, the officer in charge only happened to be present, the representative of the Political Section only carried lists, and still another only came with the keys" (qtd. in Arendt, *Responsibility* 232).

While Barbie's behaviour was somewhat more measured in the Lyon courtroom, his arrogance, and certainly his disdain for the court and indifference to the suffering of his former victims who were testifying, were manifest in his refusal to answer questions or react with anything more than a "no comment" to their testimony. At no time did he express any remorse. In the hundreds of pages of direct interrogations of Barbie, and so-called confrontations with his victims conducted during the *instruction*, Barbie was equally dismissive and disdainful of their testimony. He accused them of possessing too vivid an imagination and denied flatly having committed the crimes of which he was being accused. In most cases, Barbie claimed that he had never met his accuser or that he had forgotten him or her if he had. At the conclusion of one such confrontation, Barbie lamented on the record: "Everybody knows me, but I don't know any of these people." The only difference between Barbie's claims of total ignorance to similar claims by the Auschwitz defendants was that, with the additional twenty plus years intervening, he could more reasonably claim to have "forgotten" virtually everything.

Reflecting on some of the moral issues raised by the proceedings in Frankfurt, Arthur Miller pointed to evident paradoxes as well as what he described as "enigmas" he witnessed. Miller was struck, for example, by the courtroom behaviour of one of the defendants, Oswald Kaduk, whom Miller described as a "real sadist" whose "violence seemed to show in his quick, roving eyes" (63). Miller goes on to describe Kaduk's drunken murderousness at Auschwitz and then notes that, after the war, Kaduk went to work in a hospital. There, Miller writes, he was so kind and gentle with his patients that he was affectionately known by them as "Papa Kaduk." Miller accounted for this seeming paradox and for Kaduk's belligerence in the courtroom by suggesting that Kaduk had come to believe that he really was "Papa Kaduk" and not the brutal Auschwitz guard.

At the Barbie trial and in the *instruction* leading up to it, more than a few of Barbie's victims stressed the almost demonic hatred and cruelty in Barbie's eyes. At the same time, however, in a few fleeting moments in the trial, Barbie showed flashes of tenderness, not to his victims but concerning his family. More than once he looked out into the crowded hall and smiled gently at his daughter, Ute Messmer. In discussing the untimely death of his son in a hang-gliding accident, Barbie, as noted, momentarily lost his composure and fought back tears (13 May, Hearing 3). As the previous chapter shows, however, there is no evidence to suggest that Barbie underwent the kind of transformation or change in self-perception that Miller believes Kaduk underwent.

In reflecting on the Auschwitz trial, Miller also focused his attention on what he described as an "enigma to many foreigners," and that is the German people's "capacity for moral and psychological collapse in the face of a higher command" (65). And, Miller added, the fact that the "German soul" "finds honor and goodness and decency in obedience" (66) meant that the German spectators at the Auschwitz trial were actually torn between their sympathy for the victims and their sympathy, or even identification with, the behavioural motives of many of the accused. Miller wrote: "The problem for the Germans is that they are being called upon to identify themselves with the victims when their every instinct would lead them to identify with the uniformed, disciplined killers" (67).

Perhaps anachronistic and "essentialist' by today's standards, Miller's assessment of the reactions of the German audience in the Auschwitz trial would in any case not be applicable to the largely French audience in Lyon. Nevertheless, it is at least arguably true that the court's efforts to "understand" Barbie and his motives through questioning as well as in the testimony by psychologists early in the trial focused in the main on *individual* psychology and *personal* motivations, to the exclusion of any reflection on perceived "national" traits that might also have informed Barbie's behaviour. But then a more "French" and Cartesian perspective would, at least theoretically, focus primarily on the individual, as well as more "rational" and less communal or tribal motivations and characteristics.

Finally, and most significantly in legal terms, the legal framework within which the Frankfurt trial was forced to operate serves to underscore the greater flexibility of the French framework in Lyon, despite the latter's failings. If, as its critics claim, jurisprudence in the Barbie trial obscured the meaning of crimes against humanity, in the German courtroom the jurisprudence employed risked confusing the very notion of *criminality*, of criminal murderousness itself. As Wittman explains in *Beyond Justice*, a 1949 prohibition on retroactive legislation "made invalid all ex post facto laws (those charging individuals with crimes that were allegedly not illegal when committed)" (7). This meant that such crimes as crimes against humanity, defined and codified in the charter of the IMT, could not be applied to the Auschwitz criminals charged. Instead, the court had recourse to the 1871 German definition of murder that required proving the "subjective motivation and individual initiative of each perpetrator in order to convict him" (7).

The consequences of this, as Wittmann explains, included both a perversion of the historical record as well as any generally accepted notion of justice being turned on its head. In effect, the accused who were condemned and most harshly punished were those "who had gone *beyond* [emphasis mine] the acts of murder ordered by Himmler and Hitler" (6). So the "killing of millions in the gas chambers – the main form of murder at Auschwitz, after all – became a lesser crime, calling for a lighter sentence, than the murder of one person carried out without orders from superiors" (6). According to this framework, Adolph Eichmann, certainly as understood by Hannah Arendt, as well as other "desk killers" like him, might have gotten off or at least received a lighter sentence.

By contrast, the prosecution in Lyon had neither to deal with a ban on retroactivity nor the necessity of proving brutal personal motives on the part of the accused, although the latter were amply exposed in the courtroom testimony of his victims as well as others. And in grappling with a "bloated" definition of crimes against humanity, the Lyon court was not working within the confines of a law that might actually exonerate the accused of *all* of his crimes, but only one that ostensibly blurred the distinction between which of his victims were victims of crimes against humanity and which were victims of war crimes. While for some that distinction was crucial in historical and legal terms, it did not call into question the very premise of criminality itself in Barbie's case.

Earlier Trials of Barbie's Nazi Superiors in France: Karl Oberg, Helmut Knochen

In French memory today, the Barbie trial stands out as, among other things, the first historic trial of what some call the "Second Purge" of Nazis and French collaborators. In addition to the Barbie trial, the Second Purge also included the 1994 trial of Paul Touvier and the 1997–8 trial of Maurice Papon, and would have included the trial of Vichy chief of police René Bousquet, had he not been assassinated by a deranged gunman in 1993.

The trials of Karl Oberg and Helmut Knochen, Barbie's SS superiors in Paris, form part of the first or original Purge, commonly known as *l'Epuration*, which took place in France in the immediate post-war years, from 1945 to 1955. *L'Epuration* consisted of numerous trials and legal proceedings intended in part to curtail the many instances of "rogue" or "popular" justice that followed the Liberation. The latter included infamous acts of shaving the heads of women suspected of "horizontal collaboration" with the Germans and then parading them through the streets of French towns and villages, as well as beatings and summary executions of male collaborators.

Trials occurring during the *Epuration* took place primarily before military tribunals or before the newly established High Court of Justice. The High Court tried numerous highly placed Vichy officials, including Marshall Phillipe Pétain in August 1945 and Vichy *Président du Conseil* Pierre Laval in October of the same year. Followed closely by the public, these trials in the High Court were not without incident. Laval's trial in particular set off fireworks. Especially reviled for having publicly stated during the war that he hoped for a German victory, Laval nevertheless protested his patriotism in the courtroom and denounced officers of the High Court who not long before had served the Vichy regime. In response, members of the jury were heard to threaten the former second-in-command at Vichy, calling out to him "you won't be complaining so loud in fifteen days!" (qtd. in Théolleyre 17–18). Laval-like Klaus Barbie – more than forty years later – decided abruptly to quit his own trial to protest its perceived injustice, despite warnings from the judge that this would not help his cause. Laval was eventually convicted of treason. He was executed by firing squad, although it had been necessary to revive him from a botched suicide attempt in order to do so.

Nazi, and especially SS officials who had served in France were tried by French military tribunals, if they had not managed to escape back to Germany at the end of the war. Of the latter, several, including Barbie and a number of his SS colleagues and superiors, were tried in absentia. Some, like Barbie, were condemned to death. Others who were considered to have committed lesser offenses were given life sentences.

However, the most important SS officers in wartime France, general Karl Oberg and his adjutant, Colonel Helmut Knochen, did not escape at the end of the Occupation, at least not for long. Oberg was captured in Germany in 1945 and sent back to France for trial. Knochen, recalled to Berlin late in the war, was stripped of his administrative rank and finished the war in a combat unit of the SS. He was replaced in Paris by Kurt Lischka. Captured by American forces after the war, Knochen was eventually extradited to France in July 1947. In the interim, he had been convicted and sentenced to death in absentia in a British court for the murder of British airmen. After a lengthy investigation of their cases by French magistrates, Oberg and Knochen were put on trial together in 1954, just as the *Epuration* was winding down.

Oberg, described in *Le Monde* as the perfect caricature of the Prussian soldier, "made for the uniform," was fifty-seven years old at the time of the trial. Inflexible, arrogant, and harsh by nature, Oberg had been introduced as an SS police commander in France by Reinhard Heydich. He became good friends with Vichy chief of police René Bousquet during the war. The two men negotiated the infamous Oberg/Bousquet accords of 1942 (renewed in 1943) which, in exchange for greater French police autonomy, especially in the Unoccupied Zone, assured the Germans of French support and participation on the round-ups of Jews. (At least initially, the round-ups targeted only foreign Jews who had taken refuge in France while fleeing the Nazis.) The most infamous and immediate outcome of the 1942 Oberg/Bousquet negotiations was "Operation Spring Wind," or the July 1942 *Vélodrome d'hiver* round-up by French police of almost 13,000 Jews in Paris over a two-day period, 16–17 July. Held temporarily in horrendous conditions in terrible heat in the *Vel d'hiv* bicycle-racing stadium, some of the Jews arrested were deported directly to the East. Others, including the arrested children, were sent to French concentration camps. According to Michael Marrus and Robert Paxton, without the Oberg/Bousquet agreements, "the Germans would never have taken such a heavy toll of Jews in France" (245).

Helmut Knochen, according to *Le Monde*, was a much more "supple" man. "Polite and attentive" during the trial, Knochen spoke excellent French, which Oberg did not, and was more highly educated. Knochen held a doctorate in philosophy and had been a journalist before the war. He was Klaus Barbie's direct superior in Paris. He had given Barbie his brief "to penetrate and break the Resistance in Lyon" (Linklater et al. 67), and it was through Knochen that Barbie sent his reports, including those concerning anti-Jewish actions. Some of these reports were sent on to Berlin. According to Magnus Linklater, it was for this reason that lieutenant Barbie occasionally received telegrams from Heinrich Himmler himself.

According to the journalist Jean-Marc Theolleyre, the Knochen–Oberg trial was important because it was the first post-war trial to "offer a large-scale panorama of the Occupation, to expose the great dramas, and the principal operations of the Nazi police" (37). It revealed, for example, that Oberg, Knochen, and their operatives, many of whom were French auxiliaries, were responsible for the deportation of some 80,000 resisters. Other takeaways from the trial included the fact that many of the terms of the Oberg/Bousquet accords were not honoured by the Germans. For example, despite promises to the contrary, the Germans executed numerous French hostages handed over by French police and recruited their French auxiliaries directly, rather than through French mediaries, as agreed.

Like so many other Nazi criminals, the accused feigned ignorance of crimes committed under their authority. Oberg claimed that he only learned of the torture and death of Jean Moulin from his French investigating magistrate and that he was completely unaware of tortures carried out by SS subordinates in France. Oberg also "did not inform himself of the details" of the terrible conditions of the deportations carried out under his command. Attempting to flaunt his rank, Oberg dismissed the credibility of SS members who served under him and who testified that Oberg had ordered the executions of hostages. Oberg announced haughtily: "In my capacity as supreme leader [in France], I believe that my word must weigh more than that of the witnesses, who were my subordinates" (qtd. in Théolleyre 191).

All these protestations of ignorance and innocence were facilitated by the fact that, during the trial, the defendants were never forced directly to confront their actual victims in the courtroom. As a result, as the *Le Monde* report observed, "Oberg and Knochen recede from the picture. One is never really able to grasp their responsibility [in these crimes]. At best, one divines it" (201). The circumstances were, of course, very different in the Barbie trial, where powerful witness testimony over many days made Barbie's direct responsibility for his crimes perfectly clear.

According to the *Le Monde* accounts, two moments of the Oberg–Knochen trial were especially noteworthy. The first occurred when, in a surprise move on 28 September, defence lawyers adopted a new tack, arguing that under the 1907 Hague Convention, when a country is occupied in wartime, legal authority passes to the occupying power. Therefore, Oberg and Knochen acted *legally*, and since a foreign country cannot be tried under another's jurisdiction, the current proceedings were illegal (196). It is worth noting that among the various strategies deployed to make his client's actions appear defensible and legitimate, at least in wartime, Vergès *also* made the claim that Barbie's crimes were not illegal in Vichy France at the time of their commission.

The second remarkable moment occurred with the testimony of the star witness for the accused Karl Oberg, none other than René Bousquet. "Youthfully elegant" in his "well-fitting gray suit," Bousquet presented Oberg, along with Oberg's superior Reinhard Heydrich as loyal adversaries, even honourable men. (In his testimony, Bousquet did concede that Oberg was "too disciplined.") The former chief of Vichy police added that Oberg was the kind of man to whose grave he would send flowers, after following orders to shoot him. As for Heydrich, according to *Le Monde*'s reporter, Bousquet's testimony was so favourable that one was almost led to regret the SS leader's assassination by Resistance fighters in the streets of Prague in 1942 (205).

At the conclusion of their 1954 trial, both Karl Oberg and Helmut Knochen were sentenced to death. However, as Serge Klarsfeld writes in his memoirs, the two men must have smiled upon hearing their sentence, as both knew it was only a sentence "in principle."[12] Indeed, in 1958, the sentences were commuted by French president René Coty. In 1962, president Charles de Gaulle freed the two men as part of France's rapprochement with Germany, championed by de Gaulle and German Chancellor Konrad Adenauer. According to Klarsfeld, the liberation of Knochen in particular was encouraged and engineered by his old SS friend and comrade general Franz Six, now adjutant to Reinhard Gehlen, another former Nazi general championed by the Americans and chief of West German intelligence. In the end, both men served only seventeen years for their crimes, and Vergès would make note of these "lighter" sentences received by Barbie's SS superiors in comparison with the sentence of his client. But as Henry Rousso writes in *The Vichy Syndrome*, the seventeen-year prison terms of Oberg and Knochen were still lengthier terms than those served by most French collaborators for their wartime crimes. By the end of the 1950s, most of the latter had already been freed (62).

What is the significance of the 1954 Oberg–Knochen trial for the Klaus Barbie trial three decades later? As Barbie's superiors in France, Oberg and Knochen were more broadly responsible for and instrumental in the implementation of the Final Solution there. Given their rank and status as negotiators with Vichy officials like René Bousquet (as well as Pierre Laval and others), they were certainly better aware of the nature and full extent of French collaboration in the deportations. They also knew, despite their courtroom testimony to the contrary, that the Nazi deportations of Jews were never intended to be limited to foreign Jews but would eventually include *all* Jews in France – and Europe.

Unlike Barbie, the two men were "desk killers" rather than *bourreaux*, or henchmen. On the one hand, this permitted them greater deniability for the terrible things happening "on the ground." At the same time, however, given the elevated status of Oberg and Knochen in the SS and Nazi hierarchies, this meant that a trial dealing with their crimes and responsibilities would nevertheless paint a broader "panorama" of the Occupation and underscore the scope of French anti-Semitism and French–German cooperation.

But despite the invaluable historical lessons and revelations of the Oberg–Knochen trial, these lessons and revelations did not really "stick" as a reference point for a broader understanding to the historical context of the Barbie trial. This, at least, was the view of Jean-Marc Theolleyre, who in 1985 published a collection of reports and articles from *Le Monde* of the Oberg–Knochen trial, as well as other relevant Purge-era trials. For Theolleyre, looking back at these trials was timely because, he wrote, they offered "the beginnings of answers to questions" the youth of 1985 were asking about the Dark Years as a consequence of Barbie's capture and upcoming trial. Theolleyre also noted, perhaps as a warning, that these earlier trials "opened the dossier" on a national calamity whose "painful and tragic memories were still capable of deeply dividing the nation" (7).

Why had the Oberg–Knochen trial not remained in French memory as a permanent reference point and source of historical knowledge and understanding of Nazi and Vichy crimes during the Occupation? According to Rousso, the Oberg–Knochen trial was simply "not a suitable context for bringing to light the truth about the past" (62). Moreover, the historical moment of the trial, fall 1954, was hardly propitious for great public attention to and *absorption* of Nazi (and Vichy) crimes of the recent past. Franco–German rapprochement would soon be in the air, and the Cold War was already helping to push Nazi crimes into the background. In France, fatigue with coming to terms with France's recent traumatic past was setting in. In *The Vichy Syndrome*, Rousso notes that it was precisely in 1954 that what he describes as the phase of "Unfinished Mourning" of the traumatic wartime past was ending and the long phase of "Repressions" of that past, which lasted until 1970, was beginning. Moreover, other pressing problems were on the immediate horizon in France. The difficult and painful process of French decolonization was getting underway. Indeed, the French fort of Dien Ben Phu had fallen to Vietnamese insurgents in May of that year.

By contrast, Klaus Barbie's arrest and trial occurred during, and formed a crucial component of, what Rousso labels the "Obsessions" phase of the Vichy syndrome, when the memory of the Dark Years, and Jewish memory in particular, were in full resurgence. In his 1985 collection of *Le Monde* documents from the trials of the *Épuration*, Théolleyre asked not entirely rhetorically if this new *fin-de-siècle* France was not "masochistic" (6) in obsessing once again on the horrors of the Dark Years. Regardless, it was clear, at least in his view, that only partially answered questions about the Occupation raised in the context of the Oberg–Knochen trial were resurfacing with a new urgency. Although the charges, crimes, and the criminals in question – not to mention the respective historical moments of the trials themselves – were very different, in moving from Oberg–Knochen to Barbie, some of the same broader questions and issues emerged in different guises, as did, on occasion, courtroom strategies – and disavowals of the accused. How had the Final Solution been carried out in France? What did the accused know of the ultimate fates of the victims? As to this last question, Barbie, like Oberg and Knochen before him, claimed ignorance of their fate.

Despite the passage of three decades, there were also eerie parallels in attitudes, demeanours, and disavowals of responsibility as well among the three SS men accused. All the accused – Oberg, Knochen, and Barbie – displayed a notable arrogance, a lack of remorse, and a readiness to blame their actions on others, often trotting out the familiar "following orders" excuse. To quote Oberg: "*Un ordre ne se discute pas*" ("an order is not subject to debate"). All three men also indulged in language "games," for effect. As noted, when the tension began to rise in the courtroom in 1954, Knochen, who had earlier in the proceedings spoken in fluent French, fell back on German, forcing the awkward delays while the translators translated what he said into French for the court. Knochen also doubled down on offering long-winded and convoluted answers to questions that required a simple "yes" or "no" as answers (Théolleyre 180–1).

There is one final – and significant – parallel between the two trials that is of particular interest, in light of Barbie's statements to the court as well as those statements made by his defence lawyers. One of Oberg's lawyers, a *Maître* Doublet, argued in effect that the crimes and atrocities committed by the Germans during World War II were comparable to similar crimes by the Resistance and by the French army during World War II, as well as to crimes and abuses committed by French occupying forces in Germany after World War I. These included the killing of hostages, summary executions, etc. As the *Le Monde* correspondent wrote, Doublet's strategy was clear. His intention was to underscore the appositeness of what one of the Resistance leaders said during the trial: "The struggle was savage, but both sides scored points." The comparison, of course, suggested a certain *equivalency* of the crimes, like so many goals scored by both sides in a soccer game. All of this was, moreover, made "inevitable," the resister in question added, by "the necessities of war."

Implicitly at least, Barbie made the same claim before the Lyon court in his final statement. He affirmed that these wartime exactions were past and best forgotten: "But it was war, and the war is over." Vergès's strategy, along with those of his defence co-counsel, was also to diminish Barbie's crimes by underscoring their equivalency with the crimes of other political regimes, including Republican France in Algeria. But, of course, there was more to defence strategy than that.

Anticipating – and countering – this kind of logic just as the prosecution and civil parties lawyers would need to do in Lyon, the prosecutor in the Oberg–Knochen trial, Commandant Flicoteaux, insisted first on the *specificity* of Nazi crimes ("deportations, massive extermination, summary executions") as opposed to wartime excesses of their opponents. Flicoteaux added: "It is not because some of our compatriots committed guilty acts that the accused here today as well as others can claim that we have nothing to say them" (qtd. in Théolleyre 212). In effect, what Flicoteaux was seeking to establish were crucial distinctions that would be reaffirmed in the Lyon courtroom in 1987 in more concise legal terms. War crimes were not the same as systematic crimes against humanity, and the Nazis and Nazism itself were not of the same ilk as their/its adversaries.

To the degree that the 1954 Oberg–Knochen trial raised "the beginnings of answers" to the questions that would re-emerge at the Barbie trial, it could be argued that in certain ways it made the 1987 trial in Lyon "redundant." Moreover, the fact that it addressed the issues of Nazi crimes in France (and Europe) and official French complicity in Nazi crimes, including the Holocaust, at a *higher administrative level* would seem to diminish the importance of the Barbie trial in comparison with its predecessor.

But precisely because that predecessor, in large part as a consequence of its historical moment, had faded from view, along with the historical lessons it could have conveyed, the Barbie trial was all the more crucial. This was especially the case at a time when interest in the Dark Years was asserting itself as a national "obsession." What the historical lessons the Barbie trial conveyed will be discussed in subsequent chapters.

The 1980 Cologne Trial: Kurt Lischka, Herbert Hagen, and Ernst Heinrichson

Unlike the trials of Karl Oberg and Helmut Knochen, which took place in France a decade after the war, the trial of Kurt Lischka, Herbert Hagen, and Ernst Heinrichson occurred in Cologne, West Germany some twenty-five years later, in 1980. The long delay, as well as the location of the trial, may seem surprising, given the legal fates of their superiors, Oberg and Knocken. But unlike the latter, Lischka, Hagen, and Heinrichson had all escaped arrest in France after the war, and in Lischka's and Hagen's cases, avoided extradition back to France, thanks to shifting political tides and allegiances of the Cold War. In *Hiding in Plain Sight*, Eric Stover, Victor Perskin, and Alexa Koenig note that French efforts to extradite Lischka from West Germany to France in 1950 were foiled by British authorities in control there.[13] In September of that year,

Lischka was nevertheless tried and convicted in absentia in France and sentenced to life in prison for his crimes (K: P1/232).

Hagen and Heinrichson were also tried and convicted in absentia in French courts after the war. Heinrichson was sentenced to death and Hagen to a life of hard labour for his crimes (K: P1/232).[14] But none of the three men suffered in post-war Germany for their French convictions. Moreover, there was no question of extraditing them belatedly because the German constitution forbids the extradition of German citizens. Lischka returned to Cologne, where he had served as Gestapo chief before the war. There, he became a prosperous grain merchant. As Serge Klarsfeld remarks ironically in his memoirs, one of Lishka's favourite words during and after the war was "delivery." Klarsfeld adds: "the logistical and bureaucratic mechanism for delivery by rail of wheat or Jews is practically the same thing" (270). As for Heinrichson and Hagen, both became successful lawyers, Heinrichson in Miltenberg and Hagen in Arnsberg. Heinrichson was elected mayor of Miltenberg, and the townspeople who had elected him remained his loyal supporters despite revelations of the nature and extent of his wartime crimes.

In the 1970s, these favourable circumstances for the three men changed. In 1971, an agreement was reached between the French and West German governments according to which any Nazi tried and convicted in absentia of war crimes in France and who had not been caught and punished there could be retried in German courts for these crimes. It took four years, however, for the relevant committee in Bonn to ratify the agreement because the committee in question was chaired by Ernst Aschenbach. Aschenbach had his own reasons for delaying the ratification of the agreement. He had also served in wartime Paris and had also been sought for extradition by the French in 1947. One of Aschenbach's close wartime associates was Herbert Hagen. [15]

In France during the war, Kurt Lischka had served as deputy Gestapo chief and then had replaced Helmut Knochen as Oberg's adjutant when Knochen was called back to Germany. According to Tom Bower, a document submitted at Nuremberg stated that Lischka was fond of giving lectures to German police about his favourite interrogation methods. He counseled "patience and politeness." But, Bower adds, once he arrived in Paris, Lischka did not practise what he preached. There, "responsible for security, he organized executions of captured members of the resistance and the shooting of hostages as reprisals."[16] According to Serge Klarsfeld, Lischka was responsible for the executions of hostages at Romainville and Mont-Valérien, crimes particularly etched in the French memory of the war. As for Lischka's responsibility for the deportation and extermination of Jews on his watch, the indictment prepared against

Lischka, Hagen, and Heinrichson for their Cologne trial notes that documents held at the State Museum of Auschwitz confirm that 56,341 Jews were deported from France in 57 trainloads between 27 March 1942 and 9 February 1943 (K: P1/232). The indictment adds that this period of time "corresponds to Lischka's length of service in France." It also notes that, of those deported, proof exists that 33,592 were executed.

Herbert Hagen, who joined the SS in 1933, was a close friend and associate of Adolph Eichmann, whom he addressed in correspondence with the familiar "du." In 1937, Hagen accompanied Eichmann to Palestine in an unsuccessful attempt to meet with Zionist leaders about resettling Jews in Palestine (K: P1/232).

Hagen's first wartime assignments in occupied France were in Brittany and Bordeaux, where he later claimed that he was simply doing intelligence work. According to Tom Bower, this was not the case: in fact, Hagen was involved in the round-up of Jews.[17] In May 1942, he was transferred to Paris, where he served as Oberg's personal consultant. He was also placed in charge of Department IV of the Sipo-Sd in France, an intelligence office that, among other tasks, kept an eye on the activities of the French government and political parties. As German power and authority in France shifted away from the German Embassy and to the SS following Oberg's appointment, it was Hagen, along with Knochen, who "'pulled all the strings" in political affairs in Occupied France (Klarsfeld 280).

At the time of his appointment in Paris, Hagen was not yet thirty years old. A perfect example of the "office assassin," according to Klarsfeld, Hagen "never dirtied his own hands, he never indulged in witnessing torture, but his fanatical intelligence in the service of evil defined the parameters and constructed the structures within which men like Barbie necessarily plunged their arms in the blood of Jews and Resistance fighters." Sitting in his "bright office looking out on *Bois de Boulogne*" he composed notes and memos that "traced out for the Jews the roads that lead to Auschwitz" (280).

Hagen claimed to be only a "messenger" in Nazi negotiations with the Vichy regime at the highest level. But as the German indictment confirmed, Hagen's rank in the SS and in the Nazi hierarchy in France conferred upon him the power to actually negotiate, and documents prove that he had direct conversations with French authorities, pressing them on the denaturalization of naturalized Jews in France. Among others, he dealt directly with Pierre Laval and René Bousquet.[18] This, of course, would facilitate the deportations of more and more Jews. The German indictment states matter-of-factly that "During the period in which Hagen operated in France, (between 6 June 1942 and 18 October 1944)

73,176 Jews were deported from France to the Auschwitz–Birkenau" (K: P1/232). Hagen was also present at and drew up the notes of the fateful 2 July 1942 meeting between Oberg, Knochen, Lischka, and Bousquet. The meeting established that French police would carry out the 16–17 July round-up of Jews that came to be known as the Vel d'Hiv round-ups. On the morning of 17 July, Hagen met with French officials, including Jean Leguay (to be discussed shortly), to deal with problems associated with the lodging of the arrested Jews (K: P1/232).

According to the German indictment, Ernst Heinrichson also claimed to play an insignificant role in the SS hierarchy and in the deportations of Jews from France. He claimed to be merely a "low-level bureaucrat" with no authority in the deportations.

Part of Heinrichson's job was to go regularly to Drancy. He went there, he claimed, to respond to complaints by inmates about poor treatment and scarcity of food. Heinrichson stated that he only remembered dealing with French personnel while there. But several French witnesses testified that they had seen Heinrichson "strike and terrorize" Jews at Drancy who were not obeying orders quickly enough. Other sources report that one deportee who survived, Odette Beaticle, witnessed Heinrichson overseeing the deportation of 2,000 Jewish children between the ages of two and twelve years in two trainloads. Beaticle stated that she was haunted by Heinrichson's actions. She could not understand how he was able to do what he had done. When asked about the incident, Heinrichson responded that he was told the children being deported were being reunited with their families.[19]

Heinrichson also served as aide to Theodore Dannecker, another young SS officer (he was twenty-seven years old when he arrived in Paris) who had been given the task of organizing "a special police branch for Jewish questions – the *Judenferat* – in the Paris offices of the German High Security Office (Marrus and Paxton 5). In summer 1942, Dannecker, along with Heinrichson, made a tour of the French detention camps in the Unoccupied Zone, following Vichy's agreement on 4 July to deport foreign Jews from both zones (Marrus and Paxton 256). Although Dannecker was favourably impressed with the zeal of some local officials in deporting Jews, he was very disappointed in the number of Jews interned in the camps themselves. In part as a result of the visit and Dannecker's disappointing findings, the number of Jews demanded by the Germans was increased, and an initial leisurely timetable for the deportations proposed by the French was rejected (Marrus and Paxton 257).

As it turned out, the connection to Dannecker, not only of Heinrichson but of the other accused men in the Cologne trial, was important to the prosecution of the case. Following his summer 1942 trip south to the French camps with Heinrichson, Dannecker wrote a report of his findings to his superiors. He observed that while visiting the Milles detention camp, the camp commandant had told him that the Jewish rescue organisation Hicem would come up with "any sum" to allow Jews to book passage on any boat leaving Occupied Europe. As he wrote in the conclusion of his report: "This is a poof that the international Jewish community" was aware that "any Jew finding him- (or her-) self residing in territories under German sovereignty is headed toward annihilation."[20]

According to the indictment, the fact that Dannecker took Heinrichson on his inspection journey into the French zone and that the latter was present at the discussions with French officials and French police "shows that between Dannecker and Heinrichson a strong relationship of good quality must have existed." Moreover, when Dannecker sent his report alluding to the "total destruction" of the Jews up the ladder, Heinrichson was copied on the report and it was his duty to file it. According to the German prosecutor, Heinrichson would have "thus had the opportunity to study and read the report with care." And, the indictment affirmed, he could hardly not have comprehended its meaning. Despite the presence of his signature on the report, Heinrichson later denied ever having read it.

Kurt Lischka, for his part, claimed that he only signed Dannecker's correspondence, and this only when his superior Karl Oberg was absent. The indictment demonstrates, however, that one document (among others) from Dannecker signed by Lischka referred directly and explicitly to the extermination of the Jews as the ultimate aim of the Final Solution. The document in question is a report from Dannecker to Berlin detailing his negotiations with German transport officer general Kohl about getting the necessary numbers of locomotives and train cars for the planned deportations. Dannecker writes: "I was able to confirm his uncompromising anti-Semitism and his one hundred percent approval of a definitive solution of the Jewish problem having for its objective the total extermination of the adversary." Elsewhere in the indictment, a letter from Lischka to the ambassador of the French Delegation in Occupied Paris, Fernand de Brinon, is cited. In that letter, dealing with the recent immigration of 642 Jews to the United States and Mexico, Lischka states bluntly in the opening sentence: "Each immigration of Jews to countries overseas is not desirable." Dated 20 August 1942, the letter confirms Lishka's concern, whether directly ordered or not, that effectively no Jew should escape the Nazi net. As the indictment argues elsewhere, the articulation of this position makes it hard to believe that the person who wrote it was not aware that the ultimate goal was the total annihilation of the Jews in all occupied territories (and beyond). Otherwise, why would the Nazis care if they left?

Like Lischka and Heinrichson, Hagen, according to the indictment, was also fully aware of the ultimate fate of the Jews in Hitler's Europe. One proof of this was that, given his position in the SS hierarchy in Paris, Hagen would necessarily also have read of Dannecker's report on his trip to visit the camps in the Unoccupied Zone and his statement about the destruction of the Jews. When Hagen argued that he did not remember the report in question, the indictment noted that this was implausible, as multiple copies of the report were made and widely circulated in the SS offices in Paris.

More damning still in Hagen's case was that he followed closely the preparations for the successive deportations of Jews from France and could not have not understood their lethal implications. Hagen knew, for example, that at the outset only 10 per cent of Jews acceptable for deportation could be considered "incapable of working," thus supporting the myth that the Jews were really being sent to work camps in the East. But, very quickly, the indictment noted, more and more people incapable of performing labour were being deported, and children along with them. Unable to work, the fates of both categories could not be doubted. Indeed, the indictment points out that Hagen was present at a meeting of 17 July 1942, in which the question was posed as to what to do with some 4,000 children arrested the previous day. The answer was that they were to be divided up and deported with the successive trainloads of adults, as the central office in Berlin did not want trainloads of only children to be deported. This, clearly, would look very bad.

In his 1979 *Washington Post* article about the upcoming trial in Cologne, Tom Bower speaks of the "tragic parody" of the case of the three accused, the "faded film in which the I-was-just-following-orders line is repeated over and over again." Equally familiar when one reads the indictment are the repeated professions of ignorance by the three men as to the lethal implications of what they were up to and the stunning lapses of memory to which they were frequently subject during their interrogations. Only Hagen showed a little more creativity, arguing in effect that it was impossible to coherently describe the measures taken against the Jews as the "distorting influence of the times" made this impossible.[21]

But if the lessons of the Lischka-Hagen-Heinrichson trial were all too familiar, why were these files, translated into French on the orders of Judge Riss, included in the investigation of the Barbie case, other than because of the historical information they contained? What might they have revealed, or anticipated, that could prove helpful in prosecuting Barbie? During his many interrogations, and during the trial itself,

Barbie also claimed any number of lapses of memory when confronted with his crimes. More than once, he stated that he was simply following orders from superiors in Paris and Berlin.

But the German indictment of Lischka, Hagen, and Heinrichson also drew other conclusions that could prove helpful in prosecuting Barbie. After rehearsing the (massive) amount of evidence against the three men, as well as their frequently implausible denials, the indictment concluded that it was simply not reasonable to assume that, for three men as intelligent as were the accused, they could not have *not* understood the implications of what they were doing. The same could be said of Klaus Barbie. Perhaps more importantly, the indictment also concluded that regardless of whether Hagen, Lischka, and Heinrichson knew anything about Auschwitz (they claimed they did not), the cruelty, brutality, and deprivations of the deportations themselves made it such that all three men *had* to understand that the ultimate destination of the deportees was death. This also could have been said of Klaus Barbie, and it was a point prosecutor Pierre Truche would hammer home in his summation.

Der Befehlshaber der Sicherheitspolizei und des SD
im Bereich des Militärbefehlshabers in Frankreich
Fernschreibstelle

Aufgenommen				Befördert				Raum für Eingangsstempel
Tag	Monat	Jahr	Zeit	Tag	Monat	Jahr	Zeit	
6 AVR								
von	durch		an		durch			-7 1944
FS.-Nr.				Verzögerungsvermerk				33405
	FS.-Annahme							
an	Uhr. ab:				Uhr.			

LYON NR. 5269 6.4.44 2010 UHR == FI =

= AN DEN BDS - ABT L. ROEM. 4 B - PARIS =

= BETR: JUEDISCHES KINDERHEIM IN IZIEU-AIN =

= VORG: OHNE ==

IN DEN HEUTIGEN MORGENSTUNDEN WURDE DAS JUEDISCHE

KINDERHEIM '' COLONIE ENFANT '' IN IZIEU-AIN AUSGEHOBEN.

INSGESAMT WURDEN 41 KINDER IM ALTER VON 3 BIS 13 JAHREN

FESTGENOMMEN. FERNER GELANG DIE FESTNAHME DES GESAMTEN

JUEDISCHEN PERSONALS , BESTEHEND AUS 10 KOEPFEN,

DAVON 5 FRAUEN. BARGELD ODER SONSTIGE VERMOEGENSWERTE

KONNTEN NICHT SICHERGESTELLT WERDEN ==

= DER ABTRANSPORT NACH DRANCY ERFOLGT AM 7.4.44 ==

DER KDR. DER SIPO UND DES SD LYON ROEM. 4 B 61/43

I. A. GEZ. BARBIE SS-OSTUF==

The Izieu telegram. © Maison d'Izieu/Falco Collection

The Investigation: War Crimes, Crimes against Humanity, and the Long Road to Compromise

When Klaus Barbie arrived back in France to intense media coverage in early February 1983, anticipation ran high that he would soon face trial for crimes committed in wartime Lyon between 1942 and 1944. On the cover of its 11–17 February issue, the magazine *L'Express* featured a photograph of the former Nazi with a caption reading: "Barbie: The Tribunal of History" (Ledoux 48), suggesting that such a "tribunal" was imminent. As if to confirm that history had come full circle and that Barbie would soon face French justice, minister of justice Robert Badinter ordered that Barbie spend his first week in Lyon in a cell in the now empty Montluc Prison before being transferred permanently to the prison of Saint-Joseph. During the war, most of the Gestapo's prisoners were kept in Montluc Prison under horrendous conditions. Many, if not most, of these prisoners were tortured, murdered, or deported, or some combination thereof.[1]

But if hopes ran high following Barbie's return to France that his trial would soon take place, the reality was that it would be more than four years before the Court of Assize in Lyon called the first hearing of the trial to order. In the interim, there had been a lengthy initial *instruction*, or investigation of the case carried out by the young *juge d'instruction*, or investigating magistrate, Christian Riss. Riss submitted his final arraignment of Barbie on charges of crimes against humanity in July 1985. In December 1985, the Criminal Chamber of the Court of Cassation in Paris, France's highest court, rejected some of the conclusions of Riss's initial indictment. In the process, the court redefined crimes against humanity under French law. This necessitated an additional phase of the investigation of the Barbie case.

This chapter focuses on the difficult and often complex legal path followed by the French justice system to bring Klaus Barbie to trial in May–July 1987. It examines Riss's initial investigation of the Barbie file, and the obstacles, legal, evidentiary, and otherwise that it encountered. It also looks at the reasons for and implications of the December 1985 Court of Cassation decision. But any account of the evolution of the protracted French legal proceedings against Klaus Barbie actually begins in the immediate post-war years, and more specifically in the investigations conducted by and judgments of two military tribunals in Lyon in 1952 and 1954. Both convicted Klaus Barbie of war crimes and sentenced him to death in absentia. By the time the 1952 trial took place, Barbie, along with his wife, son, and daughter, had escaped along the infamous "Rat Line" to South America. Barbie's escape had been facilitated by the American Counter Intelligence Corps (CIC), figures close to the Vatican, and the international Red Cross (see Chronology).

First Steps: The 1952 and 1954 Trials

When Riss was handed the task of investigating the Barbie case, one of the first steps required was to review court documents, records, and judgments of the 1952 and 1954 Permanent Military Tribunals in Lyon. In both cases, the convictions for war crimes and sentences against Klaus Barbie had prescribed by 1974, as according to French law the statute of limitations for war crimes was twenty years. Nevertheless, it was necessary to make sure that for any future trial involving Barbie, *none of the crimes* for which he had been convicted by those military tribunals were included in any charges Riss would eventually draw up. This was necessary, first, to avoid the possibility of even the appearance of double jeopardy (*non bis in idem*) that Barbie might be tried for the same crime twice. Equally important, since the statute of limitations had run out on war crimes in the mid-1970s, and since crimes against humanity had been declared imprescriptible by the French legislature in December 1964 (to be discussed shortly) it was necessary that whatever crimes Barbie was charged with had to qualify as crimes against humanity. Then, of course, it was necessary to establish definitive proof that he was responsible for these crimes.

At least symbolically, the 1952 and 1954 trials and convictions of Barbie marked the culmination of early post-war efforts to come to terms with the horrors he, his superiors, and his henchmen visited on Lyon and the surrounding region between 1942 and 1944, as well as frustrated efforts over several years to bring Barbie to justice. French authorities were certainly aware by the late 1940s of Barbie's presence in the American sector of Occupied Germany,[2] and the French public knew of his whereabouts by the second trial of René Hardy in 1949. The Americans had allowed French authorities to get a deposition for the trial from

Barbie in Germany concerning the arrests of Resistance leaders at Caluire and Hardy's role in those arrests. Barbie's deposition was read aloud in court. Public outcry in France calling for Barbie to be returned to stand trial was immediate. As a result, Barbie's protection by the CIC and his intelligence work in Germany became increasingly precarious. Eventually, this would lead to Barbie's exodus from Europe in 1951.

The 1952 trial of Klaus Barbie by the Lyon military tribunal was limited in scope, certainly in comparison with the subsequent trial in 1954. According to the indictment, Barbie was charged with "assassinations, intent to assassinate, intent to burn and pillage, and the arbitrary detainment of prisoners." The only other defendant at the trial was Werner Knab, Barbie's superior in Lyon. Knab was charged with the lesser crime of the "arbitrary detention of prisoners." All crimes under consideration in 1952 were carried out in the Jura region, in small communities, including Villard Saint Saveur, Saint Claude, Molinges, Viry, as well as other villages and hamlets in the area. All the operations, in principle, were carried out against the Resistance in spring 1944.

To get a sense of the extraordinary brutality of the crimes Barbie and his men committed in the Jura, in *Klaus Barbie: The Butcher of Lyon*, Tom Bower offers the following description of Barbie's actions in Molinges:

> On 13 April, in one typical encounter, Barbie arrested Baptiste Baroni in Molinges. To intimidate the Frenchman, he pushed Baroni outside and showed him the body of Gaston Patel whom he had just executed. Where, Barbie wanted to know, was the local Maquis chief Dubail, alias "Vallin"? Baroni pleaded ignorance. Acting the part that so delighted Barbie, he ordered a heavily bruised *maquisard* to be pulled out of a nearby Gestapo lorry and asked Baroni if he recognized the man. Again, Baroni pleaded ignorance. Casually, Barbie told the *maquisard* he was free to leave. After walking a few steps German soldiers shot him down. Now Barbie dragged Baroni to a farmhouse from which Dubail emerged. "Here's your chief," shouted the exultant Barbie, ordering the house's incineration. A few hours later, Dubail was shot. Baroni was sent to a concentration camp, but he survived the war. (98)

Bower's account provides one example among many of the singular brutality and cruelty of Barbie's crimes, not only in the Jura but elsewhere as well. Moreover, it certainly helps to explain why in sentencing Barbie the court repeatedly answered in the negative to two questions submitted to it in accordance with French (military) law. These were: "Were the authors of these voluntary homicides acting in retaliation [for an attack against them]?" and "Were the acts committed on this occasion or under the pretext of a state of war justified in accordance with the laws and customs of war?" (K: EP 3/2P).[3]

When the verdict was handed down, Barbie was sentenced to death in absentia, and Werner Knab, also absent from the trial, was given a sentence of life in prison and hard labour. As it turned out, the only member of Barbie's team present at the trial was Erich Bartelmus, in prison in Lyon at the time. Following the convictions, the judgment of the court was posted on the door of the Military Tribunal's quarters. The judgment explains that if the accused were known to be in France at the time, the verdict would have been posted on the door of the *mairie*, or town hall.

Barbie's 1954 trial before the *Tribunal Permanent des Forces Armées* was a much larger affair involving a significantly larger number of accused and dealing with crimes committed in several geographical areas in the Lyon region. The charges brought against Klaus Barbie in 1954, as summarized in the indictment (K: EP 6/2P)[4] were in their general language similar to those brought against the former Nazi two years before. In the 1954 indictment, they were summed up under four headings. Barbie was accused:

- in the Lyon region, between 1942 and 1944, of having affiliated himself with an association established to commit or to prepare to commit crimes against people and property;
- of having, between 1942 and 1944 in the regions of Lyon and Grenoble, with help and assistance, of being complicit in voluntary homicides committed against French people with premeditation;
- of having, in the same circumstances and locations just described, used torture and committed barbarous acts; and
- of having, in France between 1942 and 1944, been either the author or the accomplice, without orders from the constituted authorities and outside the law, seized individuals, arrested and sequestered numerous French citizens, with the circumstances and duration of these sequestrations lasting more than a month, and submitted these individuals to bodily torture.

Included on the initial list of those accused, besides Barbie, were the aforementioned Werner Knab and Erich Bartelmus, as well as other Gestapo or SD operatives. French collaborators working with the SD were also tried as part of the 1954 trial, although early on the decision was taken to separate the prosecution of the German defendants from that of their French minions.

In 2008, Georges Cochet, a defence lawyer for one of the French collaborators accused in 1954 published a brief but revealing account of the 1954 trial and his experience of it.[5] The account serves as a stark reminder of the extent to which such trials, as well as their outcomes, can be influenced by the political headwinds blowing at the time. Ironically, in this instance, those political headwinds served the interests of many of the Nazis on trial rather than those of their French underlings.

Cochet's reflections are of interest, first, because they underscore the importance of Barbie himself to the trial. Cochet states that in his opinion the actual opening of the trial was delayed by the prosecutor's office (the *parquet*) in the hope that Barbie could be captured and brought back to face French justice (253). Also of note, according to Cochet, was the fact that, at the time the 1954 trial took place, France and Germany were experiencing a "honeymoon," a period of reconciliation in their dealings with each other.[6] As a result, the court had to tread lightly in its prosecution of the German accused. Indeed, present at the trial itself were two German lawyers, whose function was clear: "Their mute presence at the bar created a certain climate which recalled that Germany mattered again and kept a protective eye on its countrymen" (254). This, however, did not prevent members of a boisterous audience from shouting for the death of the accused. In an effort to calm the crowd, the president of the court reminded those present – as court officers would do again in 1987 – that "it was the honor of France to assure the accused a fair trial." As for the accused, according to Cochet, they sought to keep a "low profile, trying to minimize the evidence against them, and blaming their superiors or their subordinates" (254).

Cochet, as noted, along with Alain de la Servette, who would later serve as Barbie's first lawyer on his return to France in 1983, defended the Frenchmen on trial. According to Cochet, his client had been a prisoner-of-war in Germany from 1940 to 1943, and when he returned to France he misunderstood the political climate of the time in allowing himself to be recruited by the occupying Germans. Nevertheless – and even though he was merely a subordinate to the Nazis – he was given the death sentence, as most of the latter were as well.[7] But as opposed to Cochet's French client, the sentences of the Nazis present at the trial were later commuted by French president René Coty, and they would eventually return to Germany. In accordance with the tradition of the times, when Cochet's client was himself refused a pardon, the lawyer, along with the jailer and a priest, went to his cell to inform him that he would be executed. Cochet then accompanied the condemned man to a fort in the Lyon suburbs[8] to face a firing squad. For Cochet, at least, his client was the "final victim of World War II" (255).

Astute and at times moving in its recollections, Cochet's 2008 account of the 1954 trial nevertheless fails to ask one question that it inevitably raises. If present in Lyon for the trial, would Klaus Barbie, like other SD criminals, have benefited from the spirit of rapprochement with the FDR and had his sentence commuted by French president Coty as well? While the answer to the question will never be known, a closer look at the actual charges against Barbie as described in the dossier certainly make any act of clemency seem ill-advised at best.

Carried out over a large geographical region, the savagery, variety, and sheer number of the crimes committed by Barbie and his men in the Vercors, on the Glières plateau, in Grenoble, and in an around Lyon as described in both the indictment and judgment are stunning. The indictment includes more than a dozen pages listing crime after crime: pillages, rapes, murders of individuals, mass executions, torture, the burning of entire villages, hangings, and more. The timeframe of the indictment covers much of 1943 and 1944, with some of the most horrendous crimes occurring as the Liberation neared. Twenty-six wounded were taken from a hospital and executed at the *Grotte de la Luire* in July 1944. One hundred and ten hostages were arrested at Saint-Genis Laval, taken to Montluc Prison, and executed by machine-gun fire. Their bodies were later burned. The description of the crime notes that "many women" were among the victims. In late August 1944, 109 hostages, mostly from Montluc Prison and mostly Jews, were taken to Bron airfield, where they were executed and buried in craters made by Allied bombing.

The aim of these killings and other crimes was clear, according to the indictment. First, "certain categories of French" were to be exterminated, and by any means. Second a "psychosis of terror" was to be instilled in the civilian population. As part of these deliberately traumatizing actions against them, the French were also to be "deprived of their possessions." In describing the Nazis' French minions, court documents note that they were recruited among "the local lowlife" and were "richly rewarded to accomplish this sinister dirty work."

Although the indictment and judgment list many accused, the accumulated testimonies underscore the fact the Klaus Barbie stood out as particularly brutal. One translator working with the Germans, a certain Zuchner, described Barbie as the "biggest bastard on the team." Another translator, Klein, described Barbie as "particularly cruel and brutal" underneath a "jovial exterior." One of Barbie's subordinates, Ernest Floreck, stated that Barbie "never hesitated to inflict torture" to get the answers he wanted. Apart from some of their French subordinates, the other member of Barbie's team noted for his extreme brutality is Erich Barthelmus, described as "hateful and brutal," "cruel and mean"; in short, a "perfect brute." It was Barthelmus who Barbie placed largely in charge of dealing with Jews. The translator Klein states in the indictment that he even got into an altercation with Barthelmus over the latter's "mistreatment of Jewish prisoners." Clearly, whatever pardons or commutations of punishment were issued subsequent to the 1954 trial, they had to be for purely political reasons. Certainly nothing in the criminal dossier relating to *any* of the accused suggests that an act of clemency was appropriate.

The 1960s and 1970s: The 1964 Law Making Crimes against Humanity Imprescriptible and the Leguay Affair

In *The Vichy Syndrome,* Henry Rousso states that it was precisely the year 1954 when the "Repressions" phase of the evolving memory of the Dark Years began. After a decade of "Unfinished Mourning" during which the French had attempted to come to terms with the divisions of the Occupation and the "Franco-French Civil War" that concluded it, between 1954 and 1971 the divisions and traumas of the Dark Years retreated to the background in the face of a newfound national prosperity and the challenges of decolonization. From the standpoint of legal efforts to deal with the unpunished crimes of the wartime years, it would be a decade before any new developments occurred. But the long-term importance of the legal development that *did* take place in late 1964, certainly from the standpoint of the Barbie trial and the trials of Frenchmen for crimes against humanity in the following decade, cannot be underestimated or understated.

The year 1964 marked the twentieth anniversary of the end of the Nazi Occupation and the liberation of France. Therefore, in accordance with French law, this meant that the twenty-year statute of limitations on war crimes committed in France during the Occupation was about to run out. Henceforth, any Nazi who had committed such crimes in France between 1940 and 1944 could no longer be prosecuted. By most accounts, it was against this backdrop that the French National Assembly voted unanimously (471 votes to none) on 17 December to make crimes against humanity as defined in Article Six C of the Nuremberg charter imprescriptible in French law. The text of the resolution passed stated: "Crimes against humanity as they are defined by the Resolution of the United Nations of 13 February 1946 confirming the definition of crimes against humanity as they are defined in the Charter of the [Nuremberg] Tribunal of 8 August 1945, are imprescriptible [without a statute of limitations] by their very nature."

In reality, however, the circumstances surrounding the vote, as well as the factors that contributed to it, are more complex. First, as newspaper reports from the time reveal, the event that initially triggered discussion of making crimes against humanity imprescriptible in the Assembly did not concern the French situation, per se. Rather, the discussion resulted from an announcement from the West German government in Bonn that on 8 May 1965 – twenty years to the day after the end of World War II in Europe – war crimes committed by the Nazis during the war would expire. This meant, as representative Paul Coste-Floret stated in the French Assembly, that given that there were uncertainties as to whether Hitler himself was actually dead, it was possible to imagine that on 9 May 1965 the Führer himself might reappear. He could claim that the statute of limitations had run out on his crimes, and henceforth he could "pass his days peacefully, like Kaiser William the Second before him, in some foreign country." Such an eventuality, Coste-Floret argued, was intolerable. He pointed out to the Assembly that the previous June the International Association of Jurists had met in Warsaw and expressed the opinion that all nations that had signed the international Genocide Convention, including France, should subscribe to the principle that crimes against humanity are part of international law and are without a statute of limitations by nature. Coste-Floret then noted that the French Ministry of Foreign Affairs had pledged to begin negotiations to that end. But in the meantime, he explained, the present body could act on its own and declare crimes against humanity imprescriptible in domestic French law. As noted, there was no opposition to the resolution.

If developments in Germany triggered the initial discussion in the Assembly that resulted in the December 1964 imprescriptibility vote, they form nevertheless only part of a context that places the vote in historical perspective. First, it is hard to imagine from a contemporary perspective that at least for some, the French government's recent leniency towards Nazi war criminals as part of its *rapprochement* with the German Federal Republic, exemplified in Charles de Gaulle's releasing of Helmut Knochen and Carl Oberg two years earlier, still rankled.[9] Moreover, French recognition of the heroism and martyrdom of *résistants* at the hands of the Nazis was in the air, as a few days after the Assembly vote, on 19 December, the massive, nationally televised ceremony focusing on the transfer of Jean Moulin's ashes to the *Panthéon* took place. And, as an eerie reminder of a past the French nation was *not* commemorating, and was in fact attempting to forget, press reports from late December 1964 also show that where crimes committed by the French in Algeria were concerned, amnesty laws were under discussion in the Assembly alongside the law declaring crimes against humanity to have no statute of limitations. This disparity in legal and historical terms would emerge again in the Barbie trial and a decade after that in the trial of Maurice Papon.

If political and historical circumstances of the moment account for the urgency of the 1964 National Assembly vote on crimes against humanity, debates about the law that ensued in the press in late 1964 and early 1965 tended to focus more explicitly on the moral dimensions and implications of the law. These debates, moreover, would hardly be settled at the time. Indeed, they would continue to resonate in the following decades, into the 1990s and the new millennium.

The most famous statement to emerge from the 1964–5 debate about the 1964 law making crimes against humanity imprescriptible was made by the moral philosopher Vladimir Jankélévitch in his essay originally published in *Le monde* on 4 January 1965, entitled simply "L'Impréscriptible." Not the first reflection on the new law invited by the newspaper, it would nevertheless prove the most memorable, and in some ways the most controversial. As noted, like its author, it would serve as a frequent reference for civil parties lawyers during the Barbie trial two decades later.

At the heart of Jankélévitch's argument in "L'Imprescriptible," stated powerfully in the first few sentences of the essay, was the claim that Nazi crimes, exemplified in a naked human being chased into the gas chambers by guard dogs and "guards worse than their dogs" were by their very nature "crime[s] that cannot be named." They were "*infinite* crime[s]" whose indescribable horror only deepens the more [they] are analyzed." The force responsible for these crimes, this "Machiavelian atrocity" was, Jankélévitch states bluntly, "a sadism of which only the Germans are capable."

In the face of this horror, this "depthless crime," as Jankélévitch described it, it was the duty of all those who did not suffer it to devote to this crime an "inexhaustible meditation," and more. One was also compelled to "do" something for the victims. But, Jankélévitch then observed, in the strictest sense of the verb "to do," one is only capable of "futile" or "symbolic" gestures, such as, for example (as in his case), never again setting foot in Germany. But one could also "do" something in a positive sense, and that is to speak on behalf of the dead. They were, Jankélévitch wrote, "our affair." He added, "if we do not speak for them, who will?"

Turning his ire on lawyers and others who had argued for these crimes to expire and criticized those who opposed this position for their apparent inability to get over the horrors of the recent past, Jankélévitch labelled these lawyers "sophists." More pointedly, he suggested that for these individuals the past in question was never really even their "present," that they were in fact oblivious to the horrors going on around them. Implicitly, then, they were in part responsible for the crimes in question.[10]

One of those lawyers, or "sophists," at whom Jankélévitch would take aim by name in a subsequent essay entitled "L'oubli interdit" ("Forbidden Forgetfulness") appearing in the *Nouvel Observateur* on 25 March 1965 was Maurice Garçon. A novelist and playwright as well as a lawyer, Garçon had been elected to the *Académie Française* in 1946 and twice defended René Hardy in the late 1940s. For Garçon, the idea of a statute of limitations was not an invention of the mind or of human intelligence but the result of a natural instinct. It was, he maintained, a necessary part of the order of things which called for a specific, finite punishment under the law for any criminal, without which punishment that criminal would forever be consumed with remorse. Moreover, on the level of society, prescription was necessary to restore calm and encourage the settling of differences, which itself requires forgetfulness.

One criticism made at the time of Garçon's argument by fellow lawyer Paul Arrighi was that there is nothing "instinctual" about statutes of limitations, that nothing suggests that they are part of the natural order of things. Rather, the idea of a statute of limitations is a fairly recent development and a legal principle which has long been overlooked or (deliberately) under-utilized in cases involving "atrocious crimes."[11] But from Jankélévitch's perspective, the problem was less a legal or juridical one than an ethical one. As he stated in his comment about Garçon's position in "L'oubli interdit," where Nazi crimes are concerned, "M. Garçon believes that making them without a statute of limitations poses a problem in law. But does the law have anything to do with this business?" Indeed, for Jankélévitch, according to François Azouvi, imprescriptibility is "an ethical imperative before it is a juridical category" (qtd. in Jankélévitch 180).

While a number of commentators agreed with Jankélévitch that the horror of Nazi crimes required that no statute of limitations apply to them[12] and that it was the shared responsibility and duty of all to remember and speak for the victims, many strongly disagreed that these crimes should be laid exclusively at the feet of the German people. For some, the problem at hand was not the sadism of a specific national people but the massive and mechanized violence of war. For others, those characteristics of the German people that made them subject to the yoke of Nazism were by no means exclusively their own. "Fear of power, submission to orders, passive complicity cannot be the heritage of one cursed people alone." Still others recognized a danger which Jankélévitch's unequivocal condemnation of the Germans obscured: the complicity of many of the French in Nazi crimes and their own crimes in places like, more recently, Algeria, which "millions of French don't want discussed and for which they never feel responsible."[13]

From the vantage point of the Barbie trial that took place more than twenty years later, it is interesting to note the extent to which many of the issues that would emerge as points of contention and debate during that trial – the legitimacy of the absence of a statute of limitations under the law, French complicity in Nazi crimes, and France's own crimes in Algeria – were also contested in the debate over the 1964 law. Moreover, in at least arguably placing Nazi crimes against Jews front and centre in his essay and insisting on their unprecedented – and unique – horror, Jankélévitch, in the context of the 1964 debate, helped shift the focus of Nazism's most horrific crimes away from *Resistance* victims and on to their racial victims. This transition or transfer would repeat itself during Riss's *instruction* of the Barbie case after 1983.[14] Following the 1985 high court decision, it would, as noted, open a rift between Jewish and Resistance victims that would play out in the press at the time and indeed resonate through the trial. Perhaps the only theme articulated in Jankélévitch's 1965 essay that did not persist, or at least find strong expression during the 1987 trial, was the notion that Nazi criminality was the direct by-product of a "sadism" unique to the German people. But then, as Arthur Miller's comments made about the German people in the context of the Auschwitz trials discussed in the last chapter suggest, the idea that Nazism was an outgrowth of the peculiarities or perversity of the German people, while fairly common in the 1960s, was arguable less so in the 1980s.[15] Indeed, in her 1985 novel *La Douleur*, to be discussed in more detail in the next chapter, Marguerite Duras observed: "If one makes Nazism a German destiny, and not a collective one, one reduces the victim of Bergen-Belsen to the dimensions of only a regionally defined human being. The only response to this crime is that it is everybody's crime. It must be shared. The same holds true for the ideas of freedom and fraternity. To withstand this crime, to tolerate the idea of it, one must share the crime."[16]

If the idea prevalent in the 1960s that Nazism and its crimes were indelibly linked to the character of the German people had at least arguably been eclipsed by the 1980s, the issue of a statute of limitations, and the wisdom or folly of applying it, had not. It would emerge again in polemics in the French press in the late 1970s, this time in relation not to crimes committed by Nazis or Germans but in the context of charges of crimes against humanity brought against a Frenchman and agent of the Vichy regime, Jean Leguay.

Following Henry Rousso's chronology in *The Vichy Syndrome*, by the late 1970s the memory of the Dark Years in France had changed significantly, if not radically. In the early 1970s, the controversial success of films like Marcel Ophuls's powerful documentary *Le Chagrin et la pitié* and Louis

Malle's scandalous *Lacombe Lucien* had ripped apart comfortable myths about a "nation of resisters." They had also begun to foreground not only widespread collaborationism with the Germans but also official French complicity in the persecution of Jews and in the Holocaust itself.[17]

The case of Jean Leguay is an interesting one and related to the Barbie trial in at least one important way. Although a plaque in Lyon's *Palais de Justice* confirms that the first man convicted of crimes against humanity in France was Klaus Barbie in 1987, the first man *indicted* for crimes against humanity in France was Jean Leguay, on 12 March 1979. This fact is often overlooked because, despite the date and year of Leguay's indictment, it would not be until 1989, two years *after* the Barbie trial, that Leguay would finally face the actual prospect of being tried in a court of law. But in the interim, Leguay had become very ill. He died on 27 July 1989. As Rousso points out, "In a break with custom, the statement declaring the case closed by virtue of the defendant's death alluded to Leguay's *guilt*: 'The investigation established Leguay, Jean, did participate in crimes against humanity, in July 1942 [the Vel d'Hiv roundup], August and September, 1942" (*Vichy Syndrome* 151).

Leguay, a wealthy businessman who sat on numerous corporate boards at the time he was indicted for crimes against humanity in 1978, had been a senior official in the Vichy regime who served as chief of French police René Bousquet's representative in the German "Occupied Zone," including Paris in 1942 and 1943. In that capacity, Leguay dealt frequently with German authorities. Although he claimed to have "no power," to have just been Bousquet's "messenger" or "mouth piece," (*porte-parole*) documents produced at the time of his indictment by Serge Klarsfeld confirm a more active and indeed autonomous role. For example, it was Leguay who, as head of the French delegation in Paris, requested that Jewish children be deported along with their parents. Later, in September 1942, he requested of German authorities that Latvian, Lithuanian, Estonian, Yugoslavian, and Bulgarian Jews be deported along with Jews of other nationalities. The Germans agreed, and more than 150 Jews of these nationalities were deported in mid-September from Drancy. Asked in 1979 about the request to deport children with parents, Leguay is quoted in *L'Evénément* of 13 March 1979, "The decision about the children was taken over my head. It was Pierre Laval himself who took charge of this matter."

It was against this backdrop that, later in spring 1979, the writer and journalist Gilbert Comte took it upon himself in the pages of *Le monde* to once again raise the question of a statute of limitations. In an article entitled "The Devil's Return," dated 30 May 1979, Comte first dismissed the notion that his call for prescription for Leguay's crimes was out of sympathy or mercy for the recently charged Leguay. Leguay, according to Comte, had in his lack of remorse already shown himself to be a "mineral block" with a "dry heart." The issue lay elsewhere. "Sooner or later," Comte wrote, "the conscience of the public will refuse to accept the idea that after so many hecatombs occurring around the globe before or after 1945 the law only strikes in one case, and always the same case." Then, revising Garçon's argument cited earlier, Comte maintained that "Nature itself" teaches prescription in its constant erasure of what came before the present. Only "vengeance," Comte continued, excludes forgetfulness. Moreover, crimes like the July 1942 *Vel d'Hiv* round-up of Jews, considered in the context of 2,000 years of bloody French history, should not be singled out, as Serge Klarsfeld had done, as the "darkest and most shameful moment in all of French history." Given the long view, according to Comte, the *Vel d'Hiv* roundups are a crime like other horrors and atrocities in French history, just another manifestation and by-product of "our fratricidal hatreds." Then, addressing the 1964 law directly, Comte wrote, "it is a cruel irony of fate that the Parliament responsible for the 1964 law on 'imprescriptible by nature' let disappear two years before without worrying itself overmuch some three thousand French citizens and some 30,000 Harkis in the clandestine prisons of Algerian Algeria."

In subsequent essays appearing in *Le monde* up through Klaus Barbie's arrest and return to France in 1983, Comte continued to hammer at the ideas elaborated in "The Devil's Return," while offering additional reasons why imprescriptibility where Nazism's crimes against Jews were ill-advised, unfair, and simply wrong.[18] But already in the 1979 essay just discussed it is not difficult to detect a blueprint, of sorts, for Vergès's defence of Barbie and his denunciation of the hypocrisy of the French legal system prosecuting the old Nazi. As will be discussed in chapter seven, Vergès's insistence that he wanted to bring crimes against humanity "into the present" would touch on the majority of Comte's points. These included the idea that no statute of limitations was wrong, "unnatural," that it was unjust to try Nazi crimes when so many crimes, especially by Europeans against indigenous peoples elsewhere, went unnoticed and unpunished, and that ultimately figures like Barbie and Leguay before him were "scapegoats" for the sins of others.

There is one final legal development of the 1970s that did not involve French law or French legal decisions. Nevertheless, it needs to be discussed briefly here because, at least indirectly, it led to Klaus Barbie's return to France while also producing a key piece of evidence against him. In *Hunting the Truth*, Beate Klarsfeld reports that while she was conducting archival research at the *Mémorial de la Shoah* in summer 1971, the director of the memorial approached her and handed her a document he thought would be of interest to her. The document in question was an official West German announcement, *not* released to the press. It stated that the Munich prosecutor, Dr. Wolfgang Rabl, had decided to close the prosecution file on Klaus Barbie due to lack of evidence. There was no evidence, he claimed, that Barbie knew the ultimate fate of the Jews he deported. Such knowledge was necessary under German law at the time if the Nazi under investigation was to be prosecuted.

For Klarsfeld, this decision was in keeping with the "official version of the Final Solution, limiting those who knew the truth about the Jewish genocide to a microscopic minority of Nazi dignitaries and thus absolving the German people as a whole" (231). But there was more to the decision than that. In February 1971, as noted, some four months before prosecutor Rabl's decision in the Barbie case, a Franco–German legal agreement made it possible for German courts to retry Nazi criminals who had previously been found guilty of crimes *in absentia* in French courts for crimes committed in France. Many of these criminals had escaped back to Germany, where they were living comfortably – and in many instances, prosperously. (e.g., Lischka, Hagen, and Heinrichson, discussed in the previous chapter). The agreement, however, had yet to be ratified by the German parliament, or *Bundestag*. Beate Klarsfeld, along with her husband, Serge, reasoned that if the French allowed the German legal system to drop the case against Barbie, the most notorious of *all* Nazi war criminals who had committed crimes in France, then this would be proof that the French really did not care about such prosecutions. And if this were the case, why should the Germans, for whom all prosecutions of Nazis were fraught and potential sources of unrest within West Germany?

Mobilizing protests and a press campaign within France that spilled over into the Federal Republic, Klarsfeld eventually travelled to Munich to confront German authorities about Rabl's decision. But before leaving France, to counter the Munich prosecutor's claim that Barbie had no knowledge of the fate of Jews he deported to Drancy, the Klarsfelds had located a lawyer who had served as the German liaison with the UGIF leadership in France and who, as it turned out, was able to speak to Barbie's knowledge (as well as that of other Gestapo Section 4-B leaders) as to the fate of the Jews they deported. The lawyer's name was Kurt Schendel, and he lived in Paris. When interviewed by the Klarsfelds, Schendel expressed his strong belief that all these SD leaders were "in the know," so to speak, about the fate of deported Jews. Moreover, he added at a meeting with UGIF's Board of Directors, during the war one of these directors stated that he had recently visited Klaus Barbie because the latter was summarily shooting without trial many Jews he was arresting. When asked if there was not another way to deal with the Jews – deportation evidently being the only other option – Barbie had reportedly said to the UGIF director, "Shot or deported, what's the difference?" The name of the UGIF director in question was Raymond Geissmann.

When, shortly afterward, Beate Klarsfeld was able – after considerable effort – to confront prosecutor general Manfred Ludolph[19] in his Munich office, he told Klarsfeld that if she could get solid proof that Barbie had indeed made the statement attributed to him, that would be evidence enough of his knowledge of the fate of the deported Jews to reopen the Barbie file. Back in Paris, the Klarsfelds located Geissman, who was willing to make a statement. When presented with this evidence, Ludolph did in fact reopen the Barbie case and assigned one prosecutor Steiner to work with Beate Klarsfeld. Steiner corresponded with Geissmann, whose declaration to the German prosecutor is included in the documents assembled for the Barbie investigation included in the Klarsfeld files. Geissmann's "Declaration" to Steiner, dated 24 September 1971, states in part: "If I go back thirty years to the dramatic climate of the period, I must say that we all held the deep-seated conviction that these torturers, in whose hands rested the life or death of my co-religionists, knew perfectly well the fearful fate that awaited those they arrested. I remember well Barbie frothing with hatred against the Jews and voicing the phrase, 'deported or shot, it's the same thing.' It was one of the expressions he used in my presence and that I reported back to my colleagues in Paris" (K: P1/382).[20]

In fact, prosecutor Rabl's decision to reopen the Barbie file obviously did not lead to the latter's eventual arrest and prosecution in the German Federal Republic. However, it did help considerably in publicizing Barbie's crimes in the international media as well as the fact that the "Butcher of Lyon" was still at large. Over the next ten years, Beate Klarsfeld would track Barbie to South America and Bolivia and, after more than a decade of efforts on her part and those of Serge Karsfeld, finally witnessed Klaus Barbie's expulsion from Bolivia and return to captivity in Lyon in February 1983. And as the presence of Raymond Geissman's statement in Barbie's criminal dossier confirms, that statement would serve as a significant piece of evidence in the prosecution's efforts to confirm that Klaus Barbie knew of the ultimate fate of the Jews he deported. Without convincing proof of this, Barbie could not be found guilty of crimes against humanity under French law.

February 1983: The *Instruction* or Investigation Begins

Given the considerable legal and historical complexities of the Barbie case, not to mention the passage of time and twists and turns of Barbie's life, as well as efforts to bring him to justice, it is not surprising that investigating magistrate Riss's initial investigation of the Barbie case took as long as it did. By definition, a French criminal investigation must be exhaustive in every way. Every step taken or request for information made by the investigating magistrate, as well as requests made of that magistrate in correspondence s/he receives, must be meticulously documented, researched if necessary, and included in the criminal file. As a result, one finds in the Barbie file seemingly banal or innocuous documents, such as those officially appointing certified translators, requests to archives in France and abroad for documents of interest to the investigation, and even official requests to airlines to transport gendarmes to Cayenne to arrest Barbie on his arrival there from Bolivia. (Needless to say, the reason the gendarmes were being sent to Cayenne is not stated!) They also include a letter from the Croatian National Congress to Riss angrily denouncing Barbie's claim, reported in the Lyon press (*Le Progrès*) on 12 February 1983 that although he never tortured anyone, his Yugoslavian (Croatian) SS subordinates probably did so. Following the (lengthy) letter from the Croatian National Congress, an essay is included in the file examining Croatian SS units and their activities during the war. There is also an official request by the Dutch government to interrogate Barbie for alleged crimes he committed in Holland before arriving in Lyon (see next chapter).

More germane to the prosecution at hand, Barbie's criminal dossier also includes the court records and judgments of his 1952 and 1954 convictions in absentia before Lyon military tribunals, discussed above, as well as post-war interrogations of his French collaborators, many of whom were executed after the war. Also included are French translations of the records and judgments of German courts that judged Barbie's immediate SS superiors Kurt Lishka, Herbert Hagen, and Ernst Heinrichson, discussed in chapter two here.

But of greatest interest in the dossier are documents relating to the building of the case against Klaus Barbie for his upcoming trial for crimes against humanity. These include the records of multiple interrogations of the accused with his lawyers present. They also include "confrontations" between Barbie and witnesses to and victims of his crimes located by Riss with the help of François Lafforgue, his gendarme assistant and commander of the investigative division of the Lyon-Ducherre region; letters and petitions from Barbie's lawyers to Riss; and photocopies of crucial documentary evidence, much of it examined and discussed at the trial.

What the interrogations of Barbie and "confrontations" with victims and potential witnesses reveal in the first instance is an absolute refusal on the part of the accused to acknowledge responsibility for any of his crimes as well as a lack of remorse that would become brutally and even shockingly apparent during his 1987 trial. In Barbie's eyes, as he told Riss on numerous occasions, he was himself the victim of an injustice and not the perpetrator of one. In the first interrogation (*Procès-verbal d'interrogation*) by French authorities conducted on 5 February 1983 in a hangar of the Cayenne airport in French Guyana (K: P1/6), Barbie was clearly confused by what was happening to him. He nevertheless maintained his composure well enough to state that he had been expelled from Bolivia without being notified as to the reason for his expulsion. He then stated – after a "minute of reflection," according to the record of the interrogation – that "I am a German national, I thereby fall under German jurisdiction." In fact, according to Hammerschmitt's recent biography of Barbie, he had been required to renounce that citizenship in order to become a Bolivian citizen. This he apparently did.[21]

During his first interrogation in custody in Lyon on 5 February, Barbie expanded upon what he now referred to as his "illegal juridical situation" as a result of having been expelled without notice by the Bolivian Ministry of the Interior (K: P1/7–8). The issue, he maintained, was his imprisonment by Bolivian authorities over a bad debt that he had, he claimed, subsequently paid. So, in fact, in his view, he had been wronged on not one but two counts by the Bolivian government.

In a second interview conducted on the same day (K: P1/12–13), Barbie was confronted for the first time with specific crimes for several of which he would subsequently be charged with crimes against humanity. These included the so-called last convoy, or last train of deportees to leave Lyon on 11 August 1944, just before the liberation of the city. The train contained some 650 prisoners, roughly half Jews and half members of the Resistance. Barbie was also asked about the round-up of some eighty Jews at the offices of the *Union Générale des Israélites de France* on 9 February 1943. Finally, Barbie was asked about his role in the arrest and deportation of the children of Izieu. In *all* cases, even those concerning crimes for which he was not ultimately charged, Barbie denied responsibility. Either he did not remember the crime in question or he blamed a fellow member of the Lyon SD for committing it. On occasion, Barbie also minimized his own role, claiming to be a lowly subordinate just following orders. In more than one instance, Barbie also disavowed any role in the deportation of Jews, as these activities, he claimed, were carried out by others, including his subordinates who were acting on direct orders to them from Adolph Eichmann in Berlin. However, just in case such deportations *could* eventually be ascribed to him, Barbie became more loquacious, and for good reason. In being questioned about the 11 August 1944 convoy that included Jews and resisters, the accused understood full well that he could only be found guilty of crimes against humanity if it could be proven that he was aware of the ultimate fate of Jewish prisoners sent to Nazi death camps to the East. Therefore, in addressing the deportations, he stated: "I knew the trains were leaving for Germany, but I did not know their destination. I knew only that the Jews were deported to concentration camps, but I had never seen these camps with my own eyes. I did not know what went on in these concentration camps. You know that many people returned alive from them. After the war, I simply saw reproductions and photographs of what was supposed to have happened in them." As the last sentence indicates, in denying he knew what happened in the camps, Barbie also took the opportunity to cast doubt on what actually *did* happen there by referring to these crimes as only *supposed* to have happened there. After all, as he affirmed disingenuously in the previous sentence, "many people" did survive the camps.

In his many confrontations with victims and witnesses during the *instruction*, not only were Barbie's familiar denial of responsibility and/ or amnesia on display, so too were a lack of remorse coupled with disdain for the witnesses themselves. This was most often expressed in insults, ironic or insincere compliments, challenges to witnesses' credibility, or simply refusals to answer questions about their claims. Among the first witnesses interviewed was Alice Joly Vansteenberghe, who from her cell in Montluc Prison had seen Barbie in the hall of the prison on 11 August 1944. Later, as prisoners were being rounded up for deportation and assembled in the courtyard, she had seen Barbie again with the assembled prisoners. Vansteenberghe had witnessed this while standing on a shelf in her cell and looking out her window. In his confrontation with Vansteenberghe in the presence of Christian Riss and in the presence of his lawyers (except Vergès) 19 May 1983 (K: P1/27), Barbie denied he was present at the prison that day. Barbie added ironically, "I admire this woman's prodigious memory," and then stated that he did not recognize her. Barbie would repeat the performance on 19 July 1983 (K: P1/34) with another witness, Anne-Marie de Sainte-Marie Lenoir, this time praising her "rich imagination" (which implied that her story was all the more unlikely) and affirming that he did not remember her either. Like Vansteenberghe, Lenoir had also seen Barbie in the prison courtyard as prisoners were being rounded up for the 11 August convoy. In a second interview on 19 July (K: P1/33), Barbie was confronted with Elie Nahmias, whom Barbie had arrested in the streets of Lyon. After claiming that he would never arrest people in this fashion, and that there was a contradiction in the dates cited by Nahmias,[22] Barbie haughtily announced that he had nothing else to say and that his lawyers would answer any other questions posed to him. For once, however, the tables were turned on the accused when, near the end of the interview, Nahmias announced that if Barbie would not answer questions posed to him by the investigating magistrate, he, Nahmias, would not answer any questions posed by Barbie's lawyers.

As the confrontations between Barbie and witnesses and victims included in the dossier also confirm, there were moments in which Barbie broke the pattern of his typical panoply of set responses to reveal a more sinister side. In a lengthy confrontation with Simone Kadosche-Lagrange on 20 July 1983 (K: P1/36), during which Barbie predictably denied having ever seen or arrested her, he suddenly changed his tune and announced to those present: "When one is in prison, this woman is still pretty enough to look at." To all appearances a back-handed compliment which attested to Kadosche-Lagrange's attractiveness while at the same time stressing her advancing age and implying that she was only attractive to a man locked away in prison, Barbie's remark was more loaded than that. First, it attested to his predilection for "cat and mouse games," a predilection the psychiatrist Daniel Gonin would later associate in his courtroom testimony with individuals like Barbie, supposedly frozen in the "sado-anal" phase of development. Kadosche-Lagrange had stated that Barbie had complimented her looks when he had questioned her in front of her parents during the war, and in repeating the compliment here, Barbie clearly hinted that he *had* complimented her during the war. This would mean, of course, that he *had* interrogated her in the past and that he *did* recognize her, despite his claims to the contrary in the same interview. Moreover, in seemingly repeating a statement he had made to her when she was a terrified teenager under his complete control during the war, Barbie, it appeared, was seeking to establish once again his control over her through the power of intimidation. In her response to Barbie in the interview, Kadosche-Lagrange pushed back, so to speak, stating that she took his compliment as an insult and reminding those present of his wartime compliment to her. Barbie's message, nevertheless, was clear. Not only did he feel no remorse (quite the contrary), he would also use any means at his disposal to unsettle and intimidate those who would testify against him. No wonder, then, that some of Barbie's victims who were confronted with the aging and frail ex-Nazi during the *instruction* were still so disturbed and even traumatized in his presence that they expressed to the investigating magistrate after the interview their preference *not* to be called as witnesses in the trial. They would only do so if needed.[23] As the film of the trial reveals, during the trial some of his victims who testified when Barbie *was* present in the courtroom at least initially seemed to have a hard time looking at him directly. Among those in attendance at the 1983 interview who also witnessed Barbie's exchange with Kadosche-Lagrange was Serge Klarsfeld, who was one of Kadosche-Lagrange's lawyers. Certainly, the impact and implication of Barbie's provocation was not lost on him in that instance. Barbie, he knew, would be a difficult opponent in court. Klarsfeld would later write in his memoir that he, for one, was pleased when Barbie absented himself from his trial, as Vergès, whatever his talents and reputation, would be easier to handle and less formidable than his client.

Legal Developments One: Initial Stages 1983–5

From the documents assembled in Klaus Barbie's criminal dossier, as well as other sources, including articles in the French press at the time, it is possible to sketch out in general terms the evolution of the charges of crimes against humanity that would eventually be brought against the former Nazi. These documents also make it clear, especially in relation to the December 1985 Paris Court of Cassation decision, why the nature and content of these charges stirred such controversy. The fact that Barbie, through his actions, personified the terrible and tragic fate during the war of Jews and Resistance members alike at the hands of the Nazis made it seem inevitable that both groups would be acknowledged in the charges finally brought against Barbie and that both groups would feel that justice had been done if the former Nazi was successfully prosecuted for crimes against both.

But from the outset of the investigation and the appointment of Christian Riss as investigating magistrate on 12 February 1982, it was made clear to the young magistrate that this perception did not correspond with the views of many French legal authorities, especially justice minister Robert Babinter. For the latter, crimes committed against resisters and indeed against the most symbolically important *résistant*, Jean Moulin, were not to be investigated, as these were war crimes and not crimes against humanity. In a deposition before Judge Riss dated 3 February 1983, François Lafforgue, the aforementioned gendarme investigator who worked closely with Riss in locating and producing witnesses, also confirmed that these had been his instructions from his superiors as well. Therefore, during the entirety of the investigation Riss conducted, he would attempt to honour this crucial distinction by limiting himself to investigating only crimes against Jews and not Resistance fighters.

Despite Riss's intentions, however, early developments in the case unfortunately muddied the waters almost immediately. On 5 February 1983, Riss confronted Barbie with the initial list of crimes being investigated for potential charges against him, as noted above. The charges, as well as Barbie's responses to them, were widely reported in the press. Given the apparent public confusion about the nature of the charges against Barbie, the Lyon prosecutor's office released a communiqué intended to clarify matters on 23 February 1983 (AR: A/12, 7). As it turned out, the communiqué itself only added to the initial confusion. Following a first item reaffirming that crimes covered in the 1952 and 1954 judgments against Barbie were excluded from the current investigation, Item Two of the communiqué turned explicitly to the distinction between crimes against humanity and war crimes. Crimes against Resistance fighters, it affirmed, were war crimes, and therefore not subject to the current procedure underway: "Not included in the investigation undertaken for crimes against humanity committed by Klaus Barbie are acts committed by Barbie against the persons of resisters. These acts constitute war crimes, and are today expired, as they do not appear to be crimes against humanity responding to the definition in Article 6 C, 2 C, of the Charter of the International Tribunal at Nuremberg, to which the law of December 1964 refers in declaring crimes against humanity 'not subject to a statute of limitations by their very nature.'" The communiqué then added: "Because they rose up against the Vichy regime and the [German] army of occupation, resisters are by definition voluntary combatants, a status they have always loudly claimed and which has been legally recognized [cf. especially in Article 28 of the Amnesty Law of 5 January 1951 declaring that they constitute part of the French army, according to Article 30 of the Press Law.] Juridically, therefore, they cannot be assimilated into a 'civilian population' subject to the treatments described by article 6C ... of the Nuremberg Charter."

But when the communiqué turned to the list of the eight crimes under investigation and that had already been presented to Barbie, the distinction so carefully laid out between war crimes and crimes against humanity became much murkier. To be sure, the majority of the crimes listed were explicitly crimes against Jews. These included the UGIF roundup (Item C); the arrest and deportation of the children of Izieu (Item H), as well as the execution of seventy Jews buried at the Bron airfield and "other Jews" murdered at Saint-Genis Laval (Item G). Additionally, Item D referred to the execution of forty-two people, forty of whom were Jews, in the Lyon area in 1942 and 1943.

Three items, however, referred to crimes whose victims were not explicitly identified as Jews. Item A referred to the arrest and torture of a French commissioner of police, Jules Cros, and the murder of twenty-two hostages in January 1944 following an attack on two German gendarmes during summer 1943. Item B addressed the "arrest and torture of nineteen persons during summer 1943." Finally, Item E, the most vexed of the crimes under consideration for charges of crimes against humanity, concerned a round-up conducted at the workshop of the SNCF at Oullins on 9 August 1944, in which "at least two people were killed, many more wounded, and others arrested whose fate had not been determined."

Especially where the Oullins round-up and murders were concerned, potential charges of crimes against humanity would be highly problematic, as the Gestapo raid was, to all appearances, a raid carried out against the *Resistance*, so therefore precisely against those "voluntary combatants" who could only be victims of war crimes. As Alain de la Servette, Barbie's first lawyer, suggested at the time, the potential charge related to Oullins should be dropped "if the investigation establishes that Barbie and his men acted that day in consequence of a denunciation informing them that Resistance cell existed there." (qtd. In Linklater et al. 325).

There was, additionally, one more fly in the ointment, so to speak. This concerned Item F, the "last convoy" that left Lyon on 11 August 1944. As already noted, of the approximately 650 persons deported, "half … were Jews," as the 23 February release observed. But what about the other half? Most were resisters, and most suffered the terrible deprivations of being imprisoned at Fort Montluc. Moreover, like the Jewish victims in the convoy, they also experienced the horrors of deportation in extremely overcrowded and unsanitary railcars to destinations unknown to the East. At the German border, it is true, the train was divided, with Jews going to an almost certain death at Auschwitz-Birkenau, while Resistance women went to the theoretically safer "concentration camp" of Ravensbrück and Resistance men were sent to Struthof. But as moving courtroom testimony by Marie Vaillant-Couturier and especially Geneviève de Gaulle-Anthonioz would show (see chapter five here), the experience of horror at Ravensbruck itself was so devastating in its revelations of Nazi inhumanity that the distinction between war crimes and crimes against humanity seemed, at best, a legal artifice. In 1983, of course, that testimony had yet to take place, but as the initial list of crimes under consideration for charges of crimes against humanity laid out in the Lyon prosecutor's release revealed, there were potential cracks in the façade already.

As it turned out, and as Riss's final arraignment of Barbie submitted to the prosecutor's office on 15 July 1985 indicated, the initial list of crimes under investigation described on the 23 February communiqué from the prosecutor's office was actually compiled not by Riss but during an earlier investigation launched in April 1980 and carried out by police authorities. The list was compiled from documents in German provided by the *Centre de Documentation Juive.* To all appearances, this investigation was not constrained by the distinction between war crimes and crimes against humanity to which Riss's investigation would adhere. Moreover, as Riss's own investigation would reveal, several of the most problematic crimes listed in the 23 February 1983 communiqué could be dismissed for other reasons. Item A, involving the murder of twenty-two hostages in January 1944 following an attack against two German gendarmes had been covered in the convictions of 1952 or 1954 (the arraignment does not say which conviction). The same was true of Item D, the execution of forty-two hostages in 1943–4; and Item G, the murders at the Bron airfield and of two priests at Saint-Genis-Laval.

As for Item E, the attack on the SNCF workshops at Oullins, this was indeed a war crime, as Alain de la Servette had suggested. According to Riss's arraignment, the same was true of the arrest and torture of police commissioner Jules Cros, listed in Item A.

Finally, and most controversially as it turned out, Riss addressed Item F, the 11 August 1944 convoy of some 650 persons, approximately half Jews and half Resisters, deported to the East. According to the arraignment, the Jews deported were victims of crimes against humanity, whereas the deportation of Resisters, because they were active adversaries of the Occupant, was a war crime.

To return briefly to the 23 February 1983 communiqué from the Lyon prosecutor's office, it is important to stress that whatever confusion it might have sown at the time, it nevertheless laid down two clear challenges that future efforts to include crimes against resisters among Barbie's crimes against humanity would have to contend. First, the communiqué argued that the Nuremberg definition of crimes against humanity on which French law relied at the time did explicitly exclude resisters as victims of crimes against humanity, since, as the communiqué reminded the French public, crimes against humanity can only be committed against "civilian populations." Therefore, if the communiqué's prescriptions were to be put aside, the Nuremberg definition of crimes against humanity would have to be re-interpreted or worked around. Second, if former resisters now demanded to be included as victims of crimes against humanity, at least implicitly through their actions they would have to renounce their hard-earned and cherished status as combatants on a level with the regular French army.

While the language of the February 1983 prosecutor's communiqué implied that these two matters were resolved and indeed set in stone for the future, this would not ultimately prove to be the case. When Riss's July 1985 arraignment including only Jewish victims as victims of crimes against humanity was confirmed by the Lyon *Chambre d'Accusation* on 4

October, Resistance organizations decided to appeal the decision to the criminal chamber of the Paris Court of Cassation, the final arbiter in the matter at hand. On 20 December 1985, that body handed down its decision. It not only overturned crucial components of Riss's arraignment, allowing some of Barbie's Resistance victims to be included in crimes against humanity charges against Barbie, it also took up the other challenge contained in the 23 February 1983 communiqué by rewriting the definition of crimes against humanity under French law.[24] As will be discussed, in historical as well as legal terms, the repercussions of the Paris Court of Cassation's decision would be felt not only in debates in the press and in the Barbie trial itself but also in the subsequent French trials of Paul Touvier and Maurice Papon. These repercussions were, moreover, not always constructive, as the 1994 trial of Paul Touvier would later demonstrate.

Legal Developments Two: The 1985 Paris Court of Cassation Decision and Its Impact

After the considerable, indeed extraordinary, effort put in by Christian Riss in formulating his charges in his arraignment and the subsequent confirmation or ratification of that arraignment by the Lyon *Chambre d'accusation* on 4 October 1985, the question arises as to *why* the Court of Cassation in Paris took the controversial steps that it did. As the Paris court well knew, its decision would require reopening an already exhaustive investigation and delaying yet again the beginning of the Barbie trial itself. Among other risks, Barbie, as the judges certainly knew, was frail and ill, and he might die in the interim. For some, at least, this could suggest that the delay was deliberately fabricated precisely *to allow Barbie to die*, and therefore be unable to reveal his secrets in court.[25] But this was pure speculation, as the judges had other motives for – and pressures on – their decision.

First, as noted above, Resistance members had good reasons to want to see Barbie tried as well for his crimes against the Resistance, and their organizations had been committed to this objective from the outset. And, as Sébastien Ledoux has pointed out recently (Ledoux 2017), given the composition of the Court of Cassation and the ages and experiences of its judges, these organizations and their members had reason to be optimistic. Ledoux notes, for example, that "Pierre Arpaillange, who had been general prosecutor for the Court of Cassation since 1984, was himself a Resistance veteran [and] a recipient of the *Croix de combatant volontaire de la Résistance*." Arpaillange, in fact, agreed to meet with the Resistance organizations before the ruling was issued. Additionally, "all nineteen counselors in the criminal chamber had been born between 1917 and 1930," and they had therefore had firsthand experience of the war and German Occupation themselves. Moreover, they were "contemporaries of the activists submitting petitions" and, according to Ledoux, "they were [also] members of a generation" that was "very attached to the idea that the 'France of the Resistance' should be represented in Klaus Barbie's trial" (Ledoux 51).

In their decision, of course, the judges did not discuss these pressures or cite their own personal or sentimental reasons for breaking with at least some of the judgments of the investigating magistrate and the lower court. In their (frankly turgid) decision, the Paris judges cited legal considerations, some proposed, as they noted, by the Resistance organizations that petitioned them. One such consideration essentially concerned consistency: if according to international law *all crimes* defined in the Nuremberg charter were without a statute of limitations, why single out crimes against humanity *alone* of the crimes articulated in Article 6C to be made imprescriptible in French law? Article 6C also defined "crimes against peace" and "war crimes." A second consideration concerned the nature of the Resistance and members themselves. First, the court observed, somewhat speciously, persons simply *suspected* of belonging to the Resistance (and who the Nazis readily pursued) had not, strictly speaking, given up their status as civilians and could therefore be considered to be victims of crimes against humanity under Article 6C of the Nuremberg charter.

But in responding directly to the decisions of the lower court and investigating magistrate Riss, the Court of Cassation took a different tack. It argued in effect that the earlier decisions were flawed because they had read Article 6C as defining a *single category of crimes against humanity*, whereas in reality it articulated *two categories*. The first category focused on the crimes: assassinations, exterminations, deportations, etc. The second category focused on persecutions and the motives for them, political, racial, and religious. The Court of Cassation then went on to argue that the lower court's and investigating magistrate's decisions had concluded wrongly that only the *second category* was valid in determining the victims of crimes against humanity. That is to say, the only victims of crimes against humanity were the victims of persecution for reasons of race or for their political or religious beliefs. According to the Court of Cassation, this automatically excluded "combatants," that is to say, all Resistance members, from consideration as victims of crimes against humanity, as they could be considered only under the first category, "assassinations, exterminations, deportations, etc."

Whether or not this kind of legal hairsplitting in the Court of Cassation's decision accurately captured the thinking of Christian Riss and the lower court in their decisions is open to question. Under any circumstances, ultimately it proved to be a moot point. Rather than reaffirm the validity of the definition of crimes against humanity provided in Article 6C in French law, the Court of Cassation ultimately rejected that definition and, in the conclusion of its decision, handed down a *new* definition of crimes against humanity with which French courts would have to deal henceforth. Crimes against humanity would now comprise: "Inhumane acts and persecutions which, in the name of a regime practicing a policy of ideological hegemony and are committed in a systematic fashion, not only against persons because of their appurtenance to a racial or religious collectivity, but also against adversaries of this policy, whatever the form of their opposition."[26]

Before concluding with how the December Paris Court of Appeals affected the subsequent investigation of the Barbie case and which crimes specifically would be added to the list of charges against Barbie, it is important to stress that at the time of its announcement the 1985 decision precipitated another explosion in the French press which, in the range and substance of the issues it addressed, was comparable to the controversy that followed the 1964 vote making crimes against humanity without a statute of limitations in French law. Because of its subsequent impact on the 1987 trial, the controversy needs to be discussed here. Not only well-known public figures but also civil parties lawyers directly involved with the Barbie case quickly became embroiled in very public and heated exchanges about the decision and its implications. And although the different positions taken were all fundamentally reasonable and certainly heartfelt, the trial itself would reveal that these 1985 exchanges in the press two years earlier had left tensions and animosities between lawyers that occasionally erupted in the courtroom to disturbing effect.

At the centre of the debate over the 20 December 1985 decision of the Court of Cassation was Serge Klarsfeld and the positions he took vis-à-vis that decision. Quoted in *Le monde* on 24 December under the heading "A Regrettable Decision," Klarsfeld criticized the decision on several counts, most significantly for its betrayal of the spirit of Nuremberg. Because Klarsfeld's choice of language in his statement along these lines would itself prove controversial, the statement is worth quoting in full:

This decision will be the subject of criticisms, above all in the Anglo-Saxon world, where the concept of crimes against humanity was [first] elaborated in order to protect all populations and communities susceptible to be the victims of systematic and inhuman persecutions, even though they have committed no act of opposition against the powers that be. In introducing the active adversaries to these powers into the category of potential victims of crimes against humanity, the judges of the Court of Cassation have weakened the protection of the innocents, as the latter were understood by the authors of the Nuremberg Charter.

As for the situation of Klaus Barbie, who will be subject to new charges as a result of this decision, this is secondary to the broader impact that a more exemplary decision could have had, delineating more precisely the concept of crimes against humanity rather than inefficaciously diluting it.

Several days after Klarsfeld's statement in *Le monde*, on 3 January 1986, Henry Noguères, a former Resistance member and himself a civil parties lawyer for Resistance organizations during the 1987 trial, responded emotionally to Klarsfeld's criticisms of the Court of Cassation's decision in an essay entitled "Victims and Perpetrators (*Bourreaux*)." After expressing "regret" at having to distance himself from Klarsfeld, for whose moral and physical courage he expressed his admiration, Noguères turned to what he considered to be the heart of the matter, Klarsfeld's choice of the term "innocents" to describe those who were persecuted by the Nazis for religious or racial reasons, and in the context of the Barbie case, Jews.

For Noguères, the choice of the term "innocents" established a dangerously false dichotomy, as it implied that all those who did not fit into this category (Jews) would in some way be "guilty under French law," if the Court of Cassation had acted differently and had in its decision followed the spirit of Nuremberg as Klarsfeld saw it. More concretely, Noguères stressed the wisdom, indeed the exemplarity, of a decision "that will undoubtedly remain one of the great criminal decisions handed down by our Supreme Court, whose impact will be felt far beyond the miserable person of Klaus Barbie."

Why was the decision exemplary? According to Noguères, the court had legally recognized that "there can be both at the same time and in the same instance war crimes and crimes against humanity, especially when atrocious acts proceed from a state doctrine that has institutionalized crime in its most abject form." In other words, what mattered was not the religious or racial identity or the opposition or passivity of the *victim* but the ideological aims of the *state* that destroyed him or her.

Klarsfeld was not long in responding. Challenging Noguères' clearly rhetorical ploy of distinguishing between Jewish "innocents" and the "guilty" others, in this case *résistants*, Klarsfeld noted that his distinction was not at all intended to inculpate the latter. Rather, it was simply to underscore the fact that, as opposed to noncombatant Jews, or Roma, for that matter, the Resistance fighters represented a very real threat to the security of the occupying power.

But for Klarsfeld, the heart of the matter lay elsewhere. What the authors of the Nuremberg Charter intended was not simply to protect the Jews, as "innocents," but rather to protect "an infinity of human victims" who could be targeted for similar reasons for exterminatory practices in the future. Then, homing in on the new definition of crimes against humanity imposed by the Court of Cassation, with its insistence on systematic crimes carried out by an ideologically hegemonic state, Klarsfeld observed that another crime, this one involving imaginary resisters *who were also perpetrators*, was actually conceivable for adjudication in a future Barbie trial. Imagine that a group of resisters had captured some "simple German soldiers," disarmed them, tortured them, and then executed them summarily. Captured by the Gestapo, these men were then deported to concentration camps, survived, and returned to France. It would then be possible for these same resisters, according to the new definition of crimes against humanity – and despite their own horrendous wartime actions – to be included as civil parties in Barbie's future trial. Why? Because not acting on behalf of an ideologically hegemonic regime, the resisters' crimes could not be considered crimes against humanity but only war crimes and so would have lapsed as such. But their own arrest and deportation at the hands of the Nazis, on the other hand, would *not* have lapsed, as it constituted a crime against humanity under the law.

By way of concluding, Klarsfeld turned not to an imaginary scenario but to a concrete historical comparison that pointed to a real distinction that underscored the difference between crimes against humanity and war crimes. He noted that, throughout the war, only Jews and Roma had been sent, not to concentration camps, but to death camps. Moreover, of these deported, only 3 per cent returned, as opposed to 30 per cent of non-Jewish or non-Roma deportees. Finally, Klarsfeld stated, while Jewish and Roma children were deported at will by the Germans, no non-Jewish or non-Roma child was deported from France during the war. However, one chose to recategorize the victims of crimes against humanity or the nature of the regime that could commit such crimes, these historical distinctions remained real.

In a final rejoinder to Klarsfeld, the celebrated Resistance hero and novelist Vercors (real name Jean Bruller), who had written the underground "bestseller" *The Silence of the Sea* during the Occupation, offered his own perspective on the debate in *Le Monde* on 22 January 1986. Comprehensive in scope, Vercors's statement sought essentially to bridge the gap between the two positions articulated by Klarsfeld and Noguères while at the same time making clear Vercors's disagreement with the use of the term "innocents" in this context as well as with some of Klarsfeld's facts. Vercors noted, first, that his own father was Jewish and that he had lost many relatives in the death camps. For him, the fate of the Jews and Roma at the hands of the Nazis was the "most monstrous" of their crimes against humanity. But that did not mean, he continued, that the Nazis did not commit other crimes against humanity as well. These crimes were not against Klarsfeld's "innocents" but against others, resisters and especially their families, even their children. Addressing Klarsfeld directly, Vercors noted that when the Nazis could not find a resister they sought, they took members of their families, *including children,* and many of these were deported to their deaths. The Nazis had committed other horrors, other crimes against humanity, against non-Jews as well. Three million French had been captured by the Nazis and placed, according to Vercors, in "death camps" from which only one-fourth returned. But if the imprisonment itself constituted merely a "war crime," what the Nazis did to them in the camps was indeed a crime against humanity. The sufferings and debasements they experienced there destroyed their humanity. Many "strangled each other for their food" or "howled like dogs" in their dehumanization. In concluding, Vercors chose the most controversial case of all, that of Jean Moulin, to make his point: "That a Jean Moulin (unarmed) and countless others were shot, that was war. But tortured to the point of being turned into human rags, I would like to know according to what moral criterion one can deny this is a crime against humanity."

Finally, perhaps lost in the shuffle in the polemics involving Klarsfeld, Noguères, and Vercors was another statement to the press, this one made by Roland Rappaport, whose clients were Sabine Zlatin, the director of the school where the children of Izieu were hidden, and Doctor Reifman. Given who he represented, it would not be surprising if Rappaport had taken a position similar to the one taken by Serge Klarsfeld. But perhaps aware of the degree to which the Paris Court of Cassation decision was dangerously dividing civil parties lawyers and therefore potentially the prosecution itself, Rappaport struck a conciliatory note. He offered an optimistic reading of the import of the decision, not only for Barbie's victims but for a more just and expansive understanding of the definition of crimes against humanity itself: "It was because they were Jewish, and only because they were Jewish that the children of Izieu were deported and massacred. And it was because they rose up against the Nazi State that so many resisters experienced the same fate. The Paris Court of Cassation, without losing sight of what distinguished them, decided that they were united in the same suffering. In refusing to do a triage of the victims, the court has retained the nature of these crimes. It has thus given its full reach to the notion of 'crimes against humanity' as it is understood today."

Given the horrors both Jews and Resistance fighters had experienced at the hands of Barbie and the Nazis and to which many later testified so eloquently in court, Rappaport's perspective articulated in *Le Monde* in late 1985 proved more prescient than he knew.

***

In terms of the charges that were ultimately brought against Klaus Barbie, what was the impact of the Court of Cassation's December 1985 decision? Following that decision, the Lyon Court of Appeals added two more charges, both for crimes committed against former Resisters (Ledoux 53). The first concerned Marcel Gompel, a professor at the prestigious *Collège de France*, a Resistance member and a Jew who had been tortured and killed by Barbie and his men at Montluc Prison. Gompel's wife had petitioned to be included as a civil party attached to the prosecution, but as Riss stated bluntly in his 15 July arraignment, "His actions in the Resistance make it impossible to retain the charge of crime against humanity against his person" – despite the fact that Gompel was also a Jew.

The second concerned Lise Lesèvre. Lesèvre's circumstances were quite different from those of Gompel. A Resistance courier arrested at the Perrache train station in Lyon by the French Militia members and taken to Gestapo headquarters, she had been personally tortured by Barbie and then deported to Sarrebruck, then Ravensbrück, and finally Liepzig. During the subsequent "death marches" to which the SS guards submitted many internées at the end of the war, Lesèvre had escaped and been found by American troops before being repatriated to France in May 1945. Her husband, George, and her son, Jean-Pierre, had not been so fortunate. Both were arrested and deported by Barbie because Lise Lesèvre had refused to talk, even under torture. George Lesèvre died of typhus at Dachau, whereas Jean-Pierre Lesèvre disappeared on the Cape of Arcona on Lubeck Bay, apparently killed by Allied bombardments there in May 1945.

Finally, what of the "last convoy" of 11 August 1944, whose deportees were almost evenly divided between Resistance members and Jews? In his 3 January 1986 response to Serge Klarsfeld, Henry Noguères had angrily rejected Christian Riss's decision in the case as a "sordid triage" between Jews and "everyone else, Resistance or not." It was frankly difficult not to take Noguères's point and to see Riss's reading of the law in this instance as both artificial and arbitrary. In the end, the Paris Court of Cassation made it possible to include Resistance fighters deported on the convoy as victims of crimes against humanity as well. And even before the powerful testimony of many of the victims, Jews and resisters alike, of the convoy given at the 1987 trial, the arraignment itself had made clear the shared suffering of *all* of those on the train. The experience, clearly, was harrowing. At five in the morning on 11 August, prisoners were rousted from their cells at Montluc and hustled forcefully into the courtyard. (The German guards were apparently angry because the prisoners were singing the *Marseillaise*.) There they were handcuffed two by two, resisters on one side and Jews on the other. Crowded into military vehicles, all were taken together to Perrache train station to freight-loading platforms. The prisoners were then put into third-class wagons, often under the blows of SS guards. All the windows were closed and the curtains drawn. The passengers were then told to take their seats, which they were forbidden to leave or they would be shot. No food or water was provided. At four in the afternoon the train finally departed. After multiple stops along the way, some of which lasted up to two days, the train arrived in Germany. Many of the deportees had died on route. Once in Germany, suffering from thirst and lack of nourishment, they were divided and sent to different camps. Along the route, townspeople at the stations where they stopped, witnessing their pitiable condition, tried to provide some refreshment and relief but were able, in the end, to do little. In this light, separating these victims into two distinct abstract legal categories seemed all the harsher.

But however one reacts to the brutal realities of the 11 August 1944 "final convoy" from Lyon, in legal terms, at least, the stage for the 1987 trial was set. It would now be up to the magistrates and lawyers at the trial to debate the merits and legitimacy of the charges in court, as well as the substance and weight of the evidence brought to bear. And it would be up to the prosecution, and especially the witnesses, both expert witnesses and victims, to make the charges compelling and convincing and to give the jury and the audience a very real and intimate sense of what the phrase "crimes against humanity" actually meant, even more than forty years on. These were challenges indeed. And even though these challenges may well have been taken fully into account by the prosecution and the court at the outset, there was no way to anticipate all obstacles that might arise, especially those thrown up by defence counsel – and the accused himself.

President André Cerdini and his two associate judges or "assessors." Serge Mouraret/Alamy Stock Photo

Chapter Four

The Barbie Trial Begins: Opening Rituals and the Departure of the Accused

22 Yrs
AFTER
WWIIEND

The trial of Klaus Barbie on charges of crimes against humanity began early in the afternoon of Monday, 11 May 1987. It was intended to last eight weeks, according to the schedule laid out by president Cerdini.[1] The trial would meet that objective and satisfy as well the desire of most of the French, expressed in polls taken at the time, to see Barbie judged for his crimes. In Lyon, the results of these polls, reported on 9 May in the press, confirmed that 78 per cent of the townspeople of Lyon thought it was "preferable" to try Barbie, whereas only 16 per cent were in favour of "forgetting."

The atmosphere in Lyon, which had initially been one more of curiosity than concern, had become increasingly tense in the days leading up to the trial (*Le Monde*, 12 May). Protests as well as commemorations multiplied. Moreover, numerous indicators showed that the political, historical, and cultural animosities associated with the Barbie trial and the Barbie affair more generally were making their presence felt in Lyon and beyond. Indeed, the Barbie trial seemed to act as a vortex, bringing disturbing realities and developments to the forefront of French life at an ever-increasing rate.

As to the protests, these were most notably carried out by extreme right, neo-fascist groups. On the weekend before the trial opened, neo-fascist protestors paraded through Lyon to commemorate the annual celebration of Joan of Arc Day. While not violent, the protests reinforced security fears at the *Palais de Justice* itself. As a precaution, snipers were placed on the roof of the *Palais* as well as surrounding buildings, and automobile and other traffic was rerouted so as to prevent vehicles from approaching the building too closely. In addition to anxiety about neo-fascist activists, there were concerns about the security of the accused as well. Once the trial began, Barbie was to be brought to court like "precious porcelain" (*Le Monde*, 12 May), protected by a special police unit, the *Groupement d'intervention de la police nationale,* or *GIPN* ("Intervention Force of the National Police). Inside the courtroom, a glass partition eighteen millimetres thick had been installed in front of the box of the accused to protect Barbie. Not quite the glass box used at the Eichmann trial but good enough, a court official confirmed, to protect Barbie from any object thrown from the audience (*Le Monde,* 12 May).

In addition to political protests, grim reminders of France's troubled past during World War II and the ever-present horrors of the Holocaust emerged regularly in the form of significant developments announced in the press. On 11 April, Primo Levi, the Italian Holocaust survivor and eloquent chronicler of the experience and its meaning for humankind, committed suicide. The next day, René Hardy died, virtually destitute. In the minds of many, Hardy had become the very symbol of treachery within the ranks of the Resistance, a subject Vergès had been fond of raising in the press for years. At the same time, Hardy's death must have been a painful reminder to those who had wanted the trial to deal with the martyrdom of Jean Moulin, France's great Resistance hero, that this was not going to happen. As discussed, the decision had already been taken that the Caluire incident and the torture and death of Moulin were war crimes and therefore not to be treated during Riss's investigation leading up to the trial. A final effort to bring Moulin into the trial failed as well, as will be discussed in this chapter.

Then, on 3 May, Vergès, who would soon be installed in a suite in Lyon's luxury Hotel Sofitel[2] for the duration of the trial, was found guilty of defamation of character of three Resistance heroes, Raymond and Lucie Aubrac and Pierre Gullain de Bénouville. Vergès had accused all three of having played important roles in Moulin's betrayal to Klaus Barbie in Claude Bal's film *Que la vérité est amère* ("How Bitter the Truth," 1985), a film which had itself been sanctioned. Vergès was sentenced to heavy fines of 15,000 francs to be paid to each of the former resistance leaders. He was also ordered to pay 50,000 francs in damages to the court. But regardless of the court's verdict, the accusations against the Aubracs would linger and eventually explode in controversy in the mid-1990s (see the conclusion here). Indeed, in a statement attributed to Barbie three years after the trial's conclusion, dated July 1990 and delivered to judicial authorities by Vergès, Barbie stirred the pot anew by describing in detail the supposed treachery of the Aubracs and their central role in the arrests at Caluire.[3]

Vergès's conviction in no way detracted from the defence counsel's increasing notoriety and visibility as the trial approached. On 10 May, a profile of Vergès appeared in *Le Monde.* It was one of many[4] in the French and international press to evoke Vergès's colonial background, his service in the French army of liberation during the war, his mixed racial heritage (his father was from Réunion and his mother was Vietnamese), and his early career as a controversial lawyer defending Algerian and FLN militants and terrorists.[5] The profile also discussed his dismissal from the Paris Bar for disrespectful behaviour and his mysterious eight-year-long disappearance, about which he would never speak.[6] In the profile, Vergès took the occasion to speak provocatively of his tastes: "I love subversion, I love silk, I detest vulgarity." He also revealed that another well-known French *provocateur*, the author Jean Genet, had written to him to express his enthusiastic approval of Vergès's agreeing to defend Barbie: "I have learned that you are defending Barbie. More than ever, you are my friend."

In discussing Barbie's defence in the *Le Monde* profile, Vergès insisted that from the criminal dossier dealing with the many crimes of the accused he would create "a work of art" of judicial history. He added condescendingly that the chief prosecutor, Pierre Truche, would be expected to perform a similar task, although the outcome in Truche's case would inevitably be a *roman de gare*, or pulp fiction novel, because he would be obliged to follow chronology and respect the "commonplaces of society." By contrast he, Vergès, would operate under no such constraints: he would write a "new novel."[7]

But while Vergès seemingly basked in all the press attention he was getting, civil parties lawyers associated with the prosecution were experiencing a different and more chilling form of notoriety. Several lawyers for Jewish victims as well as Resistance plaintiffs reported having received a political tract from the self-described "Collective of Lycée Students Nancy-Lyon-Strasbourg 87" denying "the Jewish genocide and the existence of the concentration camps" and championing the theses of the "historian" Robert Faurisson (Faurisson was trained in literature, not history). In addition to the lawyers, a copy of Faurisson's theses were also distributed to the citizens of Izieu on 26 April, the date of a commemoration of the deportation of forty-four Jewish children sheltered there. One of the civil parties' lawyers, Gustave Berman, speculated that this dissemination of negationist materials was in all probability intended to be "one element, among others, of Barbie's defense" (*Le Monde*, 29 April 1987).[8]

Elsewhere in France, the tide of negationism seemed to be rising as well. On the first day of the trial, *Le Monde* reported that the debut issue of a new journal, the *Annals of Revisionist History*, had appeared on press kiosks around France the day before the trial opened. Featured authors included Robert Faurisson, of course, along with other French negationists and the Italian Holocaust denier Carlo Mattogno. Two years before, evidence that proponents of the denial of the Holocaust could be found in the upper reaches of French higher education was confirmed when an agronomic engineer, Henry Roques, defended a doctoral thesis at the University of Nantes containing negationist themes or claims. The chair of Roque's doctoral committee, Jean-Claude Rivière, was a professor of medieval literature who had no expertise in modern European history. Members of Roque's doctoral committee included Robert Faurisson and other negationists. A year after the defence, Alain Devaquet, the minister of higher education, revoked the doctorate granted to Roques and suspended professor Rivière, who, conveniently, was on a research sabbatical. It is worth stressing, however, that the doctoral thesis was annulled thanks to an administrative error. Otherwise, there was no way to rescind the granting of the degree by the jury. Eventually, however, measures were taken by government education officials to ensure that no embarrassment like this would happen again.[9]

If these proofs of a resurgent racism against Jews in the form of denying the Holocaust were disturbing enough, certainly equally disturbing was the violent emergence of a French racism with a different target: Arabs. On the night of 7–8 May, the office of the *Jeunes Arabes de Lyon* was vandalized and sacked by right-wing militants. On the desk of the office was left a photograph of Klaus Barbie, and 4,000 francs were stolen. The files of the organization were ransacked. Before leaving, the attackers had painted a Celtic cross and left slogans on the wall that read: "Joan of Arc will be reborn from her ashes," and "No armistice with the Arabs."

In part, perhaps to counter these manifestations of racism, and certainly those that took the form of denying the Holocaust, a number of commemorations of Holocaust victims also took place in and around Lyon. On Sunday, 26 April – a French day of commemoration set aside for the remembrance of the deportations – commemorations of Barbie's victims, and specifically the children of Izieu, were held at Izieu and in two surrounding villages. At Izieu, several dozen young people carried signs with the first names of the deported children inscribed on them. Seated in front of the monument to the children in the village sat two of the mothers who had lost children in the Izieu round-up, Fortunée Benguigui and Ita Halaunbrenner. At a ceremony there, the rabbi René Samuel recalled that the children of Izieu "suffered martyrdom and died solely because they were born Jews." Present at the ceremony as well was the Cardinal of Lyon, Albert Decourtray, who had earlier on 18 April gone on the radio to state that, in his view, the Barbie trial offered the "occasion to remember the horror" and also for the French to "look the concentration camps in the face." In the nearby villages, other commemorative gestures were made. In the village of Nantua,[10] a new plaque was unveiled on which, for the first time, the word "Jew" figured next to the names of the Izieu children deported. At Brégnier, less than three kilometres from Izieu, the mayor announced that a memorial to the Izieu children, erected in the village 1946, was to be inscribed with a phrase concerning Barbie's responsibility (*Le Monde*, 21 April and 28 April).

On the *Place des Terraux* in Lyon, a more substantial monument to Jews deported during the Holocaust was set up. At the behest of writer and sculptor Marek Halter, a massive steel cube twenty metres high was erected. Inside, visitors could walk through a labyrinth of sorts intended to suggest the experience of internment. Along the walls of the labyrinth were placed drawings made by the Jewish children interned at Theresienstadt and photographs of the Nazi death camps, all on loan from the Yad Veshem museum in Israel. The cube was completed, and the exhibit opened the first day of the Barbie trial. By the end of the trial two months later some 250,000 people had visited the exposition (Mérindol 17).

Predictably, with the trial at hand, politicians, government officials and others, including the most visible and media-savvy lawyers involved in the case, weighed in in the press with their opinions on what the Barbie trial was really about and what lessons should be learned from it for the future. Interviewed in *Le Monde* on 12 May, the minister of culture François Léotard observed somewhat cryptically that the trial should be "a moment of truth for the French" and should oblige them to think about what should be "acceptable" and what should be "rejected." Somewhat more concretely, former prime minister Pierre Mauroy stated that the trial should inform the French specifically about the horrible crimes committed during the war and punish those culpable (Barbie, presumably). Others, like André Rossinot, preferred to speculate more broadly about the trial's meaning. Undertaking this trial, he observed, was "risky" for the nation. But, he added, one measured the strength of a democracy according to the risks it takes. Finally, and not unexpectedly, Jean-Marie Le Pen volunteered a contrarian view, stating, "We are forty-five years removed from World War II, [and] in the process of scratching old wounds" (qtd. in *Le Monde*, 10 May).

As for lawyers involved in the case, the two most outspoken were Vergès and Serge Klarsfeld. For Klarsfeld, as he stated at the moment of the commemoration of the forty-four Jewish children at Izieu, "the trial will not be about Vichy's anti-Jewish laws, or about collaborationist France, but about the martyrdom of children," symbols of what Klarsfeld described as "absolute innocence." Vergès, as was his wont, chose to describe the trial in more grandiose and harshly critical terms. On 9 May, on radio *France Inter*, Vergès called the upcoming trial a "legal lynching" as well as the "trial of an ideology, not a man." He further insisted that the trial had no legal basis, as it represented a "violation of the fundamental rule of the necessity of statutes of limitations." Finally, and most provocatively, Vergès stated that the trial would be about "the genocide of one million Algerians" whose French killers had already been amnestied by the French government. This, of course, was wishful thinking on his part, although, as will be discussed, Vergès and his defence team made every effort to drag France's Algerian past into the courtroom. Typically, Vergès did not mention his client, or his view of the trial. However, the *Le Monde* court reporter Jean-Marc Théolleyre observed that, for Barbie, the faithful Nazi to the end, this would be his "last act of war" (*Le Monde*, 10 May). Clearly, however one chose to view the upcoming trial, there was no consensus about its ultimate meaning.

On Monday 11 May, the day the trial opened, the large crowd outside the *Palais de Justice* watched as those who were allowed to enter the court – reporters, witnesses, victims, and a fortunate if limited number of spectators admitted to the trial – filed past security. On the bottom steps of the courthouse, forty-four bouquets of flowers had been placed, one bouquet for each child deported from Izieu. In addition, a banner admonished the court (and the public) not to forget the four hundred Roma deported to their deaths from Lyon by the Nazis during the war. Meanwhile, Lise Lesèvre, one of the trial's most memorable witnesses (and recently added civil parties) spoke to reporters about her confrontations with and interrogation by Barbie during the war. According to *Le Monde* the next day, Lesèvre's son distributed photocopies of a hostile and anonymous letter she had received which stated: "Those were the good times, you bitch!"

Inside the courtroom, preparations had been made for the very large crowd expected to enter. As noted, the entry hall, or colourfully named *salle des pas perdus*,[11] had been transformed into a vast courtroom.[12] Additionally, balconies had been installed along the side of the hall and at the back of the makeshift courtroom to accommodate civil plaintiffs and those invited to the trial. Numbered places for these seats were assigned (Merindol 21). At the far end of the courtroom and facing back towards the river, a large multitiered stage or podium had been installed. On the top tier and facing the courtroom sat president Cerdini, his assistant judges or "assessors," and the nine jury members, along with substitute jurors. Cerdini sat in the middle of a lengthy table, and on either side of him sat his assistant judges. The nine jurors were arrayed out along the table next to the assistant judges. Behind them sat the substitute or replacement jurors, who were required to be present throughout the trial should one or more of the nine seated jurors become incapacitated.

When testifying, the witnesses in the trial, as in other Assize court proceedings, stood on the lower level of the podium, facing president Cerdini. In his role as president, Cerdini questioned the accused as well as the witnesses first, but in the Barbie trial, the witnesses were also obliged to answer questions from defence counsel, the prosecution, and civil parties lawyers. Jurors were also allowed to pose questions, although none did. All spoke on permission from president Cerdini. The opposing lawyers were not to address each other, although on occasion this rule was violated.

The defence occupied a box on the right side of the court, if one were facing the president and jury) and the prosecution and civil plaintiffs' lawyers sat on the left side (to the right of the president). These boxes were raised slightly above the level of the podium where the witness testified. Witnesses were not permitted to address the accused directly (although several did). According to numerous accounts, many in the large audience had difficulty hearing witnesses, as the latter were facing away from them in the vast courtroom. Behind defence counsel, and a level up from them, stenographers transcribed all the courtroom deliberations. However, these transcriptions were not for general consultation, as only the president of the court and two stenographers were allowed to see them.

In addition to reconfiguring the entry hall for the proceedings, other preparations had to be made as well. Behind the stage, on the right and now hidden from view, stood the original Assize court, which had been transformed into a waiting area or "green room" for witnesses. In an adjoining room, a medical station had been set up, staffed by a doctor and three nurses. The accused was old and ill. So, too, were a number of the witnesses. In addition to other maladies, Barbie, according to Vergès, suffered from blood cancer.[13]

In terms of the numbers of the French and international press corps present, Le Monde reported that there were, by nationality, 138 French reporters, 136 American reporters, 59 West German reporters, and 54 reporters from Great Britain. The Le Monde reporter observed ironically that there were no Bolivian reporters present. Apparently, the Bolivian press at least was no longer interested in the fate of its former countryman.

At this stage, it is necessary to look more closely at the workings of the French Assize court and its function in the French judicial system, which is a civil law system as opposed to a common law system. The most fundamental difference between the two systems is that in civil law, the court applies codified laws, and the judge – the central figure in the trial – serves as the chief investigator during the trial and establishes the facts and then applies the provisions of codified law. In an Assize trial, the presiding judge or "president" applies the provisions of the *code pénal,* or criminal code.[14] In a common law trial taking place in the United States or Canada, for example, the court relies on precedent. The judge plays a more passive role, relying on arguments made before her or him.

The French Assize court only tries serious felonies, as opposed to lesser crimes, or *délits,* which are handled by correctional courts. In the past, the major felonies in question have involved sentences of five years or more in prison, hard labour, and – before the 1981 elimination of capital punishment – the death penalty. Traditionally, Assize courts are located in the capital of a French department and carry the name of that department. Hence, in Lyon, the *Cour d'Assizes du Rhône.* A court of Assize does not sit at all times, but rather is called in to session periodically.

In an Assize trial, it is the president of the court who dominates the proceedings from beginning to end, much more so than an American judge. While the president in principle shares his or her authority with two *assesseurs,* or assistant judges, the latter do not play a significant role. In the Barbie trial, to all appearances the asessors served only as occasional sources for consultation for president Cerdini. At least traditionally, they do not participate in the questioning of the accused or of witnesses before the court (Ferrari 43).

The Court of Assize is the *only French court* that includes a jury. While current law mandates six jurors,[15] at the time of the Barbie trial nine jurors were chosen. Jurors are chosen by lot from electoral lists, as are substitute jurors. As they are at present, at the time of the Barbie trial, the jurors were *full voting members* of the court. To return a guilty verdict in a trial under the common law, unanimity is required. In a French Assize trial operating under a civil law system, this is not the case. For a conviction in an Assize trial today, six out of nine votes are required for a conviction. In the Barbie trial, a majority of eight votes out of twelve was required, as noted in the introduction here. Since a majority of only eight votes was required to convict or acquit, and since in the Barbie trial, where there were *nine* jurors, it was conceivable, at least, that the *jurors alone* could have acquitted Barbie. This, of course, would have been highly unlikely, as the nine jurors sat with the three judges, who also voted and who were present in part in the deliberations to make sure the criminal code was properly applied. Nevertheless, the presence of the nine jurors who were *not* legal specialists helps to explain why Vergès and his defence co-counsel, as well as chief prosecutor Pierre Truche, frequently addressed themselves so *explicitly and directly* to the jury.

As opposed to American courts, not all witnesses are placed under oath. Civil parties plaintiffs and expert witnesses called to the bar, such as psychologists and psychiatrists, are excluded. Others take an oath that they will "speak without hatred or fear" and that they will speak "the whole truth, and nothing but the truth."[16] Additionally, as opposed to a trial in a common law system, there is no cross-examination of the witnesses by opposing counsel in an Assize Court in the Anglo-American sense of the term. However, lawyers for the defence and prosecution are allowed to question the accused with the assent of the president, who may nevertheless disallow the question. Given these procedures, when civil parties lawyer Charles Libman appeared to address Barbie directly at the beginning of the trial about choosing to identify himself as "Klaus Altmann," Vergès took it upon himself to remind Libman tersely that direct cross-examination of the accused was not part of Assize court procedures.

Witnesses for the prosecution and the defence are called by the prosecution, the civil parties, and the defence, but the president also has the right to call any witness s/he feels is important to ascertain the truth. That witness does not have to take an oath. As opposed to other witnesses called, the president does not have to notify the accused twenty-four hours in advance of that witness's forthcoming testimony.

In addition to the president of the court, there are two key participants in an Assize trial: the chief prosecutor and the defence counsel. The chief prosecutor has several functions. First and foremost, it is his or her role to defend the interests of the French nation and the French Republic during the trial.[17] In the Barbie trial, this function was particularly fraught, as Vergès and his team intended to challenge the authority and legitimacy of the French Republic from the outset. It is also the chief prosecutor's role to effectively deliver to the jury "the argument for conviction." [18] Again, in the Barbie trial, this function was crucial, not only given the complexity of the legal and historical issues at hand but because both defence counsel and civil parties lawyers indulged at times in lengthy technical debates. All too often both deployed a "legalese" that Truche felt obliged to decipher for the jury.

According to American legal scholar Damon Woods, the "second most active" (Woods 329) figure in an Assize court trial is the defence lawyer and this was largely if not entirely true of the Barbie trial. The defence lawyer has the right to question witnesses (although only when permission is given by the president, as noted). Defence counsel is also given the last word in any courtroom debate, although it is the accused him- or herself who has the right to address the court last at the close of the trial. (Barbie availed himself of this right, as noted.) During the president's interrogation of the accused, generally at the outset of the trial (as was the case at the Barbie trial), it is the accused who must answer the president's questions. Defence counsel may not answer for the accused.

For some American legal scholars, there are clear advantages to the French Assize system in its broad outlines. The alacrity with which the jury is selected is impressive, as is the freedom allowed to witnesses while testifying. Also impressive is the fact that the president's rulings are rarely objected to, which facilitates the speed with which the trial progresses. There is, moreover, a virtual "certainty" that a verdict will be reached because the vote of the jury does not have to be unanimous. Finally, given the pedagogical function of the chief prosecutor, the clarity and simplicity with which the issues are generally presented to the jury in an Assize trial is worth stressing as well (Woods 325).[19]

However, other Anglo-American legal scholars have formulated substantial criticisms to the Assize court trials. For these critics, the procedures and practices of an Assize trial run counter to Anglo-American notions of fairness and equity. For example, while in theory the president remains impartial in his treatment of the accused, such impartiality is, these critics believe, impossible. Therefore, the accused "is immediately put on his defensive before the evidence against him has been presented" (Ferrari 45).[20] To all appearances, this could well have been the case at the Barbie trial. The sheer number and horror of Barbie's crimes made it reasonable to assume that *any* president presiding over Barbie's trial would have a hard time remaining neutral.

As concerns the jury, there are other potential impediments to a fair trial, certainly from an Anglo-American or common law perspective. When the witness approaches the witness stand, the judge confirms his or her identity. Then, rather than pose a series of precise questions to her or him at the outset, the president simply asks the witness to say what s/he knows about the case at hand or what s/he has to say to the court. Without guidance from the president, the jury is left to determine the credibility of the witness and sift through their accounts of events for themselves. This arguably loose approach, moreover, can also apply to the evidence presented, which may be laid out to the court in a "jumbled" fashion.

Where the power of the president in an Assize court trial is concerned, it is true that president Cerdini in many ways dominated the Barbie trial while his *assesseurs* remained, to all appearances, little more than spectators. Nevertheless, throughout the trial Cerdini maintained the decorum of the courtroom – the "dignity," he called it – as well as a firm control of his emotions, certainly during most of the trial's most trying moments. He made sure that the trial as well as the witness testimony stayed on point. Even the expert witnesses and so-called witnesses of general interest were gently admonished by Cerdini when they veered off track. Patient with the press as well, Cerdini gave photographers and television cameras ample time to photograph the accused at the historic moment of his entry into the courtroom. Most important, at no time did Cerdini put Klaus Barbie "on his defense,"[21] despite the fact that Barbie remained uncooperative and clearly disdainful of the proceedings from the outset.

Throughout the trial, Vergès sought to provoke courtroom incidents and elicit emotional reactions from Cerdini as well as others by insisting on the trial's unfairness and injustice. Vergès repeatedly lamented the fact that he, as defence counsel, was alone and unfairly outnumbered by the overwhelming numbers ranged against him on the benches of the prosecution. He would try other strategies as well to disrupt and unsettle the court. But despite these provocations, as well as pressure from some civil parties lawyers who did not keep their cool in conflictual moments and requested to have Vergès reprimanded, Cerdini kept an even hand. Indeed, by most, if not all, accounts, Cerdini's attitude was consistently one of "cordiality and credulity" in keeping with the dignity, and pressures, of his position (Ferrari 45).

What of the criticism made that, in an Assize trial, the evidence is often presented in a haphazard or "jumbled" fashion? In at least one important instance in the Barbie trial, this certainly appeared to be the case. Whereas challenging the evidence at hand is often an integral element of an Anglo-American trial in one instance, at least in the Barbie trial just such a challenge gave rise to vitriolic and distracting exchanges between the lawyers and even between the civil parties lawyers themselves. Rather than clarify the matter at hand, these exchanges seemingly obscured them.

The evidence in question was Exhibit 79, the telex Barbie had sent to his superiors in Paris announcing the round-up of the children of Izieu on 6 April 1944. The matter of the authenticity of the Izieu telex was crucial. It had been contested by Barbie and his lawyer from the outset. Originally, only a copy of the telex had been located during investigating magistrate Riss's investigation. Even though its authenticity at Nuremberg and at the German trials of Barbie's superiors had not been questioned when copies of the telex were presented in evidence in these trials (this was confirmed by experts during the investigation), Vergès had won what Henry Rousso describes as a "small symbolic victory" early on, when a higher court agreed with his demand to disallow it as a potential forgery. Afterwards, with the help of *Centre de Documentation Juive*, Serge Klarsfeld had been able to locate the original telex, which had been misclassified in the wrong file after having been used in another case (see Rousso 204, and Klarsfeld 329–30).

During the trial's fifth audience on 15 May, the original of the telex was produced in court as part of the presentation of the evidence. Chief prosecutor Truche asked that it be removed from its plastic cover so as, it turned out, to make a point about the document he would discuss later (see chapter six here). Vergès then asked to examine the telex removed from its plastic cover, and president Cerdini acquiesced. At that moment, Serge Klarsfeld protested, arguing that should something happen to the telex in Vergès's hands, the hands of a man who had contested its authenticity all along, this could give rise to claims that Vergès had damaged or destroyed it deliberately. While not unreasonable in its assumption, in the moment Klarsfeld's protest was greeted with expressions of outrage by other civil parties lawyers, who considered Klarsfeld's remarks an insult to the dignity of a colleague. Recognizing his advantage, Vergès continued to provoke Klarsfeld, who retorted in kind. If the incident accomplished anything, it only exposed the uncomfortable divide between Civil Parties' lawyers, while in no way validating a key piece – the key piece – of evidence in the trial. As another distraction to the court, it also fully exposed the simmering animosity between Klarsfeld and Vergès. Indeed, only a few days before Vergès had accused Klarsfeld, quite scandalously, of "chasing after rewards" in tracking down a Nazi like Barbie rather than going after France's homegrown criminals against humanity, like René Bousquet. Near the end of the trial, Klarsfeld refused to shake Vergès's hand when Vergès sought to congratulate him following his moving closing statement to the court about the children of Izieu (to be discussed). Klarsfeld also absented himself from the trial during Vergès's closing statement because, as he writes in *Hunting the Truth*, "I had no doubt it would be so despicable that remaining silent, as I had to do out of respect for the court, would have been unbearable." Klarsfeld adds, "He [Vergès] was our enemy, and I was not at the theater" (345).[22]

Finally, where the rights of defence counsel are concerned, American critics have argued that here as well the balance tilts towards the court and prosecution. One criticism is that although defence counsel has the right to question witnesses, this is done at the moment when the president allows it, and not spontaneously or at a moment when questioning the witness might prove particularly helpful to the defence.

There are, these critics argue, other disadvantages for the defence as well. For example, the defence counsel does not have the right to carry out an independent investigation of the case. This is done, as noted, by the investigating magistrate and the police assigned to that magistrate. Nevertheless, defence counsel does have a significant role to play during the investigation because s/he is allowed to be present for the interrogation of witnesses and the "confrontations" between the victims and the accused. In the Barbie investigation, his lawyers were allowed to question the witnesses against his client, a privilege they exploited.[23]

Despite these impediments, however, the defence in an Assize court trial has formidable weapons at its disposal. As in a common law trial, the defence lawyer makes his or her closing arguments last. Moreover, while in theory, in an Assize trial, defence counsel is expected to refer primarily to the criminal dossier and the case as a whole, in reality, s/he can say "anything he [or she] pleases" (Ferrari 53). The same, moreover, applies to the accused himself. As Michel Zaoui, Noëlle Herrenschmidt, and Antoine Garapon explain in *Mémoires de Justice: Les procès Barbie, Touvier, Papon*, "the accused can organize his defense as he pleases in an attempt to convince the judges [of his innocence]. He takes no oath to tell the truth. He has the right to lie" (80).

In the Barbie trial, Vergès as well as his co-counsel, Jean-Martin Mbemba and Nabil Bouaïta, took full advantage of the latitude of defence counsel to say "anything they pleased," in many instances much to the shock of the court and opposing civil parties lawyers, as will be discussed. (The defence's statements, and strategy, will be discussed in chapter seven here.) Moreover, as opposed to Assize procedures of earlier decades, in the Barbie trial the defence co-counsel did, as noted, have the right to call its own witnesses. It was also granted considerable leeway in questioning civil parties who testified as well as witnesses called by the prosecution.

In calling its witnesses, however, Barbie's defence team did itself no favours. The witnesses called clearly formed part of an attempt to muddy the legal and historical waters of the trial, but this backfired, sometimes spectacularly. Among the most visible of the witnesses called by Vergès was the novelist Marguerite Duras, who had during the war been part of François Mitterrand's resistance network. In 1985, two years before the trial began, Duras had published, as noted, a brilliant and provocative novel presented in episodic form of experiences taken, in principle, from her wartime past. Among the characters one encounters in *La Douleur* are a youthful, seductive, and innocent-seeming member of the *Milice,* Vichy's paramilitary and fascist militia, with whom the narrator admits she would like to have sex; a vexed and tormented Nazi spy; and, most disturbingly, an episode entitled "Albert de Capitales," in which Resistance fighters, and not their enemies, torture a suspected Gestapo agent to get him to confess to working for the Germans. The advantages to the defence of bringing these characters and episodes from *La Douleur* to the attention of the court were obvious. However, in the event, Duras refused to appear and announced her refusal to the press and in a letter to president Cerdini. In the trial's first audience, Vergès admitted, when asked by the president, that he had only learned of Duras's refusal to appear through the newspapers. She had apparently not communicated with him directly.

Also called to testify by the defence was Régis Debray, an advisor to president Mitterrand who had been heavily involved in lobbying Mitterrand to bring Barbie back to France to stand trial. A colleague of Ché Guevara, the Cuban revolutionary murdered by Bolivian security forces reputedly trained by Klaus Altmann, Debray had also been a captive of Bolivian authorities. He was later ransomed by the French government. At the Barbie trial, Debray proved "evasive" in answering the court's summons (Mérindol 25). In the end, he never testified.

The last witness of real significance to the trial called by Vergès was the Resistance hero Raymond Aubrac, precisely the man who, along with his wife, Lucie, Vergès had recently denounced as responsible for the betrayal of Jean Moulin. Aubrac's testimony, as it turned out, was hardly helpful to the cause of the defence.[24] In fact, given Aubrac's dignity, clarity, and effectiveness in countering every one of Vergès's efforts to turn his testimony against him, Aubrac's performance was nothing short of disastrous for the defence.

First, Aubrac stated his stupefaction upon receiving a request to testify for the defence. He clarified to the court that while he was called *by* the defence, he was not testifying *for* it. Aubrac added that he was in fact testifying out of respect for the justice system of his country, precisely that system and its laws that Barbie and his lawyers flouted repeatedly during the trial.

Turning to his experiences with Barbie, Aubrac remained completely calm and in control of his emotions in describing Barbie's utter brutality and evident sadism, both of which Aubrac had experienced first-hand. Every interrogation Aubrac was subjected to (he guessed roughly ten of them) was punctuated by blows form Barbie, using every instrument of torture at his disposal. Fortunately, Aubrac continued, he passed out during each interrogation, only to be awakend by more blows. As for Barbie himself, Aubrac was equally concise. Barbie, he stated, took real pleasure in administering pain to demonstate his power and superiority, occasionally in front of a woman, the nature of whose relations with Barbie was clear.

When Vergès's opportunity to question Aubrac arrived, he cited an interview in *Paris Match* in which Aubrac had been more precise in his description of the woman in question, describing her as beautiful, heavily made up, and sitting in Barbie's lap. Was there not a contradiction between the two descriptions Aubrac had given of the woman? Vergès asked. Aubrac responded that there was not and that he had been less explicit in his testimony at present out of respect for the decorum of the courtroom. Then Vergès asked Aubrac if the fact that his decription of Barbie as brutal and sadistic was not in contradiction with the courtesy with which a Gestapo officer had allowed the Aubracs to get married while Raymond was in prison? Not at all, Aubrac responded. The Gestapo officer in question was not Klaus Barbie. Having failed to rattle Aubrac or to demonstrate contradictions in his testimony, Vergès was reduced to admonishing Aubrac not for his memory lapses or "holes" from which all suffer, Vergès acknowledged, but for filling these "holes" too fancifully (at least in his view). To all appearances, the defence counsel's "lesson" to the witness fell flat, and Aubrac's courtroom performance certainly did nothing to benefit Vergès's client.

An Assize court trial like the Barbie trial opens with a series of established procedures that set the stage for the trial to follow. In the Barbie trial, these procedures included the selection and swearing in of the jury; the incorporation of civil plaintiffs not duly constituted during the investigation; the presentation of witnesses, including expert witnesses and those who would testify as civil plaintiffs; the presentation and questioning of the accused; and the reading of the *acte d'accusation,* or indictment. Then, following witness testimony and the presentation of evidence against the accused, the civil plaintiffs' lawyers begin their *plaidoiries,* or closing statements, before the court. The *réquisitoire,* or summation, of the chief prosecutor is then made before the court. Finally, defence counsel makes its closing statement. The accused is then invited to speak in his or her defence before deliberations of the jury begin. At that point, the court retires to deliberate on the verdict and sentence. In an Assize trial, the president and his assessors, as noted, deliberate and vote with the jury, their job being in part to advise the jurists on the intricacies and applicability of the law, as laid out in the French Penal Code. A series of questions is presented to the jury, and they are to vote "yes" or "no" on each question. As stated, a guilty verdict based on the answers to these questions does not require unanimity. If a vote on a question is split, that vote then counts in favour of the accused. An appeal of the verdict may be made. At that time, a second Assize trial may take place. [25]

In a trial of the magnitude of the Barbie trial and with the extraordinarily large number of civil parties and lawyers, the scheduling of the trial was, of necessity, weighted heavily towards the closing statements of the lawyers. In the event, there were thirty-nine closing statements made by civil parties lawyers, including the head of the Lyon Bar, Bernard de Bigault du Granrut. Then, chief prosecutor Truche pronounced his summation and Vergès bookended his closing statement around the statements of his two colleagues for the defence, Nabil Bouaïta and Jean-Martin Mbemba. Both lawyers arrived at the end of the Barbie trial, from Algiers and Brazzaville, respectively. Both would depart at the trial's conclusion. Given the sheer number of lawyers who were to speak, it was no wonder that of the thirty-seven audiences of the Barbie trial thirteen were devoted to the closing statements of civil parties lawyers, defence co-counsel, and the chief prosecutor. Varying in length and effectiveness, the lawyers' statements lasted from 17 June to 3 July. Given the number of civil parties lawyers, Vergès was correct in remarking in court on the disparity between the time given to the prosecution versus the time given to the defence in the trial. But then, the sheer number of Barbie's victims among Jews and Resistance members absolutely justified the number of civil plaintiffs and their lawyers. According to Pierre Mérindol, the total number of Barbie's victims included 4,342 murdered, and 7,591 Jews and 14,311 Resistance members deported.

Although many of the most prominent civil parties lawyers, and most notably Serge Klarsfeld, had remained consistent in their aims and ambitions for the trial and had, moreover, been associated with the investigation of the case from or near the outset, the same could not be said for Barbie's defence counsel. Indeed, the latter had experienced important changes in personnel and approach to the trial during the investigation of his case. By the opening of the trial, the defence team included *not one* of Barbie's original defence lawyers. As lawyers changed, so did the defence strategy.

When Barbie arrived in Lyon following his expulsion from Bolivia in 1983, according to French judicial procedure it was up to the Head of the Lyon Bar at that time, Alain de la Servette, to choose Barbie's defence counsel. Ideologically "liberal" in American terms and enjoying a reputation of not playing politics in court, Servette chose himself to represent Barbie, with the latter's consent. Servette then promptly added an assistant, the Jesuit lawyer Robert Boyer. The two men wanted, above all, as fair a trial as possible for someone as notorious as Klaus Barbie. They intended as much as possible to seek the sympathy and indulgence of the court for their client.[26]

Enter Jacques Vergès, and before him the Nazi Swiss financier François Genoud. Well-known in circles of former Nazis as well as terrorist groups and individuals from the Algerian *Front de Libération Nationale* (FLN) to Carlos, whom he had bankrolled for decades, Genoud learned of Barbie's arrest and return to France on television in his home near Lausanne. He described it as "shameful." Springing into action, Genoud contacted Vergès, whom he knew through the latter's earlier defence of Algerian causes. Genoud asked him to consider serving on Barbie's defence team. Within forty-eight hours, Vergès agreed. Then, making contact with Barbie's daughter, Ute Messner, Genoud secured her consent to add Vergès to the defence team. With these pieces in place, Genoud then travelled to Lyon to meet with Alain de la Servette. As recounted in Pierre Péan's

L'Extrémiste, Genoud reported that Servette readily agreed to Genoud's proposal to take Vergès on, stating that Vergès was "a great lawyer, and one worthy of this great cause" (371).

Other accounts of Genoud's efforts on Barbie's behalf differ, however. According to one source, Genoud first proposed to Servette that he, Genoud, pay for Barbie's defence. Servette declined but agreed reluctantly to add Vergès to the team. Whatever the circumstances, this new arrangement did not last long. Vergès was appointed to the defence in a letter to the judge by Barbie dated 27 May, and by mid-June Servette, followed by his assistant, Boyer, were forced out. Both resigned on 15 June. In the case of Boyer, a Jesuit, his service was made more problematic by the fact that the Archbishop of Lyon, Albert Decourtray, publicly expressed concern that a Jesuit was serving on the defence team of Klaus Barbie, after having denounced Barbie on French radio, as noted. (*Le Monde*, "Mon client est présumé innocent," Laurent Greilsammer, 17 June 1983). In the end, Vergès, along with his defence strategy, won the day. Even though he was jokingly referred to in some quarters as *Maître Guillotine* for sacrificing his clients for his own political ends, Vergès would remain Barbie's lead lawyer throughout the trial and afterwards. Although Vergès denied it, by many accounts it was François Genoud who footed some, if not all, of his fees and expenses.[27]

The Trial Begins: Opening Rituals, Opening Salvoes

At precisely 1:01 p.m. on 11 May, according to the video recording of the trial, the bailiff of the *Cour d'assizes du Rhône* climbed the stairs to the podium specially constructed for the Barbie trial, took a microphone from the lengthy table facing the courtroom behind which the judges and jury would sit, and announced *la cour*, "the court," for the first time. Immediately, two central, massive doors at least three times higher than the judges opened, and president Cerdini, followed by his two assistants and their substitutes, entered the courtroom.[28] The audience and other members of the court, already present at or in their seats (the main doors of the *Palais de Justice* had opened at 11:30 a.m.) rose to their feet. A murmur of anticipation and excitement was audible in the vast hall. Immediately upon taking his seat, Cerdini asked the audience to be seated and then ordered security personnel, or the *services d'ordre*, to bring in the accused.

As noted in the introduction, the man who entered hardly fit the bill of the imposing Aryan superman, even in an elderly incarnation. Indeed, he was small and decrepit. But as the Lyon journalist Pierre Mérindol

warned, for those who seemed to detect "a servile politeness and coop-
erative attitude in the face of the judicial apparatus" in Barbie's gaze and
appearance, they were sorely mistaken. For Mérindol, Barbie's "ascetic
face," with its "piercing eyes" and "frozen smile," reflected, rather, an
attitude of "determination and irony" (23). That attitude would not
change throughout the trial.

After allowing photographers onto the podium to photograph Barbie, Cerdini ordered the press to withdraw[29] and asked the defendant to
rise. Cerdini then asked Barbie if he wanted a German interpreter. The
accused responded in the affirmative, although he answered the first few
questions about his date and place of birth in French before switching to
German in describing his occupation, "merchant" and giving his address
in La Paz. In stating his name, Barbie referred to himself as "Altmann,
Klaus." When pressed by Cerdini as to when his name became Altmann,
he explained that he had been naturalized as a Bolivian citizen in 1957
under both names, "Klaus Altmann" and "Klaus Barbie."

With that formality apparently out of the way (it was not), Cerdini
proceeded to the selection of the jury. Nine names drawn by lot from
an urn were accepted. The jury chosen comprised four women and five
men. Their average age was thirty-nine and two-tenths years. Given their
ages, the members of the jury had either not experienced the war and
Occupation directly or had only experienced it as very small children.
Their supposed "neutrality," therefore, made them uncontroversial,
even if their combined socio-professional profile made them appear "a
banal image of the middle class" rather than "an illustration of *la France
profonde*" – the traditional notion of a "true France," including peasants,
artisans, etc. (Mérindol 22).[30] Mérindol reported that prior to the drawing of the names, both the prosecution and defence rejected only one
juror each, purely "as a matter of form" (23).[31]

The jury selected, all were called onto the podium. The nine desig-
nated jurors assumed their places alongside the judges facing the court.
The reserve jurists took their places behind the judges and jurors and to
the side. Cerdini then read the oath to the court, and each juror then
stated "I swear it" in turn. The oath read:

> You promise and swear to examine with the most scrupulous attention
> the charges brought against Klaus Altmann, (and here Cerdini paused to
> correct himself) Klaus Barbie, alias, Altmann, to betray neither the interests
> of the accused or the society that accuses him, to communicate with no
> one after you are sworn in, and to listen neither to hate nor meanness, nor
> fear, nor affection, to make your decision only on the basis of the charges
> and the means used by the defense, following your conscience and your

intimate conviction, with the impartiality and firmness that are appropriate to a free person of probity, and to maintain the secrecy of the deliberations, even after your service has ceased.

As opposed to an American jury, the jury in an Assize trial is not sequestered for the duration of the trial. Now, with the jury duly constituted – the true opening of the trial, according to Mérindol – Cerdini returned to the interrogation of the accused and the rehearsal of his curriculum vitae.

Two points are worth noting at this stage. The first is that, in an Assize trial, extenuating circumstances, at least since the mid-nineteenth century, have played important, if not crucial, roles in that they allow the jury to lessen the punishment meted out to the defendant if the circumstances of his or her life merit it. The rehearsal of the accused's CV, which in effect covers his or her *entire life*, allows the jury to consider external factors to the crime or crimes that may attenuate the responsibility of the accused in committing those crimes. For example, as was already widely known at the time the trial opened, Barbie had been badly abused by his alcoholic father as a child. In theory, at least, this could have been raised and emphasized during his questioning by Cerdini to mitigate Barbie's subsequent cruelty and murderousness. But at no point during the interrogation did Barbie attempt to elicit the president or the court's sympathy. Quite the reverse. Indeed, given Barbie's clear lack of repentance, several of the civil parties devoted their closing statements in part to underscoring the fact that there should be no extenuating circumstances, given Barbie's attitude.[32]

The second point is that, as the reaction of several civil parties confirmed, Barbie's identifying himself as Klaus Altmann was a deliberate provocation. It indicated that, as he and his defence counsel would maintain throughout the trial, as a Bolivian citizen who should enjoy the privileges and protections thereof, Barbie had been brought to France illegally. Challenged by Charles Libman, one of the civil parties' lawyers representing the children of Izieu, to acknowledge that many times during the investigation he had admitted to being and had spoken as Klaus Barbie the accused refused to answer. Libman's point was that Barbie was lying then or he was lying now. In other words, Libman was already making the point at the very outset of the trial that Barbie was a liar and that nothing he might say could be trusted. In an effort to bring the matter to a close, chief prosecutor Truche affirmed that whatever identity Barbie claimed now was insignificant, as he had already acknowledged being the Nazi Klaus Barbie who operated in wartime Lyon from 1942 to 1944. Truche also observed ironically that Barbie would have been an honourable name to claim until 1933. But at present, it was understandable that the name Barbie would be "a heavy name to bear."

The matter settled, at least for the moment, Cerdini turned to the roll call of the witnesses. As Mérindol reports, there were 101 witnesses called. Some, like Marguerite Duras, declined to appear, whereas others were unable to do so for medical or other reasons. As the bailiff stated at the outset, the roll call and the presentation of each witness was intended to let the president know "with whom he is dealing." Given the number of witnesses scheduled to appear and taking into account their own busy lives, Cerdini, Mérindol reported, had prepared a schedule with the date for the appearance of each witness in advance. Cerdini then informed the few witnesses in attendance for the roll call that unless they were also constituted as civil parties or plaintiffs, they would be required to absent themselves from the trial until their scheduled testimony.

The next stage of the procedure to be dealt with, the "constitution" or incorporation of the civil parties, was more fraught. After an initial reading by the bailiff of the names of 110 victims, relatives, or organizations representing one or both which had already been duly constituted as civil parties during the investigation, the criminal code allowed for the incorporation or ratification of additional civil parties. The procedure itself, Mérindol observed, was both monotonous and one which "demonstrated the extent to which the horror had become routine" (25) during Barbie's years in wartime Lyon. Some of the civil parties added were uncontroversial, such as twenty-four victims or their relatives successfully added by Serge Klarsfeld and who had already been heard during the investigation. Others, however, were not. Represented by her lawyer, the sister of Bruno Larat, one of the *résistants* arrested at Caluire along with Jean Moulin, claimed that her brother had been the victim of crimes against humanity. As the court fully realized, to constitute Bruno Larat or his sister as a civil plaintiff would require redoing the investigation and introducing the events of Caluire into courtroom debates. This was impossible because the decision had already been taken during the initial investigation that what happened at Caluire was a war crime, not a crime against humanity. It was therefore not investigated. As a result, it had not been affected by the 1985 Court of Cassation decision, as only matters already examined and included in the dossier of the investigation could be added as new charges against Barbie. In the moment, Vergès agreed as a matter of respect for legal procedures, although he took the opportunity to stress that Caluire could never be "evacuated from history." For all intents and purposes, however, it had been successfully "evacuated" from the 1987 trial.[33]

The second petition seeking incorporation as a civil party came from Bruno Ravaz, a young lawyer representing Robert Cohen. Cohen's uncle and aunt had been arrested at a hotel in the village of Saint-Claude and deported to their deaths at Auschwitz. Thanks to the good offices of his aunt, Robert Cohen himself had apparently escaped deportation. Regardless, Ravaz demanded of the court that before undertaking the trial of Klaus Barbie for the crimes of which he was accused an investigation of the Saint-Claude affair needed to be reopened. Among other difficulties – including the fact that, as Truche pointed out, this would be entirely unfair to the defence – the affair at Saint-Claude had already been included among the crimes for which Barbie had previously been judged. To reopen the Saint-Claude affair, then, would reactivate the condemnations of 1952 and 1954, and since they would have expired, Barbie would have to be freed (Mérindol 26). Not informed of Ravaz's intentions beforehand, the other civil parties lawyers were caught by surprise. Some expressed their disapproval. One of these lawyers described Ravaz's manoeuvre as what, in football, "one calls a 'suspicious pass' against one's own team" (Mérindol 27).

Following the successful negotiation of two potentially hazardous impediments to the trial in the form of civil parties applications or petitions, the court then turned to the reading of the *acte d'accusation*, or indictment. The indictment read comprised, first, the indictment of the Indictments Chamber of the Lyon Court of Appeals, followed by the indictments of the same body of the Paris Court of Appeals. Monotonous, but most thorough in its content, the text of this final indictment was some 120 pages long. It was read by what Sorj Chalandon harshly described as "gignolesque" scribes. Meanwhile, Barbie sat in his box, at times impassively, at other times with looks of irritation or disgust on his face.[34]

In its very nature a pedantic exercise both in its extraordinary, not to say excessive, attention to detail and in the flat, legalese language in which it is written, it is easy to understand how the reading of the indictment could be cited as evidence of the inherent monotony and lack of drama of a French Assize court trial. But if one listens carefully to it, it can and does reveal the thoroughness, indeed the exhaustiveness, of the investigation carried out by the investigating magistrate. In the case of the indictment in the Barbie trial, the indictment not only meticulously documented the details of Barbie's life and career, it provided a succinct assessment of the evolution of SD authority in Occupied France, the specifics of Barbie's crimes, and the exhaustive efforts to authenticate the evidence against the accused. As one example, it put the lie to Barbie's claim during the rehearsal of his CV that Dutch authorities who wished to interview Barbie in prison in Lyon for deporting three hundred Jews from Amsterdam to their deaths at Mathausen before coming to France had dropped their attempt for lack of evidence. The indictment noted that, in reality, Barbie simply refused to answer their questions.

Much more central to the trial in Lyon, the indictment also dealt in detail with the Izieu telex and provided further evidence of its authenticity. It maintained, first, that a forger would have had to have known that three of those Barbie described as "personnel" at Izieu were, in fact, Jewish children, aged fifteen, sixteen, and seventeen, so easily confused with supervising adults at the time.[35] Then, addressing Barbie's claim that he had been fighting the Resistance on the day the children were arrested and therefore unable to carry out that arrest, the indictment stated that Barbie would have had plenty of time to carry out his activities against the Resistance and still have been in Izieu for the round-up of the Jewish children. Finally, the indictment also reminded the court that the document's authenticity had *not* been challenged when it had been brought in evidence at Nuremberg and later in the trials of Barbie's superiors in the Federal Republic of Germany. So, in effect, when Vergès tried to challenge the authenticity of the Izieu telex again during his closing statement, the rug, so to speak, had already been pulled out from under him. In the indictment, the same thoroughness and attention to detail was also brought to the evidence for other crimes against humanity with which Barbie was charged.

Perhaps in part an attempt to distract the court and jury from the litany of crimes, victims, and pieces of evidence confirming Barbie's responsibility included in the indictment, Vergès chose the moment of its conclusion during the second audience of the trial on 12 May to demand the trial itself be immediately stopped. The procedure against his client, he stated, needed to be annulled. Vergès's argument was that the crimes imputed to Barbie in the current trial had already been included in the judgment of 1954. Essentially, then, the current trial was one involving double jeopardy, and no legitimate legal system in the world allowed a criminal to be judged twice for the same crime.

But Vergès's argument – as well as his aim to disrupt – were much more far-reaching than simply making an awkwardly timed case for double jeopardy. In a language laced with legal terminology and references to legal theories and judicial decisions with which the jury and the courtroom were undoubtedly unfamiliar, Vergès almost systematically extended the scope of his topics and historical references to arrive at what was among his stated goals in pre-trial interviews: the indictment of the French nation for its hypocrisy for trying Klaus Barbie for such crimes when Frenchmen working for Vichy and guilty of similar crimes were walking around as free men.

But there were important stages in his argumentation and a historical detour to be made before Vergès arrived at his goal of denouncing
the French nation, past and present. To make the claim that the 1954
judgment covered all of Barbie's French victims (the 1954 judgment covered only *French* victims), and so presumably all the victims of Barbie's
crimes at issue in the current trial, Vergès argued that the crimes covered
"limitatively" and "analytically" in the indictment just read were covered
"globally" in the 1954 judgment. The latter, Vergès argued, embraced all
crimes committed by Barbie in Lyon *as well as the surrounding region.* And
since the earlier judgment was indeed "global" in nature and, moreover,
acknowledged the authority of the *Ordonnance du 28 Août 1944 relative
a la répression des crimes de guerre,* this meant that it did not distinguish
between adults and children. Therefore, the children of Izieu (a village
in the Lyon region, after all) could be considered as included in the
verdict.[36]

Vergès then drew a stunning comparison to demonstrate what he
meant by "globally." He cited a ruling handed down in the case of Pinkus
Chmilenicky,[37] relating to the "commandant of Birkenau." The problem
in that instance, Vergès maintained, was that since all the commandant's
victims could never be identified individually, and all had died in the geographical constraints of the camp and in the same ways, individual indictments for each victim were neither possible nor necessary. Therefore a
"universal" or "global" indictment was drawn up. Commenting on this
conviction, Vergès then proposed his comparison with Barbie's 1954 conviction: "You will note here that the unity of action, the circumstances of
time and place are defined in the same manner here as, mutatis mutan-
dis, they were defined by the Permanent Military Tribunal of Armed
Forces of Lyon as concerns the 1954 case against the accused Barbie."[38]

Finally, before being interrupted by civil parties lawyers raising objections to his claims or pointing to its unforeseen implications that were in
fact detrimental to the defence counsel's argument, Vergès offered one
more comparison. In this, he took direct aim at Serge Klarsfeld. Vergès
acknowledged that while Jean Leguay, the subordinate of René Bousquet, Vichy's chief of police who had played a major role in the round-up
and deportation of French Jews, was being legally pursued by Klarsfeld
for crimes against humanity, Bousquet himself was not. Wasn't it the
case, then, Vergès wondered, that Bousquet was benefitting from the
fact that he had been tried during the Purge in 1949[39] and that the judgment issued then covered any subsequent charges? If this was indeed
true, why, Vergès asked ironically, should a "foreigner" like Klaus Barbie
not also benefit from the 1954 judgment, as Bousquet had from his own
1949 condemnation?

The Barbie trial, it appeared, had arrived at a perilous moment. In raising the spectre of Jean Leguay and especially René Bousquet, Vergès was dramatically underscoring official French complicity in the Holocaust *at the highest level* for the first time in court. To all appearances, the issue could only serve Vergès and the defence well for several reasons. First, while Bousquet's connection to the Final Solution (and following the 1978 publication of an interview with Louis Darquier de Pellepoix, his reputed direct responsibility for the infamous round-ups in Paris and deportations to their deaths of some 13,000 Jews in summer 1942) was generally known, the specifics of the case and the complicated reasons why he had not yet been indicted were in all likelihood not so well known or understood. The same, moreover, would hold true for the specifics of Bousquet's 1949 trial. In establishing a (false) parallel between that trial and Barbie's 1954 conviction, Vergès was striking directly at the heart of the trial underway. Specifically, he was taking aim at the very notion that in Lyon, now, justice in any abstract, universal, *and legitimate* sense of the word was being served. Were there not in fact *deux poids, deux mesures*, two "weights and measures" in effect here, one for a foreigner, and one for a Frenchman?

Additionally, Vergès was attempting to place Serge Klarsfeld in a bind. Klarsfeld had been pursuing Leguay publicly for crimes against humanity since 1978 but for a number of legitimate reasons would not bring charges against Bousquet until 1989, after the Barbie trial was over. In the moment, this put Klarsfeld in the uncomfortable position of challenging Vergès's claims, which he did, and attempting to offer explanations to the court as to where the Bousquet investigation stood and why there was as of yet no indictment. This was, needless to say, a distraction from the matter of Barbie's crimes, and an unsettling one at that.

Klarsfeld was not the only civil parties lawyer to be drawn in by Vergès's efforts at diversion. Responding in kind to the defence lawyer's legalistic rhetoric and his pretensions to a mastery of the penal code, Paul Vuillard[40] noted that an argument pertaining to the double jeopardy or "authority of what has already been judged" at this stage was being made either too early or too late. It should have been raised before the trial got underway or introduced at the end of the trial, when the accusations pending against the accused would already have been thoroughly explored during the trial. Vuillard added, moreover, that under any circumstances the notion of *l'autorité de la chose jugée* did not apply when one was dealing with crimes subject to statutes of limitiation on the one hand and crimes with no statute of limitations on the other. Vergès, true to form, challenged Vuillard's distinction and advised him haughtily to go back to his law books. Wishing to offer his own challenge to Vergès's call for a dismissal, Charles Libman argued that Vergès had overlooked the fact that some of the Izieu children were not French citizens but were in fact foreign nationals and therefore were not even covered by the 1954 judgment, which concerned only French citizens. But in the moment, this only complicated matters: henceforth, would only those Izieu children who were foreigners be considered the victims of Barbie's crimes against humanity and not the others?[11]

Clearly sensing that the trial was getting off track and that the jury was no doubt confused by the lawyers' protracted debates over procedure, chief prosecutor Truche rose and addressed the members of the jury directly. He stressed the fact that the issue Vergès had placed before the court was a serious one and one that did concern them directly. But rather than engage in legalistic arguments like those deployed by his colleagues, Truche, as he would do throughout the trial, attempted to reduce the matter at hand to two central legal principles or precepts that could be easily grasped with *le simple bon sens*, "simple good sense." The first was that one cannot be tried for the same crime twice. The second, codified in Article 236 of the French Penal Code of the time, was that one cannot try an individual for a crime which has not been investigated during the investigating magistrate's investigation and included in the criminal dossier of the trial. Truche then proceeded to enumerate the elements in the current criminal indictment that had *not* been included in the 1954 conviction. He emphasized the fact that both appeals courts, in Paris and Lyon, had read the 1954 conviction assiduously, and no mistake had been made, no crime covered by 1954 conviction had slipped into the current dossier.

But the strength of Truche's arguments lay as much in the *manner and language* in which he spoke to the jury as it did in his calm and convincing recitation of the facts and legal realities. More than once he insisted that these were matters easily grasped with "simple good sense" and that the facts themselves were *évident*, obvious. Moreover, casting himself as the voice of reason and of fair-mindedness where others had been caught up in high-flown legal distractions of the defence, Truche insisted: "I detest juridical and judicial over-reaching (*acharnement*). It is in some cases as condemnable as therapeutic [medical] over-reaching." In essence, Truche was arguing, the cure could be worse than the disease. And this, he stated, was "clear" and "evident" as well. To a jury and a courtroom that had already been subjected to the full array of shortcomings for which French Assize trials and the Barbie trial in particular had been criticized – the monotony of the indictment, the pedantic, confusing, and distracting arguments of lawyers, not to mention an accused who clearly felt no obligation to respond respectfully and/or honestly to questions asked of him – Truche's intervention must have seemed both necessary and a relief. This was certainly the impression made on some of the journalists present.[42]

But if the prosecutor general had won one battle in the ongoing confrontation with the defence in successfully countering Vergès' argument to dismiss, Truche's clarifications did not account for the deliberate obfuscations and exaggerations, the "diversions" then offered up by the accused himself. Asked by Cerdini if he agreed with the arguments of his lawyer, Barbie chose a different historical and legal proceeding than that used by Vergès in which to couch his response. Given the accusations against him in the indictment, Barbie told the court, he felt as if he were "at Nuremberg," that he was presented as having conducted himself as a "madman" in wartime Lyon, caught up entirely in arresting and deporting Jews to Drancy. He reminded the court that he was part of a commando unit of 120 men, that Dr. Werner Knab was the man in charge, and that he, Barbie, had not been the "master of Lyon," as he had been presented as being. Concluding his remarks, Barbie stated that he had recently read in *Der Spiegel* about the case of an SS general whose son was the current president of the Federal Republic of Germany. The general in question had been given seven years in prison because while working in the Reich office of Foreign Affairs he had written a letter to his French subordinates demanding the acceleration of the deportation of Jews from France.

Not so subtly, Barbie was painting himself, as Vergès had done, as a victim. In the process, he trotted out all the clichés other Nazis and SS had used after the war: he was only following orders, he didn't know the ultimate fate of the Jews he deported, indeed, he had no real authority. In punctuating his statements with a reference to Nuremberg and to the SS general much more responsible than he for the deaths of French Jews, Barbie was underscoring the fundamental unfairness in his situation. First, he was being placed legally on the same footing as the Nazi leaders most responsible for the devastation of the war. Second, he was being made a "scapegoat" for perpetrators of much more egregious crimes against the Jews than he was charged with, and these perpetrators were getting off more lightly because of social privilege and apparent protection in high places.

No matter how strategic or hypocritical Barbie's claims, for the jurors who had just sworn to protect the "interests" of the accused and to demonstrate "impartiality," Barbie's comments – those of a visibly aged and apparently sickly old man – must have resonated, certainly more than the legalistic arguments of Vergès and the civil parties lawyers. It would take the testimony of Barbie's victims, still several days away, to put the full horror of the accused's own crimes in wartime Lyon in their proper perspective.

If the second hearing of the Barbie trial on 12 May had its share of powerful rhetorical performances by lawyers and included Barbie's lengthy self-exoneration near its end, it was during the third hearing of the Lyon trial that the first major *coup de théâtre* occurred. As argued in the introduction, the event in question marked the end of the first phase of the trial and from the standpoint of historic trials of Nazis, set the Barbie trial apart, launching it in effect into uncharted waters. The event in question was Klaus Barbie's abrupt departure from his own trial.

As the third hearing got underway, president Cerdini resumed his interrogation of the accused concerning his life and career. Having covered Barbie's work with American intelligence in post-war Europe, his escape from Europe on the infamous Rat Line, and his activities in Peru and Bolivia, including his links with Bolivian dictators, Cerdini turned to Barbie's departure from Bolivia and return to France. At that point, at 3:30 in the afternoon, Barbie abruptly announced that he was leaving his trial and asked to be taken back to his cell in Saint-Joseph Prison.

For seasoned courtroom observers and reporters like Jean-Marc Théolleyre, Barbie's departure did not come as a surprise, given who his lawyer was. Indeed, one of Vergès's earlier, highly visible clients, the Algerian militant Georges Ibrahim Abdallah, had also quit his trial. In Abdallah's case, as opposed to Barbie's, Abdallah was protesting what he perceived to be the judges' prejudice against him. For Barbie, "kidnapped" as he claimed to have been from Bolivia, the Lyon trial in its entirety was illegitimate and unjustifiable under Bolivian and international law. It was therefore dramatically appropriate that Barbie chose to announce his departure at precisely the moment he did. Barbie had just told Cerdini that his removal from Bolivia was illegal and that he considered himself a "hostage" rather than a prisoner. He then read from a written statement to all appearances handed to him at that moment by Vergès.[43]

Barbie's announcement created a veritable storm of protest in the courtroom. Civil parties lawyers expressed outrage, noting, among other things, that Vergès had slipped the note to Barbie containing the words the accused was to articulate. Others pleaded with president Cerdini not to allow Barbie's departure. Vergès, who seemed to have orchestrated the *coup* from the outset, defended his client's decision. From the standpoint of the international press in attendance as well as critics of the trial, Barbie's departure meant that the trial had suddenly lost its "dazzle." For some, the move only reinforced their opinion that the trial was futile from the outset.[44] If anything, it had just become even more of a "bore."

But for lawyers participating in the trial, Barbie's announced departure meant a variety of different things, or proved a number of significant points. For some, including especially chief prosecutor Truche, it was proof that the brutal and domineering "triumphant" Nazi Klaus

Barbie was now the "shameful" one who did not have the courage to look at his own past. Truche reminded Barbie ironically that some fifty years earlier in Lyon "one did not have the right to absent oneself from [Nazi] interrogations" not to one's taste. Truche added, again dramatically, that it was "the honor of French justice to give an accused the right to answer his or her accusers in court" and face an "unprejudiced jury." But when given this opportunity, *Monsieur* Barbie had opted to become "*Herr Nein, Monsieur Non.*"[45]

For others, however, Barbie's departure was advantageous to the trial. Civil parties lawyer Henri Noguères, for one, expressed his pleasure that now the court would be spared "certain lies" the accused would surely tell. When the court applauded Noguères's words, Cerdini pleaded with the audience: "I beg you, we are not at the theatre." Noguères was not alone in expressing the view that Barbie's departure had in fact facilitated the prosecution of the accused. Years later, Alain Lévy stated that, in his opinion, the trial was all the more powerful symbolically because where the former Nazi once sat there was now an empty chair and not a decrepit old man who, for some, at least hardly seemed to "measure up" to his crimes. In his memoirs, Serge Klarsfeld saw further advantages. First, "it was a lot easier dealing with Vergès than with Barbie" because "the lawyer had a poor grasp of the dossiers and objected to only a few witnesses; he let the others talk, and they impressed the jury with their dignity and their horrific accounts of physical and psychological torture. Without Barbie, they were able to express themselves freely" (344). Indeed, in reading the statements of witnesses as they were confronted with Barbie during the investigation or after the confrontation was over, it is clear that many were traumatized to be placed face to face with their tormentor again. As in court, Barbie showed no remorse or regret during these confrontations, contenting himself with challenging their credibility and in most cases denying he had ever seen them.

For the man who, to all appearances, had staged Barbie's dramatic move, Vergès, the former Nazi's departure afforded him the opportunity not only to cast himself in a heroic light but to reiterate and reinforce what he had been saying about the trial all along. Rather than address what Barbie's departure said about the accused, Vergès chose to denounce the chorus of lawyers on the opposite side of the courtroom. While they "howled with wolves" intent on destroying Barbie, Vergès affirmed, "it is my honor to defend this solitary man" in the face of this "lynching." Never one to miss the opportunity to provoke and disrupt, Vergès also denounced Alain Lévy, the civil parties lawyer who had called the court's attention to Vergès slipping Barbie the note, as a *délateur* – "stool pigeon." In using the term, Vergès was fully aware of how charged it was, especially in a trial about a Nazi policeman who depended on much of his wartime success on the French being willing to denounce and betray other French. For good measure, Vergès compared Barbie's "kidnapping" in Bolivia to Napoleon Bonaparte's having the Duke d'Enghien arrested in the Rhineland, secreted back over the border into France, tried on trumped-up charges, and executed in 1804. Then, as now, Vergès implied, an "innocent man" was being railroaded by a despotic regime.[46]

When the accused's turn came to speak, Barbie denied the accusations that he was a coward and reiterated his claim that the trial was illegitimate due to his abduction from Bolivia. He added, moreover, and clearly for effect, that the lawyers seeking to prosecute him had themselves acted illegally. Had not Serge Klarsfeld put up $5,000 to have him kidnapped in the early 1970s, and with the help of Régis Debray, now president Mitterrand's senior advisor? To this chief prosecutor Truche responded that Barbie did not seem capable of absenting himself from the court, after all, and that rather than face the accusations against him all he could manage to do in turn was "accuse, accuse, accuse." Barbie was, Truche added, attempting to "divert, to go elsewhere" rather than confront the matter at hand. Truche would return to the notion of a defence "'by diversion" at another crucial moment in the trial.

If Barbie's departure ended with more of a whimper than a bang, that is, with a bit of posturing and rhetorical flourishes from both sides, it also, as noted, marked a caesura, a "before and after" moment whose implications could not be fully recognized at the time. In the two and a half audiences that had taken place before Barbie's exit,[47] virtually *all* the crucial elements that would come to define the Barbie trial were put on display, and some uncertainties or dilemmas hanging over it resolved. In the first instance, these included the key strategies and rhetoric of the defence and prosecution, the procedural rules to be followed, the weight and validity of the evidence, and the contested issues at the heart of the trial. Among these contested issues were the impact and legal implications of Barbie's earlier convictions for war crimes and the difference between crimes against humanity and war crimes. In the second instance, the spectre of Caluire and the torture and murder of Jean Moulin which still hung over the trial in certain quarters was effectively sidelined for the duration of Barbie's trial. This occured, as noted, during the petitions for inclusion of additional civil parties. In this way, despite early obstacles to its focus and continuity, the Barbie trial managed to remain on track. With this accomplished, the court could turn to its second phase, the review of the evidence and, most importantly, the often wrenching testimony of witnesses, which would produce risks and obstacles of its own.[48]

Chapter Five

The Witnesses

One hundred and seven witnesses testified at the Barbie trial between 14 May and 15 June 1987. Compared to other trials, and certainly any "normal" French Assize court trial which chief prosecutor Truche insisted that the Barbie trial was, this was an extraordinary number of witnesses. Called to testify by the court, the civil parties lawyers, as well as defence counsel, the witnesses included Barbie's surviving victims, other victims of Nazism and especially camp survivors, former Resistance members, psychiatrists, historians, jurists, philosophers, diplomats, politicians, a former American intelligence officer, and even a successful language school director from New York. As noted earlier, witnesses who were also civil parties attached to the prosecution did not have to take the witness oath, whereas all other witnesses did.

As in virtually any trial, and certainly in an historical trial of the magnitude of the Barbie trial, some witnesses and testimonies are more memorable and compelling than others. Moreover, given the range in backgrounds and expertise as well as the reasons for which the witnesses were called to testify by the different parties, by no means did all the testimonies of these witnesses serve the ends of the court and prosecution. More specifically, some of the most important and impactful witnesses strongly challenged the definition of crimes against humanity handed down by the Court of Cassation in accordance with which the accused had to be judged. Some of these same witnesses as well as others also made clear their dissatisfaction with what they viewed as the false or erroneous distinction between crimes against humanity and war crimes as established by the high court decision. This is not to say that *all* the witnesses who spoke to these matters simply muddied the legal waters. Some in fact offered insightful analyses of these crimes that undoubtedly proved helpful and perhaps even enlightening to the court and jury. But as will be discussed, what ultimately gave substance and meaning to the idea that *both Jews and resisters* could be the victims of crimes against humanity was the comparability, the similarity of their experiences and suffering at the hands of Klaus Barbie and the Nazis. Through the power of their combined testimony, as the *Le Monde* reporter Jean-Marc Théolleyre observed, the court came to understand and appreciate the moment in the trial when, after their testimonies, crimes against humanity were "no longer just words."

Given the number of witnesses who testified as well as the fact that some of the testimonies given were ineffectual, self-indulgent, or simply not germane to the matters at hand, not all these testimonies will be discussed here. Some of the testimonies, specifically those of the psychiatric team that examined Barbie as well as the witnesses for the defence, have already been discussed in earlier chapters. Of the testimonies that will be examined in this chapter, these will be divided into three categories. The first category discussed in Part One comprises primarily, but not exclusively, those witnesses who encountered the accused directly and personally during the war, and who suffered physically, psychologically, and/or morally at his hands. The second category, discussed in Part Two, is made up of the testimonies of key witnesses who chose to make the subject of their statements their thoughts on what war crimes and crimes against humanity were and were not. Prodded by defence counsel Vergès, several of these witnesses also discussed the applicability of these definitions to crimes committed more recently by other nations, and especially Western democracies and Israel. Finally, Part Three comprises testimonies of expert witnesses who provided much-needed historical background and contextualization, as well as informed opinion on the validity of key, indeed crucial, evidence used to establish Barbie's responsibility for the crime in question. Despite Vergès's best efforts to challenge them, these testimonies proved convincing, and indeed quite damning to the defence.

Part One: The "Era of the Witness" and the Bottomless Well of Human Suffering

In her influential study *The Era of the Witness*, French historian Annette Wieviorka writes that the moment in modern history when the victim-as-witness became the central figure in modernity's turn to a culture of commemoration and remembrance was the trial of Adolf Eichmann in Jerusalem in 1961. In that trial, the trauma of the Holocaust, what Susan Sontag called the "supreme tragic event of modern times"[1] was for the first time conveyed or transmitted not by mountains of historical documents and documentary footage accumulated, for example,

The Resistance survivor and trial witness Lise Lesèvre

The Jewish survivor and trial witness Simone Kadosche-Lagrange

at Nuremberg, but through the testimony of the victims of that catastrophe. Indeed, aside from the debates it sparked, the Eichmann trial is best remembered for the moving and powerful testimony of Jewish survivors of Hitler's Final Solution from all walks of life and from all over Europe. It was this testimony that helped Israelis already living in Israel understand for the first time the horrors experienced by their new neighbours and integrated that experience into the narrative of Israeli identity in the present and for the future as well.

Wieviorka also observes that, despite widespread belief to the contrary, the victims' testimony at the Eichmann trial was not spontaneous, something that simply emerged from their mouths as they faced questioning in the courtroom. In fact, these witnesses had gone through a veritable "casting call," having been chosen and screened by chief prosecutor Gideon Hausner on the basis of first testimonies and interviews he conducted with them. It was in fact an "honor to testify" in front of hundreds of journalists from around the world, and Hausner wanted to be assured that at least in principle only the most "effective" and compelling witnesses representing the horrors perpetrated against European Jewry as a whole would get the chance to speak and recount their experiences. Only the "immediacy" of such powerful, first-person accounts could "burn through the 'cold-storage' of history" (Geoffrey Harman qtd. in Wieviorka 70).

This did not mean, however, that *every* surviving victim of the Holocaust living in Israel at the time wished to testify, or that Hausner's "casting call" necessarily predicted who would prove to be an effective or compelling witness. Nor for that matter was everyone present in the courtroom convinced of the value and power of victim testimony itself. In *Eichmann in Jerusalem*, Hannah Arendt famously dismissed that testimony as inadequate, misleading, and even a distraction.[2] As for the reluctance of some victims to testify, Hausner wrote in his memoir that this was "partly due to an attempt to forget events that in any case came back often enough to plague them in their dreams" and also due to the fact that they were "afraid they would not be believed" (qtd. in Wieviorka 71). Finally, where the effectiveness or power of the testimony itself was concerned, this could not be entirely predicted in advance or manufactured at the behest of the prosecutor's questions. Indeed, unquestionably one of the most memorable witnesses at the Eichmann trial was the poet K-Zetnik (Yahiel Dinoor), whose imperviousness to Hausner's questioning and chilling evocation of the "planet Auschwitz" followed by his courtroom collapse stand out as one of the Eichmann trial's most memorable moments.

In the Barbie trial, there was no "orchestration" of witness testimony by a single person as there had been at the Eichmann trial, nor was there a "casting call' which permitted the prosecution to pick and choose among a throng of witnesses ready and willing to testify. None of this was among the prerogatives of the prosecution or the president of the Assize court, although, as noted, Cerdini did have the power to call witnesses and did set the order of testimony. But Cerdini was not alone in calling witnesses, as this right was shared by civil parties lawyers and, of course, defence counsel. And neither chief prosecutor Truche nor Cerdini participated in the pre-trial questioning of witnesses, as had Gideon Hausner in Jerusalem some twenty-five years earlier. That task fell to investigating magistrate Christian Riss and his gendarme assistant, François Lafforgue.

But if the Barbie trial differed from the Eichmann trial in the ways just described, the two trials did share a number of commonalities where witness testimony was concerned. First, even though the individual witnesses were not "rehearsed" in the same way that they were in the Eichmann trial, in the Barbie trial as in the Eichmann trial witnesses, including many who had no connection to the accused, were called to the stand to furnish historical and legal contextualization. But whereas in the Eichmann trial these were primarily Jewish victims of the Holocaust from all over Europe, in the Barbie trial they were comprised of an extraordinary number and variety of expert witnesses and "witnesses of general interest." These included German legal experts, historians, celebrated former Resistance leaders and public figures, well-known politicians and statesmen, survivors of concentration camps (one witness, Marie-Claude Vaillant-Couturier, had testified at Nuremberg), and, finally, an American CIC operative, Erhard Dabringhaus, who had been one of Barbie's American "handlers" in post-war occupied Germany. To the degree that the Barbie trial relied *both* on the testimony of many of Barbie's victims *as well as* expert witnesses with no connection to him, the Barbie trial could at least arguably be considered an improvement on the Eichmann trial as far as witness testimony was concerned. Because the Eichmann trial relied so heavily on victims of the Holocaust and not victims of Eichmann himself, in Hannah Arendt's critical view, "it was built on what Jews suffered and not on what Eichmann had done" (Arendt, *Jerusalem*, 6).

In terms of the order of testimony at the Barbie trial, the first witnesses called appeared on the third day of the trial, following Barbie's abrupt and dramatic departure. These witnesses comprised the psychological team that had examined Barbie whose testimony is discussed in chapter one here. The next day, two foreign witnesses testified, the aforementioned Erhard Dabringhaus and Gustavo Sánchez-Salazar, who had been the Bolivian minister of the interior in 1983 and who had arranged for Barbie's expulsion. The fifth day of the trial was devoted to the presentation of the charges against Barbie, and on the sixth day, two expert witnesses were called to testify as to the authenticity of the evidence presented against Barbie as well as to the accused's knowledge and understanding of the purpose of the deportations and the fate of the Jews he deported.

Following this expert testimony, the next eleven sessions were given over to the testimony of Barbie's victims. The testimony of these witnesses was grouped, generally speaking, around the three major charges against the accused, starting with the round-up at the UGIF in September 1943, followed by the Izieu roundup in April 1944, and concluding with the last convoy to leave Lyon on 11 August 1944. Not all witnesses, however, were directly linked to these crimes, nor were they segregated according to whether they were Resistance or Jewish victims. Indeed, two of the most powerful and widely anticipated witnesses, Lise Lesèvre, who was arrested for Resistance activities, and Simone Kadosche-Lagrange, a Jewish victim denounced along with her family by a neighbour, testified on the same day, 22 May. Neither was linked to the three major crimes for which Barbie was charged. Finally, among those who testified in relation to the arrest and deportation of the children of Izieu was perhaps the most celebrated witness of the Barbie trial, recently named Nobel Peace Prize laureate (1986) Elie Wiesel, who had himself been deported by the Nazis from his native Romania as a fifteen-year-old.

From 9 June through 12 June (the last day of witness testimony, 15 June, was given over to the testimony of witnesses for the defence, described earlier), a series of witnesses of "general interest" appeared before the court. A number of these individuals had had celebrated Resistance careers, including the aforementioned Marie-Claude Vaillant-Couturier as well as Charles de Gaulle's niece, Geneviève de Gaulle-Anthonioz, who had been deported to Ravensbrück. On 11 June, Jacques Chaban-Delmas, a strikingly handsome former Resistance leader, presidential candidate, and current president of the National Assembly, testified along with several other Resistance fighters, most of whom had had no direct contact with Klaus Barbie. Also included among the expert witnesses were scientists (a geneticist and Nobel Prize-winning mathematician), an historian, and also an expert on the Final Solution, as well as two additional psychological experts, although the two men in question, Tony Lainé and Robert Pagès, had not been involved in developing the psychological profile of the accused for the court.

Before Geneviève de Gaulle-Anthonioz, the first witness of "general interest" gave her testimony on 9 June, the prosecutor general Pierre Truche rose and, facing the jury, explained who the new witnesses were and why they had been called to testify. Truche stated that, ordinarily in an Assize trial, only witnesses who can speak directly to the crimes of the accused, his or her personality, or his or her psychology are called to testify. Other witnesses, for example, those with a broader knowledge of the crime in question but no knowledge of the accused and his or her crimes, have traditionally not been allowed to testify. So, in the recent trial of a rapist, Truche continued, an expert on rape, its commission, and how to legislate against it was not allowed to testify, and this was a "good thing." Otherwise, the effect of the testimony would have been to "place on the shoulders of the accused all the rapes of creation." Regardless of whether Truche's example and argument were convincing to the jury, he went on to point out that under any circumstances the trial at hand was about to pass into a new phase and consider crimes against humanity in their broader sense. As defined by the Allies at the end of the war, Truche stated, crimes against humanity were the result of a plot, and that plot, as the Court of Cassation has recently clarified, was carried out in the name of a state practicing a "politics of ideological hegemony." The purpose of such a hegemonic politics, Truche concluded, was the destruction of entire peoples. It was in this context that these witnesses of "general interest" were being called. They were there to enlighten the jury (and the audience) as to the realities of the regime in whose name Klaus Barbie had acted. In closing, Truche admonished the president of the court to allow these witnesses to speak only about Nazism as they had studied it or experienced it directly and not to indulge in unhelpful digressions. Otherwise, the trial would veer seriously and dangerously off course. As it turned out, the testimony of the very first "expert witness" confirmed that Truche's fears were well-founded. That witness, Guy Serbat, had repeatedly to be called back to the matter at hand by president Cerdini, as Serbat's discussion of Barbie's actions against the Resistance covered crimes for which Barbie had already been judged.

As these last remarks suggest, the fact that the Barbie trial, like the Eichmann trial before it, relied heavily on witness testimony subjected it to many, if not most, of the pitfalls often associated with such courtroom testimony. For example, witnesses like Serbat repeatedly wandered off course, distracting from the focus of the prosecution and the coherence of the trial itself. Other former Resisters indulged the same tendencies and had also to be called to order by a visibly impatient Cerdini. On 12 June, Marie-Madeleine Fourcade, the wartime leader of the Alliance Resistance network was called to testify by the *Comité d'Action de la Résistance*. Fourcade, like Serbat, came to court to speak of the heroism and suffering of her network's members and when questioned by Cerdini admitted that she knew nothing of the charges of crimes against humanity pending against Barbie, either as concerned the UGIF and Izieu

round-ups or the 11 August 1944 convoy. When reminded by president
Cerdini that her Resistance activities and those of her fellows were irrelevant to the charges at hand, Fourcade expressed her disapproval and
indeed outrage at what she perceived to be Cerdini's dismissal of her service.[3] Despite his admonitions, Fourcade continued to sing the praises
of her subordinates who had suffered at the hands of "your Barbie" and
concluded by stating that she did not understand the difference between
crimes against humanity and war crimes. As something of a parting shot,
Fourcade added that in Germany they did not make what was clearly, in
her view, a false distinction between the two crimes.

Another risk or pitfall of courtroom testimony is that the demeanour
of a given witness on the stand may add to or subtract from that witness's
credibility, regardless of whether or not the witness is telling the truth.
The most notable example of this phenomenon in the Barbie trial was
Michel Kroskof-Thomas. A Polish-born former Resistance member (by
his own account), Kroskof-Thomas then volunteered in the French and
US armies during the war and later became a US intelligence operative.
Kroskof-Thomas was the only witness to claim that he had personally
seen Barbie at the UGIF round-up. After the war, Kroskof-Thomas went
to New York and later to Los Angeles to found language schools that
used his special method for learning a foreign language in three days.
Kroskof-Thomas's celebrity client list supposedly included Grace Kelly,
Woody Allen, Barbra Streisand, and many others. When he appeared
in court in Lyon on 21 May, unlike a number of witnesses who were
frail or handicapped as a result of their wartime encounters with Barbie, Kroskof-Thomas appeared vigorous, dapper, and self-confident, certainly well-prepared and capable of handling any challenge the defence
might throw up.

But when Kroskof-Thomas began to testify, a different image of the
man emerged. In highly melodramatic and indeed histrionic terms,
Kroskof-Thomas described his encounter with Barbie at the UGIF headquarters on the day of round-up of Jews on 9 February 1943. Barbie, he
stated, was an "angel of death," and every moment one spent in his presence was an "eternity." Indeed, each instant with Barbie left "wounds"
that while they might "scar up" would "never heal." Asked to describe
Barbie physically, Kroskof-Thomas noted that one distinguishing feature
was the very "effeminate" way he held his baby finger apart. Kroskof-
Thomas then testified that after the war he had recognized Barbie in
a photograph of the Gestapo chief he had seen in *Time* magazine in
1972. The picture penetrated him, he testified, like a "lightning bolt."
The old wounds now burst open, the trauma of his meeting with Barbie
returned.[4]

When Vergès was given the opportunity to question Kroskof-Thomas, he stated ironically that he was obliged "to break the charm of this testimony that has captivated all of us" and ask some "down-to-earth questions." He noted that Kroskof-Thomas had testified during the *instruction* that he had been told by someone that there would be a distribution of essentials at the UGIF on the day of the round-up, and he asked Kroskof-Thomas to state the name of the person who had informed him of the distribution. Visibly irritated, Kroskof-Thomas asked if Vergès could recall the names of people he met in passing forty-four years ago. Then, after hazarding a few names, Kroskof-Thomas shook his head, said he could not recall any, and reminded the court that he was in the Resistance and not associated with the UGIF. Pressed now by president Cerdini rather than Vergès, Kroskof-Thomas raised his voice, affirming that even if he knew names he would not state them in court. When Vergès got the chance to question him again, he noted that Kroskof-Thomas had stated that at the UGIF, where he had ostensibly gone to recruit more resisters, he had been worried that some he had contacted might recognize him and make a sign to him. Could the witness give any of the names of some of these people, Vergès asked. Again, Kroskof-Thomas, visibly angry, refused to answer. In a final follow-up, Vergès asked Kroskof-Thomas how he came to be in both the French army and later the American army during the war. When Kroskof-Thomas claimed that he had been an interpreter in the American army, Vergès, seizing the moment, observed that when one volunteered for the French army during the war (as he, Vergès, had) one pledged to serve until the end of the war, and three months beyond. His credibility and perhaps even his reputation in tatters, Kroskof-Thomas was thanked by the court and left the podium. Reflecting on Kroskof-Thomas's testimony, Annette Kahn wrote: "Why is such vivid testimony so embarrassing, so unconvincing? Michel Kroskof-Thomas is no doubt sincere, but he is so theatrical, so grandiloquent! In a few days, another witness will evoke ... the affectations of [Barbie's] pinkie, and he will be believed on the spot" (Kahn 123). Pierre Truche, for one, did not share Kahn's faith in Kroskof-Thomas's credibility. During his closing summation, he would ask the jury to ignore the language school director's testimony.

Finally, in a trial like the Barbie trial, or for that matter the Eichmann trial, the testimony that some witnesses give may prove to be so horrendous and overpowering in nature that the jury and court are simply overwhelmed or numbed by it. They are incapable of taking in or even in some instances *believing* what they have heard.[5] In a well-known historical example of the latter phenomenon (but not in a courtroom setting), Jan Karski, a Polish Resistance hero and author of a best-selling memoir, *Story of a Secret State,* reported that he had been sent by the Polish government-in-exile to Washington, DC, to report on Polish Resistance efforts. Karski was also sent to tell American leaders what he had witnessed firsthand in Nazi death camps and Jewish ghettos. Once in Washington, Karski was sent by president Franklin D. Roosevelt to describe the Nazi camps to Supreme Court Chief Justice Felix Frankfurter. According to Karski, after completing his narrative, Frankfurter told him that he was sorry but that he did not and could not believe him. Frankfurter explained that his experience of humankind simply did not permit him to believe such horrors were possible.

In the Barbie trial, multiple witnesses described scenes of unimaginable sadism and cruelty that appeared to paralyse the court or provoke responses that seemed inappropriate or incongruous but which were nevertheless entirely understandable under the circumstances. One example was Francine Gudefin, who on 4 June testified that Klaus Barbie was present at the departure of the last convoy that left Lyon on 11 August 1944. But Gudefin's testimony along these lines paled in comparison not only to her physical appearance (one side of her face had been hideously disfigured by beatings she had received at the hands of the Gestapo and their French minions) but to what she described witnessing in Gestapo headquarters. Brought into a room where Nazis were torturing their victims, she testified that she saw her brother naked in a bathtub. He was, she testified, being drowned. As he was modest by nature, she knew that he was embarrassed to be seen by a woman, even his sister, in this condition. Unable to contain herself, Gudefin cried out "Courage my Pierrot." She then confessed to the stunned courtoom: "I will tell you something, I began to pee. To pee everywhere. All down my legs, I peed and I peed. I couldn't hold myself back. Then a German said, 'Look at this bitch, she's peeing in our office.' Then they started to slap me, to hit me with their fists." As the *Libération* reporter wrote about the audience response to Gudefin's testimony, "In the courtroom, there was nervous laughter. Laughter, tears." One of those who laughed apparently rushed from the courtroom.

On 25 May, Mario Blardone,[6] a Resistance member who had been assigned to kill Barbie and his French minion Francis André but who had been arrested before he could complete his mission was called to the stand. If possible, Blardone's testimony was even more horrific than Francine Gudefin's testimony. Following his own torture at the hands of the Gestapo, which he declined to describe in detail, Blardone testified that what had affected him the most was what he had seen Barbie do to several women prisoners. Upon entering the room where Blardone was being interrogated, a young woman carrying her baby had the baby ripped away from her by Barbie, who then threw the baby into the hallway as if it were "a used Kleenex" (Kahn 152). Most likely, Blardone continued, the baby died on the spot. The mother was then ordered to strip, and Blardone reported, Barbie laughed while she cried. Barbie then forced her to run around the room as his dog chased her. A second woman was then brought into the room and forced to get on all fours so the dog could mount her.[7] Later, Blardone testified, as the prisoners were descending the stairs to the basement and their cells, Barbie would gratuitously shoot the occasional prisoner in the back of the head. According to Blardone, Barbie did this four times in eighteen days (Kahn 153).

These were by no means the only accounts of utter horror in the Barbie trial, nor was gut-wrenching testimony by witnesses and victims confined to tales of purely physical abuse and murder. Shortly before Blardone testified on 25 May, André Frossard, whose testimony will be discussed in detail shortly, spoke of a Jewish shopkeeper and prisoner who became the "personal scapegoat," the *tête de Turc*, of an SS officer. Even though the shopkeeper could not speak German, the officer made him learn to recite in German a sentence to the officer whenever the latter ordered him to do so. The sentence was: "Every Jew is a parasite who lives on the skin of the German people, and it must be extirpated." Whenever the Jew made a mistake in pronunciation or grammar, the German hit him. Frossard reported that eventually the shopkeeper became so traumatized that whenever the door of the Jewish Barrack of Montluc Prison opened, he would stand and pace back and forth, reciting the sentence over and over. When he was being dragged in front of a firing squad, the Jewish shopkeeper was forced to recite the sentence one last time (Kahn 155).

If the eleven audiences of the trial largely (but not exclusively) given over to the testimony of Barbie's victims seemed almost to outdo each other in the tales of horror recounted, one day in particular, 22 May, at least to some observers, appeared to surpass all the others in the suffering and humiliation recounted. In her memoir of the trial, Annette Kahn prefaced her summary of the accounts of that day's victims in writing: "At the Barbie trial, no sooner do those of us in the audience feel that, word by word, we have reached the limits of the nightmare than we realize we have been optimistic. It has no limits" (133).

The first person to testify that day was Irène Clair-Frémion, a plump, kindly looking former resister who had been arrested in 1943 and later deported to Ravensbrück. Clair-Frémion first described the conditions in Montluc Prison, where there were eight women per cell, where there was inadequate space to lie flat, and where the toilet facilities consisted of a small chamber pot in the middle of the cell. Like many other witnesses, what clearly affected Clair-Frémion the most was not her own suffering, but that of someone else, in her case her commanding officer in the Resistance. When she saw him in Gestapo headquarters after she had been taken there, Clair-Frémion testified that the man whom she knew to be thirty-four years old now looked eighty. He had been tortured by every conceivable method. Clair-Frémion then stated that in her mind's eye she saw the man in that pitiable state every day since.

The second witness on 22 May was Lise Lesèvre, whose status as a potential victim of crimes against humanity had been confirmed near the end of the pre-trial investigation. Lesèvre's name, and indeed her image, had long been associated with Klaus Barbie. She had been a witness at the 1952 and 1954 trials of Barbie in absentia[8] and had written a memoir, *Face à Barbie: Souvenirs-Cauchemars de Montluc à Ravensbrück*, with a preface by Geneviève de Gaulle-Anthonioz. Given her public visibility, she had also been a target of Vergès well before the trial began.

As she testified in court, Lesèvre had managed to keep a diary of sorts during her ordeal, writing notes on bits of paper about her travels as a deportee and her experiences as a prisoner in Lyon and at Ravensbrück. A kindly German, she stated in court, had stapled the bits of paper together for her, and when she returned from captivity, she transcribed the notes into a small *carnet*, or notebook. According to Vergès, this notebook, like the Izieu telex, was a fraud. Lesèvre, he claimed, had written the whole thing up after the war in order to accuse Barbie. The notebook was under seal as evidence in the trial, and Lesèvre anxiously told the court it was of great value to her and asked to have it returned to her as soon as possible.

Lesèvre appeared in court in a blue dress that accentuated her silver hair. She had to be helped to the podium and used a cane because, as she explained to the court, on the last day of interrogating her, Barbie had shattered her spine with a kind of mace. In giving her deposition, Lesèvre occasionally lost track of her story, at one point asking president Cerdini, "Help me, I've lost the thread." But Lesèvre's memory, when it came to specific details of her own experience and what she had seen, was razor sharp. In fact, unlike most other witnesses, Lesèvre was well aware of the fact that what she was recounting was so horrific as to be difficult, if not impossible, to believe. She described how, in Hamburg near the end of the war, she had witnessed forty Jewish children and the French doctor who tended to them hung on meat hooks to die. She told the court that she knew that what she was recounting was so horrible that in telling it "one gives the impression of having made it up." Ravensbrück she described as a "horror film" unrolling before her eyes.

But perhaps the most poignant part of Lesèvre's testimony concerned her husband and sixteen-year-old son, both of whom Barbie had arrested in an attempt to force her to talk. When she did not, the two were deported to their deaths, the son disappearing during an Allied air raid at the end of the war (but, as she told the court, he had already contracted tuberculosis in a concentration camp) and the husband dying of typhus and exhaustion at Dachau. As for Barbie himself, Lesèvre described him as sadistic, "a savage" who had a whip or other instrument of torture with him at all times. When he didn't have a victim to strike, he struck the side of his boot repeatedly. Prisoners would know he was coming by the sound of whip on boot.[9] When Lesèvre realized Barbie was not in the courtroom, as others had done, she condemned his cowardice.

The testimony of the next witness, Ennatt Vitte-Léger, contrasted sharply with Lesèvre's poised delivery. In her rush to describe how she was tortured at Barbie's hands, she interjected phrases like "Ooh! La! La!" and protested to the court the horror of what she had experienced, as if it were continuing in that moment. Barbie and his men had broken her front teeth and split her lip wide open by ramming a bottle into her mouth. At Ravensbrück her mouth became infected, and she was forced to repeatedly spit out pus so the infection did not worsen. Her teeth were only repaired on her return to France after the war. Like Lesèvre, Vitte-Léger had also published a memoir with the unappetizing title of *Connaissez-vous la cuisine de la Gestapo* ("Do You Know the Cuisine of the Gestapo?"), a question she stated Barbie had asked her as she was about to go through the experience of torture.

Along with Lesèvre, Simone-Kadosche Lagrange was one of the Barbie trial's most iconic victims and witnesses. Like Lesèvre, after the trial she became a principal and powerful witness in Marcel Ophuls's film *Hôtel Terminus*, giving – somewhat surprisingly – a lesson of hope of sorts at the end of the film. In a final conversation within the film, Kadosche-Lagrange tells Ophuls that while being led from their apartment by the Gestapo after being denounced as a neighbour, another neighbour had tried to pull her into her apartment to save her. *Hôtel Terminus* is dedicated to such "neighbours."

However, in the trial itself, Kadosche-Lagrange's testimony hardly concluded with a message of hope concerning good neighbours, although she testified in court that the very day she and her parents were arrested began with the Allied landings in Normandy. This had caused her family great joy. But if the day began with hope, it did not end that way. Kadosche-Lagrange and her parents were interrogated by Barbie who, for the adolescent she was at the time, initially appeared rather kindly, as he was carrying a cat.[10] For Kadosche-Lagrange, as she stated, children are not suspicious of adults who are kind to animals. But after Barbie was unsuccessful in getting the location of the Kadosche-Lagrange's other children from them (they were hidden in the countryside, and the parents themselves did not know their locations), Barbie turned violent. Grabbing hold of Kadosche-Lagrange by her long hair and wrapping it around his wrist, Barbie struck her repeatedly in front of her parents. She had, she stated, never been hit before. When the interrogation was done for the day, the family was taken to Montluc Prison, where the father was placed in the Jewish barracks while mother and daughter were put in a regular cell. Because the floor of the cell was covered with straw, she testified that she was afraid rats were in the cell. This, Kadosche-Lagrange told the court, was another "child's idea," but one which kept her awake at night. That same night, she saw through the spyhole in the prison door trucks containing other Jewish families arriving at the prison.

The next day, Barbie came in person to get the adolescent girl. He took her back to Gestapo headquarters, where she waited all day. From time to time, Barbie would come and ask her where her siblings were. When she did not answer him, Barbie struck and kicked her repeatedly, "opening new wounds on top of old ones." In the evening, he would return her to prison, throw her into her mother's arms, and say, "See what you have done to your daughter!" Despite her suffering, Kadosche-Lagrange testified that her mother's suffering was worse, as "moral torture is the worst of all." This lasted for seven days. Reflecting back on this experience, Kadosche-Lagrange told Cerdini that, given Barbie's importance and responsibilities, this seemed strange in retrospect but that it testified to the intensity of his fanaticism and his cruelty. She added, "Trying to track down two children [to deport them] by martyring a third is intolerable."

Under questioning from president Cerdini, Kadosche-Lagrange went on to testify how she had identified Barbie by seeing him on television in 1972 and concluded by describing her confrontation with Barbie in prison during the investigation a decade later. During that investigation, she told the court, Barbie had insulted her by telling her that for a man in prison even in her fifties Kadosche-Lagrange was an "appetizing" woman. When, as noted, she protested that he was insulting her, she stated that he had responded by laughing and saying that she did not understand "the joke."[11] For her, someone who had "killed her parents" as well as other relatives had no right to make pleasantries with her. As will be discussed, although Vergès did not challenge her testimony at the time, he would try to turn Kadosche-Lagrange's natural dignity, and indeed her apparent decency, against her at the end of the trial.

Given the numerous tales of horror recounted at the Barbie trial, what made Kadosche-Lagrange's testimony stand out, perhaps above all the others? Most obviously, like Lise Lesèvre and arguably a few other witnesses, Kadosche-Lagrange had emerged from the suffering and indignities Barbie and then later the concentration camps had heaped upon her and her family (she had seen her father killed in front of her, and her mother was gassed the day Paris was liberated) with her evident kindness and dignity intact, indeed, seemingly enhanced. But there was something else in her testimony that was virtually unique to the trial, and that was the fact that she had attempted to convey what a child, an adolescent, had experienced *firsthand* at Barbie's hands during the war, and what her own suffering had done to her parents. While for many the very meaning of the trial had come to centre on the suffering of innocence in the form of the children of Izieu, a point forcefully made by Sabine Zlatin and later Serge Klarsfeld in his closing statement before the court, not one of these children had survived to tell the tale, so to speak. Therefore, it fell to Kadosche-Lagrange to reveal to the court how the crimes inflicted by Barbie appeared to an adolescent who, as her testimony confirmed, had never even been struck before in her life until Barbie struck her. This made Barbie's cruelty all the more repugnant and Vergès's attempt to destroy her testimony and reputation at the end of the trial all the more horrifying.

There were three more witnesses who testified at the end of the 22 May audience, but one, like Lesèvre and Kadosche-Lagrange was particularly notable for what he had experienced and what he had to say. This was Marcel Stourdzé, a Jew accused of "terrorism" by Barbie. In fact, Stourdzé testified, he had only assisted refugees. Stourdzé came to the podium with a large neck brace running up his neck and cradling the back of his head. He testified both as to what he had experienced at Montluc and, later, in Nazi camps. Upon being confronted with Klaus Barbie for the first time following his arrest in summer 1943, he noticed Barbie's sharp uniform and "shiny boots." Barbie approached and slapped him twice, as hard as he could. Stourdzé explained to the court that at the time, he, Stourdzé, was "very much of a snob" and wore a monocle. Barbie, Stourdzé testified, detested him for his snobbery, a sign perhaps of his self-esteem, and struck him for this reason. When Barbie hit him, the monocle did not fly off.

Despite his own suffering, the heart of Stourdzé's testimony concerned others, and specifically the suffering of women at the hands of Barbie and the Nazis. Following on the four women who testified before him that day, Stourdzé told the court that their "discretion" had prevented them from describing their special humiliation as women at Montluc, but he would do so. Men and women, he testified, were crammed together in a single cell. They drank water from two rusty preserves cans and were forced to use these same cans to relieve themselves. Summer 1943 was torrid, Stourdzé stressed, which made living conditions all the worse. As all the prisoners were arrested with no possessions, the women had no sanitary products for their periods, so the men gave them their shirts to use. When they had to relieve themselves, other women would hold whatever item of clothing they could find to use as a sort of partition. "Such was Montluc prison for women," Stourdzé concluded. But, as the testimony of Mario Blardone and later Geneviève de Gaulle Antonioz and Marie Claude-Vaillant-Couturier, who would speak later during the trial of their respective experiences at Ravensbrück and Auschwitz, this was just the tip of the iceberg. Many of the women imprisoned in Montluc were later deported to the Nazi camps.

Given the traumatic content of such testimonies, it is not surprising that their impact was felt not only by those present in the courtroom but by the witnesses and victims who recounted them as well. As the film of the Barbie trial reveals, many witnesses were forced to pause during their testimony and compose themselves. Others cried or sobbed openly, often visibly overwhelmed from one moment to the next. On 26 May, Fortuné Lanfranchi, a well-dressed former member of the Resistance, described being taken by his SD captors into an interrogation room whose walls were splashed with blood. Seeing that, Lanfranchi told the court: "I told myself, 'you are in for one really lousy quarter-hour.'" Then suddenly Lanfranchi began to sob uncontrollably and collapsed into the chair behind him on the witness stand. After a few moments, Cerdini informed Lanfranchi that he could remain seated during his testimony if he wished. In a visible effort to recover his composure as well as his dignity, Lanfranchi rose and stated, "I wish to remain standing."

While witnesses like Lanfranchi fell victim to the power of their own grief, seemingly reliving on the stand the trauma that they had experienced some forty years earlier, others became enraged (again) at the crimes Barbie and his minions had perpetrated. Sabine Zlatin, the founder and director of the Jewish children's home at Izieu, became visibly angry as she concluded her testimony and, raising her voice, demanded what harm the Jewish children deported from Izieu could possibly do to the German army, the organization Barbie claimed to be protecting in committing his crimes? Similar expressions of anger, even outrage, were especially notable among those witnesses who were given the opportunity to confront Barbie in person in the courtroom. As determined by president Cerdini after Barbie's abrupt departure from his trial, while the accused did not have to face those witnesses that he had already faced during the investigation of his case, he would have to face witnesses who had not seen him at that time. This was done so the latter could see him face to face and identify him. On 26 May, Barbie was returned to the courtroom for the first time. Among those who confronted him were Mario Blardone, Robert Clor, another Resistance member tortured by Barbie, and Raymonde Guyon-Belot, a soft-spoken, thoughtful Resistance survivor who had not been tortured by Barbie but who had been deported to Ravensbrück. All three formally identified Barbie, and when asked if he had anything to say, Barbie responded repeatedly "No," or "nothing." While Guyon-Belot seemed to accept Barbie's response with a tired and resigned expression, Blardone and Clor became visibly angry. Clor, who had testified that he had seen Barbie rape a young woman with a whip handle, dismissed him derisively in court as a "phony" (*faux jeton*). Later in the trial, on 5 June, when Barbie was forced once again to return to the court to face another series of witnesses, one of the men he confronted was André Courvoisier. Upon realizing Barbie was in the box, Courvoisier turned angrily towards him, berating him outside the range of the microphones as he stepped towards the accused. President Cerdini had to call Courvoisier to order more than once. It was at this moment that Pierre Truche, seemingly finally losing patience with the accused and his obstinate silence, asked Barbie directly about how he had become the SS he had become. As discussed, Barbie refused to answer.

Given what so many of these witnesses – and not just Barbie's victims but the so-called witnesses of general interest who were the victims of other Nazi crimes – had experienced during the war, it is not surprising that a number of them felt the effects of their testimony after they were through testifying. Indeed, as noted, one of the most memorable of the "witnesses of general interest," Geneviève de Gaulle-Anhtonioz, had to be hospitalized on the night following her appearance in court. Given what de Gaulle-Anthonioz had seen at Ravensbrück and testified to in court, this was hardly surprising.

Although Ravensbrück, the largest Nazi camp for women prisoners, was not a death camp per se, what de Gaulle-Anthonioz described having seen there was in some ways just as destructive to the humanity of the inmates as being put to death. On arrival at Ravensbrück, de Gaulle-Anthonioz described seeing prisoners returning from work details who "n'avaient pas de regard," who no longer had the ability to look at others or the world around them. These prisoners, de Gaulle-Anthonioz continued, were "human rags," they were not human beings, but only vestiges of them. They were *Untermenchen*, "sub-people."[12]

But if those in the work detail had been reduced to subhuman creatures, they were not alone in their dehumanization at the hands of the Nazis, nor was their physical suffering any less horrendous. De

Gaulle-Anthonioz noted that a number of women and girls, and especially Roma girls, had been selected for medical experimentation. These guinea pigs were known as "little rabbits." Many were sterilized, de Gaulle-Anthonioz affirmed, and twelve- and thirteen-year-old girls were given hysterectomies. Visibly struggling with her emotions as she described this, de Gaulle-Anthonioz affirmed that given her experiences at Ravensbrück in particular, combatting Nazism was "a terrible but certain satisfaction."

Despite the trauma of her testimony in the Lyon courtroom, de Gaulle-Anthonioz was fortunate in that she recovered from the experience and lived until 2002. In 2015, her remains were interred along with those of another Resistance heroine, Germaine Tillion, in the *Panthéon*. Others who testified at the Barbie trial and suffered from the experience were less fortunate. Following his testimony and his confrontation with the accused, Mario Blardone, who had stated that testifying in the trial was the most important event of his life since the war, seemed deflated, like he had "lost his reason for being," as Annette Kahn described seeing him following his testimony. Four months after the conclusion of the trial, Mario Blardone died.

When confronted with such emotional and occasionally overpowering testimony – which clearly, moreover, most often elicited the sympathy of the court – Vergès was faced with something of a dilemma. Whereas it was fairly easy for Vergès to directly challenge and largely discredit a witness like Michel Kroskof-Thomas, whose courtroom demeanour was so off-putting, with a witness like Francine Gudefin, Vergès had to tread more lightly. As his questions to her following her testimony revealed, Vergès was aware of the fact that Gudefin had contradicted herself during the investigation on more than one occasion and that her testimony given in court did not coincide with any of her earlier accounts. And while in pointing these inconsistencies out Vergès hoped to cast doubt on her credibility in the long run, he was clearly reluctant to go after her more directly or personally in court. In fact, on more than one occasion during his questioning of Gudefin Vergès was quick to reassure her that he was aware of the extent of her suffering and believed in her "sincerity." Where Sabine Zlatin was concerned, the transcript of the trial indicates that Vergès asked no questions of her at all, perhaps because of Zlatin's stature among those who testified, or perhaps because Zlatin was quite blunt in her utter distaste for Vichy and Philippe Pétain. She testified in fact that, in her opinion, a full 70 per cent of the French were ardent supporters of the Marshall and that when in Montpellier, where she was at the time of the Izieu arrests, she had witnessed the entire town rush to see Pétain when he had visited there. When she had received word of the arrest of the Izieu children, Zlatin had rushed to Vichy itself to ask government officials to intervene on behalf of the children. A highly placed government official she met with asked Zlatin, "Why do you concern yourself with these dirty kikes?" Because, as she testified, her identity card was not stamped with the word "Jew," the official in question did not realize that Zlatin herself was Jewish. If nothing else, Zlatin's powerful denunciations of Vichy in the Lyon courtroom served – at least briefly – to distract from the crimes of Klaus Barbie and the specifics of the arrest and deportation of the children of Izieu.

With Mario Blardone, however, Vergès would take a different tack entirely. In this case, Vergès apparently decided that Blardone's account of Barbie's demonic cruelty and sexual sadism were, even in a courtroom which had become a recitation hall of a seemingly endless stream of unspeakable horrors, literally *too much* for the court to absorb, even to *believe*. So rather than look for inconsistencies or gaps in Blardone's account, Vergès decided to turn Barbie's supposed sexual perversions against his accuser, the witness himself.

Vergès's challenge to Mario Blardone's testimony did not occur immediately after the witness had given it, but rather during his closing statement before the court at the end of the trial, on the afternoon of 3 July. That way, Vergès likely reasoned, it would have the greatest impact, not being subject to president Cerdini's interruptions or admonitions. After initially addressing the three major charges in the dossier against his client, Vergès announced that in concluding his statement he would examine the charges related to *cas individuels*, or "individual cases." But rather than focus initially on specific testimonies and their possible inconsistencies or contradictions, it was the *dramatic power* of these testimonies, Vergès claimed, that was fraudulent. The entire point of such horrific testimony was to convince the jury and the court that even if Barbie could not be proven guilty of one or more specific charges with the evidence at hand, the overall impact of the witnesses' tales of woe and suffering would make the jury believe that *he must be guilty of something.* This "manipulation," this "intoxication" Vergès warned the jury, was proof that, despite appearances to the contrary, the court and prosecution took them for "gullible well-meaning yokels," (*bons bougres*). Simply stated, Vergès insisted, the court "despised" them.

Having stunned those present in the courtroom with this obvious breach of decorum, Vergès then turned to the credibility of the testimony of the witnesses, most pointedly that of Mario Blardone and – certainly surprisingly for many – the testimony of Simone Kadosche-Lagrange. Vergès began his assault on the two witnesses by stating that, as is well known in the human imagination, torture is always linked to sexuality.

Moreover, he continued, while humans are capable of sexual perversion, animals are not. A man may voluntarily have sex with a sheep, he stated, but the reverse is not the case. All animals have sex *only with their own kind.* Then, taking direct aim at Blardone's testimony, Vergès stated bluntly that no dog will have sex with a woman unless that dog is incited to do so by the woman. And a woman lying prostrate was unlikely to enact such incitement.

As the video recording of the trial reveals[13], at this stage members of the audience, including especially Barbie's former victims, began to protest, shaking their heads in disgust or covering their eyes. Although barely audible in the film, Blardone protested loudly that he had told the truth. Apparently satisfied with the disruption he had created, Vergès then haughtily admonished the court to leave Blardone "to his obsessions" and turned his attack to Kadosche-Lagrange, now sitting in the audience with her grandson.

In retrospect, it seems surprising, not to say counterproductive and even suicidal for Vergès to go after Kadosche-Lagrange, for reasons already discussed. Nevertheless, in his zeal Vergès seemed intent not only on destroying Kadosche-Lagrange's credibility but, as he attempted to do with Blardone, on making her appear in the eyes of court as a sexually depraved pervert, guilty in fact of the same kind of deviant impulses long associated with the Nazis themselves (see chapter one here). Moreover, as opposed to Blardone, both as a thirteen-year-old in wartime Lyon and during the investigation of Barbie's case, Kadosche-Lagrange had been subjected by the accused to offensive sexual innuendo that, during the investigation at least, Vergès had witnessed firsthand.[14] So there was clearly an element of *intentional* cruelty in his attack on Kadosche-Lagrange.

First, Vergès stated unequivocally that Kadosche-Lagrange's claim that Barbie was holding and caressing a cat during his wartime interrogation of her was false because cats were the quintessential animal traditionally associated with erotic fantasies of all types, and Barbie's cat was obviously a figment of Kadosche-Lagrange's over-wrought imagination. Warming to his subject, Vergès then referred to a supposed interview in the press Kadosche-Lagrange had given, in which she complained that during the *instruction* Vergès himself had repeatedly rolled a cigar along his thigh before lighting it and blowing smoke in her face to intimidate her. At this stage, Kadosche-Lagrange, in tears, tried to protest out loud, but president Cerdini admonished her not to interfere. Distraught, she hugged her grandson as those around her tried to comfort her.

Viewing the film of this moment in the trial and the outrage that followed Vergès's most egregious provocation – speaking in response to

Vergès on behalf of the civil parties lawyers, Bernard de Bigault du Granrut, visibly enraged, informed Vergès that "Everything that is excessive becomes derisory" – it is difficult to imagine, at least at first glance, what Vergès thought he was accomplishing in these attacks. If anything, in its sheer "excess" to quote Granrut, Vergès's harangue had shored up the credibility of Blardone and Kadosche-Lagrange, as the jury (and audience) in their sympathy for the two following Vergès's assaults on their integrity would likely *want to believe them*. For Sorj Chalandon, the only explanation for this aberrant behaviour was that Vergès was now simply talking to himself, in a kind of self-induced delirium: "No more criminal dossier, no more facts, no more guiding thread" (147). Reporters asked each other, "What is he talking about?" But after a few more sarcastic comments about Barbie's Gestapo office being turned into a "menagerie" by the fantasies of the victims and now witnesses, Vergès finally got to the point he was attempting to convey. Following a brief and heated exchange over procedural issues with Granrut, whose outcome, announced by Cerdini, was that the penal code favoured the civil parties in the matter at hand,[15] Vergès addressed the jury and court, asking ironically, "What can we do but submit?"

Given Vergès's choice of verbs, his intent was clear: he deliberately used the verb *subir*, often used for sexual submission. But now, the sexual submission in question was not that of Barbie's wartime victims but that of the court, *of the French people as whole*, in the here and now. Barbie was just a devil "made to measure," Vergès explained, and the trial itself was just the latest act of expiation for the dark shadow that had haunted the French people for decades: the humiliation, the abject *submission* of the nation following France's defeat at the hands of the Germans in May–June 1940. And now, Vergès told the jury, they had the opportunity to save the French from themselves, to put the shadow of the past to rest by acquitting Barbie. In the audience, there were audible groans.

In a subsequent chapter, the incident just described will be discussed in the broader context of Vergès's defence strategy and the radical philosophical and judicial ideas that undergirded it. Suffice to say for the moment that Sorj Chalandon was wrong in his assumption that Vergès was going off the rails, so to speak, or coming unhinged in his seemingly gratuitous attacks on Mario Blardone and Simone Kadosche-Lagrange. But in attacking them as he did, Vergès proved that he was willing to forego any benefits that might have accrued to his client by carefully dissecting and exposing the contradictions and inconsistencies of their testimony or arguing *persuasively* that their recounted experiences were simply too horrendous to be believed. Additionally, the passage of more than forty years made the accounts of other witnesses, especially those who were very old and feeble, shaky and arguably unreliable to begin with, and Vergès could have made more of an effort to cast the testimony of these two witnesses in that lot. But as it was, he let the moment pass. Clearly, for all of his reputation as a brilliant lawyer, Vergès had squandered some potentially valuable opportunities in the responses he chose to give to witnesses' testimonies.

On the whole, what was the impact on the court and on the audience of the emotionally charged testimony of Barbie's victims, many of whom showed the indelible physical traces of Barbie's and the Nazis' brutal treatment of them decades earlier? Apart from stirring in those present in the courtroom feelings of profound empathy, or possibly numbness, or even the distancing effect of disbelief, had that testimony forwarded the aims of the prosecution and the civil parties lawyers? In other words, had the testimony of these witnesses helped the court and jury understand in a deep, visceral sense what crimes against humanity *actually were* and that the accused was fully guilty of just such crimes? Where the law, and specifically the controversial December 1985 Court of Cassation decision was concerned, in the eyes of the court and jury did the testimony of these victims, Jews and former resisters alike, justify the argument that crimes against humanity should not be limited in their application in French law to racial, religious, or ethnic minorities, but in some instances should be extended to embrace certain crimes committed against resisters, that is, enemy combatants?

In an essay entitled "Retour sur le contexte général du procès Barbie" ("Return to the General Context of the Barbie Trial"), written for a commemorative volume for the twentieth anniversary of the Barbie trial, the historian Laurent Douzou offered an essentially optimistic response to these questions. The "essential" truth of the trial, Douzou stated, "was that which appeared in common between Simone Kadosche-Lagrange, deported to Auschwitz, and Geneviève de Gaulle-Anthonioz, deported to Ravensbrück, of whom Jean-Marc Théolleyre wrote at the end of the trial that they were sisters" (17). In other words, the testimony of all these witness-victims, resisters *and* Jews, taken together, underscored their proximity, their intimacy, their *identity* in suffering. Moreover, citing Théolleyre's article in *Le Monde* of 23 May – one day after the testimonies of 22 May described above – Douzou noted that on that day, for Théolleyre as well as the packed courthouse, "the words 'crimes against humanity' had ceased to be simply words." Reflecting on the meaning of Théolleyre's observation, Douzou wrote, "It is one thing to know that tragic events have taken place, but it is quite another to hear their description emerge from the mouths of women and men who have been crushed by them" (12).

But if Douzou's assessment of the impact of the testimony of witness-victims is reasonable and indeed convincing in retrospect, it is important to stress that by no means did *all* the witnesses, including some expert witnesses or "witnesses of general interest" reinforce during the trial the uncomplicated clarity and unity of the message Douzou later detected. Nor, for that matter, were all these witnesses concerned, explicitly or specifically, with championing or reinforcing the court's understanding of crimes against humanity. Quite the contrary. In the Part Two of this chapter, complicating as well as divergent opinions about what crimes against humanity were and are, voiced by key witnesses at the trial, will be discussed in some detail. Especially given the credibility and prestige of the witnesses who articulated them, these definitions represented a real challenge to the prosecution's case that would have to be dealt with and overcome. To be sure, the counterweight of the combined force of witness-victims testimony as just described was most helpful, but this did not mean that the contradictory testimony, especially of figures like Elie Wiesel, could be or was dismissed out of hand. And because in making their arguments about what crimes against humanity and war crimes were involved reference to other geographical locations, other times, and other victims, these will be discussed here briefly as well.

Part Two: Debating Crimes against Humanity and the Wages of Comparison

The December 1985 decision to include resisters among the victims of Barbie's potential crimes against humanity, accompanied as it was by a new definition of crimes against humanity under French law, not only divided the appeals courts in Lyon and Paris at the time, it also divided civil parties lawyers at the 1987 trial itself.[16] Many of these lawyers in fact remained as fiercely committed to their earlier stated positions pro or contra the decision during the trial as they had been at the time the decision was announced. This meant that there remained an undercurrent of tension and division about the matter in the Lyon Assize court. To add to this tension, when called to testify, many prominent witnesses also expressed their disagreements with the 1985 decision. This, of course, afforded the defence an opportunity to challenge one of the fundamental premises of the trial, and Vergès exploited this opportunity, often provocatively.

The first and perhaps the most memorable of these dissenting witnesses was André Frossard, who testified on 25 May during the trial's eleventh hearing. Frossard testified at the request of Sophie Gompel, the daughter of Marcel Gompel, a Jew and a resister who had been tortured to death by Klaus Barbie. Frossard had in fact seen Gompel die in horrendous circumstances, as he, like Gompel, was also a prisoner in the infamous "Jewish Barrack" at Montluc Prison. Frossard had written a book about his experiences there, entitled *La Maison des otages*, the "House of Hostages." After the war, he had become a distinguished journalist and illustrator and was elected to the *Académie Française* in 1987, the year of the Barbie trial. Frossard had also become a proud convert to Christianity, and to Catholicism specifically. At the age of twenty, he had entered a chapel in Paris as a "young skeptic and atheist of the extreme left" and had emerged a few minutes later as an "apostolic Roman Catholic" (qtd. in *Le Monde*, 20 June 1987). Frossard had also published a number of books about his Christian faith, as well as a dialogue with Pope John Paul II, entitled *N'ayez pas peur* ("Don't Be Afraid"). While all his thinking and writing were indelibly marked by his faith, Frossard's testimony in the Barbie trial was, for the most part, Cartesian in its methodical and logical clarity.

In a calm and confident voice strikingly at odds with the emotional testimony of some of Barbie's victims, Frossard took the oath as a witness, swearing that he was testifying neither out of fear nor hatred – the latter a sentiment he said he had never known – and then began his deposition. After describing his experiences in the infamous "Jewish Barrack," Frossard turned to the subject of what he considered crimes against humanity to be. He explained that he had begun to understand the reality and substance of such crimes while witnessing what the SS officer had done to the Jewish merchant prisoner described earlier, forcing him to repeat the same obscene and degrading phrase right up to moment his death. Frossard affirmed that "a crime against humanity has been committed when one kills another human being simply for being born, for coming into the world. That person has come into the world against the doctrine, he has no right to exist." But Frossard continued, referring directly to the Jewish shopkeeper, before the victim is put to death, he or she must be humiliated, debased, stripped of his or her personhood, his or her humanity. A crime against humanity, he concluded, is distinguished from war crimes as well as all other crimes by these two elements.

Admirable in its concision and clarity, Frossard's definition of crimes against humanity was matched in its simple eloquence by his analysis of how criminals against humanity become who they are, in short, how "Barbies are made." Such criminals are first and foremost mediocrities who "give up their consciences to the party." Such donations, he continued, are "total" and represent a "complete abdication of the notion of a personal, individual conscience." Once given, moreover, these individuals can never recover their own consciences in their lifetimes.

In exchange, the party, in this case the Nazi party, "designates [for these individuals] both good and evil" and gives to them the power of life and death over their fellow human beings. This surfeit of power, Frossard added, is something they could never obtain on their own. With this acquisition, the transaction is complete. In concluding, Frossard explained that the abdication of one's conscience in exchange for power also explains why the "Barbies of the world" never feel remorse and never repent. Their consciences, Frossard affirmed evocatively, have died with Hitler in the wreckage of his Berlin bunker.

Impressive as was Frossard's analysis, and as appealing in its simplicity and straightforwardness as it must have been to those present in the courtroom, it nevertheless also opened up opportunities for the defence, and indeed for anyone who wished to challenge the legalistically unwieldy definition of crimes against humanity handed down by the Paris Court of Cassation. Anticipating that the defence would attempt to underscore the fact that Frossard's definition of these crimes and the Court of Cassation's definition were at odds and then exploit that disparity to invoke other crimes, such as France's own crimes in Algeria, it was a civil parties lawyer who raised the issue first. Alain Feder, the lawyer in question, asked Frossard bluntly if Barbie's crimes as a Nazi policeman in Lyon were "assimilable" to the torture of Algerian resisters attributed to "certain French officers" during the conflict there. First expressing his surprise that the question had come from "that side" of the courtroom, Frossard responded emphatically in the negative. He stated, "It is not the same thing to torture a resister as it is to attempt to abolish an entire people, it is not the same thing at all." Then, addressing the second "element" of his definition of crimes against humanity, the dignity, the "personhood" of the victim, and provocatively invoking the name of Jean Moulin, Frossard continued: "Torture does not debase the resister; it did not humiliate Jean Moulin, it weakened him and diminished him physically, but it did not debase him morally. Quite the opposite: it elevated him." And Frossard concluded, the same was true of those Algerian resisters tortured by French officers, an action that he, Frossard, had loudly and publicly protested at the time.

If Feder's questioning of Frossard was intended to anticipate and therefore silence in advance the defence's efforts to exploit Frossard's testimony, the strategy did not succeed. After expressing his admiration for Frossard's past denunciations of French crimes in Algeria,[17] Vergès nevertheless raised the comparison anew, pointing out that Hubert Beuve-Méry, the founder and editor of Le Monde, had in 1957 expressed the view that after French crimes in Algeria the French no longer had the right to condemn the Nazis for what they did to the martyred village of Oradour, or for the tortures inflicted by the Gestapo against resisters. In responding, Frossard noted first that Beuve-Méry's opinions were not his own, and then drew a further distinction between the Nazi and French crimes at issue, noting that there was a massive difference between "violence born of fire, violence born of combat and of the fear that combatants inspire reciprocally in each other" and a "violence of extreme cold-bloodedness," carried out, for example, against the children of Izieu. This had not been war, Frossard added, and there were no "veterans of Izieu," there was no "Battle of Izieu."

Rather than address the distinction drawn by Frossard, Vergès chose a different angle of attack, raising in the process the issue of race for the first time. Anticipating the line that he and especially his defence co-counsel Jean-Martin Mbemba and Nabil Bouaïta would later take during their closing arguments at the end of the trial, Vergès read to the court and to Frossard the Martinique-born writer Aimé Césaire's famous dictum: "That for which the bourgeois humanist refused to pardon Hitler was not his humiliation of mankind as a whole, but the crime he committed against the white man, the humiliation of the white man, and for having applied to Europe procedures that previously had only been applied to the Arabs of Algeria, the coolies of India, and the negroes of Africa."[18] What, Vergès asked, was Frossard's reaction to that?

For the first time in their exchanges, Frossard admitted his frustration, indeed his irritation with the defence counsel. But as the film of the trial reveals, he remained cool and calm just the same. Frossard noted first that the question he was addressing was the distinction between war crimes and crimes against humanity and that under any circumstances there was hardly a valid comparison to be made between the situation of Jews and resisters in occupied wartime Lyon and FLN and other revolutionaries in Algeria. First, in Lyon resisters and Jews were a tiny minority, struggling for their survival against an overpowering external occupier. By contrast, the Algeria Arab population from which the rebels arose outnumbered the French there ten to one. And under any circumstances, if a logical comparison was to be made, one needed to address Barbie's very specific methods, which Vergès had not done. Finally, in prosecuting Barbie, an exemplary criminal, the trial underway was not just "exorcising" Nazi "demons" like Barbie (here Frossard's religious beliefs infused his language) it was also exorcising all the other demons "against which we have always fought," including, presumably, those French who tortured Algerians.

The exchange between Frossard and Vergès concluded on a conciliatory note. Nevertheless, in legal terms, it clearly *did not* serve the aims of the prosecution or reinforce in any way the hybrid definition of crimes against humanity handed down by the Paris court of Cassation and in effect in the Lyon court. Indeed, at the end of their exchange, Vergès asked Frossard if he understood that his definition of crimes against humanity was at odds with the definition of crimes against humanity of the Court of Cassation. Frossard acknowledged that it was and added: "I regret that the Court of Cassation has encapsulated in its definition certain crimes that are traditionally placed under the rubric of war crimes." Then, addressing president Cerdini and the jury, Frossard stated again. "I regret it." Vergès, obviously satisfied, told the court, "That is all."

A week later, on 2 June, Elie Wiesel, another distinguished witness and discordant voice where the court's definition of crimes against humanity was concerned, took the stand. As opposed to Frossard, whose tone and presentation were objective and deliberately analytical, Elie Wiesel spoke at least intially in a highly personal and evocative fashion. His testimony eschewed the analysis of legal definitions and the motivations of the killers to emphasize first that, in his view, those who had not lived through the Holocaust could never truly understand it. He had written thirty books, he testified, but was always reluctant to address the subject of the Holocaust in them because "no one will understand." All the surviving witness that he was could do, therefore, was "capture an image [of it] here, a fragment there, a small spark." Second, for Wiesel, the Nazi killers were best understood not in terms of the kinds of banal psychological motivations Frossard had described, but rather as metaphysically inspired assassins who wished to "take God's throne away from him." Nazism was less an ideology to Wiesel than a "new religion," one of "cruelty" dominated by inhuman forces. That this religion should emerge from "the most civilized nation on earth" only added to its mystery, in Wiesel's view. The same mystery ultimately obtained where the Nazis' visceral hatred of the Jews was concerned. The suffering of the latter was, after all, the "oldest in the world." And the fact that the Jews – and the young adolescent that Wiesel had been in Hungary at the time – wished only to serve God and do well by other men meant that they were unprepared for the scourge of Nazism when it arrived.

When it came to subjects like the dimensions of the crime that the Holocaust represented and the guilt of the Jew in the eyes of the Nazis, Wiesel's language became more deliberately analytical. Echoing Frossard, Wiesel stressed that, for the Nazi, "to be [born] a Jew was a crime deserving of capital punishment," and this is why the Nazis set out to annihilate him. Indeed, this aim was the Nazis' highest motivation. It took precedence even over winning the war. The trains filled with Jews and destined for Auschwitz, Wiesel affirmed, took priority over military trains carrying troops being sent to repel the invading Soviets to the east.

As for the Holocaust, Wiesel insisted, "in its dimensions, in its onto-logical character, and by its eschatological ambitions," it was a "tragedy that surpassed any responses to it." For the first time in history, he added, "'an entire people, from the smallest to the largest, the richest to the most disinherited, were condemned to disappear." The Holocaust, he concluded, was "unique," a "case apart," as he later put in in responding to a civil parties lawyer's question. And, he added pointedly, "If we compare it [to any other crime or catastrophe], we minimize it, we falsify the situation and the image [of it]."

For Wiesel, the purpose of the Barbie trial, as he saw it, was less to render justice for the accused than it was to provide for the *rescapés*, the surviving witnesses, a "justification for their survival." Here it was apparent that Wiesel was referring to Jewish survivors. As he stated, "As a Jew, it is impossible for me not to accentuate the burden on my people during these travails." By way of clarification, Wiesel added, "all of Hitler's victims were not Jews, but all Jews were victims." The Jewish children of Izieu playing in the schoolyard before their deportation in 1944 were "already dead," Wiesel stated, "because they were seen as dead in Berlin." Pressed by the civil parties lawyer Alain Jakubowicz, who had convinced him to testify, Wiesel stressed anew the uniqueness of the Holocaust as a crime in history, and it was that uniqueness, and the *recognition* of that uniqueness, he added, that allowed it to serve as an obstacle to further genocides.

Although Elie Wiesel did not explicitly testify in the Lyon courtroom that, for him, crimes against humanity should be reserved for Nazism's "innocent" victims and not be expanded to include Barbie's and Nazism's Resistance victims, the import of his testimony was nevertheless clear. Indeed, in an interview on *Radio France Inter*, Wiesel had stated explicitly that "A crime against humanity is always a crime against the innocence of the world, against the soul of humanity and the innocence of the souls of children." Poetically evocative in its language, Wiesel's definition nevertheless emphasized the notion of innocence, which, as the context of the 1985 debate between Serge Klarsfeld, Henri Noguères, and Vercors had made clear, distinguished Jewish victims and explicitly the children of Izieu from those resisters tortured and deported by Barbie.

For Vergès at least, Wiesel's position was very clear. When his turn came to question the witness, Vergès set out to demonstrate what he perceived to be the narrowness and selectiveness of Wiesel's admittedly Judaeocentric perspective and testimony. But Vergès also wanted to demonstrate that Wiesel's perspective was ultimately inseparable from a wilful ignorance (and indifference to) the suffering of non-white peoples and a blinkered devotion to the hegemony of the West and its Israeli ally. Vergès first asked Wiesel if he was aware of a report supposedly written by Michel Rocard in 1958 that 15,000 Algerian children were dying per month of exposure in French detention camps.[19] When Wiesel responded that he was not aware of the report because he had left France by that time to take up residence in the United States, Vergès responded archly, "I conclude then that the death of 15,000 children per month, and their cries of pain didn't cross the Atlantic; indeed sometimes, I have to inform the witness, these cries don't even cross the Mediterranean."

Then, homing in on the West and American crimes, Vergès asked Wiesel what he thought of the fate of children in Vietnam, and especially the children of My Lai and the fact that their killer (the aforementioned William Calley) was living free in the United States. After Wiesel responded that he had organized a protest of writers, lawyers, and others against the massacre, Vergès arrived at the subject of Israel and Israeli crimes: "the witness has affirmed his solidarity with Israel. I would like to ask him this question: has he heard about the massacre of [Palestinian] children at Deir-Yassin shortly after the end of the 1948 war?"

With this question, Wiesel had had enough. He announced that he did not want to "create an incident in the courtroom," and president Cerdini then intervened, stating,"it is true that we are moving outside the issue at hand in our trial." Then Wiesel concluded, "I am solidary with Israel. Thirty-nine years ago Israel had accepted the idea of sharing Palestine. The Arabs refused. I am not justifying an act of barbarism that was indeed committed. I only wish to rehabilitate, and not to divide. I find it deplorable and regrettable that the lawyer who defends the man accused of the crimes of which the defendant is accused accuses in turn the Jewish people" (Mérindol 135).

After his testimony at the Barbie trial, in the interview on *France Inter* radio mentioned above, Wiesel would reiterate his anger and indeed outrage at Vergès's questioning. He stated that what he remembered of the trial was the "abject questions of the lawyer for the defense who took pride in dishonoring the United States, France, and Israel in comparing them to Nazi Germany."[20] In all likelihood, Wiesel's outrage at Vergès, as well as the questions themselves, contributed to the impression voiced by Alain Finkielkraut as well as others that Vergès and his defence team had succeeded in turning the Barbie trial into the trial of the white man and his crimes against colonized people, and not the crimes of the Nazis. But from the standpoint of the civil parties lawyer Michel Zaoui, who would write about the episode much later, Vergès's performance on 2 June actually served in the long run to undermine one of his *other* cherished ambitions for the Barbie trial, and that was to turn the trial into a "trial by rupture." The idea of the "trial by rupture" as fully conceptualized by Vergès in works like *De la stratégie judiciaire* will be discussed in chapter seven here. But in questioning Elie Wiesel as he did, Vergès, Zaoui speculated, had essentially abandoned the defence of his client to launch into a political discourse whose "aims were totally at odds with the reality of the crimes committed by his client Klaus Barbie" (*Mémoires de justice* 85). For a "trial by rupture" to be successful, Zaoui continued, the defence lawyer must argue for the "nobility of the actions of his client" in order to set them in opposition to the corruption of the court and the state that it serves" (85). But in raising the issue of French, American, and Israeli crimes and implicitly comparing them to Nazi crimes, Vergès was instead engaging in a "great leveling of the atrocities humanity had known, notably confounding war crimes with crimes against humanity" (86). In other words, rather than expose and fully exploit the limitations of Wiesel's own definition and understanding of crimes against humanity, Vergès had, through his questions and comparisons, further muddied the historical and legal waters in a way that made the nature of his defence of Barbie *less clear* to the jury. From the standpoint of French law as it applied in the case, the argument was irrelevant, anyway.

The testimonies of André Frossard and Elie Wiesel, and their respective exchanges with Jacques Vergès remain, in the subsequent documentation of the Barbie trial, perhaps the most memorable such exchanges and testimonies when it came to conflicting definitions of crimes against humanity and their historical and geographical reach. They would also help stoke later debates related to the "competition of the victims," the comparison of Holocaust victims with those of other political crimes carried out by modern democracies and especially by France, the United States, and Israel. However, as the testimonies of other "witnesses of general interest" who spoke later in the trial would make clear, the testimonies of Frossard and Wiesel were not the "last words" on these matters in the trial. Other testimonies would prove at least equally incisive, and some more prescient as to what future historical debates and comparisons would emerge later. For example, following the publication in October 1997 of *Black Book of Communism*, a compendium of the crimes of Communist regimes worldwide, the comparison of the crimes of the two predominant forms of totalitarian regimes of the first half of the twentieth century was the subject of considerable debate, and for several months. In his testimony at the Barbie trial on 9 June, Léon Poliakov, the distinguished historian of anti-Semitism raised precisely this comparison in order to address the specificity of Nazi motivations and Nazis' crimes. Taking a position that would later be highly contested during the *Black Book* controversy, Poliakov testified in the Lyon courtroom that although

Stalin had killed "thirty million people" and Mao more in China, these crimes were not comparable to Nazi crimes because they were committed in the name of "an ideal of universal justice." With racist crimes committed in the name of a "racist utopia" like Nazism, on the other hand, there are no such higher motives: those who do not belong to the race were inevitably "reduced to the status of slaves" or exterminated. Besides, Poliakov concluded (inaccurately), children were not killed by the Communist regimes at issue.

Given the range of historical issues and comparisons, implicit or otherwise, that *did* arrise during the Barbie trial, it is interesting to note that the question of the absolute "uniqueness" of the Holocaust among genocides and indeed the unprecedented criminality of the Nazi regime itself never came up directly in the Lyon courtroom. This is surprising not only because the testimonies of witnesses like Frossard, Wiesel, and Poliakiov implied that both *were* "unique," whereas the defence's clear assumption was that they were not, but because accross the Rhine, in West Germany, these questions were being intensely debated in the media and had been for many months. Indeed, at the heart of (West) German *Historikerstreit* or "Historians' Dispute" that involved in fact historians, philosophers, and others were a number of crucial questions that in many ways hovered over the Barbie trial in Lyon. Specifically, according to Charles S. Maier, did the Holocaust have "a claim to special horror in the annals of twentieth-century? If it was special, why?"[21] Was national socialism itself usefully considered "a specimen of a more inclusive poltical or ideological phenomenon whether fascism or totalitarianism" (Maier 3), or something entirely different, apart? Third, was the Holocaust an "originary" event, or as the historian Ernst Nolte asked provocatively, was it inspired by Hitler's fear that the Soviets might visit an "Asiatic deed" on the German people, like the Armenian genocide? As Nolte phrased it in his essay "The Past That Will Not Pass": "Did the National Socialists of Hitler perhaps commit an 'Asiatic' deed? Was the Gulag Archipelago not primary to Auschwitz? Was the Bolshevik murder of an entire class not the logical and factual prius to the 'racial murder' of National Socialism?"[22] While Nolte's question, provocative as it was, may have been more specific to German history and in fact extraneous to the case against Klaus Barbie, the other two questions articulated by Maier *were* clearly germane to the issues and debates in the Lyon Assize court. In fact, according to Maier, the Barbie trial (and presumably, the long investigation leading up to it) formed part of a nexus of issues (along with the Waldheim scandal and Ronald Reagan's visit to the Bitburg cemetery) that helped launch the *Historikerstreit* in the first place (Maier 7).[23]

Where the distinction between crimes against humanity and war crimes, Nazi crimes, and French crimes in Algeria, as well as the motivations of the accused were concerned, other witnesses besides Frossard and Wiesel added valuable insights as well. On 17 June, the last day of "witness of general interest" testimony before witnesses for the defence took the stand, Laurent Schwartz was called to testify. A Fields Medal winner in mathematics and a resister "of the first hour" against Nazi oppression, as Rolland Rappaport, the civil parties lawyer who called him to testify explained to president Cerdini, Schwartz began his testimony by criticizing the ways in which he perceived the defence was manipulating these issues to the advantage of the accused. First, to the defence's implicit argument that it was unfair and perhaps useless to judge Barbie if other criminals against humanity, perpetators of war crimes, etc. had gotten away with their crimes, Schwartz retorted that if one uses that as a reason not to try Barbie, then "there is no hope that any future condemnations of war crimes or crimes against humanity will take place." Second, to those who argued that Barbie was just a *lampiste*, a "subordinate" or "underling" in the Nazi hierarchy who was therefore not responsible for Nazism's crimes, Schwartz responded that the round-ups at the UGIF headquarters and of the children of Izieu, as well as ordering the last convoy of 11 August 1944, were hardly the crimes of a *lampiste*. They were in fact the crimes of a fanatically committed and powerful Nazi. As proof, Schwartz observed that "the acts of torture committed with the brutality one has heard described in this courtroom, these are not the acts of torture committed by someone who is simply following orders but who doesn't believe in those orders."

Then Schwartz turned to the comparison of Nazi crimes to French crimes in Algeria. Here again, he drew distinctions Frossard and Wiesel in their testimonies had not. There were, Schwartz stated, war crimes committed when Algerian rebels were arrested and tortured for information. And there were also, Schwartz conceded, in all likelihood crimes against humanity committed as well. But then, comparing French exactions in Algeria not to Nazi crimes but to the more recent Argentinian "disappearances" of political enemies, Schwartz noted that the Argentinian authorities arrested their victims with the intent to torture *and* to "disappear" or kill them. In Algeria, by contrast, the French arrested opponents with the intent to torture but *not* kill them. Of course, he continued, when these victims of torture were too badly wounded, too "unpresentable" to be released to the public, they were then executed. This was a "horror without name," Schwarz testified, but there had nevertheless been "no intent," no "hegemonic" plan, to wipe out or destroy an entire people, one of the qualifications of a crime against humanity in French *and* international law. There was simply never a "system to annihilate Algerians" as a whole. While Schwartz's testimony clearly did not satisfy Vergès and the defence, as the lawyer's questioning and criticisms would make clear, it did draw distinctions that Frossard and Wiesel had not, distinctions that undoubtedly in their clarity proved helpful to the court and jury.

Part Three: Historical Context and the Validity of the Evidence

In terms of the organization of expert testimony dealing with the historical context and implications of Barbie's crimes as well as the viability and legitimacy of the evidence against him, the schedule followed by the Lyon Court of Assizes presented these matters in a somewhat disjointed and arguably confusing fashion. For example, two German jurists, Alfred Streim and Rodolf Holfort, specialists on the Nazi and SS hierarchy, the Final Solution, and the authentification of the evidence, testified early in the trial on 18 and 19 May. By contrast, several "witnesses of general interest" who could also address these matters did not testify until 9 June or later. In between, there had been the often powerful and emotionally draining testimony of Barbie's many victims, and so it was perhaps difficult to change intellectual and emotional gears, so to speak, and recall the testimony of Holfort and Streim, both of whom had also been questioned at length by president Cerdini, prosecutor Truche, several civil parties lawyers, and the defence. To be sure, all these witnesses had their own busy schedules with which the court needed to work, but the effect of dispersing their testimonies was at least arguably to diminish the clarity of focus many brought to their depositions before the court.

Both Alfred Striem, who as chief of the Central Justice Service for examining Nazi crimes, had prosecuted Nazi crimes committed in France and so knew the Barbie case well, and Rodolf Holfort, a specialist of Nazi crimes against Jews in France, had been questioned earlier, during the *instruction* of the Barbie case. At that time the two men had answered important questions about the process and order of command in the SS and SD hierarchy, the extent of Barbie's likely knowledge of the fate of the Jews he deported, the extent of his power as chief of Section Four of the Lyon SD, and perhaps most crucially, the authenticity of the documentary evidence against Barbie. They were now prepared to repeat their conclusions in court.

As to the Izieu telex, both men had only seen a photocopy of the telex during the investigation, as the original had not yet been located by Serge Klarsfeld at the *Centre de Documentation Juive*. In court, therefore, both men were asked to look at the original during the trial. When Streim held and examined the original document, he affirmed that when he had earlier seen the photocopy of the telex he was virtually certain of its authenticity. Now, holding the original, he was absolutely certain of it. For one thing, he stated, the strips of paper containing the text of the telegram that were glued to the piece of paper of the original were produced by a Siemens machine of the type used by the Gestapo.

During the lead-up to the 1987 trial, the defence had, as already noted, questioned the authenticity of the Izieu telex on several counts. First, before the original was produced, Barbie and the defence claimed that the photocopy was a fraud, not only in the sense that there *was* no original but also in the sense that it had been created after the fact expressly to incriminate Klaus Barbie. Additionally, when the original was produced, the fact that strips for the telex machine were pasted on the back of a map of England made the document highly dubious, as did the fact that a *French* dating stamp, with the date in French, had been used during its transmission, rather than a German one. The defence raised two further objections as well: could not someone else have signed Barbie's name without him knowing it? Or, couldn't Barbie just have signed the telex even if the Izieu round-up had not been carried out by him, or if he had not been the one responsible for ordering it? In other words, couldn't Barbie just be the messenger?

According to Streim and Holfort, all these objections were either highly dubious or entirely without substance, given the historical realities of the period and of Nazi practices themselves. In strictly material terms, both the use of the French dating stamp and of the map for paper were common, given paper shortages late in the war and the fact that the Nazis as a matter of standard practice used such stamps in the other countries they occupied, in addition to France. As for the possibility that someone else had signed for Barbie without his knowing it, this would have been an extraordinary breach of SS and Gestapo protocol and hierarchical practices, and in all likelihood severely punished. Finally, where the claim that a clever forger had created the document out of whole cloth was concerned, notations on the telex itself cast very serious doubt on this possibility. Indeed, in examining the original telex in the courtroom, Streim noted that it contained a highly specific numerical code that identified the service concerned. No forger working after the war would have known this code.

Where the possibility that Barbie was just the messenger was concerned, there were several realities that mitigated against this argument, according to the German experts. First, as head of Section Four, Barbie would automatically have been in charge of Section Four-B, the section handling the persecution and deportation of Jews. Therefore, no head of Section 4-B would have acted independently of Barbie. What about the possibility that the orders had come directly to their homologue in Lyon from the office of Jewish affairs in the Reich Main Security Office in Berlin? This, again, was not the way the SS functioned, according to Streim and Holfort. And, finally, what of the possibility that an independent commando unit or *sonderkommando* had been sent, ostensibly from Berlin, to carry out the raid at Izieu? Here, the German experts were categorical: any such mission would have to have notified and subsequently worked with Section Four in Lyon.[24]

There were other circumstances that pointed to Barbie's direct responsibility for the Izieu round-up as well, according to the German jurists. By 1944, lacking in personnel to be sent out to aid in operations of this sort, Paris headquarters had sent a directive to Section Four leaders in regional offices encouraging them to act independently and on their own initiative to carry out the round-ups and deportation of Jews. Moreover, if there had been any instructions from headquarters directly pertaining to Izieu, a file would have been created on it there and assigned a reference code, and any subsequent communication about the Izieu round-up would bear the reference code to that file. No such reference was found on the documents in evidence.

As a result of questioning by president Cerdini and the civil parties lawyer Rolland Rappaport, two final points – both unfavourable to the accused – emerged. First, when Cerdini asked Streim if Barbie's signature on the telex describing the round-up confirmed that he had personally carried out the round-up, Streim answered in the negative. But, he added, if Barbie's signature was on the document, that indicated with certainty that he was *responsible* for the operation itself. In response to a question from Rappaport, Streim added that because actions like the Izieu round-up were viewed as "successes" within the SS and Gestapo hierarchies, it would have been especially advantageous and even prestigious for an ambitious officer like Barbie to sign his name to the telex. This, undoubtedly, gave him extra incentive to sign it.

When it came to Vergès's turn to query the witnesses, it was clear that the defence had few cards left to play, as the testimony of Streim and Holfort had offered thorough and convincing evidence of both the authenticity of the Izieu telex and of Barbie's direct responsibility for the roundup. Therefore, as he would attempt to do shortly with the likes of Mario Blardone and Simone Kadosche-Lagrange, Vergès opted to go after the witnesses by challenging the legitimacy of the German criminal justice system of which they were both representatives.

During the investigation, Streim had confirmed to investigating magistrate Riss that the photocopy of the Izieu telex had been introduced successfully into evidence at the trials of Kurt Lischka, Herbert Hagen, and Heinrichson, and that defence lawyers had not challenged its validity. Referring to this earlier testimony now in the Lyon courtroom, Vergès now asked Streim if the German courts were in the habit of using photocopies, implying, of course, that this was flimsy evidence and that therefore the system itself might be shoddy.

In framing his response, Streim noted, first, that after the war all the victorious countries had looted Nazi records, so the German courts had been forced to rely on photocopies of them. But, Streim added, because German courts had maintained good relations with (most of) these foreign powers and their archives, when a request was made by a German court for an original, this request was honoured, almost without exception. German defence lawyers, no slackers themselves, despite Vergès's insinuations, had in the past challenged the authenticity of the photocopies, as Vergès had done, but they had learned over time that such challenges were of no avail.

This line of questioning having failed (and to all appearances, to have backfired), Vergès chose another tack. Since the two German witnesses were involved in the German Federal Republic's efforts to prosecute Barbie, why had the German authorities themselves not demanded Barbie's extradition from Bolivia before 1982, even though they had long known the unrepentant Nazi was living and thriving there? When the German magistrate's long and admittedly convoluted response failed to satisfy Vergès, the defence counsel turned to the topic of what the two men knew of the *Wehrmacht* organizations, and specifically flak battalions of the kind that had been commandeered by the Lyon Gestapo to help in the round-up at Izieu. Did the German prosecutor know, for example, to what *Wehrmacht* headquarters Flak Battalion 958, the battalion that had assisted in the Izieu round-up, was assigned? Streim answered that he did not; Vergès observed sarcastically, "Monsieur le spécialiste ne sait pas!" ("The specialist does not know the answer!").

It is impossible to know with certainty, of course, what the impact of the German magistrates' testimony had on the jury and the court, or whether Vergès's somewhat strained attempt to challenge the limits of their knowledge and undermine their credibility as "specialists" had any effect. But when Vergès delivered his closing argument to the court, he clearly chose *not* to revisit important elements of the two men's testimonies or challenge them again.

As opposed to the testimonies of Holfort and Streim, who spoke early in the Barbie trial and so before the witnesses who were also victims and survivors of Barbie's crimes, the testimonies of the "witnesses of general interest" spoke after these often-harrowing testimonies were given. They therefore served more than the earlier expert testimonies to fill in the historical and political context, or in some instances to bolster, sum up, or put an explanation point to the witness testimonies themselves. Moreover, some of these witnesses filled in blanks that were not historical or political, but rather psychological. For example, the testimony of Tony Lainé was particularly helpful in that it stressed that recent studies of trauma had confirmed that remembering a traumatic event even forty years after the fact was normal and not exceptional. Moreover, Lainé stressed it was *visual memories* which often proved the most powerful, and especially memories of *facial details*. Given that many, if not most, of Barbie's victims recognized him by his eyes or by what they considered the strange shape of his ears, Lainé's testimony tended to reinforce the credibility of their claims.

In terms of filling in aspects of the historical context consonant with much of the testimony given by witnesses and victims, perhaps the most substantive and informative testimony was given by Jacques Delarue, a leading French historian of the Gestapo and SS as well as Vichy's own *Milice*, or *Militia*. Delarue's testimony was helpful in a number of important ways both in terms of the Nazi, SS, and SD hierarchies and operations in France, as well as in clarifying Barbie's role, functions, and especially his prerogatives in those hierarchies.

First, Delarue testified that Barbie was neither a soldier nor a government functionary, but rather someone entirely answerable to the party and its radical aims. Second, Delarue made it clear that not all Gestapo officers indulged in Barbie's brutal methods or involved themselves in the dirty work of rounding up and deporting Jews. There were, for example, Gestapo officers in Paris who had never practised torture during the four years of the Occupation. And in Bordeaux, the head of Section Four had succeeded in ridding his section of its own Section B, giving it to another section instead in order to concentrate on the less morally repugnant task of fighting the Resistance. The point seemed clear that Barbie *wanted* the tasks and the kind of work he carried out.

The second point, particularly germane to some of the witness testimony and to Barbie's words and actions in wartime Lyon, concerned the infamous *Nacht und Neibel* (Night and Fog) decree. Delarue explained to the court that the decree mandated that all political opponents of the Nazi regime in occupied countries were to be brought back to the Reich to be judged and dealt with and that their relatives and others were not to know of their fate. Whereas the decree was originally implemented by the *Wehrmacht*, it also became a tool of the SS and Gestapo, which, at least according to some *Wehrmacht* officers, abused it entirely. According to Delarue, the latter invoked it to carry out deportations and mass executions of victims, many innocent and chosen arbitrarily, at the whim of the local Gestapo authority and specifically the head of Section Four. Moreover, the SS commandeered criminals already tried and condemned by the *Wehrmacht* and used them to their own purposes, despite the fact that they had been opponents of the Reich. Summing up SS and SD authority, Delarue observed it constituted a "regime of total arbitrariness," answerable to no one but itself.

In his testimony, Delarue was at pains to stress, like earlier witnesses, that Klaus Barbie was no simple "cog" in the Nazi machinery. In the first place, he was appointed head of Section Four in a city that was central, and indeed crucial, to Nazi aims, not only in the struggle against the Resistance but also in that the city was near the Swiss and Italian borders and therefore an excellent location from which to block or limit the transit of refugees. Indeed, Delarue testified, when Germany moved into the Unoccupied Zone in November 1942, the *Abwehr*, or *Wehrmacht* intelligence, moved their headquarters from Dijon to Lyon for precisely this reason. Additionally, according to Delarue, local Gestapo authorities in Barbie's position had "enormous autonomy" in their postings, including, as his testimony about the Night and Fog decree indicated, the power of life and death over virtually anyone he chose. And, Delarue added, this autonomous power was enhanced because Barbie's bosses were far away in Berlin and not likely to closely surveil him or his colleagues elsewhere in Occupied France. Finally, given his position and authority, it was "unthinkable" that Barbie was unaware of the outcome of the deportations.

Under the prompting of Lise Lesèvre's lawyer, Roland Dumas, Delarue also testified that Lesèvre's personal experience which she had described in court was a perfect example of Barbie's total power and autonomy, and that of the Gestapo as well. Following her initial interrogation and torture by Barbie and his men, as a member of the Resistance, Lesèvre was then tried before a military tribunal, convicted, and sentenced to death. But Barbie had no trouble in recuperating her from the tribunal and getting her back in his hands, as he wished to continue to interrogate her. Clearly, his power as a Gestapo officer easily trumped the authority of the military authorities who held her.

There was one final witness who also testified about Barbie's autonomy and that of other Gestapo and SS officers in his position. This was Gert Bastian, a retired army general and now deputy in the West German *Bundestag*. Bastian wished to make two points. First, he wanted to insist – wrongly, certainly in light of more recent research – on the absolute distinction between the *Wehrmacht* in which he served as a very young man and the Gestapo in terms of the crimes they respectively committed.

The former, he testified, followed and honoured a military code which, implicitly at least, prevented it from committing the kinds of crimes that the SS and Gestapo routinely carried out. There were of course excesses committed by the *Wehrmacht*, but these were the exception and not the rule.

Bastian's second point concerned Barbie and the SS and Gestapo themselves. These organizations and their members, he testified, were "the killing machines of the Third Reich" and were "the instrument Hitler used to carry out his crimes against people for political, racial, and religious reasons." Those who chose to serve these organizations – and here the question of Barbie's autonomy came into play – did so *voluntarily*. And if these volunteers changed their minds, Bastian continued, nothing prevented them from resigning if they found the work too distasteful. As Bastian stated, "A member of the Gestapo, and especially one who fulfilled important functions [like Barbie] cannot pretend that he acted only in following orders, that he could not revolt against the Gestapo." Of course, this would likely mean that the "rebel" in question would be sent to the eastern front, but others had done so before Barbie.

If Gert Bastian's testimony confirmed that Barbie's "autonomy" could have been used in a more positive sense in that he could have chosen to be a fighting soldier rather that a torturer and murderer, it also opened the door for Vergès to challenge the witness effectively in ways he had been unable to do with other witnesses. Vergès pointedly asked Bastian if, as a young soldier, *he himself* had revolted against the Nazi hierarchy. Bastian responded that he had not, but that there was a difference between a naïve adolescent of seventeen when the war began, which he had been, and a mature adult like Barbie, who should have known better. Vergès then asked Bastian if he was aware that it was *Wehrmacht* troops and not SS troops or the Gestapo that slaughtered French colonial troops during the invasion of France. Bastian confessed that he did not and said that he regretted this greatly.

Certainly, from a rhetorical standpoint, Vergès had gotten the better of the German deputy. Never one to underplay his own success, Vergès even taunted the witness at the conclusion of their exchange, stating, "A lieutenant in the SS could disobey orders but the [Wehrmacht] lieutenant that he [Bastian] was could not." But, paradoxically, what Vergès did not seem to realize was that, in attempting to establish parallels between Bastian and Barbie, he had in fact underscored vast differences between two Germans and World War II veterans in moral terms. These differences in fact only cast Barbie's failings in sharper relief. While Bastian had after the war studied and acknowledged the crimes of his country while seeking to strengthen its democratic future, and while he regretted and willingly shouldered some of the responsibility for the crimes Germany had committed in the past, Barbie, who stated repeatedly that he regretted nothing and demonstrated his indifference in the face of his victims' testimonies, was *frozen* in that past. He seemed, moreover, completely oblivious or indifferent to that fact. In that Barbie demonstrably possessed virtually no capacity for empathy, he resembled Adolph Eichmann as Hannah Arendt had described him in his inability to *think*, specifically, to "think from the standpoint of someone else" (Arendt, *Eichmannn in Jerusalem*, 49). But for all Barbie's lack of empathy, for all the harm he had done his victims, one of the most thoughtful witnesses to testify during the trial, Raymonde Guyon-Belot, stated that, if given the opportunity, she would not harm Klaus Barbie or the other Nazis who had made her and so many others suffer. But it was also, she stated, her right to forgive them, and this she would not do, either.

Chapter Six

The Civil Parties and Prosecution Make Their Case

As the Barbie trial drew to a close in the final weeks of June and first few days of July, the witnesses having completed their testimony, it was the turn of the civil parties lawyers, the chief prosecutor, and finally the defence counsel to make their closing arguments before the court. According to the schedule established by president Cerdini, from 17 June through 26 June, the civil parties lawyers gave their closing statements, followed by two days (29–30 June) devoted to the *réquistoire*, or summation, of chief prosecutor Pierre Truche. The trial concluded with three days of closing arguments by defence co-counsel Jacques Vergès, the Congolese lawyer Jean-Martin Mbemba, and the Algerian lawyer Nabil Bouaïta. Immediately after Vergès completed his lengthy closing statement, the accused returned to the courtroom to make a final statement before the jury began its deliberations.

Before discussing the closing arguments of the civil parties lawyers and Truche's summation, it is important to stress that Barbie's defence team already found itself in difficult straits by the time the witness testimony was concluded. Despite Vergès's best efforts to impeach the testimony and/or discredit some of the witnesses and victims who had testified, and despite the fact that some of these witnesses were not convincing or persuasive, the combined impact of the testimony clearly elicited the sympathy and indeed empathy of many, if not most, of those present in the massive courtroom. More importantly, the sustained and repeated accounts of suffering by resisters and Jewish victims alike, especially women, tended to confirm that the definition of crimes against humanity imposed by the Paris Court of Cassation, while awkward and debatable in legal terms, appeared genuinely and entirely legitimate in moral and indeed in *human terms*.

In addition, while some of the testimony of experts and "witnesses of special interest" proved to be problematic to the prosecution, specifically

Serge Klarsfeld in 2016. Greek photonews/Alamy Stock Photo

Pierre Truche. REUTERS/Alamy Stock Photo

where conflicting definitions of crimes against humanity were presented, those witnesses who testified about the authenticity of the material evidence in the case and who addressed Barbie's likely knowledge of the fate of those deported were quite convincing. Stated simply, Vergès had little to work with from a month of witness testimony. Not surprisingly, Mbemba and Bouaïta ignored that testimony outright in their respective statements before the court. Moreover, as civil parties lawyer Gérard Welzer pointed out at the conclusion of these statements, neither Mbemba nor Bouaïta had bothered to even mention the actual crimes of which Barbie was accused.

The lack of good options for the defence from witness testimony doubtless helps to explain why Vergès resorted to a legal stratagem before the civil parties lawyers' statements got underway. If successful, the stratagem would have resulted in freeing Barbie at the conclusion of the trial, regardless of a conviction and the sentence handed down. The manoeuvre involved a French legal principle, codified in Article Five of the Penal Code and known as the *confusion des peines*, or the "conflation of sentences." The *confusion des peines* determines the sentence a felon receives if s/he is convicted of more than one crime. Because the discussion and debate over the "conflation of sentences" preceded the closing statements of the civil parties lawyers and the prosecutor general's summation, it will be discussed at the outset here.

Part One: The "Conflation of Sentences"

In viewing the film of the Barbie trial, the debate following Vergès's request that the court pronounce the "conflation of sentences" after its deliberation, judgment, and sentencing of Klaus Barbie marks one of the trial's more incongruous moments. Indeed, arguably at least, it appears in retrospect to justify those who criticized the trial as pedantic and monotonous, privileging highly technical and abstract legal debates by grandiloquent lawyers over lively and dramatic exchanges that cross-examination of the witness, for example, often affords. Nevertheless, leaving aside the posturing of the lawyers, their citing of conflicting precedents, and the application (or not) of specific articles in the French penal code, the debate nevertheless focused a sharp light on critical questions with which the court had to wrestle or would soon be wrestling. First, if the "conflation of sentences" was pronounced by the court, would this be an act of fairness granted by the law to even the worst of criminals, which Klaus Barbie to all appearances was, or would it be an example of a legal technicality taking precedence over justice itself? Second, was a crime against humanity such a special or *unique category of crime* that it could not be conflated with any other crimes, which pronouncing the conflation of such crimes entailed? Third, and on a much more pedestrian level, in raising the issue itself before closing arguments by the lawyers and before a judgment and sentence were even handed down, was Vergès just conjuring up another distraction, one to confuse the court and suggest that his client was not benefitting from all the legal rights he was due?

To answer these questions, it is of course first necessary to clarify the meaning and implications of the "conflation of sentences" as Vergès sought to have it applied to the Barbie case. As codified in Article Five in the French Penal Code,[1] the principle referred to as the *confusion des peines* dictates that "if one is convicted of multiple crimes or misdemeanors, only the heaviest sentence will be applied" (*Libération*, 16 June 1987). According to Pierre Truche, as he addressed the jury, the implications of the article could be explained with reference to the following example. An individual is caught in the act of armed robbery. This is a penal offence, for which the individual receives a ten-year sentence. It then emerges that this individual has also committed another robbery, this one unarmed. This, as Truche explained, is a correctional offence for which the individual is given a three-year sentence. So, the question arises, should the criminal now serve a combined thirteen-year sentence, or a lesser one? The answer, according to the principle of the *confusion des peines*, is that the lesser sentence should be absorbed into the larger one. As a result, in the case described, the individual will serve a ten-year sentence to cover both crimes.

As Vergès explained to the court, the principle applied in Barbie's case because the accused had already been sentenced to death in absentia twice, in 1952 and 1954. As the court knew well, the statute of limitations on both crimes had run out by 1974. If Barbie were to be convicted of crimes against humanity in the current trial, the maximum punishment he could receive was life in prison. Now, Vergès explained, the latter punishment was of course a "lesser" punishment than the supreme penalty of being executed, and so it should be subsumed or incorporated into the death sentence. And since the latter had lapsed, whatever Barbie's conviction in the current trial he would have to be released once the verdict and sentence were in.

Vergès buttressed his argument with three additional observations. First, in 1958, the Court of Cassation ruled that if a crime whose statute of limitations had run out imposed a heavier sentence than a second crime, then the lapsed sentence still absorbed the punishment for the second crime. Second, the lapsed punishment itself counted as punishment according to the same decision, which meant that if one successfully avoided punishment for the duration of the lapsed sentence, one was no longer subject to any sanction. Finally, while the 1964 Assembly vote made crimes against humanity imprescriptible under French law, it said nothing about the *sentence or punishment handed down for that crime.*

On the face of it, Vergès's move appeared both shrewd and reasonable. It was clearly intended to play on the idea that if the French justice system was as equitable as was claimed (the civil parties lawyers insisted that it was on several occasions), then Barbie should benefit from the advantages it offered just like any other person convicted of two crimes. To emphasize the validity of his claim even in international law, Vergès pointed out that at Nuremberg most of the twenty-four defendants had been convicted of multiple crimes, yet their respective sentences did not reflect an *accumulation* of sentences, one for each crime, but rather the absorption of multiple sentences into one. This, Vergès insisted, was a fine example of the "conflation of sentences" and one the Lyon Assize court should follow. As for the unusual timing of his request, Vergès explained that he wished to make it before the closing statements of the civil parties lawyers, as it would be "discourteous" to them to distract the court from weighing the import of their words.

Given Vergès's and the defence's other distractions and *coups de théâtre* during the trial (and these were not done yet!), it is not surprising that several of the civil parties lawyers protested that the request for a pronouncement of the "conflation of sentences" was just one more in a series of such diversions. It was, they argued, a ploy whose intent was to distract the court from the weight and implications of the weeks of testimony already heard. Indeed, Paul Vuillard argued that Vergès's move was both "too early and too late." The argument, he stated, should have been made either before the trial began in pre-trial hearings or at the time of sentencing in the current trial. Besides, Vuillard added, the real reason the defence lawyer was making the move now was that his own witnesses who had testified the day before had "turned against" him. Although Vuillard did not name the witnesses in question, to all appearances he was referring to Raymond Aubrac, whose testimony has been discussed earlier here. Vuillard concluded dismissively: "You are trying to mask your own defeat." To this, Vergès haughtily responded that he had submitted his request and argument to the court *before* the previous day's courtroom audience.

While such exchanges certainly had entertainment value, they also trivialized the very real and substantive implications raised by Vergès's introduction of the issue of the "conflation of sentences." These implications, however, did emerge in the reactions of other civil parties lawyers, who made a point of underscoring them and reflecting on their meaning and applicability to the context of the Barbie trial itself.

First, as noted, was the conundrum evident in the decision to pronounce or *not* to pronounce the "conflation of sentences." From one perspective (Vergès's, for example), if it were applied in Barbie's case it would be proof of the French justice system's true impartiality, regardless of the heinousness of the crimes committed and of the criminal himself. But from another perspective, it could also legitimately be seen as a gross miscarriage of justice, where a man responsible for the deaths of literally thousands of people was avoiding all punishment thanks to a technicality that would never have been possible had not Barbie succeeded in avoiding arrest and punishment in the early 1950s. And to add to the irony, as civil parties lawyer Alain Jakubowicz pointed out, the request was being made on behalf of an accused who had shown nothing but disdain and contempt for the legal system that his lawyer was now trying to exploit to his advantage.

If these considerations raised vexing questions about fairness, justice, and French law itself, a second, equally substantive matter raised by the principle of the "conflation of sentences" was the nature and specificity of crimes against humanity themselves. Following the logic of Vergès's argument, if the punishment for crimes against humanity could be subsumed in a punishment for a *lesser* crime like war crimes, then this at the very least put the crimes themselves *on the same level* as war crimes. And if this were the case, why were the former *alone* singled out in the 1964 law by not making them subject to a statute of limitations? In this light, the distinction between the two categories of crimes seemed arbitrary. And if this were so, did not the 1987 trial itself fall into the same category?

Two civil parties lawyers in particular, Alain Jakubowicz and Ugo Ianucci, took up the challenge that Vergès's request implicitly posed. According to Jakubowicz, by their very nature crimes with a statute of limitations and imprescriptible crimes could not be conflated in the manner discussed. Otherwise, this would turn an imprescriptible crime into one subject to a statute of limitations, and this would violate the 1964 law. Moreover, even if this were possible and feasible under the law, a crime without a statute of limitations would necessarily outweigh one when it came to the "conflation of sentences." Therefore, the punishment for the first would take precedence over the punishment for the second. In Barbie's case, this would of course mean that his life sentence for crimes against humanity would absorb his death sentences for earlier crimes. Therefore, he would serve the life sentence. Finally, Jakubowicz added, the fact that one sentence may lapse never intended to allow a criminal to completely avoid punishment for a subsequent conviction, as would be the case with Klaus Barbie.

Ianucci for his part took a different tack on the matter. He argued, first, that a crime against humanity was by definition *international* in scope, and therefore a sentence for committing it could not be restricted by domestic law. As concerned the French legal context itself, given the ramifications of the 1964 law on making crimes against humanity imprescriptible, that law would have halted the expiration of 1952 and 1954 death sentences. This was because all of Barbie's crimes would need to· be reexamined in light of the incorporation of crimes against humanity in French law, given that that legal category was unavailable to prosecutors bringing charges against Barbie in the early 1950s.

In the end, the complicated arguments developed in relation to the "conflation of sentences" by both the defence counsel and the civil parties came to naught in terms of their direct impact on the course of the trial and judgment. This was so because, as Truche explained with his usual clarity to court and jury, a decision by the Court of Cassation in 1980 left it up to the court and jury in question to decide *at the end of their deliberations* if the principle of the "conflation of sentences" was applicable in the case at hand. But although the issue was ultimately tabled, it had served in general terms as an opportunity for the civil parties lawyers attached to the prosecution to underscore once again the *uniqueness* of crimes against humanity in French jurisprudence, albeit in a convoluted way. As Iannucci reminded the court and jury at the outset of his comments on the question of the "conflation of sentences," this jury was not the first to have to deal with this issue, but it *was the first jury* to judge an individual for crimes against humanity under French law. This made any decision it might make all the more consequential. Alain Jakubowicz added that any inclination on its part to follow Vergès's reasoning on the matter and to assure Barbie the same treatment that other convicted criminals might receive should be tempered by one consideration. Klaus Barbie had never served *even one day in prison* in punishment for the many horrendous crimes for which he was being judged and for others for which he had already been convicted.

Part Two: The Closing Arguments of the Civil Parties Lawyers

Jacques Vergès was certainly correct in stating that he was greatly outnumbered by his opponents on the opposite side of the courtroom. In fact, there were thirty-nine civil parties lawyers attached to the prosecution who made closing statements before the court in Lyon, and this did not count the summation of chief prosecutor Truche. Although these lawyers were primarily tasked with defending the interests of their respective clients, many of them clearly worked in concert to anticipate any argument the defence might make and attempt to counter that argument in advance. The various strategies they followed and arguments they made will be discussed in this section. Given both the number of closing statements made and the vagaries of some the arguments, not all these closing statements will be discussed here.

Despite their numerical superiority and cooperation, there were still divisions between civil parties lawyers who represented Barbie's Jewish victims and those who represented his Resistance victims. Nevertheless, in their statements, they sought for the most part to present a united front. In terms of quality and substance, the closing statements of the civil parties lawyers varied greatly. While some were emotionally powerful or compellingly persuasive in addressing the law or the evidence, others were frankly vapid or maudlin in the extreme. In one of the more embarrassing moments in the trial, the lawyer for Resistance groups, Paul Vuillard, told the court and jury that he dreamed and hoped that the ghosts of those who "had answered the call of the General [de Gaulle], the bloody faces of tortured men and raped women" would be present with the jurors as the latter deliberated over their verdict and sentence.[2] Nevertheless, despite such dubious performances, the sheer range of personalities and matters discussed by the civil parties lawyers lent a plurality of voices to the trial that, as Leora Bilskey observes, the Eichmann trial as one example never enjoyed (Bilskey 109).

According to most accounts in the press – and in watching the video recording of the Barbie trial – the most emotionally powerful and convincing closing argument was the lead-off statement by Serge Klarsfeld on behalf of the children of Izieu.[3] As described by Sorj Chalandon in *Libération*, Klarsfeld "did not make a legal plea." Indeed, he "hardly seemed a lawyer at all" (111). Rather, "without striving for vocal effects," at the end of his statement Klarsfeld read "with sadness" what amounted in many ways to an "in memoriam" for the deported children. Klarsfeld cited the name and age of each child, described him or her, and, where possible, read a segment of a letter the doomed child had written to his or her parents. At the conclusion of his announcement of the fate of each child, Klarsfeld stated that he or she "never came back." As Klarsfeld explained in his memoirs, the idea for that final, haunting sentence came from his own son, Arno.[4] As Klarsfeld made his comments about each child, Chalandon described the reaction of the defence counsel: "*Maître* Vergès is tense. Leaning back against the wall, he studies the public, trying to decipher their faces. This is not the time for a smile. Not even for breathing. Vergès absorbs the blow [delivered by Klarsfeld's words]. Everybody absorbs the blow. The speaker's voice gives nothing away, recites this litany without emotion. This enormous red signpost, covered with the smiling faces of children (113).

Because of the extraordinary power of Klarsfeld's remarks about the children of Izieu, journalists like Chalandon tended to overlook in their press reports what he said at the outset of his plea. In these earlier remarks, in fact, Klarsfeld presented in concise terms not only an utterly damning portrait of the accused and the nature of Nazi criminality itself but also the reasons that the trial was as historically important as it was. Finally, Klarsfeld explained to the court in moving terms why he had such a personal stake in the Barbie trial.

Rather than indulge in the abstract and technical language generally used by some of the psychiatrists who testified at the outset of the trial to describe the accused, Klarsfeld meticulously portrayed Barbie as an intelligent, relatively cultured individual who clearly knew the difference between right and wrong. Barbie (unlike many of his victims) "had a choice" in his actions. The young man who had originally "believed in God" had *chosen* to become an SS and Gestapo member, fully understanding all that that entailed. Far from being just a pawn or a cog in the machine, in Lyon Barbie had had more power than "a *Wehrmacht* general." Exceeding even the expectations of the criminal organization to which he had sworn allegiance, Barbie had displayed a sadism and cruelty that outshone by far those of most of his fellow Gestapo members. In 1944, only Barbie and Aloïs Brunner had proceeded to empty refuges and deport Jewish children when other Gestapo authorities were no longer doing so. Late in the war, Barbie's Gestapo office in Lyon had been among the most efficient in chasing down Jews. When deportations were no longer possible following the Allied landings, Barbie chose to execute his prisoners instead of allowing them to be liberated by the Allies when the latter arrived in Lyon.

In addition, rather than being the unfortunate, hounded "victim" that Vergès insisted Barbie was, in Klarsfeld's account Barbie was extraordinarily *fortunate*. He had escaped the war largely unscathed and had been protected and defended by American intelligence, South American dictators, and even legal decisions like the one made by the Munich prosecutor who dropped the case against him in 1971. Discovered in Bolivia that same year, Barbie had first lied about his identity. When that identity *was* exposed, Barbie lived with impunity for another decade, all the while flaunting his freedom. Moreover, if the Nazi criminal organization to which he belonged had succeeded in accomplishing all of its aims without exception, Barbie would not even be on trial in Lyon in 1987, as all the witnesses against him would have been liquidated long ago.

Even as Barbie was finally facing justice in a trial for his crimes against humanity, Klarsfeld reminded the hushed courtroom, it was important not to forget all the other horrendous crimes he had committed for which *he would never be punished,* as the statute of limitations on war crimes had lapsed. So even if the Lyon Assize trial constituted the final episode in coming to terms with the "immense criminal enterprise" launched by the Gestapo in Lyon under Barbie's direction forty-five years earlier, the accused would never be fully accountable for all of his crimes. But if the full legal measure of Barbie's crimes could never be taken, on a more positive note Klarsfeld added that soon perhaps the Nazis' French accomplices, and specifically Jean Leguay and Maurice Papon, would finally face justice for their own crimes.[5]

In a rare moment in the Barbie trial, in which one of the lawyers on either side chose to speak of themselves in personal terms before the court,[6] Klarsfeld addressed his own wartime experience. He explained that, if not for the false back of a wardrobe his father had constructed and behind which the young Klarsfeld had been hidden, he would have been captured and deported to his death, as his father had been, during a Gestapo raid in wartime Nice, where the family had sought refuge. The story was well-known to the public and part of the pre-trial lore concerning the lawyer as well as a major part of his legend as a famed Nazi hunter over his long career. But in the Lyon courtroom, Klarsfeld framed the most traumatic episode of his childhood directly in relation to Barbie and his victims. Had it not been for the false back of the closet constructed by his father, Klarsfeld stated, he would have walked the ramp to the gas chambers at Auschwitz, just as had, tragically, the children of Izieu. Hidden as he was in the closet, he could hear cries of the less fortunate Jewish neighbour girls as they were struck by Gestapo officers, just as Simone Kadosche-Lagrange had been struck by Klaus Barbie.

In his relatively brief closing statement before the court, Serge Klarsfeld had succeeded in accomplishing a number of important, not to say crucial, tasks, not just in the moment but for the memory of the Barbie trial and its legacy. First, as a complement to the combined testaments of Barbie's victims, Klarsfeld had offered a compelling and convincing dissection of the criminality of the accused, not just in his personal choices but in the nature of the ideology and organizations he elected to serve. Moreover, as opposed to the analysis of how one becomes a Nazi given earlier by André Frossard, which, astute as it was, insisted on the mediocrity of figures like Barbie, Klarsfeld's analysis reckoned with the fuller dimensions of the man and his past that Truche had earlier in the trial attempted to get the accused to discuss. But for the purposes of the prosecution, this in no way made the accused more empathetic or tended to explain away his crimes. Quite the reverse. And in making the point that the trial of Klaus Barbie should not be the last such trial, and that Frenchmen likely guilty of similar charges should also be tried, Klarsfeld put the lie to the idea that Barbie was being scapegoated for these very same French that no one wished to prosecute.

Historically, of course Klarsfeld's statements during his closing statement were prescient, in that partially if not largely due to his own efforts, two trials of Vichy officials, Paul Touvier and Maurice Papon, on charges of crimes against humanity did occur in the 1990s. Both men, like Barbie, were found guilty. As noted, Jean Leguay died before he could be tried, although the French government pronounced his guilt in acknowledging his death.

In terms of the *memory* of the Barbie trial, Klarsfeld's moving *in memoriam* to the children of Izieu assured their near-sacred status in the memory of the trial and of the war itself for the French. And to the degree that in the 1990s especially the memory of Vichy would become increasingly Judaeocentric, as Henry Rousso has observed, the forty-four doomed children played no small part.[7]

A final, striking point about Serge Klarsfeld's statement before the Lyon Assize court is that, even if it is remembered primarily for its moving evocation of the Jewish children of Izieu, in its fuller scope and implications, Klarsfeld's remarks addressed *all* of Barbie's victims, Jews and resisters alike. And this despite the fact that earlier in 1985 Klarsfeld had been outspoken in his opposition to including some of Barbie's crimes against Resistance members among the crimes for which he would stand trial for crimes against humanity.

In his inclusivity Klarsfeld was not alone among the civil parties lawyers as they gave their closing statements. For example, Klarsfeld's colleague Roland Rappaport first addressed the Izieu children, noting that in Barbie's criminal dossier there was a tract published in the clandestine *Fraternité* from 1944 decrying the fate of these children while they were being held captive at Montluc Prison. The tract stated that a German officer was approached by a relief organization and asked if the children could be aided and comforted. The officer responded that there was no point in this, as the children "had to die." It was clear, Rappaport affirmed, that this German officer knew very well the fate of the Jews according to Nazi ideology and practice. And if he did, so, obviously, did Klaus Barbie.

After first addressing Barbie's Jewish victims in his remarks, Rappaport then turned his attention to Resistance victims, and specifically the women the Nazis deported to Ravensbrück. Of the 10,000 French women sent to Ravensbrück over the course of the war, Rappaport reminded the courtroom that only 3,000 had returned to France, most in terrible shape. Following the testimony of Lise Lesèvre, Geneviève de Gaulle-Anthonioz, and Marie-Claude Vaillant-Couturier, this was already painfully apparent to all those present in the courtroom. When the time came for his closing statement, Alain Jakubowicz, the lawyer for the Jewish Consistory of France, did likewise. In addressing these women directly (along with Jewish victims like Simone Kadosche-Lagrange), Jakubowicz stated: "When you spoke of the indignities and degradations that were imposed upon you, of your nudity, of the intimacy of the smells and memories that continue to haunt your nights, I wish to say to you, *Mesdames*, whatever your age, whatever the Calvary you have endured, you are beautiful, for all eternity."

While Rappaport and Jakubowicz chose to emphasize the shared suffering of Jewish and Resistance victims in expressing their solidarity with the latter, the renowned lawyer for the League of the Rights of Man, Henri Noguères, expressed the same solidarity and then went a step further. Noguères, who had earlier written a book denouncing Vergès for what he considered Vergès's calumnies against Jean Moulin and the Resistance,[8] declared at the outset of his closing statement that although both Barbie's Jewish and Resistance victims were victims of crimes against humanity there was no comparison between victims of the Holocaust and victims of the Nazis' other crimes. By the same token, there was no comparison between the children of Izieu and Barbie's Resistance victims.

Noguères did not elaborate on the distinction between Holocaust victims and other victims of Nazism before the court. He was more explicit, however, in discussing another comparison, dear to the defence, this one between Nazism's Jewish victims and France's victims during the Algerian conflict and indeed all other victims in Third World countries. As Noguères pointed out, Vergès was happy to rattle off a litany of these victims at any moment, but in doing so, he failed to mention the victims of Pol Pot in Cambodia, or of Idi Amin Dada in Uganda, or of Ayatollah Khomeini in Iran. Vergès's links to or sympathy for these figures was widely known. In not mentioning them, Noguères implied, the defence lawyer was being as selective as those whom he harshly criticized for their own supposed selectivity.

Where Algeria was concerned, Noguères, who had himself denounced French army actions there, including torture and murder, nevertheless described the comparison between Nazism's victims and French victims in Algeria as "odious." First, only *certain* army units were involved, not all. Second, there was never any intent to annihilate or exterminate an entire people in Algeria, as was the Nazis' intent where the Jews were

concerned. Most significantly – and going directly to the 1985 definition of crimes against humanity, which required that they be carried out
in the name of an ideologically hegemonic regime – Noguères underscored the fact that the French democratic and pluralistic republic was
not a regime of this sort.

Like Serge Klarsfeld's closing statement, Noguère's statement proved
to be prescient as well, but in a narrower context. More than the other
statements of the civil parties lawyers, Noguère's statement went directly
to the heart of the final defence Vergès and his colleagues would mount.
It was of course no secret that the defence counsel would seek to con-
flate Nazi victims with those of other Western and democratic regimes.
But in anticipating that move, Noguères had also made distinctions with
regard to applicable French law that in their clarity helped make these
arguments transparent and accessible to the jury. Perhaps more importantly, Noguères had correctly predicted Vergès's final move in his closing statement, which was to put France on trial instead of Klaus Barbie.
And as a final reminder of the hypocrisy of the defence's overall strategy,
Noguères pointed to the bitter irony of defending a Nazi, by definition
a believer in "Aryan" supremacy, which is to say white superiority, in the
name of the oppressed people of colour of the world.

If Noguères in his remarks sought to challenge in advance the arguments of the defence on the terrain of historical realities, comparisons,
and distinctions, Bernard de Bigault du Granrut did so essentially on the
level of the law, all the while stressing his aim of putting the jury's mind
at ease on these matters. This was necessary because from the outset
of the trial the defence had striven to give the jury, and France itself, a
"bad conscience" specifically on "three points related to the law." The
first concerned Barbie's supposed "illegal" extradition from Bolivia. De
Bigault stressed that France had issued an entirely legal international
arrest warrant for Barbie in 1982, and the new Bolivian government had
legitimately responded to it in expelling Barbie to French Guyana. Moreover, once there, Barbie himself made a fatal error that undermined in
advance this whole line of defence: he had stated that he was "of German
nationality" and so whatever protections Bolivian citizenship afforded
the accused were made null and void by his own statement.[9]

If all of this was inadequate to impeach the argument concerning
Barbie's "illegal" extradition from Bolivia, de Bigault turned to earlier
legal precedents dealing with the Nazis and their crimes, all of which
clearly related to Barbie's case. First, in the October 1943 Declaration
of Moscow, the Allies had warned the Nazis that they would be pursued
for their crimes after the war. Then, in February 1946, a UN declaration
stated that Nazi criminals were to be pursued wherever they had fled and

sent back to the countries where they had committed their crimes to be judged and punished. Bolivia had been part of the UN at the time and was therefore obliged to comply with its stated policies along these lines. In this light, Barbie's removal to France was entirely legitimate.

Second, de Bigault addressed the 1952 and 1954 convictions and defence efforts to persuade the jury and court that the crimes that served as the basis for these convictions were being retried in Lyon in 1987. This, de Bigault insisted, was absolutely not the case. The current trial focused crucially on Barbie's involvement in the *deportations* of Jews and resisters. In the 1952 and 1954 verdicts, the word "deportation," let alone the reality it represented, were nowhere to be found.

The major thrust of de Bigault's remarks in his closing statement focused on the third legal issue, the specific and indeed unique nature of crimes against humanity. In this instance, de Bigault declared, he was undertaking this discussion *both* in an effort to make the jury comfortable with the meaning of crimes against humanity *and* to remind them of the importance of their historical role as jurors in this trial. This jury, he stated, was the first French jury to ever deal with charges of crimes against humanity, and as such the jurors themselves were "creators of the law."

De Bigault began his presentation by stressing that since by their nature crimes against humanity were *international in nature* and thus transcended the national context of penal law, he well understood that the jury would have "scruples" in judging them. The problem, de Bigault observed, concerned "restricting" or limiting overmuch the crimes and victims to which the term applied, or conversely overextending or stretching its application indiscriminately to include crimes and victims which did not fit the definition itself. In addressing this matter, and leaving aside or more accurately dismissing the "derivations" of the defence as Truche had labelled them, de Bigault wanted to put the jury's and the court's minds at ease on the vexed and vexing question of including some crimes against the Resistance among the charges of crimes against humanity pending against Barbie. De Bigault reminded the court that critics of "extending" the definition in this way had already been eloquent witnesses in the trial, Elie Wiesel and André Frossard first among them. But in tracing international jurisprudence dealing with this matter all the way back to Nuremberg, de Bigault argued that Nuremburg itself did not restrict such crimes to crimes against Jews and other racial minorities. Indeed, its definition allowed for a more expansive determination. For his part, de Bigault stated, he shared the view of his "colleague" Serge Klarsfeld that in the current trial the children of Izieu were at the "summit" of such crimes. He added, however, that he also believed that the crimes against the Resistance at stake still fit the category as well. In summing up this argument for the court, de Bigault stated," just because there are gradations in the atrocious doesn't mean that the atrocious does not exist [in each case]." Referring the testimony of Marie-Claude Vaillant-Couturier, Geneviève de Gaulle-Anthonioz, and Lise Lesèvre and what they had witnessed in the camps, he added, "where the Jews were concerned they [the Nazis] wished to exterminate them immediately; as for the others, [the Nazis] needed to use them for labor for a certain time, only to liquidate them later."[10]

If the closing statements of civil parties lawyers Serge Klarsfeld, Henri Noguères, and Bernard de Bigault du Granrut stood out as arguably the most ambitious, comprehensive, and compelling statements in their range, scope, and power,[11] this did not mean that other statements, while less ambitious, failed to make substantive contributions to or score rhetorical points for the prosecution as well. Some, for example, addressed the hypocrisies of the defence and their strategies, as had Noguères and Jakubowicz, among others. Included in this group was Alain Gourion. Gourion pointed to the irony of the fact that Jean-Martin Mbemba, now defending a Nazi in the name of peoples of colour, had once praised the Jewish people. He had stated that African peoples could learn much from the latter about how to give voice to the sufferings of their people and, through this, to gain a greater degree of self-knowledge.

Other closing statements by civil parties lawyers challenged specific defence witnesses and defence arguments, or pointed to the testimony of the witnesses or the accused himself not heard in the courtroom. This testimony, they argued, confirmed either Barbie's guilt or his knowledge of the terrible fate that awaited the deportees at their ultimate destinations. On the first score, in his remarks Jakubowicz belatedly attacked the credibility of one of the defence's key witnesses, Jacques Forment de Launey. Reputed by the defence to be a well-regarded and objective historian, Forment de Launey, Jakubowicz pointed out, had written a history of World War II and in the discussion of the Vichy "not one word" on the deportation of the Jews.[12] Michel Zaoui in his statement addressed the responsibility of the accused in the UGIF round-up in 1943. While the trial had focused on the issue of Barbie's physical presence there and had heard the dubious testimony of Michel Kroskof-Thomas along these lines, Zaoui argued that this was not the crucial factor. What mattered was that Barbie was *responsible* for it. Here, Zaoui referred the court to a statement made by Barbie on 4 January 1985. While saying that he was not directly involved with the actions of the anti-Jewish section under him, Barbie nevertheless affirmed his ultimate responsibility for its actions: "When something is done, it is done. Once undertaken, I can no longer question exactions of this sort. The arrests having been made, it was necessary to maintain them" (K: P1/464). On the issue of Barbie's knowledge of the ultimate fate of the deportees, the civil parties lawyer Ugo Ianucci, unearthed surprising evidence that had not previously been mentioned in court. Ianuccu pointed out that during his interrogation, following his arrest in the immediate post-war years, Barbie's French henchman Francis André, or *gueule tordue* ("twisted mug"), told interrogators that he had told Francine Gudefin after her arrest, "you are going to die in Germany." If André knew this, Iannucci asked the court, how could his superior Barbie not know?

Other civil parties lawyers stressed anew the legitimacy or import of specific pieces of evidence, most notably the Izieu telex. In his criticism of the testimony of Jacques Forment de Launey, Michel Zaoui also criticized the historian for his claim that the Izieu telex the court had was not the original. As Zaoui pointed out, this claim was made erroneously because De Launey in his analysis had failed to take into account distortions of the original document made in the process of reproducing its image for books, pamphlets, and other publications. Zaoui's comments about the authenticity the telex as it turned out proved to be a helpful complement to Truche's own analysis of its authenticity in his summation. Indeed, by the time Vergès gave his own closing argument, the majority of the challenges to the document's authenticity appeared to be resolved. And thanks to the closing statement of the sole German civil parties lawyer present at the trial, Elfrun Andréani-Jungblut, the defence might have preferred to avoid discussion of the document altogether. In a surprisingly compelling linguistic analysis of the German language used by the author of the telex, Andréani-Jungblut underscored the disdain and indeed toxicity of that language in describing the arrest of the Jewish children, very much in keeping, she argued, with Nazism's ferociously anti-Semitic hatred. For example, in the telex Barbie described the round-up itself in language one would use for "emptying a nest" of brigands. She added that the German word Barbie used for the capture of the children was the legal term for "arrest." All this implied, she emphasized, that in Barbie's eyes the children were not politically innocent adolescents, but rather criminals fully deserving of arrest and punishment.

Some civil parties lawyers, the minority in fact, focused their remarks on their clients, stressing the latter's ongoing trauma and suffering not as part of a group but as individuals. For example, Joe Nordmann, one of Lise Lesèvre's lawyers, emphasized the extent to which his client's suffering as a result of Barbie's crimes had to be endless, and not merely in a physical sense, from the wounds she had received. Lesèvre, he speculated, must have been haunted up to the present by the thought that, had she betrayed her Resistance colleagues to Barbie, her son might still be alive. In the audience, Lesèvre betrayed no emotion.

Finally, a number of the civil parties lawyers directly addressed the duties and obligations of the court and jury in what they emphasized was an historic and unprecedented Assize court trial. In his own powerful closing statement, Zaoui asserted that notwithstanding the chief prosecutor's insistence that the Barbie trial was a "normal" Assize court, the Barbie trial was, in fact, an exception. In concrete terms, the Assize courts rarely, if ever, dealt with crimes committed forty years earlier. The usual length of time lapsed between crime and judgment was two to three years. Moreover, the crimes examined usually occurred in one or a few instants. Here, they spread over eighteen months. Finally, in the Barbie trial, the crimes being judged were, for the first time, crimes against humanity, and the CV of the accused, usually central to deliberations of the court, in this instance was "secondary" to the ideology the accused embraced. All this only reinforced the unique importance of the trial at hand.

To the argument that Barbie was an old man and that for any number of reasons the humane thing to do was to "pardon" and "forget," Alain Jakubowicz reminded the jury that their duty was not to indulge in these gestures, but rather to "judge and sanction" the accused. He added, "No sanction, no matter how heavy, will ever be commensurate with the crimes committed by Klaus Barbie." In addition, as de Bigault would emphasize to the jury in his own statement, a crime against humanity was a crime *against all of humanity*, and it was not the right or place of a small group of that humanity, like this jury, to issue a pardon in the name of all of humanity.

Finally, what of Barbie's punishment, and of extenuating circumstances that would oblige the court and jury to deliver a lesser sentence to the accused? While recommendations along these lines fell primarily to the chief prosecutor, several civil parties lawyers weighed in on these matters as well. Charles Korman, for example, noted that Klaus Barbie had always claimed to be a proud soldier of the Reich. But in this instance, not only had this soldier not admitted his crimes, he had also run away from the fight. By any standard, then, he deserved no sympathy and had given the court no evidence to support the idea of extenuating circumstances. Echoing Korman's position, Paul Lombard also asserted that there were no grounds for allowing the accused to benefit from extenuating circumstances. As a "soldier" Barbie had during the war followed a "scorched earth" strategy in Lyon. Now, forty-five years later, his strategy was that of the "empty chair." Clearly, Klaus Barbie was in no way worthy of the court's sympathy or clemency.

The Prosecutor General's Summation

In his judicial philosophy, as in his performance in the Lyon courtroom, chief prosecutor Pierre Truche was, as one admirer succinctly described him, the "anti-Vergès."[13] Whereas Jacques Vergès, following his self-described Nietzschean, indeed Dionysian aspiration to "enlighten by striking down" to "rise up through madness" repeatedly provoked and outraged the courtroom, Truche followed a more modest and measured approach that relied on reason and appeals to the court's and jury's *bon sens*, or "good sense," to be persuasive. Truche's role, as Pierre Mérindol observed, was simply "to convince" (296). Logical and empirical in his approach, Truche, as he would state repeatedly after the trial, considered the meaning and definition of crimes against humanity not to be immutably written in stone or to consist of artificial legal constructs, but to be a work in progress. Indeed, in an interview given to the *Nouvel Observateur* shortly after the trial, Truche told his interlocutor that "the Barbie trial represents one further step in our ongoing reflections on the notion of crimes against humanity."[14] Moreover, for Truche, the status of the prosecutor in a trial such as this was not that of a supreme arbiter of justice bent on retribution but that of a simple human being, acutely aware of his or her failings and vulnerabilities. In a 2001 essay, "*Juger, être jugé*," Truche affirmed that in order to perform his or her duties professionally and equitably, the prosecutor must first acknowledge his or her own fallibility. S/he must recognize the degree to which his or her own judgments, like those of any person, can be clouded by beliefs, tastes, prejudices, and especially personal bonds and relationships. Indeed, on the last two scores, Truche wrote, "It is useless to proclaim one's independence if one is not lucid about links of dependence. It is only after one recognizes this that one can achieve impartiality in having no *parti pris* for any particular party. While keeping in mind of course, that one can always be wrong" ("*Juger, être jugé*" 28–9.) The prosecutor must also remember that in civil as well as penal cases, "it is not only the facts that one judges; there is also a person being judged. As mandated by the French penal code, "every sentence handed down must be personalized" ("*Juger, être jugé*"18).

All of this is especially true, Truche emphasized, in a case where the prosecutor is confronted with "a particularly odious crime" or a "gross abuse of civil authority." In these instances especially, the prosecutor "must not allow him- or herself to be carried away by personal feelings. S/he must by all means avoid the vengeful finger of the prosecutor pointed at the accused, the glare full of disdain, and above all the words that demean and exclude" ("*Juger, être jugé*" 32).

When Truche was brought back from Marseille to his native Lyon to handle the Barbie prosecution by justice minister Robert Badinter, he had, as Maurice Szafran wrote, the reputation of a magistrate who believed integrally in the criminal dossier itself. Indeed, Truche had the reputation of "vampirizing" the dossier, of learning it down to the tiniest detail, and in a criminal proceeding, of relying on it above all else. By the time he gave his summation in Lyon, everyone present at the Barbie trial was aware of his mastery of the Barbie dossier as well. But, according to Szafran, the question remained as to whether in the Lyon courtroom Truche would rely on the dossier *to the exclusion* of other considerations, such a witness testimony. Given the emotional and persuasive power of so much of the latter, for the chief prosecutor to ignore that testimony completely would be at the very least to squander an invaluable resource for the prosecution. But on the other hand, to rely too heavily or exclusively on that testimony in making his case, given the failings of some of the witnesses, could prove risky as well.

In the event, Truche not only astutely marshalled all the resources at his disposal, in his summation he also managed to apply the guiding principles others recognized in his work and that he would discuss some fourteen years later in "*Juger, être jugé.*" Renouncing from the outset the grandiloquence and theatricality of a number of the civil parties lawyers (and Vergès in most of his courtroom pronouncements), Truche began not with the dossiern but with an homage to Barbie's many victims who had come to testify in the Lyon courtroom. He affirmed that "crimes against humanity presuppose a plunge into the inhuman," and that this was precisely what those in the courtroom had experienced in listening to the horrific and gut-wrenching testimony of these victims recounted over the past several weeks. But after a few brief references to these experiences of the "inhuman" in a voice whose emotion he visibly worked to control, Truche stated that these testimonies would not be the subject of his summation because, as he put it, "I do not have the words to say it." His silence, he added, was a sign only of his "respect" and "compassion."

Before turning to the heart of his presentation which concerned the history and nature of crimes against humanity, Nazi criminality and Barbie's involvement with it, and finally the three crucial charges and evidence against Barbie, Truche sought to dispel two myths circulating around the trial. The first concerned the notion that crimes against humanity were essentially an affair among white peoples, invented by the outraged Allies to punish the Nazis for targeting other white peoples. Truche noted that similar tribunals to Nuremberg had been established to punish Japanese war criminals, and so *not* only white peoples were concerned. He added that the Nazis themselves did not consider themselves part of the broader race of white peoples, but in fact, a superior Aryan and Nordic race.

The second myth was that the Barbie trial, like the Nuremberg trial before it, was essentially a demonstration of victor's justice. To this Truche responded by reminding the court that, following the war, a *defeated* Germany had in the late 1940s put some 6,000 Nazis on trial, and this was more than the Allies had done.

In turning to crimes against humanity, Truche's explanations were simple and straightforward. As Mérindol observed, Truche avoided both "lyricism and anathema" (296). He began by providing a brief overview of the history of crimes against humanity to explain first why Barbie was only being tried for these crimes now. The jury and court were of course already aware of the fact that such laws had only been declared imprescriptible in French law in 1964, and so in fact were not on the books, so to speak, at the time of Barbie's earlier trials in 1952 and 1954. But Truche's approach was different. He argued that although crimes against humanity were applied along with other charges to the Nazi leaders at Nuremberg, the actual *sentencing* of these men offered no clear directives for subsequent courts on either the application of such charges to an accused or what punishment was appropriate to mete out. Quoting the French judge Donnedieu de Vabres, who had been present at Nuremberg, Truche noted that following the conclusion of the trial, Donnedieu had expressed his disappointment in one aspect of its outcome. Referring specifically to crimes against humanity, Donnedieu had stated that "the category of crimes against humanity, slipped in by the back door in the statute itself, following the judgement and sentences and as a consequence of them, simply evaporated." Given Donnedieu's attitude, it was not surprising that French jurisprudence on such crimes remained "poor" in Truche's words, and so there was not even a question of applying such statutes in 1952 and 1954.

Truche then turned to the vexed issue of crimes against humanity as defined in French law and as applied in the Barbie trial. For Truche, as many in the court and press were aware, this was an especially difficult subject. When the controversy over the December 1985 decision by the Paris Court of Cassation to include some crimes against Resistance members among the charges of crimes against humanity against Klaus Barbie, Truche had sided with the lower court in Lyon, which had rejected the notion that these crimes were crimes against humanity. He had, moreover, been public with his views for which, according to Pierre Mérindol, he was "harshly criticized" (14) by the Court of Cassation. With his usual simplicity, Truche had made his position clear:

> On the one side, there is the Resistance fighter who is informed of the consequences of being arrested on his physical constitution and his life, and has courageously accepted the dangers he faces. Perhaps, he carries poison with him to end his days if the torture he knows he will face proves unbearable. On other occasions, with arms in hand, he is capable of resisting capture, individually or collectively with other fighters.
>
> On the other side, there is the Jewish child of two years of age, like the one who was deported on 11 August 1944 on the last convoy from Lyon and who doesn't even know yet what it means to be a Jew. There are old people, there are couples without means of defense who represent no threat to the occupation army and who are therefore "innocents." This means that they do no harm, that they are "non-belligerent." And the opposite of "innocence" or "innocent" is not "guilty" but "belligerent." Is it not natural that the greatest legal protections should be accorded to those who are without protection? (qtd. in Mérindol 14)

In explaining his views on crimes against humanity in the Lyon Court of Assize in 1987, Truche once again recalled the Jewish child he had referred to in his 1985 statement. Imagine being a Jewish family in 1942 Lyon, he asked the jury, expecting a child. The expectant mother is of course making future plans for that unborn child, but should she be arrested by the Nazis, the child will either be aborted or drowned after birth. The child in question, Truche continued, was in fact born on 27 April 1943. His name was Guy Haltoz. He was the youngest child deported to his death on the 11 August 1944 convoy, simply because "his path crossed that of an SS." The point Truche continued, was that from the moment of his conception he was condemned to death if he simply encountered a Nazi, despite the fact that he represented no threat and there was no value or gain to be had in harming him.

Truche then asked the jury to recall the testimony of another deportee, this person a member of the Resistance, who had testified that it was "perfectly normal" to be arrested as a member of the Resistance. And, he added, as the Resistance member Alice Joly-Vansteenberghe had testified, she knew exactly what risk she was running in joining the Resistance.[15] For these Resistance deportees, Truche continued, when they arrived at the Nazi camps it was then that they encountered a "gigantic inhumanity." But if they had not opposed the Nazis, they would in all likelihood not have met this particular fate.

The Resistance Truche observed was a "marvelous epic," all the more so because the humblest of people had joined it to build the nation of the future. Nevertheless, the lives of these individuals did not take a "turn toward the perilous" unless they were caught. For the Jews, and Roma as well, Truche emphasized, their lives were "nothing but perilous."

In choosing these examples Truche was once again making the distinction he had made in 1985, but with a difference. If crimes against humanity presupposed a "plunge into inhumanity," this was the fate of the Jew from the moment of his or her conception. But for the resister, this "plunge into inhumanity" only occurred when s/he entered a Nazi camp. Or, as Mérindol phrased it, "For the Resisters, there was no 'Final Solution.' But this did not mean that, as was the case for the Jews, the final destination of the trip was death" (305). In the end, resister and Jew alike shared, if not an identical, at least a common fate. Both were ultimately victims of crimes against humanity in their respective "plunges into inhumanity." Nevertheless a "hierarchy" of sorts within that category had been maintained.

Arguably the most compelling moment of Truche's summation concerned the issue of Nazism's intention to destroy, to obliterate, its enemies and in that context, Barbie's knowledge of the ultimate fate of those he deported. On the first score, having cited the statements by Hitler and other Nazi leaders concerning the absolute mercilessness necessary to carry out the Nazi enterprise, Truche asked the jury a simple, "common sense" question. How was it possible to imagine that, the war over, the Nazis, who believed fervently that their Reich would last a thousand years, would release the inmates of their camps? For the most part, these internees were human wrecks, barely alive, weighing no more than fifty or sixty pounds. This would be an embarrassment, a scandal the regime would never tolerate. By the same token, Barbie having tortured the likes of Lise Lesèvre to within an inch of her life and then deporting her, how was it possible to imagine that this was done with the idea that she would one day return? Clearly, this was not possible, and the jury, like the accused, understood this only too well. Besides, were such humane considerations even possible in the mind of Klaus Barbie and his fellow SS members? Where Barbie was concerned, Truche affirmed, echoing the assessments of the psychiatric team that had testified earlier, "Barbie, who was never confronted with anything outside his own mental constructions, possesses a personality of such a remarkable rigidity that it completely prevents him from having any opening on the outside world" (qtd. in Mérindol 303). As for Barbie's fellow Gestapo members in Lyon, Truche recalled to the jury that one of those who worked with them noted that following a drunken 1943 New Year's party for these members, one of the participants had gone to Montluc Prison, ordered the release of a number of prisoners, and shot them dead. As a final and crucial point, Truche asked, was it possible that in sending resisters off to the camps that, once there, Barbie believed that they would be detained in "humane conditions"? Had he as well as his subordinates not told many of those he deported that the conditions in deportation would be "worse than death"? If they were not held in "humane conditions" in these camps, Truche continued, then according to the Court of Cassation they were victims of crimes against humanity. Barbie had knowingly submitted them to this fate.

Like his discussion of crimes against humanity, the Nazi enterprise, and the attitudes and mentality of SS men like Barbie, Truche's presentation of the evidence against the accused concerning the three major crimes of which he was accused was straightforward and clear. But first, the prosecutor general addressed the reliability of the witnesses whose testimony had buttressed the material evidence of these crimes. Specifically, Truche drew a sharp distinction between those who had *suffered* at the hands of the accused through interrogation, torture, or deportation, and those who had not. Truche reminded the jury of the testimony of the psychiatrist Tony Lainé, who had told the court that when one experiences great suffering at the hands of a torturer like Barbie and his men, one is capable of recalling the exact experience many years later, and also a facial or other detail of one's tormentor. On these grounds, Truche continued, the jury should believe the testimony of those who had experienced such trauma. By contrast, the testimony those who had not directly suffered at the hands of the accused was likely less reliable, and not adequate grounds to convict Barbie. On the basis of this distinction, Truche told the jury that they should discount the testimony of Michel Kroskof-Thomas and Julien Favet. It was Favet, a humble and facially deformed farm worker who worked near the home of the children of Izieu who had claimed to have seen and been briefly addressed by Barbie on the morning of the roundup. In Favet's case Truche affirmed that he did not question his honesty or good intentions, but only his ability to remember.

Truche made his presentation of the evidence for Barbie's responsibility for the UGIF raid and round-up, the round-up of the children of Izieu, and the 11 August train convoy to the camps in the east in chronological order. Where specific documents were concerned – and Truche reminded the court that, fully aware of the reprehensibility of their actions, the Nazis had attempted to destroy these documents at the end of the war – it was necessary to put them in the proper context. In keeping with the *fuehrerprinzip*, these reflected the absolute authority of one's superior and one's own absolute authority over all those under one's command and control. As André Frossard had explained earlier in the trial, this was exactly the trade-off Klaus Barbie had bargained for in becoming a committed Nazi.

Where the round-up at the *Union Générale des Israélites de France* was concerned, there were a number of exchanges between Lyon and Paris in the form of telexes and reports, some of which existed as evidence in concrete form in Barbie's criminal file, and some of which could be surmised on the basis of the documents available. Taken together, they confirmed Barbie's absolute responsibility for the round-up, even if his physical presence there, *pace* Michel Krokof-Thomas, could not be established with any certainty. And if Barbie was in fact present, Truche pointed out, it would have been the only crime included in the accused's criminal dossier in which the Gestapo had shown the least bit of "humanity" in allowing three individuals to depart. Barbie of course denied remembering the round-up, then claimed he had nothing to do with it or that it had been carried out by a *Sondercommando*, or special commando force, sent from Paris on orders from Paris or Berlin and which had no connection with Barbie's Section Four in Lyon. These claims, as Truche pointed out only slightly ironically, "conformed with what we know of the accused."

With the help of three documents, however, Barbie's *responsibility* within the Nazi hierarchy could be absolutely established, according to Truche. The operation, the prosecutor general reminded the jury, took place on 9 February 1943. The next day, 10 February, Paris headquarters had received news of it, and the message was addressed to not just anyone but to Helmut Knochen himself. How did one know this? Because Knochen had sent a telex back to Lyon the same day asking about the deportation of those arrested to Paris. Knochen's telex had been destroyed, Truche continued, so how was its existence confirmed? Because in documents which had been sent from Lyon subsequently, Knochen's telex was referred to explicitly. In fact, two written documents were sent from Lyon on 11 February. Both were signed by Klaus Barbie. One was a telex addressed directly to Knochen, which arrived that evening in Paris. A response to Knochen's own telex, it contained details of the operation "executed from this location" and confirmed that those arrested were in the custody of German authorities. The telex confirmed two things, Truche insisted. First, the UGIF roundup had *originated* with the Lyon Gestapo and was therefore *not* an operation carried out by a *Sonderkommando* acting on orders issued elsewhere. Second, because the detainees were in the hands of German authorities, this was not an operation carried out by the French police.

The second document sent from Lyon on 11 February and which arrived in Paris the next day was a more detailed report of the operation. It was also addressed to Knochen. Signed by Barbie, it included an additional statement written at the end of the report, also signed by Barbie, and confirming that the Jewish captives would not in fact be sent to the *Wehrmacht* prison at Chalon-sur-Saône, as stated in the body of the report, but would be sent elsewhere, as that prison was full. The significance of the addition, Truche affirmed, was that it proved that it was *Barbie* who was overseeing the entire affair and that he was directly involved in this instance in arranging the *deportation* of Jews to the camps. And this Truche concluded, was a crime against humanity.

The third document, sent on 15 February and also signed by Barbie, confirmed that two of the eighty-six Jews arrested had escaped. Because Montluc Prison was full, the Jews had been sent to the *Fort de Lamothe*. Their escape had been discovered at the moment of their deportation. Barbie assured his superiors in Paris that all efforts were being undertaken to track the escapees down and, although Truche did not mention this in his summation, Barbie also stressed in the report to his superiors that it was the *Wehrmacht* and not his own Gestapo forces who were responsible for guarding the Jews when they escaped. Eager in his communications with his superiors to demonstrate his zeal in arresting and deporting Jews, Barbie revealed himself to be just as eager to avoid responsibility for developments that might bring him discredit.[16]

Truche began his discussion of the arrest and deportation of the children of Izieu by acknowledging that, as everyone agreed, it was the "gravest event," the most heinous crime in Barbie's criminal dossier. Moreover, it was undertaken because, as the psychiatrist Gonin had testified earlier, for Barbie "the 'other' is always a danger, even if that 'other' is a child."

But if Truche's presentation on Izieu began with a measured evocation of the horror of the crime and the mindset of the criminal responsible for it, the rest of the discussion was more "technical," as he warned the jury. The key to the matter, he stated, was the much discussed and disputed telex Barbie sent to his superiors reporting the action in concise and, as the German civil parties lawyer Elfrun Andreani-Jungblut described it, brutal terms.

The telex itself, Truche recalled, was first cited at the Nuremberg Tribunal, when Edgar Faure spoke of it on 6 February 1946. At the time, Faure (as Vergès liked to point out) had not mentioned that the telex was signed by Klaus Barbie, preferring instead to speak about what it revealed about the Nazi system itself: "I think that there is something that is even more striking and horrible than the concrete fact of the kidnapping of these children. It is the administrative nature of the summary of it which, moving up the administrative ladder, leads to discussions in which different functionaries discuss it calmly, as part of the normal procedures of their service. It is the fact that all the gears of the State, and I'm speaking of the Nazi state, are put into motion on such an occasion and with such an end in mind."

In Truche's more technical presentation, the implications of the telex as Faure had presented them forty years earlier gradually became clear. First, Truche noted, the fact that the telex Faure cited was authentic, and not a forgery recently concocted and designed to frame Barbie, was confirmed by the fact that copies of this telex were held in archives in the United States and The Hague (where all the Nuremberg archives were kept). It was absurd, moreover, to argue that it had been forged between April 1944, when it was written, and when it fell into French hands in 1945, as there was no need to frame Barbie then. He was safely on the run, and there were no charges pending against him or courts to try him in the final chaotic days of the end of the French Occupation and the defeat of Nazi Germany.

Truche then turned to the content of the telex, and observed, first, that there was a handwritten note at the bottom of the telex, added in Paris by Röthke after its reception there, acknowledging the arrest and stressing that normal procedures should be followed in lodging the children before their deportation. What did the addition of the note prove? Most crucially, it confirmed that in acknowledging that he was being apprised of the operation, Röthke was also confirming that he *was only now being made aware of operation itself.* That is to say, the note confirmed that the operation did not originate with orders from Paris or Berlin, for that matter. *It was rather a local operation,* initiated by the Gestapo in Lyon. Additionally, the fact that there was no reference number in the corner of the telex referring to a previously established dossier meant that *no such dossier existed.*

Truche then turned to Barbie's own typed signature at the bottom of the telex. To the suggestion that this signature had been added subsequently and was not on the original telex, Truche pointed out that this idea was contradicted by the existence of a "typographical difficulty" shared by both the body of the telex and Barbie's name. In both, the letter "B" was separated slightly from the letters that followed.[17]

Finally, where the Izieu telex was concerned, Truche stressed that Barbie was aware of the document's existence by the time of his return to Lyon in 1983. He knew that it constituted proof of his guilt and that he needed to concoct a story to deny personal responsibility for the round-up itself. In fact, Truche pointed out, Barbie was aware of the existence of the telex since 1972, when Beate Klarsfeld, accompanied by Ita Halaunbrunner, who had lost two children at Izieu, arrived in Bolivia to denounce Barbie-Altmann publicly, referring to the telex and to Barbie's signature on it as proof of his guilt. When Barbie returned to Lyon, he stated to the investigating magistrate *not that the telex was a fraud*, but rather that he was "vaguely aware" of it and that in any case it was an operation carried out by Wenzel, head of Section 4-B, on direct orders from Adolph Eichmann in Berlin. That this was a lie and that Barbie *was* responsible for the operation was confirmed by the initials "I.A." next to his signature. The letters stood for *Im Auftrag* in German, meaning "By Order of."

The final charge of crimes against humanity against Barbie to be discussed was the accused's responsibility for the "last convoy" of 11 August 1944. In this case there were no documents to prove his responsibility, but rather the testimony of several witnesses. These witnesses, Truche reminded the jury, testified both to Barbie's presence at Montluc Prison, when the deportees had been rousted from their cells early the morning of 11 August, and on the train platform as they were about to leave. The fact that their testimony varied as to the clothes Barbie was wearing as well as what he had said or did not say mattered little, as all these witnesses were were certain of his presence.

Deprived of specific material evidence or documents in discussing the 11 August 1944 "last convoy," in his summation, Truche chose to present to the jury the broader circumstances surrounding its departure and the larger role Barbie had played in the affair. First, he stressed that the situation of the Nazis themselves in France and in Lyon itself was increasingly dire at that moment. The Allies had landed in Normandy and were making progress inland, the Resistance was intensifying its activities as well as their magnitude, especially in the Lyon region. As the jury and court were aware, the accused himself had been involved in combat missions against the latter in the countryside. True to their mission to the end, the Nazis, disposing of one last train to be sent to the east, opted to fill it with Resistance and Jewish captives alike. What was Klaus Barbie's precise role in this? In addition to organizing the last convoy, in an act that rivalled the horror of the Izieu round-up, Barbie had made it his mission to gather up the Jewish children of those Jews who were to be deported. Many of these children had been dispersed to children's foyers around Lyon while their parents were in prison. Barbie then brought them back to their parents so that they could be deported as well. On the train trip to the East, in terrible conditions and even before they reached their destinations, many of the deportees died. The statistics concerning these deaths spoke for themselves. Out of 842 deportees, 373 died in route. Of these, fifty-two were children. Truche assured the jury that no Assize court in French history had dealt with a crime of this magnitude.

In fulfilling his obligation as chief prosecutor, Truche concluded his summation by addressing the matter of extenuating circumstances, a matter the jury would need to deal with in sentencing Barbie, if found guilty. Truche developed his argument against leniency for Barbie along three lines. First, at Nuremberg it had been established that following orders was no excuse for the crimes committed by the Nazis. However, "if justice demanded it" the fact that one followed orders *could* be taken into consideration. How might this option apply to the case of Klaus Barbie? For Truche, the issue came down to whether Barbie did more or less than what was required to satisfy his superiors. Based on the evidence, Truche concluded, Barbie could possibly have done more, been even more zealous, but *he could also have done much less and still satisfied his superiors.* Therefore, Barbie deserved no clemency.

Second, addressing the view that Barbie was merely a scapegoat standing in for French collaborators and accomplices who had gone unpunished, Truche referred the jury to the post-war Purge. At that time, Truche argued, many more French were punished and executed than their Nazi overlords. This argument could therefore be dismissed.

The final issue to be addressed was whether or not it was just and appropriate to try the frail and aging Nazi forty years after the fact. Here again, Truche saw no argument for clemency. First, the graves of those tortured and murdered by Barbie and his men still existed. They had not gone away. Moreover, rather than repent his crimes, the former SS lieutenant in Lyon remained outspokenly firm in his Nazi convictions. Then, referring back to Barbie's claim that the Nazi movement had been betrayed by its own members, Truche pointed out that the traitors Barbie mentioned were just the small fry. They did not include the leaders and ideologues like Himmler, Goering, and Hitler himself. These were and remained untouchable icons for Barbie. Finally, Truche noted, all of these men had paid in one way or another for their crimes. Even Barbie's direct superior, Helmut Knochen, had spent ten years in prison, whereas Barbie had never been punished. Given all these considerations, perhaps the victims themselves could cite extenuating circumstances for Barbie's crimes, but he, Truche, could not.

Jacques Vergès in 1989. Serge Mouraret/Alamy Stock Photo

Chapter Seven

Barbie's Defence Takes Centre Stage

Part One: Jacques Vergès, Devil's Advocate, and the "Trial by Rupture"

To the extent that the Barbie trial, like other historic trials, is remembered primarily for the colourful and even scandalous individuals who played important roles in these trials, it is fair to say that along with Pierre Truche and Serge Klarsfeld, Jacques Vergès stands out as an iconic figure of the 1987 Lyon trial for crimes against humanity. This is true not just because of the deliberately provocative and controversial role Vergès played before and during the trial, but also because of his well-earned reputation as a rebel, a maverick, and a politically radical lawyer (and essayist and novelist) who spent his long career defending controversial political actors and in a number of instances, political pariahs. These included revolutionaries, terrorists, tyrants, and deposed dictators. At the start of his career Vergès defended the Algerian terrorist and bomb planter Djamila Bouhared, for whom he was able to secure a presidential pardon from French president René Coty and whom he later married.[1] Vergès went on to defend Palestinian terrorists, members of Germany's radical leftist Baader-Meinhof gang, and, much later, the famed international terrorist Carlos. In the late 1990s and early 2000s, Vergès was consulted for the defence of Serbian strongman Slobodan Milosevic when Milosevic stood trial in The Hague. Vergès was also apparently consulted for the defence of Iraqi dictator Saddam Hussein after his downfall and capture.

If these clients were not enough to secure for Vergès a scandalous reputation, his friendships, expensive tastes, and lavish habits contributed to that reputation as well. Vergès was proud of his friendships with Khmer Rouge leaders and genocidal killers like Pol Pot, as well as PLO leader Yassar Arafat and the Swiss-Nazi financier François Genoud. In filmed interviews with Vergès he enjoyed showing off his large, impressively decorated office, replete with ancient statuaries, lavish carpets, and an extraordinary collection of chess sets. In these interviews, Vergès was often filmed smoking expensive Cuban cigars. At the Barbie trial, as noted, Vergès stayed at the four-star Sofitel Hotel in the heart of Lyon. When asked in 2013 what he remembered most about the Barbie trial, he stated that he recalled chocolates from the famed Bernachon chocolate maker. Proust, after all, had his *madeleines* so why shouldn't he, Vergès, have his chocolates? The lawyer added ironically that chocolates were all that was left to him in Lyon, as the prosecution and the civil parties lawyers had kept the "lofty sentiments and beautiful words" for themselves (*De mon proper aveu* 98). When asked how, as a committed leftist revolutionary, he could justify and indulge such bourgeois and decadent tastes, Vergès responded that "one could wish for the end of a world without ceasing to appreciate its poisonous flowers" (*Aveu* 104).

But if to all appearances Jacques Vergès enjoyed his scandalous reputation as well as epithets given to him, like "terror's lawyer," the "devil's lawyer," the "luminous bastard" and the "grand inquisitor," this did not mean that, at heart, he was merely a superficial showman who enjoyed his role as scourge of the *bourgeoisie* and its hypocritical institutions. Vergès was also well educated and well read. As noted, he enjoyed presenting himself as an intellectual and a man of letters, frequently showing off his literary erudition in the courtroom as well as in his writings.

Most importantly, Vergès considered himself *un homme engagé*, a committed leftist revolutionary who was deadly serious about his political beliefs and the rage he felt towards white Europeans and their allies. In short, he detested all those who colonized and continued to colonize Third World countries and exploit underprivileged people of colour everywhere. The son of a father from Réunion and a Vietnamese mother, Vergès stated that he had experienced colonialist oppression firsthand, and the humiliation of having to step out of the way to let white colonizers pass stayed with him his whole life. When it was suggested to him that he could not imagine the experience of wearing the yellow star as a Jew in Nazi-occupied Europe, he responded that his mother could, as she was yellow-skinned all over and the victim of a comparable prejudice.

In his 2013 autobiography *De mon proper aveu* (on the cover of which he is photographed smoking a cigar), Vergès emphasized several crucial ways in which his background and upbringing had shaped his attitudes and persona. These characteristics, moreover, were readily apparent during the Barbie trial. First, Vergès emphasized that the central issue of his life was what he called the "question of colonialism." This "question" he maintained, "traversed my very body, from one end to the other" (13).

Second, his background and his mixed-race heritage made him a solitary figure, not afraid, as he put it, "to affirm my humanity without feeling the need to hide my egotism." This allowed Vergès to "disdain critics whose counsels would reduce me to being a man of the herd" (14). Finally, the lawyer wrote that he did not "share the dream of some of a peaceful world where there would be no more contradiction and conflict, a vain nostalgia for a lost paradise." Having discovered through Nietsche "the hidden continent of the super human," his preference was to dazzle, outrage, and indeed provoke conflict and dissention, all the while demonstrating his own superiority.

Whatever Vergès's anti-colonialist and revolutionary convictions and Nietschean pretensions, as he reveals in *De mon proper aveu*, there was also a Pascalian and even Jansenistic pessimism concerning human nature and the human condition whose political implications seemed to ignore ideological lines that his revolutionary creed would tend to confirm. Referring to the figure of the torturer, Vergès stated that "if the torturer disturbs us as much as he does, it is because he reveals the latent duplicity that grows in us in critical moments" (100). And whereas the Barbie trial could and *should* have allowed for an exploration for this capacity for duplicity in all human beings, or as Vergès phrased it in *De mon propre aveu*, to "sound the abyss of the human heart," instead the "good souls" who ran the trial "spit derisively" into that abyss. They did this in condemning Barbie and denying the kinship that all shared with the accused (100).

Given Vergès's evident pessimism and his stated conviction that all humans have the capacity to become torturers themselves, it is not surprising that the torturers he described in *De mon propre aveu*, along with their minions as well as their hierarchical superiors, were taken from countries across the political and ideological spectrum, from democracies to dictatorships to genocidal regimes. For Vergès, moreover, these torturers were all motivated by what they perceived to be higher political ideals. Barbie, for example, was motivated by a dream of a "Great Germany"; Colonel Aussarresses, who tortured FLN prisoners for the French army, was driven by the idea of a "Great France"; and American guards at Guantanamo believed they were championing the "American way of life." Duch, the infamous Khmer Rouge executioner and director of the regime's S-21 prison, was motivated by the ideal of the "triumph of socialism" (*Aveu* 101).

Below these "professional" torturers were the "auxiliaries," those excluded from their own societies and cultures, the "amateurs and butchers" whose sadism frightened others and for whom the defeat of their country offered the possibility of avenging themselves against it.

These included Francis André, who worked for Barbie, and the Iraqis who worked for the American army. Perhaps the quintessential fiction embodiment of Vergès's "auxiliary," although he does not mention him, is the eponymous anti-hero of Louis Malle's 1974 film about a French collaborator, *Lacombe Lucien.*

Lastly, there are what Vergès labelled as the *Monsieurs les donneurs d'ordre,* the "gentlemen who give the orders." There is "no blood under their carefully manicured fingernails." Moreover, as opposed to their subordinates, who are "all of a piece," these men are "double": "elegant, intriguing, and ambivalent." In Vichy France they were the René Bousquets; in Nazi Germany, the Albert Speers; and for the Colonel Aussaresses in Algeria, François Mitterrand. For the Guntanamo guards, the "gentleman giving orders" was Donald Rumsfeld. According to Vergès, these *Messieurs* were and are above all deft survivors. For example, despite his crucial role in the Nazi genocide, Albert Speer got off with a sentence of only twenty years at Nuremberg, unlike his less adroit fellow-accused, many of whom were sentenced to death. Ever the "double," the protean figure, Speer succeeded in convincing the Allies of his democratic and anti-communist sentiments, and in a gesture of "extreme elegance," according to Vergès, Speer accepted responsibility for Nazi crimes while denying he knew anything about them (103).

Vergès's ambivalence concerning the "gentlemen who give the orders," as he described them in *De mon propre aveu,* is apparent in his evident repulsion for these men as individuals who send others to do their dirty work while avoiding the consequences their subordinates pay for carrying it out. The Barbies and Francis Andrés of the world were, in Vergès's view, ultimately the hapless and gullible victims of such men. On the other hand, Vergès volunteered, he would rather discuss Nietzsche with Speer than with Barbie, and Balzac's *Splendors and Miseries of the Courtesans* with Bousquet than Francis André. Clearly, the cultured sophistication of these "gentlemen who give orders" (at least as Vergès imagined them) appealed to the lawyer's sense of his own refinement, and especially his literary erudition.

What are the implications of Vergès's analysis of the "torturer," the "auxiliary," and the "gentlemen who give orders" for the Barbie trial itself? First, despite the horrific nature of the crimes of the "torturers" Vergès described in *De mon proper aveu,* he seemed nevertheless to respect and even admire them for being "of a piece" and willing to devote themselves and their lives to a "higher" ideal or idea. At the same time, it is clear that Vergès felt *sympathy* for them for being exploited and used by the "gentlemen" above them who never really paid, or paid very little, for their own crimes. In this perspective, these "exploited" torturers (as well as their auxiliaries) could be merged or identified with the greater masses of the downtrodden, the colonized peoples, at least when the "gentlemen giving orders" were white men. It is worth stressing that if there is a way to resolve the apparent paradox of Vergès raising the issue of colonialist oppression in defending the Nazi Klaus Barbie, this would seem a likely, or at least plausible, way to resolve it.

In addition to autobiographical reflections as well as analyses of tortur-ers and their hierarchical superiors and inferiors, in works like *De mon proper aveu* and other works written up to his death in 2013, Vergès was fond of discussing judicial theory and strategy as well as the role of the defence lawyer as he conceived that role in a criminal trial. He was also happy to present these views in interviews in the press and in appear-ances on television. In discussing both judicial theory and courtroom strategy, Vergès's political views, his radical, anti-colonialist outlook played a crucial if not *the* determining role in shaping his views. Stated simply, for Vergès a trial was a political confrontation, a political struggle, by other means.

This was certainly how Vergès, along with his defence co-counsel, Jean-Martin Mbemba and Nabil Bouaïta, viewed the Barbie trial. They did everything in their power to transform it into such a confrontation and struggle. The stakes, moreover, were absolutely *not* about the politics of the Resistance and treason within its ranks. As Vergès stated in an inter-view in the French *Penthouse* magazine, whether "there were two traitors more or two traitors less in the Resistance" was not "a matter of prin-ciple." The "essential political debate" was about colonialism.

From Vergès's perspective, as he explained in *De mon propre aveu*, once the Court of Cassation decided in 1985 to expand the definition of crimes against humanity and include Barbie's crimes against some Resis-tance members, this opened the door to include similar crimes commit-ted by colonialists against *Algerian resisters* in Algeria. Why? Because the crimes against the Resistance in World War II were *war crimes*, just like the crimes committed by Algerian resisters. Once the first of these sets of war crimes was incorporated into crimes against humanity in Lyon, the inclusion of the second set was inevitable, despite the equally inevi-table opposition of the court. As Vergès saw it, because of the necessary struggle to include crimes against Algerian resisters in the Barbie trial, the trial itself became "an enclosed field of battle where antagonistic memories confronted each other, which the passage of time had only exacerbated" (*Aveu* 99).

It is important to stress at this point that Vergès's conception of a trial as a political confrontation and struggle was not a view he came to late in his career or that only found its full expression in the Barbie trial.

Already in *De la stratégie judiciaire*, an early theoretical work originally published in 1968, Vergès had made it clear that in his view *all criminal trials were political* and that the courts and the justice system themselves were not arbiters of justice but merely tools of the state. Their real function was to preserve the power of that state and oppress individual freedoms. Or as the epigraph of *De la stratégie judiciaire* put it in a quote from Mao Zedong: "The apparatus of the State, which includes the army, the police, *and the justice system,* [emphasis mine] is an instrument with which one class oppresses another" (4).

In light of this perspective, it is not surprising that, for Vergès, "the law is never good … all that matters is [whether there is] a moribund defense or a vital one" (5). Vergès's negative view of the law held true as well for the judges who serve that court and make it function: "Good judges, like heroes, don't exist. Unless one means a good judge like Napoleon was a good general. In this light, there are in effect efficient judges to the extent that they make one forget their role as judges, which is to say protectors of order and domestic tranquility" (9). This being the case, the purpose or duty of the judge is not to render an impartial judgment, but rather to help society "recuperate its prodigal children" (16). At least arguably, from Vergès's point of view, this is what Truche had attempted to do in encouraging Barbie to open up to the court about the change he had undergone in transitioning from an empathetic Christian youth in 1934 to a fanatical member of the SS in 1937.

Given these perspectives on the law and the justice system itself, what, in Vergès opinion, was the role of a defence lawyer before the court and on behalf of his or her client? As Vergès saw it, his or her obligation was most crucially to *oppose* the law as well as the false morality behind it: "My law is to be against the law …, my morality is to be against [accepted] morality" (13). The law as it was, he maintained, strove to "halt history" and traditional morality to "freeze" or paralyse life.

What strategies are available to the defence lawyer to allow him or her to oppose the law *within the courtroom and in the trial itself,* in which that lawyer plays such an integral part? In *De la stratégie judiciare*, as well as in subsequent works, most notably *Justice et littérature*, Vergès articulated his conception of two forms of trial which the defence lawyer could seek to orchestrate together with his or her client. These are the previously mentioned "trial by rupture," which constitutes the ideal act of revolt against and rejection of the law, as well as the social order it sustains, and a second form, much less admirable in Vergès's view, the so-called trial by connivance. History, as well as literary history, Vergès affirmed, were replete with examples of both. What distinguished the two forms from one another was the attitude of the accused when confronted with what

Vergès called "public order." If the accused accepted that order, then "the [traditional] trial itself becomes possible, consisting of a dialogue between the accused who explains himself and the judge, whose values are respected" (19). Stated in more negative terms, in a "trial of connivance," "the accused shows his wounds, his weaknesses, even his flaws and misfortunes, and rather they take responsibility for his criminal destiny, he claims to be subject to it, a victim of it" (58).

To all appearances, for Vergès, the trial of Adolph Eichmann in Jerusalem was an example, if not *the example par excellence*, of a "trial of connivance." In *De la stratégie judiciare*, Vergès offered a description of that trial as just such a trial. The description is worth quoting in full because it not only stresses the role and attitude of the accused in the courtroom but also the larger *political forces* at play in the trial itself.

> The style of a trial is … the best revelation of the true nature of the opposition between the prosecution and the accused. When, in April 1961 the trial in Jerusalem of one of those principally responsible for the "Final Solution," the scientific massacre of six million European Jews took place, one would have thought that it would be the greatest trial by rupture in history. Instead, it was a trial of connivance. That which the judges condemned through Eichmann was not imperialism with which they were solidary but the form it took in Nazism. It wasn't the crime itself [imperialism] but only the most disheveled component of that crime. The horrors of Nazism in this light became the monstrous nightmare of a species of a German Marquis de Sade, an illness of the soul of which Eichmann, who had been transformed into a pyscho-pathological caricature could also claim to be the victim. (23–4)

By contrast, the noblest form of defence, the form that would theoretically at least radically alter society for the better, was the "trial by rupture," in which the accused becomes the accuser, the judge the judged, along with the system s/he serves and protects. In Vergès's telling, the earliest historical trial by rupture was the trial of Socrates, and the first such trial recorded in literature was Sophocles's *Antigone*. Where Socrates is concerned, Vergès stressed that the philosopher did not disavow the crimes attributed to him, but rather assumed responsibility for them. He did so not in the name of his own defence or because he was guilty in any real sense, but for the good of the community, of society itself. Socrates's "crime," in effect, was not a "crime" but a necessary provocation of the community to expose its hypocrisy and corruption. Moreover, once found guilty, when one of his judges proposed the death penalty, rather than plead for a lesser sentence Socrates embraced the death penalty.

According to Vergès, if Socrates had pleaded for a lesser sentence, he would have been indirectly acknowledging his guilt and thereby "entering the game" of the tribunal itself (*Stratégie* 91).

In his discussion of *Antigone* in *Justice et literature,* Vergès offered a more comprehensive analysis of Sophocles's masterpiece *as* an Assize court trial, culminating in the moment when Antigone confronts Creon. In the exchanges between the two antagonists, it is starkly apparent that no reconciliation between them and their respective visions is any longer possible. At that moment, Vergès explained, "we are now projected precisely into the framework of a trial by rupture, where no dialogue is possible and where the opposing parties each claim and embrace values that are rigorously antagonistic" (3). In Sophocles's *Antigone*, it is Antigone who emerges as the heroine, despite her death. The system Creon represents reveals itself to be oppressive and destructive. Moreover, as Vergès observed, "the dignity of Antigone, like all those accused in trials of rupture, ends up stirring the conscience" (6) of those within the community or state the accused is challenging.

How is a trial by rupture staged in the courtroom? In *De la stratégie judiciaire*, Vergès proposed three key elements or components of that defence strategy that are crucial to transforming an ordinary trial into a trial by rupture. The first is that the person and personality of the accused must become invisible, forgotten, erased. The second is that trial's deliberations must be transformed into a "pure political debate" in which the political distinctions and stakes of the trial are sharply, indeed starkly, defined and delineated. Third, the defence must remain intransigent in its posture and dealings with the court. No compromise whatsoever is possible. Moreover, Vergès concluded, it is only if the defensce adopts such a strategy of rupture that it will hold the initiative in the trial itself.

Before turning to the specific arguments made by Vergès and his co-defence counsel, Jean-Martin Mbemba and Nabil Bouaïta, in the Lyon courtroom, it is clear in retrospect that in general terms Barbie's defence team followed in their presentations (whether deliberately or not, in Mbemba's and Bouaïta's case) the basic tenets of a "trial by rupture." First, every opportunity was exploited to make the accused, and especially his crimes, fade from view, even *disappear*, to the extent that this was possible. That way, from a perversely skewed perspective, Barbie could serve as an "everyman" of sorts, challenging the injustice and oppressiveness of the "system" itself. From Barbie's orchestrated refusal to attend his trial near the outset to his refusal when present to speak other than to state the basic facts of his life or to reiterate that he had been illegally kidnapped in Bolivia, to the efforts of two of his defence lawyers to avoid discussion of the accused's crimes altogether,[2] Barbie remained almost invisible.[3]

Second, at every possible juncture, Vergès and his colleagues sought to transform the trial into a "pure political debate." This was evident early on in Vergès's questioning of witnesses such as André Frossard and Elie Wiesel and most obviously in bringing in Mbemba and Bouaïta in as part of the defence team in the first place. Not only were both men the representatives of formerly colonized countries, both were also politically active in their countries as well. Undoubtedly, as will become evident, their respective closing statements were intended to stir debate and controversy.

As for the third element, intransigence, in the Barbie trial this almost invariably assumed the form of provocation. This Vergès and his colleagues attempted at virtually every opportunity the trial afforded, especially, and perhaps predictably, at the conclusion of the trial. For Vergès, as he later wrote in *De mon proper aveu*, the three men together represented "humanity itself," and its defence, sitting on the bench of the accused (98).

Part Two: The Closing Statements of Jean-Martin Mbemba and Nabil Bouaïta

Although Jean-Martin Mbemba and Nabil Bouaïta delivered their closing statements before Vergès closed the trial with his own statement, Vergès nevertheless opted to give a "preamble" of sorts to his colleagues' statements to set the stage, so to speak. Facing his legal adversaries across the courtroom, rather the judges and jury (as had Truche), Vergès made it clear from the outset that he intended to politicize the matters at hand and attack and accuse rather than defend. On behalf of his co-counsel *as well as his client*, he insisted, he wished to pay his respects, first, to the struggle carried out by the French Resistance. Then, in the same breath, he asserted angrily that this was the *right of the defence*, as "the African peoples had been the first to engage in this struggle." He himself, he added, had "spent my youth" in the cause. Next, Vergès asserted that the defence wished to express its respect for the "Jewish and gypsy victims," and this was its right as well because, he affirmed ironically, "just imagine! We know what racism is, too!" Finally, Vergès stated, "we incline ourselves before the martyred children of Izieu, because we mourn the Algerian children who have died as well." Then, visibly attempting to stare down the civil parties lawyers opposite him, Vergès concluded that, unlike his counterparts across the courtroom, "we do not separate the victims in death."

When his turn to speak came, Mbemba picked up where Vergès had left off, essentially equating Nazism's crimes with those experienced by colonized peoples and arguing, in effect (and following Hannah Arendt in *The Origins of Totalitarianism*), that the former were in many ways the outgrowth of the latter.[4] Hitler's crimes, Mbemba asserted, "did not fall from the sky."

To make the case that he was offering an alternative context for Barbie's and Nazism's crimes than the one Pierre Truche had presented, Mbemba spoke to the court of two crimes, both deliberately chosen to offer disconcerting echoes or parallels with the Nazis' crimes as well as subsequent legal efforts to come to terms with the latter. Mbemba first described the situation in the Congo in the early 1930s in the years leading up to the advent of Nazism in 1933. Was there no link, no parallel, he suggested, between the brutal practices of the latter and what was happening in the Congo? There, the indigenous population was treated like "beasts, [and] these were beasts [the colonizers] loaded on barges, their backs bent, without cover for fifteen to twenty days, no food nor water, and no right to it [while others] were forced to walk five hundred kilometers and more on foot, many falling to the wayside and dying of exhaustion."

The second example Mbemba chose was the massacre by French military units in Madagascar of "thirty thousand indigenous peoples, some disabled veterans and former resisters." This crime having occurred a year after Nuremberg, he asked the court, how could one have a tranquil conscience in judging Barbie now, if this French crime in Madagascar had gone unpunished?[5]

If Mbemba followed Vergès's lead in comparing Nazi crimes to the crimes of colonialism, he followed that lead as well in attempting deliberately to provoke and even shock the court in the description he offered of his first encounter with Klaus Barbie. Mbemba explained that when Vergès had invited him to meet Barbie personally and join his defence team, Mbemba had expressed his reservations about both prospects to his wife. She encouraged him, he said, to meet Barbie and to "determine the place of Nazism in his head." Then, to the consternation of the courtroom which, Mbemba told his listeners, he had fully anticipated – but then, they had not "lived his experience" – he described a moving and indeed fraternal encounter between the two men in which, shaking Mbemba's outstretched hand with both hands, Barbie stated simply, "Thank you, counselor." The rest of their conversation, Mbemba stated, was "confidential." But with his own people, he told the hushed court, when one shakes hands with two hands, this is a sign, indeed proof, of one's "respect for the other man."[6] Presumably, then, for Mbemba at least, Nazism was no longer "in the head" of the accused.[7]

In another apparent provocation, this one aimed directly at the civil parties lawyer Charles Berman, Mbemba told the court that in questioning his fellow lawyer's decision to defend Barbie, Berman had reminded his African colleague that Hitler had refused to shake Jesse Owens's hand at the 1936 Berlin Olympics after the African American had won his race. Looking directly across at Berman, Mbemba told him, "you have entered my conscience too late" because he, Mbemba, had "already lived" what Jesse Owens had experienced and he continued to "live it in the present."

In closing with what might first have appeared a gesture of solidarity or reconciliation, Mbemba expressed the hope that, in moving forward after the trial, "we can all extirpate the remains of racism in ourselves," and in the future, it will be possible to say to "all massacring regimes," "never again, that" (*"Plus jamais, ça"*). But in the language he chose, Mbemba's open-heartedness was less apparent, and this was certainly not lost on many of those present in the courtroom. In choosing the verb "extirpate" to refer to the racism of *all of those present*, Mbemba chose the precise verb that André Frossard had earlier described the Nazi jailer using with his Jewish prisoner in wartime Lyon. Was Mbemba's intent, then, to suggest that the racism of all of those present whom he beseeched to rid themselves of racism *identical to Nazi anti-Semitism?* And in using the phrase *"plus jamais ça,"* a phrase synonymous with preventing another Holocaust in French, and then applying it to any and all crimes of massacring regimes, was Mbemba saying that all these crimes were the same? Whatever Mbemba's ultimate intent, the overall message (and effect) of his closing statement was hardly one that promoted reconciliation between the opposing parties.

If anything, Nabil Bouaïta's closing statement was even less conciliatory than Mbemba's and at least equally provocative or *intransigent*, as required by a "trial by rupture." Like his Congolese colleague, his choice of topics to address, and especially the vocabulary he used, were deployed ironically and even sarcastically to mock the shibboleths of the opposing side and the bases of the trial itself. In his statement, Bouaïta sought to underscore and demolish the false distinctions he detected between the crimes of colonialism and its modern practitioners and Nazi crimes against the Jews.

First, as Vergès would do in his own statement, Bouaïta reminded the court that Claude Lanzmann's *Shoah* was being shown on French television as the defence made its case. The film's message, Bouaïta insisted, was nothing less than the claim not only that the Holocaust was unique but that in comparison with it, *all other crimes and misfortunes in the world were not even worth remembering.* "Bannish from your memories all other preoccupations, all other misfortunes of this world, there is only *one* misfortune, just as God himself is unique."

Then, referring to a recent interview with the *pied noir* popular singer Enrico Macias, whom he quoted as saying that he preferred the word "pioneer" to "colonizer," Bouaïta told the court that Macias was "faurisson-izing" France's colonial past, just as the real Robert Faurisson was attempting to erase the Holocaust from history. Later in his closing statement, Bouaïta once again invoked the name Faurisson, this time casting members of the "new wave of intellectuals like Pascal Bruckner" as burgeoning "Faurissons" intent on "denying," in toto, "the aggression, the guilt, the criminality of colonialism and inviting the West to put aside its guilt complex." Bouaïta added that, "to the best of my knowledge Pascal Bruckner's thesis has not been banned." Indeed, while Bruckner was currently the darling of France's television stations, Faurisson was being "gagged and insulted."[8]

In turning to the law being applied in the Barbie trial, Bouaïta's statements and language were more measured, but equally critical. He began by recalling the testimony of Marie-Madeleine Fourcade to the effect that the distinction between crimes against humanity and war crimes as applied in the trial was "*un peu gros*," a bit phony or artificial. More substantially, Bouaïta observed that crimes against humanity did little to favour "peace" among peoples because, he claimed, they only applied to *some* peoples. As for absence of a statute of limitations, this made these crimes timeless and thereby encouraged a perpetual "thirst for vengeance" and even "hatred" – presumably this was just what was happening in the current trial.

To the extent that Bouaïta's closing statement was memorable and crucial to the memory and legacy of the Barbie trial, at least according to critics like Alain Finkielkraut, it was in the Algerian lawyer's insistence in his closing remarks that Israel was the new Nazi Germany. Its crimes against Palestinians, moreover, were equivalent to Nazi crimes against Jews.

Bouaïta began with the general observation that, in his view, there was little difference between crematoria and phosphorous bombs, as both killed "innocents." To the extent that the two crimes differed, he argued, the difference lay the fact that the killer operating the crematorium was obliged to see the murders he was committing, whereas the pilot was not. In this light, the pilot seemed almost worse than the crematorium operator, as he did not have to *assume responsibility* for his crime in the same way. Then, following brief references to American crimes in Vietnam, like the My Lai massacre and those of Australians against the aborigines, Bouaïta turned to Israel.

It is possible, although unlikely, that if Nabil Bouaïta had not dwelt on Israel and Israeli crimes at such length and in such provocative detail that his statement would not have provoked the reaction it did nor the incident that followed. But in making that presumption one must assume that Bouaïta and his defence co-counsel were not in fact *seeking* to provoke such a disruption, one very much in keeping with the tenets of a trial by rupture, where the accused, or his defence counsel in this case, becomes the accuser. Of course, this ignores the fact that the Lyon Assize court, and France itself, were hardly answerable for the actions of Israel. Nevertheless, Bouaïta implied that the court, and by extension French law, *were responsible*, as it required an act of "mental alchemy" to be "silent" on the "genocide" of the Palestinians and the Armenians before them and sanction only the crimes of the aging Nazi in the Lyon courtroom. Indeed, Bouaïta continued, if he had been present earlier in the trial and been involved in the selection of witnesses for the defence he would have called the director of the Israeli League of the Rights of Man, who would have denounced Israeli crimes before the court. Citing a list of other prominent Israeli and French Jewish critics of the Israeli state, Bouaïta claimed that they, too, would denounce the "Nazification of the Israeli people," Israeli complicity in the murders at Shabra and Shatila, which Bouaïta labelled an "Israeli Babi Yar,"[9] and the murderousness of Israeli leaders Menachim Begin and Ariel Sharon. In closing, Bouaïta stated that on the "white page" of the history of the trial on which Roland Dumas wished to see inscribed the names of the children of Izieu he, Bouaïta, would add the names of the Palestinian children of Shabra and Shatila and those of the children of Soweto as well.

As both the transcript and film of the trial show, before Bouaïta had completed his closing statement the civil parties lawyer Michel Zaoui rose to protest the line of argument that the defence lawyer was following, along with its implications. President Cerdini then quickly stepped in. He admonished Zaoui that "You do not have the choice of arguments the defense is allowed to make, you will allow the defense to express itself." Visibly upset, Zaoui responded: "It is completely intolerable to have to listen to such arguments!" When Cerdini told him to be seated, Zaoiu protested again, "this is inadmissible!"

After Bouaïta had completed his closing statement, Zaoui was allowed to address the court. He demanded a suspension of the proceedings in order that he and some of his civil parties colleagues could formulate a response to the defence's condemnation, specifically of Israel. He was not Israel's lawyer, he added, but where Shabra and Shatila were concerned, the incident had been reported and condemned by the international community. Besides, he stressed, Bouaïta had only reported selectively on crimes committed in Lebanon. What of the massacre of Christian militias by Shiite militias at Anaour El Sadate? Why had the Algerian lawyer not addressed that crime? Concluding, Zaoui asserted: "The problems of our times are not in the exclusive purview of the defense."

Zaoui's remark hit a nerve, certainly among the civil parties lawyers. François La Phuong, a lawyer for Resistance organizations who had earlier upbraided Mbemba and especially Bouaïta for arriving in the courtroom so late (and, in Bouaïta's case, missing the most crucial element in the trial, the victims' testimony) rose angrily and exclaimed: "I am not a lawyer for Israel!" Then, addressing the judges and jury, he continued: "It is up to you to say what is good and bad in the arguments of our adversaries, not us." At this point, the courtroom erupted in applause, and Cerdini, visibly angry for one of the very few times in the trial, ordered the courtroom to be silent. He told the court guards to apprehend the individual who had also whistled loudly if they were able locate that person and remove him or her from the courtroom.

Once order had been restored, other civil parties lawyers were invited to speak. Alain Jakubowicz denounced Bouaïta's statements as "ignominious," and seconded his colleague's request for a recess. Other lawyers for Jewish plaintiffs followed suit. However, several lawyers for Resistance groups took a different tack. Ugo Iannuci declared that in an Assize court, the defence should be absolutely free in its choice of arguments. But at the same time, the defence also had to assume the "risks and perils" of the arguments made. Under those conditions, he continued, he deplored the interruption of the defence by Zaoui. When his turn to reply came, Vergès noted that the defence counsel had not interrupted the endless stream of statements made by the civil parties lawyers, even if the defence considered some of these arguments inadmissible as well. Moreover, condescending to give a legal lesson to his opponents, he stressed that they were allowed only to challenge factual errors in the case presented by the defence, not the substance of its arguments. Besides, he stated, his opponents were always too late with their rebuttals, and if they were allowed the recess and time for rebuttal they requested, this would only be the first step of many in their apparent efforts to disrupt the trial.

At the conclusion of these exchanges, president Cerdini ordered a ten-minute recess, as Pierre Mérindol reported, to "calm tempers" rather than to allow time for Zaoui and his colleagues time to prepare a lengthy rebuttal. The matter seemed closed, and its significance limited to tense but brief exchanges. Indeed, Mérindol reported on the incident matter-of-factly, and Sorj Chalandon in his daily report for *Libération* did not mentioned the episode at all.

But for the critics of the Barbie trial like Alain Finkielkraut, the lawyers' exchanges at this point in the proceedings marked a watershed moment, exposing a deep fissure among the civil parties that contributed significantly to the trial's ultimate failure. According to Finkielkraut, when François La Phuong exclaimed "I am not a lawyer for Israel," he was indicating "that Mr Zaoui, himself was, that his gesture was motivated not by concern for the truth but by self-interest and by the image of the country he was representing in the courtroom. Only a militant Zionist – and further, a hypersensitive one – could contest the defense's right to identify the Palestinian refugee camps of Sabra and Shatila with Auschwitz, phosphorous bombs with crematoriums and the Jewish notion of the 'chosen people' with Hitler-style racism" (43).

In effect, for Finkielkraut, Zaoui's interruption, along with its seconding by Jewish lawyers and La Phuong's protest seconded by lawyers for the defence put the civil parties of the Resistance "on the same side of the fence" as Vergès and his defence co-counsel. Defence and civil parties lawyers for the Resistance now shared an "offended nationalism" and "separately and severally led the same battle to dislodge the Jews from their position of uniqueness and to wrench crimes against humanity away from this who would monopolize them" (43). And if proof were needed that there was a double standard operative among civil parties lawyers for the Resistance, Finkielkraut wrote that when Henri Noguères "interrupted" the defence "on behalf of the members of the Resistance," La Phuong and his colleagues did not protest, whereas "it was deemed sacrilegious" when Zaoui spoke up on behalf of the Jews.

Years after the Barbie trial was over, Zaoui echoed many of Finkielkraut's views on what the latter labelled the "incident." For Zaoui as well, Bouaïta's provocation, his own intervention, and La Phuong's assertion that he was "not a defender of Israel" had the effect of "tragically dividing" the civil parties into two camps, aligning the lawyers for the Resistance with the defence against the lawyers for Barbie's Jewish victims. But for Zaoui, this was at least partially inadvertent on the part of La Phuong and his colleagues. In protesting Zaoui's interruption of Bouaïta, they simply *failed to understand the implications* of what they were doing. Like Finkielkraut, Zaoui also noted that a double standard was evident in the fact that no one had spoken up when Noguères had intervened to warn Vergès not to overstep the bounds of decency in attacking the Resistance, but they *had* protested when Zaoui defended Israel and the Jews.

With respect to Alain Finkielkraut and Michel Zaoui, there is another way to interpret the "incident" in retrospect, based on the trial transcript and especially the film of the proceedings. First, while it is possible to argue that La Phuong's statement that he was not Israel's defender implied that Zaoui was, it is also possible to view his *complete* statement in a different and less partisan light. Coupled with his criticisms of Mbemba and especially Bouaïta for their tardy arrival in court, it seems clear that in his criticism of Zaoui La Phuong was insisting first and foremost on the need for *both sides* to respect the customs and traditions of the Assize court, as well its unwritten code of courtesy. Otherwise, the trial itself could not be conducted fairly and without prejudice. Indeed, as La Phuong continued his statement, he reminded the court that it was up to the judges and jury, not the opposing lawyers, to determine "good and bad" arguments and consider what was acceptable and unacceptable.

As to Finkiekraut's claim that two different standards were applicable when La Phuong and his colleagues failed to criticize Noguères for his "interruption," the fact is that Noguères *did not interrupt the defence*, but rather made his warning to Vergès during his own closing statement. In this, he had not violated any courtroom protocol or code of conduct. While this might seem a "technicality," it nevertheless lends support to the idea that La Phuong was primarily concerned with upholding procedures when he responded to Zaoui's interruption. Indeed, as Zaoui himself wrote later about the "incident," he had committed the "crime of *lèse-défense* "in interrupting Boaïta, and he did fully believe that the 'rights' of the defense are sacred, and that it is the ultimate expression of democratic justice" (86).

At least equally important, it should be stressed that the comments of other civil parties lawyers both for Resistance organizations as well as Jewish victims confirm that they did not hew to a "party line" or establish the kind of stark dichotomy Finkielkraut described. Alain Lévy, the lawyer for the Jewish Resister Gilberte Jacob, agreed with La Phuong in criticizing Zaoui's interruption, and Ugo Ianucci in his comments clearly implied that while he supported the defence lawyer's absolute right to his arguments, those arguments, when freely expressed, were subject to their own "perils." In other words, the freedom Bouaïta enjoyed in voicing his provocations might well backfire and prove detrimental to the cause of the defence. Indeed, to the extent that as part of an overall strategy of disruption or "rupture" it failed to sway the jury in its verdict, this turned out to be the case. As Zaoui would also write years after the trial in referring to the "incident": "What is this argument that consists of expropriating the sufferings of some on the pretext that others are not sufficiently recognized in their own misfortunes? What an infamy!" (87–8).

Part Three: Jacques Vergès Closes for the Defence

In his closing statement before the Lyon Assize court that began on 2 July and concluded the next day, Vergès made it clear that, although unlike his two colleagues he *would* discuss in detail the charges and evidence against his client, like Mbemba and Bouaïta he would also address the court defiantly and provocatively. As he stated in *Le Salaud Lumineux*, "comfortable in my own skin, I always conduct myself as an accuser, never as the accused" (286). But in the tone Vergès took and the language he used, especially in castigating his opponents and even some of the victims themselves, there was, as Zaoui later recalled, a "verbal violence" in Vergès's closing argument that Zaoui described as simply "inadmissible" in an Assize court trial. However, Zaoui also confessed that sitting in the Lyon courtroom he was worried that that very verbal violence might unduly "impress" the court and jury. Whatever one might think of the defence lawyer, Zaoui added, in an Assize trial Vergès was a "swashbuckler" who knew "all the strings" that one might pull to his own and his client's advantage (Zaoui et al. 83).

Although occasionally obscured by rhetorical fireworks, Vergès's closing statement was nevertheless clearly organized and divided into several parts. He began by casting Barbie not as an executioner but as a victim and then moved to a denunciation of the legal system and the legalities in play. Next, the lawyer addressed the main charges against Barbie, reversing the chronological order of the Izieu round-up and the 11 August 1944 convoy in order to address Izieu on the final day of his statement before the court. Vergès concluded, as one would expect in a "trial by rupture," with a denunciation of the French nation itself. As already discussed, as he neared the conclusion of his statement and to the outrage of many present in the courtroom Vergès also attacked the character of several of Barbie's victims who had testified against him during the trial.

In characterizing the accused himself before the court, Vergès began by insisting that, far from being the "monster" painted in much of the courtroom testimony, Klaus Barbie was in fact simply an "old man," "without illusions." And he added, when Barbie committed the so-called crimes of which he had been accused he had "the law on his side."[10] Moreover, Barbie had been arrested and then deported in harsh and de-humanizing circumstances from Bolivia ("a cowl had been placed over his head" as he was led to the airport, Vergès explained) in a process in which France had flaunted Bolivian law. This was not surprising of course because, for the arrogant French, Bolivia was just another "banana republic," read Third World country. The whole process of Barbie's arrest and return to France, Vergès continued, was cloaked in a "juridical fog," the details of which, he implied, even president Cerdini was unaware. And in an historical trial like the trial at hand, the "little German officer" was hardly important enough in historical terms, and certainly in terms of the Nazi hierarchy itself, to merit such an extravagant production. Barbie, Vergès told the court, was merely an "ersatz Goering."

In turning to the legalities of the case, Vergès's claims at least in part seemed more compelling. He stressed, first, that prosecuting Barbie according to a law that had not been on the books at the time he committed his crimes was "unconstitutional."[11] The principle of prescription or a statute of limitations on all crimes, he added, had been incorporated into French law from Roman law, so it had been there for centuries. Ironically, Vergès continued, the political regime that had legally transformed the foundational legal principle of *nullum crimen sine lege*, "no crime without the law" into *nullem crimen sine poene* – "no crime without punishment" was none other than Nazi Germany itself. Should a French Assize court follow a Nazi example to punish a Nazi criminal? In raising these issues, of course, Vergès was essentially rejecting the legitimacy of the 1964 law as well as challenging international jurisprudence since Nuremberg. At Nuremberg, the crimes of the Nazis were considered to be unprecedented, and therefore any law applied to them would have to be new and applied retroactively. For Vergès, as he stated on numerous occasions, the jurisprudence established at Nuremberg was fraudulent to begin with. Moreover, there was nothing unprecedented about Nazi crimes in his view. Besides, if the chief prosecutor was right in his earlier statement before the court that the jurisprudence involving crimes against humanity was effectively a work in progress, why should Klaus Barbie have to serve as a guinea pig in that process? In concluding, and again in keeping with the spirit of a "trial by rupture," Vergès reminded the jury that in this matter their authority and power were beyond those of "the rulers of this country." In effect, he implied, they possessed a *revolutionary* power.

In the third part of his closing statement, Vergès turned to the first main charge against his client, that of organizing the round-up and deportation of eighty-four Jews as a result of the raid on the *Union Générale des Israelites de France* on 9 February 1943. To the extent that, as Zaoui later claimed, Vergès's closing statement went beyond the pale, so to speak, and became "inadmissible," this was first readily apparent in his discussion the *UGIF* round-up. Stated simply, in much of his presentation Vergès's remarks were tinged with anti-Semitism, if they were not overtly anti-Semitic in tone and content. As the journalist Pierre Mérindol observed, "Everything that is excessive becomes derisory [to quote de Bigault], and the sort of delight Vergès took in humiliating the Jewish community stripped much of the credibility that could have been gained from his larger presentation" (333).

In discussing the *UGIF*, the lawyer began, one had to address the painful reality of Jewish collaboration with the Nazis in their own destruction. Even after the war, he continued, Jewish intellectuals, including

Pierre Vidal-Naquet, had denounced the *UGIF* leaders, including especially Raymond Geissman, whose own testimony, as noted, forced the
Munich prosecutor to re-open the Barbie case in 1971. Having deliberately sounded a note that had unleashed massive controversy over
Hannah Arendt's *Eichmann in Jerusalem* some twenty-five years earlier,[12]
Vergès then proceeded to invoke a "Jewish conspiracy" of sorts, whose
fomenters were the *Centre de Documentation Juive Contemporaine*, in concert with Serge Klarsfeld. All the archives of the *UGIF* were held in the
Paris archives and, Vergès implied, they would reveal the extent of Jewish
collaboration with the Nazis if they were brought to light. The man with
privileged access to the *CDJC* and its holdings was of course the "rat of
the archives," Klarsfeld himself. For anyone familiar with Nazi as well as
Vichy propaganda, the rat figured frequently in dehumanizing charac-
terizations of the Jew, as did evocations of a Jewish conspiracy.[13] Where
the round-up at the *UGIF* was concerned, Vergès concluded, should
"Jewish responsibility be blamed on Barbie?"

Then changing his approach and tactics, Vergès went at the *UGIF*
round-up from a different direction, this one intended to diminish Barbie's role and responsibility by casting him as merely a small cog in the
much larger Nazi war machine. The *UGIF* operation, the lawyer now
maintained, was not an independent or autonomous operation but part
of a much larger operation carried out by the Nazis to limit the flow
of refugees as well as German army deserters into Switzerland. In these
circumstances, there was no question that if he had indeed carried out
the *UGIF* raid Barbie was only following orders. Moreover – and here
Vergès referred back to Pierre Truche's reference to the "closed chamber of horror" maintained by the Lyon Gestapo – this broader context
belied the Sartrean *Huis Clos* in which Truche had maintained Barbie
operated.[14]

In discussing the witnesses, or more precisely the one witness who
claimed to have seen Barbie at the *UGIF* headquarters on the day of the
raid and round-up, Vergès turned his attention to the aforementioned
Michel Kroskof-Thomas. Seizing on the fact that Truche had dismissed
Kroskof-Thomas's testimony as unconvincing in his summation, Vergès
rehearsed that testimony at length, emphasizing Kroskof-Thomas's many
embarrassing lapses in failing to answer the defence counsel's questions.
Then, veering once again into anti-Semitic rhetoric, Vergès angrily
claimed that Kroskof-Thomas (and, at least implicitly, the [Jewish] civil
parties lawyers who called him to testify) believed that in testifying the
defence would not dare challenge him because, "in his lovely wig and
make-up," he testified as a Jewish resister, a kind of sacred cow. In the
end, Vergès concluded derisively, the outright lies Kroskof-Thomas told

in court proved that the anti-Semitic writer Louis-Ferdinand Céline was right in telling his lawyer that if he, Céline, returned to Paris from exile after the war, there would be "twenty witnesses who would claim that I had been Hitler's mistress."

Vergès's comments on the 11 August 1944 convoy were more perfunctory, if no less acerbic. Given that no documentation or order related to the convoy existed, Vergès contented himself with attacking the witnesses' testimony. That testimony, he claimed, was essentially all over the place, riddled with glaring contradictions in virtually every detail. Some witnesses claimed that the train had departed from Perrache train station in the heart of Lyon, while others said that it left from a different station in the city's suburbs. On another matter, how long did the train's numerous stops in towns and cities along the way to Germany last? Two hours? Two days? The testimony was contradictory on this point as well, Vergès maintained. As for Barbie's presence at Montluc Prison when the prisoners were gathered up to be deported, and later on the train platform at the moment of departure, these testimonies dealing with what Barbie wore, how he behaved, and what he said were contradictory, too. Should the court believe the two key witnesses, Alice Joly-Vansteenberghe and Anne-Marie de Sainte Marie, just because they were medical doctors, Vergès asked? Of course not! This was all part of a process of deliberate "intoxication" of the court and jury in a time when "intellectual tyranny was running rampant." As examples of that "intellectual tyranny," Vergès noted that the young Jesuit lawyer who was originally part of Barbie's defence team was told by Lyon Cardinal Decoutray that he could not serve on the defence because the accused refused to admit his crimes. As another example, why should anyone believe that Lucie Aubrac could go and visit Barbie during the Occupation when her husband was imprisoned by him and believe that she could walk out free, as she claimed? And yet this was an article of faith that no one was supposed to challenge.[15]

In addressing the round-up of the children of Izieu on the second day of his presentation, Vergès relied more heavily on documentary evidence and especially the infamous telex Barbie had sent to his superiors in Paris right after the raid, whose authenticity Vergès and his client of course rejected. It is fair to say that at this stage the defence lawyer's options where the telex was concerned were quite limited, given the extent to which the testimony of expert witnesses and the detailed analysis of the telex by chief prosecutor Truche had to all appearances firmly established the document's authenticity. Nevertheless, as was his wont, Vergès forged ahead with his challenge anyway, but not before strategically offering up a red herring of sorts in an apparent attempt to mislead the court as well as attacking the veracity of Julian Favet, the one witness who claimed to have seen Barbie at Izieu. The potential persuasiveness of Vergès's efforts on the last score were bolstered by the fact that Pierre Truche had already discounted Favet's testimony in his summation, but for different reasons, as noted earlier.

The red herring in question was Lucien Bourdon, the Frenchman from Lorraine known to have betrayed the Izieu Jewish children's refuge to the Germans. Bourdon had employed one of the Izieu adolescents at his farm nearby, discovered the boy was in fact a Jew, and then denounced the Jewish refuge to the Germans. Bourdon was also known to be a Nazi sympathizer and frequented the German officers present in the area. After the round-up of the children had taken place, the Germans moved Bourdon's family, along with their possessions, back to Lorraine. Bourdon himself went on to Germany, where he became a camp guard. After the war, Bourdon returned to France, working as a gardener in Lorraine. Where his role at Izieu was concerned, he had been evasive about the entire affair when contacted by journalists in the lead-up to the 1987 trial.[16]

If as was already established Bourdon had in fact been present at the raid after having led the Germans there, he would certainly have seen Barbie there if he was in fact present. This being the case, Vergès asked pointedly, why was Bourdon not required to testify at the trial?

Having raised the issue of Bourdon's absence from the trial, Vergès then left the matter in abeyance, noting only that during the investigation Bourdon had been questioned but that he had not confirmed Barbie's presence at the round-up. Clearly, the implication was that the prosecution did not *want* to hear Bourdon's testimony for fear of what he might say.

In reality, matters were more complicated than Vergès let on, and his account of the affair skewed. In point of fact, Lucien Bourdon had been tried after the war in 1947 for betraying the children's refuge to the Germans. He was found guilty, and, in a period when putting the Occupation behind was the mindset of the day, Bourdon had been sentenced only to "National Indignity," with no prison term. During his trial Bourdon had lied repeatedly, saying that the Germans sought him out instead of the other way around and that they had forced him to betray the Jewish children's whereabouts.

According to Vergès in *Un Salaud lumineux*, had he been called in 1987 Bourdon would have testified that *other* German officers had been present at Izieu, but *not* Barbie (308). This was not at all certain, however. Bourdon had in fact been questioned during the instruction of the case on 25 February 1983 (K: P2/VIII/18), and what he actually stated was quite different. Bourdon stated that he was at the Izieu round-up but that he had viewed it from a distance of some three hundred metres. He testified that he was unable to determine at that distance who the German officers present were and what their ranks were. He also stated that he did not know Barbie and that he had seen him on television years later for the first time. However, Bourdon *did not affirm that he had not seen Barbie at the roundup.* Moreover, one of the witnesses for Bourdon's *own* trial had seen Bourdon at the round-up along with the Germans present. Eusèbe Perticoz, a local farmer, testified on 10 May 1946 during the instruction of Bourdon's case that he had seen Bourdon there in the company of "two German officers and two men in civilian clothes, members of the Gestapo of Lyon, one of the German officers told me" (K: P2/VIII/35).

Given these realities, it seems clear why Vergès was content merely to point to Bourdon's absence in the hope of convincing the court that something was amiss in the trial. But under any circumstances, given Bourdon's track record of lying, there was no way to be sure what he would say, and whether what he said was true. Additionally, from the standpoint of some of the civil parties lawyers, as they told the journalist Antoine Spire, bringing Bourdon to testify would only be a distraction.[17] And in fairness to Bourdon, he had already been judged and punished (in a manner of speaking) for his crime.

In the case of Julien Favet, Vergès's tone in discussing the witness was mocking and ironic. This seemed especially cruel, in light of the fact that the farm labourer was severely disfigured, that Vergès had already attacked and humiliated him during his testimony in court, and that Truche had dismissed Favet's testimony as well. In his closing statement, Vergès described Favet as "this fellow with a great head wound," implying that this would certainly have impaired the reliability of his powers of observation at the raid. In fact, Favet had received the wound in an accident that occurred *after* the war. Pointing to inconsistencies in Favet's testimony as he told his story over the years, Vergès dismissed the very idea that Favet, working in the fields at the time of the Izieu round-up, had seen Barbie with Bourdon and the German troops there as the latter carried out the operation. Who, in the end, was this witness who appeared "by magic" at this trial thirty-five years after the fact, and why had he not discussed what he had seen in the intervening years? Vergès raised the last point twice in his closing statement, clearly in an effort to suggest that Favet was being opportunistic in the present trial in order to seek publicity. In fact, Favet had been available to testify at Bourdon's trial decades earlier and had so testified earlier in the trial at hand. Favet stated at the time that he had been "shocked" not to have been called to testify in 1947. But, at least according to Spire (120–1), because the court in 1947 wished to put the Dark Years behind, as noted, it did not seek Favet out. Moreover, Spire speculated, the court was uninterested in the testimony of a "domestic worker" and "farm hand" like Favet (111). Besides, the testimony of other witnesses clearly established Bourdon's culpability.

In turning to the telex itself, Vergès was certainly aware that his options for challenging its authenticity were limited. However, being a "swash-buckler" of the Assize courtroom as Zaoui described him, he voiced his objections to it confidently, all the while denouncing those he said had perpetrated this glaring fraud. But while the defence lawyer performed his indignation and even outrage admirably, a close look at the claims he made underscores their tenuousness or facticity. This was certainly the attitude of the civil parties lawyers and the prosecutor general, who frequently shook their heads or grinned as Vergès analysed the telex.

As for the tenuous claims: despite the fact that expert testimony had confirmed that due to paper shortages maps of England were often used as backing for telexes by German intelligence services, Vergès argued that the backing of the Izieu telex could not have been from an invasion map. Indeed, the map in question was of Scotland and the New Hebrides Islands, not England, where the invasion was to occur. Moreover, there were no German markings on the document, so how could it have been used by German forces? Vergès's comments in this instance clearly pre-supposed that the Germans would only have used their own maps, and that all these maps would detail the English landing sights.

Vergès's claims for what appeared on the front of the telex were equally questionable. First, on the original telex there was a gap between the text and Barbie's typed signature from which, Vergès maintained, a strip containing the name of one of Barbie's superiors actually respon-sible for the raid had been removed. Earlier in the trial, when the telex was removed from its protective covering to be inspected by the lawyers, Vergès included, Pierre Truche had made a point of running his finger over the empty space to confirm that there was no trace of glue pres-ent. Besides, next to Barbie's name were the initials I.A., signifying *In ordanen*, which, as noted, the Gestapo used to indicate the individual responsible for the action taken. This, clearly, had been the accused. But, Vergès persisted, massive historical frauds had been perpetrated before, most notably the discovery of Hitler's secret diaries. Despite the fact that renowned historians had confirmed the authenticity of the dia-ries, only a chemical analysis of the paper confirmed the fraud. The same was necessary here, Vergès maintained, but the court essentially refused to carry out such a test.

There was more, Vergès continued. The telex was marked as having been received in Paris on 7 April 1944. In the body of the text message, the date it was sent from Lyon was indicated as 6 April. However, Vergès now argued, there was another date on the telegram next to Barbie's signature indicating that it was sent in the year 1943. What more telling evidence of a fraud could there be? The only problem with this, as the jury would have the opportunity to verify, was that the numerical figure "forty-three" was not part of a date, but rather part of Gestapo coding.

To all appearances at this stage, Barbie's lawyer was clutching at straws. This did not deter him, however. Broadening the focus of his challenge and raising the spectre of an unnamed conspirator or conspirators, along with Klarsfeld and the CDJC of course, Vergès stressed the evident chaos of the archives of the CDJC, since the so-called original of the telex had been found in the file marked Otto Abetz, the former German ambassador in Paris. How could such an archive, and those associated with it, be trusted? Vergès then noted again that the French representative at Nuremberg, François-Poncet, had discussed the telex but had made no mention of Barbie, although this issue had already been addressed. Then, in a new twist, Vergès went after the German expert witnesses. They had confirmed the authenticity of the telex *even when they only had the copy of it to examine.* Nevermind that they had reiterated the authenticity of the telex in court, especially after they had seen the original. Under any circumstances, Vergès concluded, they, like all Germans, could not be trusted in these matters. Still wracked by guilt over Nazism and the war itself, the German people would not dare challenge the authenticity of a document provided by a *Jewish organization* like the CDJC. Besides, asking Germans to confirm the authenticity of the telex in the first place was a sign that the French legal authorities themselves had doubts as to its authenticity. The whole affair, Vergès concluded, was an "immense fraud," a "monstrous stupidity" orchestrated by a "great and unknown manipulator."

Vergès, having identified – while not identifying – a "great manipulator" pulling the strings behind a grand conspiracy of sorts, it was time for the court to recognize at last that Klaus Barbie was a scapegoat. It was also necessary to discover the source, the wellspring of that conspiracy, as well as why it was being carried out it the first place. In preparing to name this source, Vergès did not seek to implicate the Jewish people again, as he had earlier in his closing statement. Rather he began by reminding the *French people as a whole* of their own humiliation in the nation's ignominious defeat in 1940, when the supposedly mighty French army had collapsed in the face of the German onslaught. Only France among all the European nations suffered from what Vergès described as a "strange historical delirium," the ongoing guilt and shame which that defeat had produced and which had lasted up to the present.

Now, Vergès was ready to name the manipulators. In staging the Barbie trial, Vergès accused his adversaries across the courtroom, the court, and the Republic it served of both stoking this delirium among the French people and, in sacrificing Klaus Barbie, of preventing the nation as a whole from truly coming to terms with its guilt by blaming someone else for its failure in 1940. For the French nation to recover its honour in its own eyes and in the eyes of the world, it was necessary to break this cycle of guilt and denial and, in effect, free the nation from its past by pronouncing Klaus Barbie innocent.

Given the degree to which the troubled memory of France's World War II past – what Henry Rousso so aptly labelled the "Vichy Syndrome" – would come to dominate the national stage over the next decade and more (to be discussed in the conclusion here), Vergès's closing remarks seem eerily prescient in retrospect. But from the standpoint of the trial itself, the lawyer's aims were less prophetic and arguably more pragmatic. In attempting to erase Barbie's crimes while claiming that he was ultimately the expiatory victim, the scapegoat of a monstrous hoax, Vergès was seeking to transform the ex-Nazi into the righteous victim of a "system," a "state" whose corruption and subterfuges had now been exposed. The stage was set, so to speak, for the final act necessary if the Barbie trial were to be successfully transformed into a "trial by rupture." But that act would require the acquiescence of the court, and especially the jury, in finding the accused innocent on all charges. Despite his self-confidence and rhetorical firepower before the court, Vergès certainly knew this was an unlikely outcome. But his client apparently did not. When the guilty verdict was announced and Vergès turned to his client, Barbie told his lawyer that the verdict was "unbelievable" (*Salaud lumineux* 316).

A memorial marking the location of the "Baraque aux juifs" in the courtyard of
Montluc Prison. Photograph by Richard Golsan

Conclusion

Part One: The Verdict

It is fair to say that, in the end, the 1987 trial of former SS lieutenant Klaus Barbie was not, *pace* Jacques Vergès, "a sad spectacle of which there was much to be ashamed" (*Le salaud lumineux* 315), but rather a largely successful effort to serve the ends justice and history. Nevertheless, one central question about the trial remains. On what grounds did the three judges and nine jurors find the accused guilty on all counts, with no extenuating circumstances?

To be sure, the power of much of the witness testimony was overwhelming, and closing statements by some of the civil parties lawyers, most notably Serge Klarsfeld, were extraordinarily memorable and compelling as well. Moreover, the evidence presented was highly persuasive, if not – depending on one's point of view – entirely conclusive on all counts. In the end, despite their provocations and histrionics, Vergès and his defence co-counsel had done little to counter any of these elements that weighed strongly in favour of the prosecution.

At the same time, however, the swirling tensions in the courtroom, the legal complexities of the case, the complicated and complex historical backdrop from more than forty years in the past, not to mention the magnitude of the occasion itself in France and internationally hardly lent themselves to a serene, detached unequivocal judgment. Indeed, the trial itself closed in a most dramatic fashion. Within minutes of Vergès's stunning personal attacks on the credibility (and dignity) of the witnesses Simone Kadosche-Lagrange and Mario Blardone described in chapter five here, Assize court procedure required that the accused himself have the opportunity to address the court last. Almost immediately, Klaus Barbie was brought handcuffed into the courtroom. At this stage of the trial, the mere appearance of the accused was itself a dramatic, if not a disruptive, event. When asked by president Cerdini if he had anything to say, Barbie stunned the hushed court by responding "Oui, quelques mots en Français" ("Yes, a few words in French"). Then, in effect, Klaus Barbie pleaded "innocent" to the crimes of which he was accused for the first and only time during his trial. He stated that he had not ordered the Izieu round-up and added that he had fought the Resistance "with harshness" (*avec dureté*) but that he "respected" them just the same. Barbie then concluded: "Mais c'était la guerre, et la guerre, c'est finie" ("But it was war, and the war is over"). In other words, Barbie had done nothing against the Jews, and the rest of his crimes were best forgotten. Clearly, after two months of hearings and in his final statement before the court, the accused had no intention of giving the judges and jury anything with which to work. To refer back to Vergès's categories of criminal trials discussed in *De la stratégie judiciare*, Barbie clearly followed the model of an accused in a "trial by rupture" rather than a "trial of connivance." Unlike Adolph Eichmann, he did not excuse or dodge responsibility for his actions (against the Resistance, at least), nor did he become complicit with the court in his own condemnation in an effort to seek the court's mercy.

Given this decidedly unsettling conclusion to the trial and, at least according to the journalist Antoine Perraud, the fact that Vergès had easily taken the measure of what Perraud saw as the ego-driven performances and "muddleheaded" arguments of the unruly "crowd" of civil parties lawyers,[1] what led the jury to such a decisive and unequivocal verdict of "guilty"? The most obvious answer, as Perraud also argues, is that in his duel with chief prosecutor Pierre Truche, Vergès, talented *comédien* or actor though he was, ultimately lost out in his effort to win over the minds and hearts of the jury in a trial of occasionally overwhelming emotional power as well as substantial challenges to the intellect. Indeed, for Perraud (as well as others) the "extraordinary hero" of the Barbie trial *was* Truche, whose sheer charisma and elegance, whose "genuine physical beauty" apparently mesmerized the courtroom. Truche was, for Perraud, an Alain Delon[2] who rather than contemplate his own navel (as supposedly did Delon) contemplated justice instead. When he spoke, Truche was the *koryphaeus*, or leader, of the classical chorus of the trial, addressing not only those present in the vast courtroom but posterity itself.

Such effusive praise (and aesthetic appreciation) of the chief prosecutor may explain some of the latter's sway and persuasiveness in the courtroom. But it does not really address the content, and especially the effectiveness, of what Truche had to say, either in his summation or in his efforts to counter the arguments of Vergès, Nabil Bouaïta, and

Jean-Martin Mbemba, arguments which Alain Finkielkraut, among other critics of the trial, found so (disastrously, in Finkielkraut's case) effective. For the jurist Denis Salas, who, like Perraud, commented on the trial in a 2011 film entitled *A propos du procès Barbie*,[3] the crucial component of Truche's success lay in the fact that in his summation he had responded "point by point," and in advance, to the arguments made by the defence. In the process, Truche had done a masterful job of "reading" the Izieu telex in such a way as to reveal the full extent of Barbie's initiative, responsibility, and understanding of the ultimate fate of the Izieu children, and therefore the full dimensions of the crime he was committing.

While Perraud and Salas are certainly correct in their statements of Truche's effectiveness in his confrontation with Barbie's defence, there is also a broader dimension to that confrontation. This involved what Leora Bilsky would call a clash of "competing historical narratives," referred to in the introduction here. But the broader dimension of that confrontation also included deep philosophical and temperamental differences as well. To understand why Truche ultimately prevailed, these differences need to be briefly examined here. Although it was Vergès who addressed the court last, as Denis Salas points out it was chief prosecutor Truche's job to refute that argument, essentially in advance. Therefore, in order to assess the effectiveness of both arguments in their proper context, Vergès's closing statement, and specifically its historical and philosophical implications, will be analysed first.

In his defence of Barbie, Vergès's most basic strategy was, as noted, to transform the Lyon trial into a "trial by rupture." But this strategy ultimately proved unsuccessful because, as Michel Zaoui, among others, observed, for the strategy to succeed the defence would have been obliged to persuasively cast the crimes of the accused as noble actions in defence of a worthy cause. This was of course impossible because the "worthy cause" in question was Nazism (Zaoui et al. 84–5). But beyond the confines of the "trial by rupture," Vergès and his defence co-counsel also sought to articulate a coherent and *global* vision of history. This vision of history was designed to attenuate and even efface Barbie's crimes while also exposing the hypocrisy, as they saw it, of the French Assize court, the French Republic, and the "white race as a whole." For the prosecution of Klaus Barbie to be successful, and for the Barbie trial to prove legitimate in the eyes of posterity, this vision would ultimately have to be successfully countered. As he well understood, this task would fall to Pierre Truche.

What were the specifics of the global historical vision articulated by Barbie's counsel? In the first instance, as already noted, Vergès and his colleagues proposed a *tiermondiste* conception of the world and of history whose implications and ramifications were moral and legal as well as historical. In simplest terms, according to this view, the Barbie trial was a farce because it glossed over the very real crimes of the world in the present as well as during the centuries of Western oppression of peoples of colour. The Congo, Algeria, Madagascar, Vietnam, and indeed Sabra and Shatilla were just so many signposts along the way pointed out by the defence counsel. As long as the thousands, indeed millions, of crimes and acts of violence committed in this context went unaddressed, trying an aging Nazi for crimes, and especially for crimes against humanity, was ludicrous. The crimes against humanity that needed urgently to be addressed according to this vision were those crimes occurring now, in the present. Moreover, these crimes in the end were as horrific as the crimes of the Nazis. This comparability between them was underscored by Nabil Bouaïta in particular, with his comparison of phosphorous bombs and crematoriums.

In its obvious affinity with a traditionally French revolutionary idealism, Barbie's defence team's *tiermondisme* not surprisingly appealed to many on the left and far left in France, as some responses in the press to the three defence lawyers' closing statements clearly indicated.[4] But there was also another dimension to the historical vision articulated by the defence counsel that seemed to run counter to a strictly political *tiermondiste* reading of it, and, arguably, at least undercut that reading. In insisting on the *radical equivalency* of the crimes of the Holocaust and those of colonialist oppression, the defence counsel was also, in effect, "leveling all the atrocities humanity has known" (Zauoi et al. 86) and, as Finkielkraut observed, reducing them all into so many undifferentiated drops in "an ocean of human suffering." Taken to its logical conclusion, this implied that, in the end, all modern political crimes were and are just so many manifestations or symptoms a globalized, very human capacity for violence and political violence, in particular, capable of erupting at any moment. In this perspective as well, all perpetrators are equally innocent or guilty, in that they are all mere agents or, more accurately, transmitters of a violence that so readily and often destroys human communities.

But in a broader context, despite this extraordinary capacity for violence, human communities have survived, and indeed thrived. How has this been possible? In the early 1970s, the French philosopher René Girard, following in the steps of Émile Durkheim, among others, began to articulate his theory of mimetic violence and the practice of scapegoating that achieved extraordinary notoriety, especially in France, with the publication in 1978 of *Des choses cachées depuis la foundation du monde.*

According to Girard, since the origins of human culture communities and indeed larger societies have staved off the spread of all-destructive contagions of violence by collectively designating a *bouc émissaire* or scapegoat as the "originator" and sole culprit of that violence. Through the destruction or removal of that scapegoat, moreover, that community can rid itself of its violence. In reality of course, since all in the community are ultimately responsible for the spread of violence, the designation of the scapegoat is artificial, a fraudulent practice. The scapegoat is in reality neither *more nor less guilty* of originating the violence than anyone else. But, according to Girard's theory, the scapegoat bears distinguishing marks that set him apart as an "outsider" who can effectively be blamed for the troubles for which all in the community are ultimately responsible. As long as the artifice of scapegoating remains concealed, the practice proves efficacious, and the community is all the more unified by focusing its collective animus on one "guilty" outsider.[5]

In articulating his theory of mimetic violence and scapegoating, Girard relied initially on examples taken from ancient myths, global mythology, and great works of Western literature, like Sophocles's *Oedipus the King* and Shakespeare's tragedies. But in *Le Bouc Emissaire*, published in 1980, Girard applied his theory of scapegoating to modern political practices as well. Most notably, he stressed that Jews provided literally "reservoirs" of scapegoats for the Nazis. They were after all easily singled out as "other" in European culture, bearing physical marks of difference (exaggerated or made up by Nazi propaganda), followed different religious, dietary, and (often different) clothing traditions, and yet were enough "inside" the community to be blamed for its internecine strife. They were of course not "guilty" of or responsible for that strife or violence, but if Germans could nevertheless agree collectively that they were, their "sacrifice" would prove beneficial in uniting the rest of the community.

Girard's theories concerning scapegoating and collective violence may seem far removed from the Barbie trial. But their applicability becomes apparent if one considers the implications of Vergès's deliberate and repeated insistence that Klaus Barbie was a *bouc émissaire*. First, in accordance with both the political and more broadly philosophical parameters of the historical vision sketched out by the defence, Barbie could serve as an effective scapegoat because in a world given over to violence, he was no more "guilty" or "innocent" than any other agent or transmitter of that violence. This would include a French paratrooper in Algeria, an American foot soldier in Vietnam – the possibilities were limitless. But at the same time, within a European and French context, he was *the worst of all killers, a Nazi executioner*. That fact served to mark him out as radically "other" and therefore as a perfect conduit and scapegoat for *all* the violence of recent French history, from the Occupation to Algeria and beyond. If punished for his crimes, if "sacrificed" in Girardian terms, he could effectively stand in for and assume the burden of guilt the French people felt over their own killers, their own transmitters of violence, from French collaborators and killers who worked for Vichy and the Nazis to French soldiers who tortured and killed "resisters" in Algeria. If this were not enough, Barbie's "sacrifice" would also assuage French guilt over the nation's disastrous and humiliating 1940 defeat. Of course, such a "sacrifice" would be an enormous act of bad faith, as it would allow the French people to ignore their own criminals and *their* crimes, but it would also, by the same token, be an extraordinary *temptation*, not just for the jury in Lyon but for the French people who awaited Barbie's conviction. In telling the jury that it was up to them to save the honour of France by declaring Barbie "not guilty," it was this scenario, if not precisely articulated in these terms, that Vergès had in mind.

***

It is hard not to imagine that, despite the utter horror of Barbie's crimes, given the picture Vergès had painted and his calls for the jury to save France's honour in freeing Klaus Barbie, at least some in jury and certainly in the larger courtroom were receptive to what he had to say. And in making his case to the Lyon Assize court, there is no doubt that Vergès was making his case to a much larger public opinion, and to posterity as well. Regardless, when Pierre Truche rose to give his summation before the Lyon court immediately prior to the closing statements of defence counsel, he had a very different story to tell, and one motivated by an historical and moral vision much less grandiose and frankly pretentious in its reach than the one Vergès and his colleagues would soon articulate. Pierre Truche, unlike some of his colleagues among the civil parties lawyers as well as the defence, had always maintained that the trial of Klaus Barbie, despite its visibility and importance, was a *normal* Assize court trial. That is, there was an accused, an individual, on trial for crimes with which he was charged. The issue at hand was to judge *that individual* on the weight of the evidence and testimony presented rather than weigh his guilt or innocence in relation to that of all other political criminals who had committed other crimes in other contexts, no matter how horrendous or despicable these crimes and criminals might be.

It is in this light that, even before he gave his summation, Truche had challenged before the court the very idea and application of the "trial by rupture," as Vergès and his colleagues were seeking to enact it. First, he noted the fact that, as alluded to earlier, a "trial by rupture" presupposes the nobility or "dignity" of the actions of the accused and that these actions are carried out on behalf of a worthy cause or regime. But as Truche observed, "Nobody ever said we should speak of Barbie's dignity, or the dignity of Nazism, or the dignity of the acts he committed." Then, by way of context, Truche stressed the fact that Barbie himself had begun to set the groundwork for a trial by rupture as far back as 1971. At that time, the former Nazi had stated, "I didn't do more than others did in Algeria."

At the heart of Barbie's defence, Truche explained to the court, was not in fact a "rupture" with a supposedly corrupt system or order, but rather, literally, an effort to "transport the trial elsewhere," that is, to make it about everybody *except* the accused. So, in questioning the German magistrates Holfort and Streim, Vergès had not pursued the evidence against Barbie about which they had been called to testify but had rather pointed the finger at them, and the Federal Republic itself, by asking them why Barbie wasn't being pursued legally *there*, in Germany, instead of in France. But then, as Truche observed, to distract from Barbie and his crimes in the present, in the Lyon Assize court, "it was necessary to pursue simply everybody."

The message the defence wished to send to the jury, Truche continued, followed along the same lines. "You cannot judge me," Barbie and his defence team were arguing in effect, "because of what your own government did in Algeria." But, of course, the members of the Lyon jury had absolutely no responsibility for what happened in North Africa a quarter of a century earlier. If one accepted the defence argument and followed it to its logical conclusion, all control would be lost, and "disrespect for the right of others to a defense would be complete."

In concluding, Truche underscored the fact that in seeking to turn the Barbie trial not into a "trial by rupture" but rather into what he labelled a "trial by derivation" or distraction, literally any comparative tactic, any distortion, was possible, including grossly inflating numbers of dead when that was convenient. Referring back to Vergès's bitter exchanges with Elie Wiesel, Truche noted that Vergès's figure of 15,000 Algerian dead per month in French camps was totally fallacious. As a kind of *coup de grâce*, Truche then demonstrated how Vergès had concocted his magical numbers. He warned the court and jury, "once Vergès leads you outside the confines of this trial, you are obliged to doubt what you hear." Vergès's only response was to observe that "today it is the trial of Monsieur Vergès."

If a first step at dismantling Barbie's defence in advance consisted of exposing the subterfuges and fallacies of the "trial by rupture," in his summation Truche, as noted, relied more on his own judicial philosophy as well as on a more pragmatic, rational, and empirical vision of history. Where that historical vision was concerned, Truche avoided precisely the kind of dubious or problematic comparisons and conflations that would serve as the basis for the historical vision that the defence would articulate. Moreover, in his summation the prosecutor focused meticulously, as noted, on the precise political and historical backdrop and context in accordance with which Barbie's crimes needed to be understood and judged. What emerged from Truche's presentation was that Klaus Barbie was, as Truche affirmed in an interview after the trial, "no scapegoat." Barbie had, moreover, and on his own initiative worked diligently to please his superiors, doing more than was necessary to achieve that end. And in making his case, Truche avoided precisely the kind of judicial theatricality, histrionics, and overreach that characterized the performances of the defence counsel, and especially Vergès and Mbemba (recall the latter's description of his handshake with Barbie). Such antics were clearly anathema to the prosecutor. For Truche, the role and demeanour of that prosecutor required most crucially that s/he keep an eye on his or her own prejudices and partialities, and then that s/he must never point an accusatory or demeaning finger at the accused, or presumably, anyone else in the courtroom. This is of course precisely what Vergès had done in launching his final salvoes at Simone Kadosche-Lagrange and Mario Blardone.

Still, in purely abstract terms, all of this does not fully explain the *decisiveness* of the jury's verdict, of its conviction of Klaus Barbie. And, to be fair to Vergès and his defence co-counsel, the appeal to what might be described as the *revolutionary spirit* of their case to a French jury, for whom the spirit of 1789 was such a fundamental part of its national identity, could not have fallen on completely deaf ears. So what did Truche's arguments, in their content, spirit, and vision, have to offer that the defence's arguments did not?

In its most basic assumptions, Truche's arguments of course conformed more closely to the basic tenets of the French justice system, and in fact any other justice system worthy of the name. In such justice systems, an individual must be accountable for his or her actions before the law. And despite Vergès's and his colleagues' best efforts, the idea that one crime must go unpunished because other crimes have gone unpunished is untenable for even the most unsophisticated mind. As Primo Levi had written: "No juridical system absolves an assassin under the pretext that there are other [unpunished] assassins in the house next door" (qtd. in Zaoui et al. 86).

But in countering the defence's appeal to the "revolutionary spirit" of the jury and through it, to France's long and proud revolutionary heritage, Truche offered the court and jury something that was equally a part of French traditions and culture. In his demeanour, arguments, and *presence* in the Lyon Assize court, Truche, whether consciously or not, appealed to the traditions of French rationalism and humanism, dating from the sixteenth and seventeenth centuries and extending up to the present. Those traditions required, first and foremost, a rational approach to the testimony and evidence in the trial that respected at the same time the limits of human understanding and knowledge. This was evident, as noted, in Truche's absolute commitment to studying and understanding Barbie's criminal dossier, something which, at least according to Serge Klarsfeld, Vergès did not adequately master. Moreover, when Truche confronted the jury with his conviction that Barbie knew full well the fate of the Jews he deported, he appealed to the jury's *own* powers of reason. He insisted that it was illogical and unreasonable that the Nazis, Barbie included, would set these deportees free after the war to be allowed to return to tell their tales of horror.

Equally important to Truche's character and presence in the court-room – what Perraud and others called his "humanism" – was an awareness of his own limitations. This was evident in his visibly mod-est demeanour, certainly in comparison with Vergès's all too apparent egotism and disdain for others, and in his insistence on the dignity and humanity of others, including the accused himself. It was, after all, Truche and Truche alone who invited Barbie to explain himself in "human" terms, all the while underscoring the fact that Barbie had not always been the brutal Nazi he had become but had once been an indi-vidual as capable of empathy as anyone else. For Truche, clearly – and to quote Paul Bénichou on the fundamental vision of French humanism – "the name 'humanity' in and of itself designates not only the quality of being human, but also the sentiment that obliges one to respect that quality wherever it is found."[6]

In the name of that "humanity," that "quality of being human," in sum-mer 1987 the Lyon Assize court found Klaus Barbie guilty on all counts.

Part Two: The Complex Legacies of the Barbie Trial in the 1990s and Beyond

Given its global visibility and resonance, as well as the debates and con-troversies historical, legal, and otherwise, it stirred up, it is not surprising that the Barbie trial's legacies are somewhat mixed, although most fall on the positive side of the ledger.

In the long term, within France, Vergès was right in his prediction that the nation would have to reckon with the guilt and humiliation it still felt over its disastrous defeat to the Germans in May/June 1940. It would also have to deal with the indignity of four years of Nazi occupation and Vichy's abjection in, among other things, its willing participation in the Nazi Final Solution of the "Jewish Question." Indeed, it is fair to say on this score that the Barbie trial in many ways prompted or unleashed more than a decade of French soul-searching and reckoning with the troubled past of the so-called *années noires*, or Dark Years. Here the signposts were numerous: scandals over the troubled pasts of prominent public figures, captains of industry, and political leaders, culminating in the 1995 scandal over president François Mitterrand's own youth as an extreme right-wing and anti-Semitic student and especially his long service to the Vichy regime. Mitterrand was in fact awarded the Vichy regime's highest honour, the *francisque*. The socialist president had glossed over and minimized his past for many years, and the fact that he was France's first socialist and left-wing president in decades made the revelations over his right-wing past all the more galling, as many of his fellow socialists and others acknowledged.[7]

At the same time the nation was rocked by scandals like the Mitterrand scandal, important novels and films attempted in a variety of ways and contexts to come to terms with the weight of the Dark Years in the past and present. France's greatest filmmakers of the era, including Marcel Ophuls, Louis Malle, Claude Chabrol, Claude Berri, and François Truffaut, among others, made stunning and powerful fictional films and documentaries about the Occupation. These ran the gamut from personal experiences and recollections of the war and its impact on subsequent generations, to denunciations of the cowardice and passivity of the French people at the time, to the brutally anti-Semitic practices of the Vichy regime and its role in the Nazi Final Solution. Indeed, as Henry Rousso pointed out in *The Vichy Syndrome* and many subsequent works, in the 1980s, and arguably at least, especially in the wake of the Barbie trial, "Jewish Memory" of the conflict moved front and centre and certainly dominated much of the discussion of the Vichy past in the 1990s and into the new millennium.

In terms of the Barbie trial's impact on subsequent legal and judicial efforts to deal with the troubled legacies of the Dark Years, Vergès was spectacularly wrong in his predictions that France would never come to terms with its own *French* criminals against humanity. These men had served Vichy and/or the Nazis, and specifically those who had participated in one way or another in forwarding the aims of the Nazi Final Solution. Thanks in considerable measure to the continuing efforts of Serge Klarsfeld and others, especially journalists like Annette Lévy-Willard at *Libération*, who unearthed important evidence against these men, in the early 1990s three individuals – René Bousquet, Paul Touvier, and Maurice Papon – stood on the verge of facing trial on charges of crimes against humanity. The most important of these individuals was undoubtedly Bousquet, who served as secretary general of Vichy police during the Occupation and had personally negotiated with Barbie's superior, Karl Oberg, the infamous *Vélodrome d'hiver* round-up on 16–17 July 1942. In that roundup, French police who had prepared in advance lists of foreign Jews living in Paris swept through the city and arrested some 13,000 men, women, and children and had taken them to the bicycle racing stadium, the *Vélodrome d'hiver*, where they were kept for several days in horrific conditions before most were deported to their deaths. After the war, Bousquet was tried in 1949, but not for crimes against humanity, of course, since these statutes did not exist in French law at the time. He was found guilty of "intelligence with the enemy," but received no prison sentence, as he was credited with providing help to the Resistance. After the war, he became a wealthy businessman and a close friend of François Mitterrand. In July 1993, as the final legal obstacles to his prosecution were removed, Bousquet was assassinated by a deranged gunman who had earlier attempted to kill Klaus Barbie in prison in Lyon.

The first Frenchman to be tried for crimes against humanity for his crimes during the Occupation was Paul Touvier, who stood trial in the Yvelines Assize court in Versailles in spring 1994. The eleventh child of a right-wing Catholic family of modest means, Touvier had been essentially a n'er-do-well before the war. With France's defeat, he joined a pro-Vichy veterans association and then joined Vichy's paramilitary police force, the *Milice*, or Militia, when it was created to fight "France's enemies" in 1943. The *Milice* was openly fascist and anti-Semitic and worked closely with the Nazis in fighting the Resistance and in persecuting and murdering Jews. Touvier climbed quickly through the ranks of the organization and eventually became head of the Second Service (intelligence) for the Savoy Department. Known, like Barbie, for his brutality, Touvier robbed his Jewish victims, lived lavishly in a stolen apartment, drove a stolen car, and murdered Resistance members and Jews alike. After the war, Touvier went into hiding, aided by high-ranking figures in the Catholic Church. Travelling under the alias of "Paul Lacroix," Touvier hid out in monasteries throughout France. In the early 1970s, Touvier's high-placed friends and Catholic authorities secured a pardon for Touvier from then president Georges Pompidou. When that pardon became known, public outcry drove Touvier back into hiding. He was finally arrested in a right-wing *intégriste* monastery in Nice in 1989, by which time he had been charged with crimes against humanity.

It is at this stage, and in the years leading up to Touvier's 1994 trial, that the legal legacies of the Barbie trial began to impact the Touvier case directly. In April 1992, to the shock and consternation of the nation, the Paris Court of Appeals, dominated at the time by right-wing judges, acquitted Touvier on all charges of crimes against humanity pending against him. In its decision the Appeals Court essentially rewrote history. It argued first – and wrongly – that the Vichy regime, unlike Nazi Germany, was *not* a state practising a "politics of ideological hegemony." Therefore, applying the logic inherent in the definition of crimes against humanity handed down by the Court of Cassation in December 1985 in the Barbie case, the court reasoned that since Paul Touvier was a member of the *Milice*, any actions he took in that capacity were carried out on behalf of Pétain's French State. Since crimes against humanity could only be carried out on behalf of an ideologically hegemonic regime, according to the 1985 decision, Touvier's crimes could only be construed as "war crimes," on which the statute of limitations had run out. Therefore, Touvier could walk.

Clearly, in this instance, the December 1985 Court of Cassation definition of crimes against humanity that had roiled the Barbie investigation and put stress on the prosecution and civil parties during that 1987 trial was now, ironically, making it possible to free a Frenchman guilty of committing crimes like those of his Nazi predecessor. In the event, in December 1992, a higher court partially overturned the Paris Appeals Court decision, allowing Touvier to face trial for one crime alone. Touvier had ordered the murder of seven Jewish hostages at the cemetery of Rilleux-la-Pape near Lyon on 29 June 1944. This crime was supposedly carried out according to Touvier himself on *German* orders. In its decision, the higher court opted, wisely or unwisely depending on one's perspective, *not* to challenge the Paris Court of Appeal's wrong-headed historical assessment of the political nature of the Vichy regime.

As it turned out, the December 1985 Court of Cassation decision threw up one more serious obstacle to Touvier's prosecution for crimes against humanity, once the trial itself got underway. A more thorough investigation of the crime suggested that Rilleux had *not* in fact been ordered by the Germans, so in effect it was a *French* crime. Therefore, it could not be a crime against humanity. How was the court to handle this dilemma? During the trial, notable historians who had earlier argued that it was a French crime now changed their tunes so that the prosecution could move forward with the case. One civil parties lawyer, however, resisted this argument, insisting that Rilleux was indeed a *French crime* after all. The lawyer in question was Arno Klarsfeld, who had replaced his father in representing his association in the Touvier trial and subsequently in the trial of Maurice Papon. But despite his contrarian stance, Klarsfeld also offered the court a solution, a way out of the dilemma. Klarsfeld argued that, because Joseph Darnand, the head of the *Milice*, had sworn a personal oath of loyalty to Adolf Hitler, the *Milice* itself could *also* be considered a Nazi organization. Therefore, crimes committed on its behalf could be considered as crimes carried out in the name of a regime practising a politics of ideological hegemony. In this way, Klarsfeld "squared the circle," so to speak, and Touvier was convicted and sentenced to life in prison. Like Barbie before him, Touvier died in prison several years after his conviction.

Although, like the Barbie trial, the conviction of the accused was generally treated positively in the press, decisions taken during the investigation and prosecution of Klaus Barbie ultimately hindered rather than helped the efficient prosecution of Paul Touvier. Moreover, for Touvier to be found guilty, the law and certainly history had to be massaged or manipulated. This, decidedly, had been an unfortunate outcome and one directly attributable to the December 1985 Court of Cassation decision in the Barbie case. The final irony was that, in attempting at last to try a Frenchman for crimes against humanity, to find him guilty the only regime in whose name that crime could ultimately be committed was not French, but German.[8]

In looking back on the French trials of the 1990s, the 1997–8 trial of Maurice Papon stands out as more substantive and significant than the Touvier trial if for no other reason than the fact that Maurice Papon was a well-placed and important civil servant of the Vichy regime. He was not a corrupt and brutal policeman like Touvier – "political rabble," as François Mitterrand labelled him. More importantly, as a Vichy subprefect in Bordeaux, Papon had been directly involved in the most memorable and *iconic* aspect of the Final Solution, certainly in Western Europe: the round-up and deportation of tens of thousands of Jews to their deaths in the East. Indeed, when Papon was found guilty of crimes against humanity in April 1998, he was found "complicit in the "illegal arrest" and "arbitrary detention" of some one hundred persons in the context of deportations by train convoys from Bordeaux headed to the East between July 1942 and January 1944. However, Papon was acquitted on charges of complicity in the murder of those deported. As a result, he received only a ten-year sentence, which he immediately appealed.

How was this possible? How could one be found guilty of complicity in crimes against humanity but innocent of criminal responsibility for the fate of those deported, that is, innocent of complicity in murder? Given the importance during the Barbie trial of proving that Barbie knew the fate of those he deported, if he was to be found guilty of crimes against humanity, this seemed unbelievable. Even the "political rabble" Touvier had been found guilty of in ordering the killing of Jews, even if many had come to believe that the Rilleux killings were merely an act of personal vengeance and therefore not a crime against humanity.

The explanation for this apparent paradox can be found in a decision taken by the Court of Cassation in January 1997. Some six months before the Papon trial opened, the court decided that it was not necessary that an "*accomplice*" to a crime against humanity adhere to the politics of ideological hegemony of the regime carrying out these crimes, or to an organization that regime sponsored, like the SS. This was code for saying such an accomplice *did not have to know the aims of that politics*, which in this case meant the knowledge that deported Jews would be exterminated. Under any circumstances, Papon could always plead ignorance of having *knowingly* sent Jews to their deaths. This claim would be more credible in his case than that of a Nazi and SS member like Klaus Barbie. However one viewed the 1997 Court of Cassation decision, the point was that French courts had once again massaged French law to accommodate the prosecution of an individual charged with crimes against humanity or complicity therein, either in allowing Resistance civil parties to "add on" to the prosecution of Klaus Barbie or in making a conviction of a Maurice Papon possible through a kind of legal splitting of hairs.

If one considers the status and stature of the accused – Maurice Papon was a *grand bourgeois* – the nature of the crimes committed, and in the verdict and sentence handed down, the Papon trial bears little resemblance to the trial of Klaus Barbie ten years earlier. Nevertheless, the ghost of Jacques Vergès and the shadow of Barbie's defence *did* make their presence felt when the memory of France's colonial past suddenly erupted in the Bordeaux courtroom. As part of the procedure in an Assize court trial, as described earlier, the biography or *curriculum vitae* of the accused is rehearsed through the questioning of that accused by the president of the court. During that questioning in the Papon trial, the bitter memory of Papon's tenure as a prefect of Paris police in the late 1950s and early 1960s was raised and discussed, especially his role on the night of 17 October 1961 in the brutal, and indeed murderous, suppression of Algerian protestors in the streets of Paris. The protest that night had been called in response to a harsh curfew on Algerian workers imposed by Papon that made it difficult, if not impossible, for many to get to their jobs. Tens of thousands of Algerians protested, and in response French police, acting apparently on orders from Papon, beat thousands of protesters and killed anywhere from fifty to three hundred people.[9] Some were beaten to death, others shot, and some were thrown in the Seine River, where they drowned. Their bodies were fished out over subsequent days. Additionally, thousands of Algerians were rounded up and taken to detention centres in and around the French capital, including the infamous *Vélodrome d'hiver*, where some 13,000 Jews had been detained in 1942. When the public became aware of the fate of the Algerian protesters, outraged critics compared French police tactics to those of Vichy and the Nazis some two decades earlier.

During his trial Papon denied that Paris police had killed any Algerian protestors in October 1961, blaming the deaths on clashes between rival Algerian liberation movements. This denial of responsibility in 1997 for what had happened in 1961 only served to intensify public outrage over an event many had forgotten and others were too young to know about in the first place. As for its impact on the trial itself, the re-emergence of October 1961 served primarily to roil the waters. The distinguished French historian Pierre Vidal-Naquet, himself a Jew, stated that Papon's actions as chief of Paris police against Algerians were *also* crimes against humanity, and that he should be charged with these crimes as well. And as opposed to the Barbie trial, where the crimes of European colonizers, the United States and Israel raised by the defence had no real relation to the accused, here the accused was *directly linked* to one of the worst examples of French oppression of colonial peoples, even if the colonial peoples in question resided in Paris.[10]

In many ways, the controversy that arose over 17 October 1961 early in Papon's trial serves as a perfect example of the "competition of victims" that the Barbie trial played a major role in promoting. Indeed, if the 1990s were deeply marked in France by the recognition of a "duty" to the memory of the Jewish victims of the Holocaust and France's role in their deportation and destruction, other victims now emerged to claim their right to recognition as well. Most prominent among the latter were formerly colonized peoples.

Despite the best efforts of of Vergès and his colleagues during the Barbie trial to make the colonial past *the* central issue in the trial itself, Nicolas Bancel and Pascal Banchard write that it was not until the 1990s that the tramautic memory of colonization and decolonization truly came into its own. This was the case, they affirm, for several reasons. Most importantly, in their view, before the 1990s the past was seen as a "permanent source for the edification and consecration of national values" (138).[11] In this context, "the colonial episode and its postcolonial consequences" were "in practical terms of no 'usefulness' and were even counter-productive" (138). To add to this, France's colonial past itself had also become a source of nostalgia for the extreme right and the emerging National Front. But with the Judaeocentric turn of the memory of Vichy and the shift from edifying memories of the Resistance to traumatic memories of the Holocaust and Vichy's role in that event, the nation's focus turned to other past traumas rather than sources of national pride and celebration. And there were many traumatic memories associated with colonialism and decolonization that needed to be reckoned with. In addition to 17 October 1961, which, once recalled so jaringly in the Papon trial, generated new histories of the event as well as novels and films, there was the use of torture by French troops in Algeria,[12] the disgraceful abandonment of the *harkis*,[13] as well as other painful memories to be dealt with. Throughout the 1990s and into the new millennium, the traumatic memory of colonialism and decolonization would assume centre stage, perhaps even more so than the memory of Vichy itself, although this is debateable.

Then there were the victims of other repressive and murderous ideologies in addition to Nazism that needed addressing as well. As the Papon trial was picking up steam in late October 1997, the eruption of another traumatic memory on the French stage occurred when the publisher Fayard released the *Livre noir du communisme*, or *Black Book of Communism*. An enormous volume featuring essays by many of France's leading historians, the *Black Book*, published on the seventieth anniversary of the October Revolution, chronicled the crimes and genocides of Communist regimes worldwide. In a controversial introduction that echoed the type of uncritical and deliberately provocative historical comparisons and amalgamations used by Vergès and the rest of Klaus Barbie's defence team a decade earlier, Stéphane Courtois argued, among other things, that the number of those killed by Communist regimes worldwide far outnumbered those killed by the Nazis. In Courtois's telling, Communist crimes therefore essentially dwarfed Nazi crimes. Courtois also affirmed that the life of a Kulak child killed in the Stalinist famines was "equivalent" to that of a Jewish child who died in the Warsaw ghetto, without drawing any distinctions between the two. Finally, Courtois demanded, why had there never been a "Nuremberg" for Communist crimes as there had been for Nazi crimes? It was, he insisted, time for the world to fulfil a duty to the memory of Communism's victims. And in the fall of 1997, the sheer enormity to Communist crimes reported in the *Black Book* made Maurice Papon's crimes seem almost inconsequential in comparison. Under any circumstances, as the ever-pessimistic Alain Finkielkraut wrote in October 1997 in *Le Monde* a week after the Papon trial opened, it was simply "too late" to try Papon for committing his wartime crimes (qtd. in Golsan, *Papon*, 190).

In a year, 1997 in which so many troubling memories were re-emerging and assuming centre stage, it is perhaps only appropriate that, a decade after the Barbie trial, the memory of the Resistance should re-emerge, and spectacularly as well. The "memory" in question was the wartime past of iconic heroes of the Resistance Raymond and Lucie Aubrac, who, as discussed earlier, were accused by Vergès as those truly responsible for the betrayal of Jean Moulin to the Gestapo. Vergès's claims at that time in the 1980s, recorded in Claude Bal's film *Que la vérité est amère*, had been put to rest when the Aubracs had won a defamation suit against the two men.

The occasion in 1997 was not a film but the publication of a book, Pierre Chauvy's *Aubrac, Lyon, 1943*. In his book, supposedly a work of objective history, Chauvy published in the appendix documents from German police files as well as Klaus Barbie's "Memoir," supposedly written in 1991 and accusing the Aubracs of being Moulin's betrayers. The overall impression created in Chauvy's book was that the carefully cultivated narratives of heroism recounted in the memoirs of both Aubracs were "tainted," that something was not right. Given the status of Raymond and Lucie Aubrac as living icons of French heroism during the war and the fact that their legends had only grown in the decade since the Barbie trial, such a challenge to their credibility and integrity could not go unanswered. In May 1997, the newspaper *Libération* agreed to host a roundtable requested by the Aubracs and at which they were present, along with former colleagues in the Resistance; France's leading historians of the Resistance; and Daniel Cordier, Jean Moulin's former secretary and author of a monumental and definitive biography of the Resistance martyr.

Although the roundtable, whose exchanges over several days were recorded and published in the newspaper, began quite cordially, according to Leah Hewitt, the discussions eventually assumed the form of an inquisition. Or, as Susan Suleiman suggests, the historians began to assume the role of the *juge d'instruction*, or investigating magistrate, as the inconsistences and improbabilities in the Aubracs' accounts of their wartime actions began to pile up. By the end, the historians were, for the most part, pitted against the Aubracs. Lucie Aubrac in particular[14] came under heavy criticism for "romanticizing" facts in her memoir, *Ils partiront dans l'ivresse*, and then not admitting to this subsequently. In the end, the roundtable left a bitter taste in the mouths of the participants and created enmities that did not dissipate with time. For those, like Vergès, who had long wished to impeach the credibility of Resistance heroes like the Aubracs, their discomfiture and shaken credibility must have been most satisfying.[15]

What of the new millennium, what "legacies" might be attributed to the 1987 Barbie trial that, for some at least, belong to a different century and different era? Arguably, the relatively recent effort to deal *in legal terms* with a traumatic past by defining the crimes that took place at that time retroactively as "crimes against humanity," an effort that resulted in the early 2000s in the passage of several controversial "memory" or "memorial" laws is an "indirect descendant" of the Barbie trial. But if this is the case, the import and consequences of this "descendant" or "legacy" laws are vexed as well. The first so-called memory law, the 1990 Gayssot Law, was passed in the wake of the Barbie trial and constituted a direct response to one political phenomenon that the Barbie trial sought to challenge – the denial of the Holocaust, or "negationism." The Gayssot Law incriminated the denial of the Holocaust, with sanctions including incarceration for up to a year and heavy fines for one found guilty of the crime.

Following upon the precedent set by the Gayssot Law, in the early 2000s several more memory laws were passed, all of which soon came to be criticized as overtly political and as responses to pressures from various influential constituencies in contemporary France. In 2001, two such laws were passed, the first officially recognizing the Turkish mass murder of the Armenians in 1915 as a "genocide." The second memorial law, the so-called Taubira Law, recognized slavery since the fifteenth century and the institution of slavery itself as a "crime against humanity." Then, in 2005, another memorial law was passed, the so-called Meckachera Law, which recognized the "positive role" played by French colonists in former French possessions, in North Africa in particular.

It is not hard to recognize that the proliferation of laws like France's memory laws poses dangers to the law as well as to history and historical truth. Indeed, a group of concerned historians, whose organization was named *Liberté pour l'histoire*, or "Freedom for History," underscored the fact that if an event in the past was labelled a "crime against humanity" or a "genocide" by law, to challenge this classification could incur legal sanctions. This would have the chilling effect of pre-empting further research on that event, as no historian would relish fines or jail time for doing his or her research and publishing the results. From the standpoint of the law, what real substance or meaning would terms like "crimes against humanity" or "genocide" have if they could be applied willy-nilly and as a result of partisan pressures to events even centuries in the past? This impulse, in fact, had already begun to manifest itself in the form of petitions, for example, to label the revolutionary suppression of rebels from the Vendée at the turn of the eighteenth and nineteenth centuries a "genocide." There were many other such petitions as well. It is hard to imagine that anyone in the Lyon Assize court in 1987 could have foreseen that the incorporation and application of "crimes against humanity" statutes in French law could eventually lead to developments like this. [16]

Finally, what were and are the legacies of the 1987 Barbie trial for international law? Any in-depth discussion of this topic is beyond the scope of the present study, but a few statements along these lines from French as well as American sources seem pertinent. For example, in a 1989 *University of Colorado Law Review* essay on the Barbie trial, Nicholas R. Doman wrote that the December 1985 Court of Cassation decision allowing Resistance members to attach themselves to the Prosecution represented "an important contribution to international law with respect to crimes against humanity." This was so because it stipulated that "acts that may fall under the definition of war crimes can also be crimes against humanity if carried out 'in the name of a regime practicing a political system'" (456).

For Michel Zaoui, Noëlle Herrenschmitt, and Antoine Garapon, the legacy of the Barbie trial, coupled with those of its two French sequels, the Touvier trial and the Papon trial, goes further still. The French trials, they argue, did nothing less than "reawaken the spirit of Nuremberg" and "inspire the International Criminal Court itself" (142). It is not inconsequential, they write, that between the Barbie trial in 1987 and the Papon trial a decade later, the ad hoc International Tribunals for the former Yugoslavia and for Rwanda were established and had begun to function. Then, in June 1998, the Statute of Rome for the creation of a permanent international tribunal was signed, and any number of international tribunals, truth and reconciliation commissions, and other fora of justice for political crimes have become operative since.

To conclude, and to return to France. As this conclusion is being written, another historically important Assize court trial is taking place in Paris. The trial involves those accused of aiding and abetting two Islamic radicals, the Kouachi brothers, who in January 2015 carried out attacks on the satirical journal *Charlie Hebdo*, resulting in the deaths of twelve journalists and security individuals. Several days later, an ally of the Kouachi brothers, Amédy Coulibaly, killed five and injured ten more people at a kosher grocery store near the *Porte de Vincennes*. All three terrorists were killed, but the trial of the accomplices is intended to help the French come to terms with the memory of the trauma and the subsequent, much bloodier massacres carried out by Islamic extremists in November of that year.

The *Charlie Hebdo* trial does not involve charges of crimes against humanity. But, like the Barbie trial, it does serve as a public forum where witnesses and victims can describe the horrors they experienced and achieve some form of catharsis for themselves and others. As for the French people, in principle, at least, they will gain a better understanding of politically, racially, and ethnically motivated crimes that shook the nation and underscored the nation's divisions. In a different time, and with different issues of national concern, the Barbie trial did much the same thing.

In 2014, in a trial that did involve charges of crimes against humanity, a former Hutu genocidaire, Pascal Simbikangwa, was tried and convicted for his role in the 1994 Rwandan genocide that killed close to a million people, mostly Tutsis. France had an especially close relationship with the Hutu regime in Rwanda, whose most fervent adherents organized and carried out the 1994 genocide. Subsequently, two more Hutus involved in the genocide have been tried and convicted of crimes against humanity in French courts. All three trials would not have been possible had not a legal decision by French courts in 1996 made it possible to try non-French citizens in French courts for crimes against humanity committed elsewhere. Like the Barbie trial, the trials of the Rwandan genocidaires were filmed. The *Charlie Hebdo* trial is being filmed as well.

In expressing their ambitions and hopes for the Barbie trial in the courtroom, in their writings as well as in the media afterward, the two central antagonists of the Barbie trial, lead defence counsel Jacques Vergès and chief prosecutor Pierre Truche, were clear about what the Barbie trial needed to accomplish or set in motion for the future. For Vergès, crimes against humanity trials, moving forward, should not be about political and/or racist crimes of the past but about those of the present and future. For Truche, what was crucial was that crimes against humanity were understood to be "works in progress" and that trials in the future that worked with these concepts had a responsibility to develop and refine them as they were applied to different crimes and different situations.

In the new century, in circumstances they might not have expected, each man, it would seem, got his wish.

Chronology

25 October 1913   Nikolaus "Klaus" Barbie is born in Bad Godesberg, Germany. His parents, Nikolaus Barbie and Anna Hees, are both schoolteachers. The couple are not married when Anna Hees gives birth to Klaus but are married soon thereafter, on 30 January 1914. Nicholas Sr. joins the army and spends four years at the front. He is severely wounded in the neck and in pain most of his life. An alcoholic, be beats his son and wife. He is also physically violent with his students. According to Hammerschmidt, the beatings the young Klaus absorbs lead to both a "loss of confidence in paternal authority" and a "passionate longing" for a "charismatic leader."

1923   French and Belgian troops invade and occupy the Ruhr, an episode which triggered Barbie's lifelong hatred of the French.

1925   Barely twelve years old, Barbie leaves the family home to become a resident student at the Freidrich-Wilhelm Gymnasium in Trier. Barbie embraces the strict discipline of the school, where he enjoys a camaraderie he never experienced at home.

1929   Barbie returns to live at home in the family apartment in Trier. The domestic situation has not improved, and Barbie joins a number of organizations, including the *Deutsches Jungvolk* ("German Youth") and the *Deutsche Jungcraft*, a Catholic sporting organization. He also joins a Christian charitable association, the *Bahnhofsmission*, which serves prisoners and the homeless. It is to this period in Barbie's life that chief prosecutor Truche refers in asking Barbie how a young man with charitable impulses became an SS member.

1933   Barbie's father and his mentally incapacitated younger brother, Kurt, both die. On 1 April, Barbie joins the Nazi Party and is from the start a devoted and indeed fanatical member. At the encouragement of his superiors, Barbie begins to spy on the other members of youth organizations to which he belonged.

1934   With his father's death, Barbie no longer has funds to pursue his studies. He volunteers for the New Nazi Labour Force and works in the northern province of Schleswig-Holstein. He returns to Trier in October, an even more fervent Nazi than before.

1935   On 1 February, Barbie becomes the adjutant of an important party leader in the Trier region. He begins to work in the Security Service of the SS Reichsfuehrer (SD) and on 26 September becomes a full-time, paid member. Barbie's membership number is 272284.

1936–7   Barbie's training and early career in the SD are fairly typical. He trains in the suppression of the "State's enemies": Jews, Communists, homosexuals, Jehovah's Witnesses, and prostitutes. He also serves in the various branches of the Berlin police. He learns the techniques of extreme physical force, which he does not hesitate to use against women. He also undergoes further indoctrination at the SD School in Bernau, where his instructors include Reinhard Heydrich and Adolph Eichmann.

1940   On 20 April, Barbie is promoted to the rank of second lieutenant in the SS. Shortly thereafter, he marries Regine Willms, a devout Catholic and fanatical Nazi like her husband. With the outbreak of war Barbie is sent to occupied Amsterdam. His zeal and brutality in persecuting Jews, German emigrants, and Free Masons earn him a promotion to the rank of lieutenant on 9 November 1940.

1941   The Barbies' first child Uta (Regina Maria) is born on 30 June 1941. Although the evidence is not clear, and although Barbie claims to have served in the Soviet Union following the Nazi invasion of summer 1941, it appears that Barbie continued to serve in Holland through 1941.

1942–4   In May, Barbie arrives in France. He serves initially in Gex, on the French–Swiss border. Following the Allied invasion of North Africa and the German invasion of the "Free Zone" in southern France, Barbie is assigned to Lyon. He arrives on 11 or 12 November, although he has apparently visited the city clandestinely earlier to get "the lay of the land." Although Barbie is not officially in command of the Lyon Gestapo, most witness accounts claim that he was the man in charge. In Lyon, Barbie lives as a kind of Mafia boss. He walks his German Shephard, Wulf, regularly along Lyon's riverbanks, apparently feeling no fear for his personal safety. He frequents Lyon's finer restaurants and nightclubs and keeps a mistress, although he frequents other women as well. Barbie's efficiency and cold-blooded brutality earn him the fear and respect of his subordinates, both German and French.

Upon arrival, Barbie takes up residence at the *Hôtel Terminus*, a stone's throw from Lyon's central Perrache train station and an easy walk to Lyon's central plaza, the *Place Belcour*. The upper floors of this high-end hotel are turned into interrogation chambers where, according to Barbie's victims, torture is carried out.

In June 1943, the Gestapo requisitions the *Ecole Militaire*, not far from the Montluc Prison, where most Resistance and Jewish prisoners are kept. Most SD interrogations are now carried out at the *Ecole Militaire*. When the *Ecole Militaire* is bombed by the Allies, Gestapo headquarters are moved to an address near the *Place Belcour*.

In late summer 1944, with the Allies rapidly approaching Lyon, Barbie and his men are ordered to pull back and abandon the city. During the retreat, Barbie is badly wounded in the foot. Back in Germany, after a stint at the military hospital at Bad Peterstal, Barbie joins the fight to protect the homeland. Initially captured by the Americans, Barbie escapes. He manages to trade his SS uniform for civilian clothes.

1945–6   Barbie is reunited with his family in October, in Bursfelde. With the help of former SS members, the family relocates to Marburg. Barbie enrols in the university there under the name "Klaus Becker."

1947–8   In the spring, Barbie is hired by the US Army's Counter Intelligence Corps (CIC). He establishes a network of spies and, among other responsibilities, keeps an eye on French activities in the occupied zone. Meanwhile, the French have become aware of Barbie's whereabouts and his work for the Americans.

1949   In June, French authorities formally request American help in locating Barbie.

1950   American authorities allow the French to question Barbie about the incident at Caluire which resulted in the arrest and eventual death of Jean Moulin. The occasion for the interrogation is the trial of René Hardy, accused of having betrayed Moulin and other Resistance leaders to Barbie. Now that it is widely known that Barbie is in the hands of the Americans, pressure in France mounts to have him sent back to Lyon to stand trial for his wartime crimes there. Aware that Barbie knows a great deal about the operations of the CIC, the decision is taken by American authorities to get Barbie out of Europe.

1951   Barbie and his family, now including a son, Klaus-Jorg, are sent along the infamous "Rat Line" set up to allow Nazis to escape from Europe. Aided by the Red Cross and Catholic authorities close to the Vatican, Barbie, now "Klaus Altmann," and his family arrive in Genoa. They leave Genoa on the Italian steamer the *Corrientes* on 23 March. They arrive in Buenos Aires and on 23 April 1951 take a train to La Paz. Barbie/Altmann keeps a low profile and goes to work in a sawmill nearby, overcoming his aversion to working for the Jew who owns it. Eventually, Barbie becomes a partner at the sawmill and then buys out the original owner. Over the next several years, Barbie moves his family to La Paz and through multiple business ventures becomes wealthy. He frequents the Café la Paz, eventually becoming a fixture there.

1957   Having initially tried to renew his German passport, a request that is denied, Barbie, with the help of friends and contacts, is granted Bolivian citizenship on 7 October. He becomes friendly with highly placed officers in the Bolivian military, especially Air Force General René Barrientos.

1964   General Barrientos leads a coup and overthrows the Bolivian government. Right-wing dictators will rule the country until 1978. An expert in countersubversive measures, Barbie volunteers his services and is given an office in the Ministry of the Interior. It is with the support of Barrientos that *Transmaritima Boliviana*, a Bolivian shipping company is created. Barbie becomes its director and as a result is able to travel freely. He visits France, Germany, and the United States, among other destinations. To all appearances, the *Transmaritima Boliviana* is involved in weapons trafficking, among other illegal activities.

1971   Colonel Hugo Banzer Suarez, from a wealthy Bolivian family involved in the drug trade, comes to power following a successful coup. Barbie's prospects continue to improve, as does his role in repressive activities and his involvement with far-right politics on an international scale.

1980   Following another coup, general Luis Garcia-Meza comes to power. By most accounts, his dictatorship is among the bloodiest and most

corrupt in Bolivian history. Klaus Barbie played a major role in secur-
ing weapons for the coup, among other services. Out of gratitude for
his service, Barbie is made a lieutenant colonel in the Bolivian army
in July. The regime of Garcia-Meza proves to be short-lived. Originally
supported by the United States, that support was dropped as the role of
the Bolivian government in cocaine trafficking became clear. General
Garcia-Meza's minister of the interior, Colonel Luis Arcé-Gomez, was
presented to American audiences in an episode of *60 Minutes* as the
"Minister of Cocaine."

1981   Klaus Barbie's son, Klaus-Jörg, dies in a hang-gliding accident.

1982   In October, a left-wing government committed to human rights comes
to power in Bolivia. Barbie is now officially a *persona non grata*. The
Socialist government in France under François Mitterrand begins
negotiations with the new government to have Barbie expelled.

1983   On 25 January, Barbie is arrested and jailed for swindling $10,000 from
Transmaratima Boliviana. Efforts to pay off his debts by his friends are
successfully blocked. On 4 February, Barbie is officially stripped of his
Bolivian citizenship for lying about his past when naturalized in 1957.
At nine o'clock that night, he is led by two officers from prison and
taken by car to an airport where a transport plane awaits him. He is
flown to French Guyana, where French authorities await to arrest him.
The Bolivian pilots refuse at first to open the plane to let his passenger
out. They receive bribes and then release Barbie. Barbie is then taken
into an airport hangar and officially told of his arrest and the charges
pending against him. He is then flown to France and taken to Lyon.
After a brief stay at Montluc Prison, where his wartime captives were
held, Barbie is transferred to Saint-Joseph Prison, where he will remain
during his trial and up to his death in 1991.

1991   On 25 September, Klaus Barbie dies in prison. He is seventy-seven years
old. His remains are cremated and scattered in one of Lyon's rivers,
according to Hammerschmitt, although which river is not mentioned.

A Note on the Sources

In writing *Justice in Lyon*, I have relied on several important archival sources. These include, first, the video recording of the trial; second, trial archives held at the *Archives du Rhône* in Lyon, which became available to researchers in 2017; third, the typed transcript of the trial held in the archives of the United States Holocaust Memorial Museum; and fourth, Klaus Barbie's criminal dossier prepared by investigating magistrate Christian Riss for the *instruction*, or investigation, of Barbie's case and generously loaned to me by Serge Klarsfeld. Below, I provide a brief description of these sources, how they were used, and how they are indicated in the text of the book.

Following the examples of the Nuremberg Tribunal and the trial of Adolph Eichmann in Jerusalem in 1961, the Barbie trial was filmed in its entirety following the passage of a law on 11 July 1985 to that effect and proposed by the minister of justice Robert Badinter. However, strict conditions were imposed on the video recording of the trial. Four cameras were placed in approved locations in the courtroom. Behind Klaus Barbie and the box of the defence, a first cameraman was positioned to record the box of the prosecution and civil parties lawyers across the courtroom. A second cameraman was positioned behind the box of the prosecution and civil parties lawyers. His primary responsibility was to film the defendant and the box of the defence. A third camera was attached to a pillar behind the president of the Assize court, André Cerdini. This camera was controlled remotely by a third cameraman. Its main function was to film witnesses as they gave testimony at the witness stand, which was located at the centre of the court and faced the judges and jury. Finally, a fourth fixed camera not controlled by a cameraman was installed over the entrance to the courtroom facing the podium where judges, lawyers, and the defendant were seated. The function of this camera was to film broad-angle shots of the front of the courtroom. A glass control booth was situated in the courtroom itself, behind the defence. In the booth, a film director was seated alongside a representative from the Ministry of Justice, whose job was to oversee the film of the trial as it was being assembled. At the end of each hearing, the video recordings were placed in the hands of the Ministry of Justice representative.

As per an agreement signed with the Ministry of Justice and the Ministry of Culture and Communication in 1993, a copy of the entire video recording was given to the *Institut National de l'Audiovisuel* (INA).

Any broadcast of the video recording of the Barbie trial in whole or in part requires the permission of the *Tribunal de grande instance* in Paris. After receiving permission from the *Tribunal de grande instance*, in 2000 the television station *Histoire* signed an agreement with INA to broadcast portions of the trial. In October 2000, *Histoire* began broadcasting two hours of footage a day. By the conclusion of these broadcasts, 70 hours out of a total of 185 hours of the trial were broadcast.

In 2009, *Arte* television received permission to prepare and market a collection of DVDs of the trial, covering approximately twenty hours of hearings. However, judicial restrictions were placed on what could be shown. Specifically, the DVD recordings needed to reflect a balance between footage devoted to the prosecution and the defence. Additionally, the booklet accompanying the DVDs states that the goal of the production team in selecting footage used was to "lose nothing of the intensity of the trial, to neither deform nor favor one side or the other" (4). This the production team accomplished admirably.

In 2017, as part of an exhibit on the thirtieth anniversary of the Barbie trial, the *Mémorial de la Shoah* in Paris received permission to show the Barbie trial in its entirety. Following the closing of the exhibit in the fall of that year, the audiovisual archives of the *Mémorial* made the film of the entire trial available to scholars.

In terms of how these films were used in the present project, during several trips to Paris beginning in fall 2017 and lasting until summer 2019 I was able to visit the archives of the *Mémorial de la Shoah* and watch important parts of the trial that were not included in the *Arte* DVDs. For example, the testimony of many of the witnesses' statements recorded on the DVDs are truncated, as are some of the closing statements of the civil parties lawyers. At the *Mémorial de la Shoah*, I was able to "fill in the gaps" so to speak, on some of the truncated testimonies and statements. For example, it was there that I watched the civil parties lawyer Alain Lévy's call for the trials of a Frenchman who committed crimes against humanity following the trial of Barbie. That said, it is fair to say that the most dramatic statements and testimonies are included in the *Arte* DVDs.

What do these official video recordings of the Barbie trial reveal about the trial? First, although there are dull moments comprising uninformative testimony or long-winded and technical arguments by lawyers, for the most part the films reveal the tension and dramatic power of much of the proceedings. The camera hung behind President Cerdini repeatedly captures the intense emotion of the witnesses, often in closeup. The cameras on either side of the courtroom often pan out to the audience and zoom in on spectators' reactions, especially, for example, when Jacques Vergès attacked the credibility of Mario Blardone and Simone Kadosche-Lagrange in his closing statement. Blardone's outrage and defiance and Kadosche-Lagrange's pain are palpable. The two cameras on either end of the courtroom often provide as well a sense of the historical magnitude of the Barbie trial in capturing the sheer size of the courtroom and the extraordinary numbers of spectators present on most days of the trial.

A final point. The video recordings of the trial are only divided by audience. At the top of the recording, the time and date are indicated. I have only indicated the exact time an event occurred when that event marked a sea change in the trial, as when Klaus Barbie announced his departure from the court on the third day.

I made two lengthy trips to Lyon to consult the archives of the Barbie trial and to visit the sites associated with Barbie's reign of terror in Occupied Lyon: Montluc Prison, the *Ecole Militaire*, where today the Museum of the Resistance is located and where glass panels in the floor allow visitors to look down into the cellar Barbie used as a torture chamber. Where I have used materials from the *Archives du Rhône*, these are indicated with 'AR:,' followed by the file number. A complete list of the *Archive du Rhône*'s holding related to the Barbie trial is available on their website.

The files of investigating magistrate Riss's lengthy investigation of Barbie loaned to me by Serge Klarsfeld include a number of invaluable, not to say crucial, documents related to this study. These include interrogations of the accused, confrontations between Barbie and his accusers, documents from Barbie's 1952 and 1954 trials in absentia, translated court documents from German trials of Barbie's Gestapo colleagues, etc. In citing these materials in the book, I have given dates where appropriate and also indicated the file numbers of the documents used for the investigation. These documents are indicated with a 'K' (for Klarsfeld) followed by the file number.

Finally, the transcript of the trial is like the video recording of it divided only by date and "audience" or hearing number. I have used the transcript to verify what is seen and said on film (sometimes, emotions garble the words of the speaker) and especially to read and study the extended closing statements of the lawyers and the summation of chief prosecutor Truche. I have found it particularly illuminating in trying to capture the "feel" of a particular statement by first reading the relatively *dry* words recorded in the transcript and contrast them with the emotional or rhetorical power of the statement as seen on film. Under any circumstances, by cross-referencing film and transcript it is possible to determine exactly what is said and to quote individuals accurately in my book.

Notes

Introduction

1 Sorj Chalandon, Pascale Nivelle, *Crimes contre l'humanité: Barbie, Touvier, Bousquet, Papon*, 148.

2 See Hugh Nissenson's description of Barbie in *The Elephant and My Jewish Problem*, 199.

3 The civil trial to award damages began immediately after the criminal trial concluded. At stake was the awarding of one symbolic franc to each of the civil parties plaintiffs following the conviction of the accused. The defence was represented by the Algerian lawyer Nabil Bouaïta, who immediately asked for a delay of a week for the defence to consider its legal options. This request was supported by some civil parties lawyers and opposed by others. In the end, President Cerdini granted a delay of one week. At that subsequent hearing, the symbolic franc in damages was awarded to each of the civil parties.

4 Quoted in Marc-Olivier Baruch, *Des lois indignes? Les historiens, la politique, et le droit*, 47.

5 In Beate and Serge Klarsfled's memoirs, *Hunting the Truth*, Serge Klarsfeld describes his actions and feelings after the verdict. The Klarsfelds of course played the central role over more than a decade in getting Klaus Barbie returned to France to face trial. As a lawyer for the children of Izieu, Serge Klarsfeld played a major role in the 1987 trial. Indeed, his final plea before the court is among the most memorable and certainly the most moving of the final pleas of the thirty-nine civil parties lawyers present. It is discussed in chapter six here. Klarsfeld writes in his memoirs: "After the verdict, about 2:00 am, after Barbie had been sentenced to life in prison for crimes against humanity, I walked to Montluc prison [where Barbie's prisoners were held] to gather my thoughts. At Montluc, I needed to be alone with the souls

of those who had suffered so much. I thanked the Almighty, the power of human will, and fate for having helped me get through the sixteen year ordeal" (345).

6 For a discussion of this transition, see especially Sébastion Ledoux, "The Barbie Trial (1987): Narrator of the Holocaust in France," 41–52.

7 In a French Assize court trial, civil plaintiffs are permitted to attach themselves to the prosecution and be represented by lawyers in the trial. These "civil parties" lawyers may represent "associations" representing different constituencies, or specific individuals. In the Barbie trial, thirty-nine lawyers represented a variety of constituencies and individuals. Some of the civil parties lawyers represented Jewish victims, while other represented Resistance victims. These civil parties lawyers were occasionally at odds inside and outside the courtroom, for reasons to be discussed.

Lévy gave his closing statement to the court during the trial's twenty-seventh hearing on 19 June. Lévy would go on to serve as a civil parties lawyer in the prosecution of Paul Touvier in 1994.

8 For the Touvier and Papon trials, see my *Memory, the Holocaust, and French Justice* and *The Papon Affair*. See also Adam Nossiter's *The Algeria Hotel*. Not long after the Touvier trial, the novelist Brian Moore wrote an excellent novel about Touvier entitled *The Statement*. The novel was later made into a movie starring Michael Caine.

9 This tendency is certainly reasonable when one considers that Klaus Barbie's presence in South America and his protection there by friends and political leaders had been revealed to the world by Beate and Serge Klarsfeld in the early 1970s. Indeed, a full decade would pass before Barbie's return to France. During that time, Barbie gave, or rather sold, multiple interviews to the international press.

10 Ted Morgan, *An Uncertain Hour: The French, the Germans, the Jews, the Klaus Barbie Trial, and the City of Lyon, 1940–1945*, 25.

11 Ryan would later write a book about his investigation of Barbie and other Nazi war criminals, many of whom were hiding in the United States: *Quiet Neighbors: Prosecuting Nazi War Criminals in America*. Ryan's full report about Barbie and the CIA can be found online.

12 Magnus Linklater et al., *The Nazi Legacy: Klaus Barbie and the International Fascist Connection*.

13 This is not to say that all commentaries on the Barbie trial in France and abroad, certainly at the moment of its conclusion, were negative. Indeed, some offered glowing praise of the trial and its outcome. In a *New York Times* op ed. published on 6 July 1987 and entitled "A Model of French Justice," the article concluded, "the weight of the evidence, the weight of truth, the weight of decency won out." The author concurs with this assessment.

14 Pierre Mérindol, *Barbie, Le Procès*, 11. Mérindol's day-by-day account of the trial published in book form as *Barbie: Le Procès* in 1987 has proven to be particularly valuable to the author. The reporter's understanding of the implications of daily developments and their importance to the aims of the defence and prosecution is remarkable. Mérindol also enjoyed a remarkable career. He served for more than thirty years as a correspondent for the Lyon newspaper *Progrès*. He covered the assassination of President John F. Kennedy, the Palestinian attacks on Israeli athletes at the 1972 Munich Olympics, the Yom Kippur War, the Cambodian genocide, as well as other historical events and trials.

15 Pierrre Mérindol, *Barbie, le Procès*, 11.

16 Vergès had made these claims most notably in Claude Bal's film *Que la vérité est amère.*

17 Bertrand Poirot-Delpech, *Monsieur Barbie n'a rien à dire*, 21. The main part of Poirot-Delpech's "trial-novel" consists of an imaginary account of the trial told by Barbie himself, who remains loyal to the *fuehrer* and unrepentant for his crimes to the end. Poirot- Delpech was certainly right about this.

18 Jacques Vergès, *Le salaud lumineux*, 300.

19 See Hannah Arendt, *Eichmann in Jerusalem*, 125.

20 André Chelain, *Le procès Barbie ou la Shoah Business à Lyon*, 43.

21 As will be discussed here, the "complicity" of the *Mémorial de la Shoah* in helping to "frame" Barbie with dubious or false documents was a regular refrain for Barbie's defence team.

22 See Henry Rousso, *The Vichy Syndrome*, 316.

23 See chapter four here for a discussion of an Assize court trial and how it differs from an Anglo-American or commom law criminal trial.

24 The film can be seen at http://www.scenariofilms.com/tv/the-trial-of -klaus-barbie/. Compared to the documentary footage of the trial itself, the BBC performance seems quite stilted. Depending on one's perspective, Ascherson's blaming the monotony of the BBC production on the Assize system is misplaced.

25 Fateful as it was in the Barbie trial, the December 1985 Court of Cassation decision would subsequently directly impact the 1994 trial of the Vichy Militia member Paul Touvier. To the degree that it also set a precedent for modifying French law concerning crimes against humanity to meet the circumstances of the moment, it also affected the trial of the Vichy civil servant Maurice Papon in 1997–8. These developments are discussed in the conclusion here.

26 In the French Assize court system, during the pre-trial investigation of the case, the accused is confronted with his accusers and victims. In the Barbie case, there were literally hundreds of victims, and not all of those who confronted Barbie testified in the 1987 trial. Some expressed their

preference not to testify, as the sight of their torturer left them traumatized all over again.

27 Guyora Binder, "Representing Nazism: Advocacy and Identity in the Trial of Klaus Barbie," 1339.

28 As will be shown in chapter six, Binder's claim that the 1985 decision forced the prosecution to focus too much on Nazi ideology is overstated. In making his summation, chief prosecutor Pierre Truche focused instead on the logical implications of Barbie's and the Nazis' actions, for example, that after torturing victims to within inches of their lives and then having them deported it was possible to imagine that Barbie and his colleagues ever imagined that these victims would return after the war, or that they would be allowed to return if the Nazis won.

29 Here again, Binder's assessment is fascinating but at least arguably overstated. Although the "innocence" of Jewish victims as opposed to Resistance fighters who were enemy combatants strongly marked the debate about the trial following the 1985 decision (see chapter three here), it is questionable that the trial itself was "sacrificial" and that its message was that the dead died not in vain but to redeem the living.

30 Judith Miller, *One, by One, by One*, 119.

31 Despite Miller's claim here, as already noted, Barbie *was* brought back to the trial several times. Moreover, Barbie's absence from the courtroom was not seen by several of the trial's participants as a negative development, but rather a positive one. See chapter four here.

32 See Michel Zaoui's comments on the Barbie trial in *Mémoires de justice*, 87.

33 Alain Finkielkraut, *Remembering in Vain: The Klaus Barbie Trial and Crimes against Humanity*, 9.

34 As will be discussed in detail here, and especially in the final chapter, Vergès's and his co-counsel's arguments were provocative and occasionally outrageous, but they were effectively countered by chief prosecutor Truche, statements made by some of the civil parties lawyers, and the weight and impact of witness testimony.

35 In October 2007, a three-day-long colloquium was held at the Ecole Normale Supérieure in Paris to commemorate the twentieth anniversary of the Barbie trial. The proceedings of the colloquium were published as *Juger les crimes contre l'humanité: 20 ans après le procès Barbie*. In his inaugural address published in the volume, the historian Pierre Douzou emphasized the positive lessons and accomplishments of the trial. Among these lessons, the Barbie trial was the first successful trial for crimes against humanity in French history. Moreover, the Barbie trial confirmed that no torturer or criminal like Klaus Barbie, no matter how far removed from his crimes in time and space, could escape punishment forever. Finally, no matter how

widespread the fear before the trial, the good name of the Resistance had not been successfully besmirched by the defence. See 7–19.

36 Tzvetan Todorov, *La signature humaine*, 236.

37 See Judith N. Shklar, *Legalism: Law, Morals, and Political Trials*, 143–92.

38 Conversation with the author, June 2018.

39 Leora Bilskey, *Transformative Justice*, 98–9.

40 To do this, Truche had to overcome his own earlier strong reservations about the 1985 decision that he expressed publicly at that time. These reservations will be discussed in more detail later.

41 Hubert Ogier, the president of the Lyon Court of Appeals and a former *résistant* himself, had opposed including Resistance members among the plaintiffs because they had been enemy combatants. After the 1985 Court of Cassation decision, Ogier, now in retirement, stated that the decision would make any future trial of Barbie for crimes against humanity "unjudgeable" (Mérindol 15).

42 A brief chronology of Barbie's life is included at the end of this book.

1 Klaus Barbie: Nazi "Idealist"

1 In June 2018 I interviewed Serge Klarsfeld and Alain Lévy, both of whom served as civil parties lawyers in the 1987 trial. When I asked them what their final assessment of Klaus Barbie was as a person, both described him simply as a *salopard.*

2 These reports can be found in the *Archives du Rhône* (AR: 4544W7, B-1).

3 This was despite the fact that Heinrich Himmler, the head of the SS, on occasion congratulated Barbie for his work in Lyon.

4 Barbie appeared to like to subject his victims to freezing cold, then scalding hot, baths, or vice versa, one after the other, according to Abendroth.

5 Barbie claimed that Moulin's injuries while being interrogated were the result of his own efforts to commit suicide by slamming his head into his cell walls. But his own translator in Lyon, Gottlieb Fuchs, says he saw Barbie drag Moulin down the prison steps by his feet. Hence, clearly, at least some of his head injuries (Linklater et al. 92).

6 Arendt, *Thinking without a Bannister*, 277.

7 See the introduction to Volker Ullrich's recent biography of Hitler, *Hitler: Ascent, 1889–1939*, 1–11.

8 Quoted in Carolyn Dean, *The Fragility of Empathy after the Holocaust*, 106.

9 For an excellent discussion of the *mode rétro* phenomenon, see Saul Friedlanders's *Reflections of Nazism.*

10 It is worth noting here that the *mode rétro* preceded the Barbie trial by only a few years. In his final defence plea before the court, Jacques Vergès deeply shocked those present in the courtroom by essentially turning the *mode*

rétro mindset on its head and suggesting that it was Barbie's *victims* who had succumbed to it by imagining – or fantasizing – Barbie's perversions and sadism. See chapter five here.

11　Harald Welzer, *Les Exécuteurs*, 11.

12　The psychologists' report is located in the *Archives du Rhône* (AR: 4544W7, B-26).

13　Jacques Vergès, *Le salaud lumineux*, 281.

14　The three men testified last during the third hearing of the trial. The account of their testimony presented here is taken from the *Arte* DVDs, which show some of the testimony, and from the HMM transcript of the trial.

15　Where the Eichmann trial in particular is concerned, this depends on whether one accepts Arendt's portrait of the accused as accurate and penetrating, or whether one accepts Bettina Stagneth's view that Eichmann was disguising himself behind a successful courtroom theatrical performance.

16　For a discussion of how this was accomplished, and under what circumstances, see Serge and Beate Klarsfeld's memoir *Hunting the Truth*, 231–2.

17　At Nuremberg, some of the accused, including most famously Albert Speer, got off with lighter sentences not only by attenuating their responsibility but by expressing their regrets, in one way or another.

18　The theory and practice of the "trial by rupture," as Vergès interpreted them, and their application to the Barbie trial itself will be discussed in greater detail in chapter seven here.

19　It is important at this stage to stress that Klaus Barbie, both in his Nazi fanaticism and in his murderousness in Lyon, was quite different from recent models of "ordinary" German police killers as described, for example, in Christopher Browning's *Ordinary Men*. The men Browning describes in the Reserve Police battalion carrying out executions of Jews in Poland were hardly fanatical Nazis, like Barbie. In fact, most did not belong to the Nazi Party itself. Finally, whereas at least initially some, if not many, of these men were disturbed by their grisly task, Barbie simply never showed sympathy or empathy for his victims.

20　See Johann Chapoutot, *La loi du sang*, 360–7.

21　According to Robert Wilson, Barbie on occasion compared himself to Napoleon Bonaparte.

22　Harald Welzer, *Les Exécuteurs*, 35.

23　In *Les Exécuteurs*, Harald Welzer makes the striking observation that "The desire to be seen as persons acting morally can be found, from what I have seen, is all executioners, whatever their level of education, their place in the hierarchy, or their intelligence" (34).

24　"Decency" was a word close to the heart of the SS and their conception of virtue. Indeed, a recent Israeli documentary on Heinrich Himmler, built around his autobiographical writings, is entitled *The Decent One*.

25 The function of a court in the Nazi world view was to protect the German race, and the French Assize court exists and judges on behalf of the French people. Moreover, Barbie was fully aware that the notion of crimes against humanity according to which he was being judged was created and applied at the International Military Tribunal at Nuremberg. For Barbie, Nuremberg was a sham.

26 When Robert Taylor described Barbie as a "Nazi idealist," he states this in part because Barbie believed that Hitler had been betrayed by other Nazis. Indeed, Barbie's outburst about his loyalty to Hitler in conversation with Schneider-Merck followed Schneider-Merck's own comment that Hitler "had betrayed the idealism of German youth."

27 See Linlklater et al. 266–302.

28 Jankélévitch is clearly referring to white, presumably European, racism here.

29 As the Lyon psychologists confirmed in their report, Barbie's intelligence was above average in some circumstances but inadequate in others.

30 It is also possible that Barbie, who sought to present himself as a "cultured" individual as discussed here, wished not to appear to embrace the kind of "vulgar" anti-Semitism that Marice Bardèche, for example, described in Louis-Ferdinand Céline. But this is hardly in keeping with the brutal and savage treatment to which he submitted Jews, including adolescents like Simone Kadosche, in wartime Lyon.

31 For the Nazi Generation described by Wildt, Barbie was also a little young by a few years. Barbie was born in 1913, whereas most of the men Wildt describes were born between 1900 and 1910 (Wildt 27). Moreover, unlike most of the Nazi leadership Wildt discusses, most of whom were highly educated, Barbie had only the equivalent of a high school degree.

2 The Historical Judicial Backdrop: From Nuremberg to the 1980 Cologne Trial of Kurt Lischka, Herbert Hagen, and Ernst Heinrichson

1 Moulin's former wife is interviewed in Kevin McDonald's film *Mon meilleur ennemi.*

2 On 9 February 1983, *Libération* published selections from an editorial published by Badinter in *L'Express* on 6 April 1961 concerning the necessity of trying Eichmann not only for his crimes against the Jewish people but against humanity as a whole.

3 Quoted in Gideon Hausner, *Justice in Jerusalem*, 323–4.

4 The circumstances and details of Raymond Geissmann's statement about Barbie, as well as its importance of that statement to the Klarsfelds' pursuit of him in the 1970s, will be discussed in chapter three here.

5 Presumably Barbie is referring here to a semi-autobiographical introduction Avner Less wrote for *Eichmann Interrogated.*

6 Robert Jackson addressed the annual meeting of the New York Bar Association on 24 January 1947. The transcript of his speech can be found at the Robert H. Jackson Center website. Its original source of publication is not indicated. All page numbers given here are to the original publication.

7 This statement comes from Robert H. Jackson, "Foreword: The Nuremberg Trial becomes an Historic Precedent," *Temple Law Quarterly*, also available on the Robert H. Jackson Center website. In her recent book *Soviet Justice at Nuremberg*, Francine Hirsch offers a very different vision of Allied collaboration at the IMT. According to Hirsch, the Soviets, who played a more substantial role in developing the ideas and legal principles that shaped the prosecution, felt marginalized or sidelined by France, the United Kingdom, and the United States during the trial.

8 According to Hirsch, this was also not accurate, Moscow being directly involved in shaping the Soviet prosecution and Soviet judges' actions at the trial.

9 See Jean-Marc Théolleyre, *Procès d'après-guerre*, 180.

10 See Hannah Arendt, "Auschwitz on Trial," in *Responsibility and Judgement*, 227–57.

11 Arthur Miller, "The Nazi Trials and the German Heart," in *Echoes down the Corridor*, 66.

12 Beate and Serge Klarsfeld, *Hunting the Truth*, 176.

13 Eric Stover et al., *Hiding in Plain Sight*, 106.

14 According to the German indictment, the French Military Tribunal in Paris sentenced Hagen to a life of hard labour in absentia in 1955. In the Klarsfeld files, the indictment is included under the headings P1/ 232–5. The Judgment of the Cologne Court is included under the headings P1/236–242.

15 Tom Bower, "They were just following Orders," *Washington Post*, 21 October 1979.

16 Ibid.

17 According to Marrus and Paxton, Hagen on occasion requested French police dealing with Jews to make arrests in Bordeaux (137).

18 See Marrus and Paxton 197, 286.

19 These incidents are cited by Bower, "They were only following Orders."

20 The activities and claims made by the three accused, as well as related correspondence and juridical assessments of the veracity of some of the claims made by Lishcka, Hagen, and Heinrichson, are discussed in both the Indictment (Sections VIII and IX) (K: P/234–5) and in the final Judgement of the Court (K: P/239–40).

21 For their crimes, the three men were given the following sentences: Kurt Lischka, ten years in prison; Herbert Hagen, twelve years in prison; Ernst Heinrichson, six years in prison (K: P1/242).

3 The Investigation: War Crimes, Crimes against Humanity, and the Long Road to Compromise

1 See *Klaus Barbie 1987: Mémoires d'un procès*, 20.
2 As photographs of documents included in the 2017 *Mémoires du Procès* volume show, Barbie also served as a witness in trials of former collaborators with the Nazis carried out by French secret services in 1948 (30).
3 The *Jugement par contumace*, or "Judgment in Absentia," was handed down on 29 April 1952. All references are to this document, included in the Klarsfeld file.
4 The *Acte d'Accusation*, or indictment, was handed down on 15 July 1954, also included in the Klarsfeld file.
5 See Georges Cochet, "Avocat au procès de la Gestapo de Lyon, 1954," *Histoire de la Justice*, vol. 1, 2008, 254–5.
6 At this moment, negotiations to create a European Defense community were underway. As a result, France's "traditional enemy" was to become potentially an ally.
7 According to the 1954 judgment included in the Klarsfeld files, of the five Nazis present at the trial, three were given death sentences and two multi-year sentences with hard labour. Of the twenty-three convicted in absentia, seventeen, including Barbie, received the death sentence and six multi-year sentences with hard labour. Bartelmus received an eight-year sentence of hard labour, and Werner Knab, in absentia like Barbie, received the death sentence.
8 Cochet does not identify the fort in question.
9 Certainly, in the debate about the 1964 law that followed in the press, many voices expressed the view that the horror of Nazism and its crimes was "timeless." See the discussion of Vladimir Jankélévitch below.
10 Jankélévitch's *L'Imprescriptible*, along with subsequent texts written by Jankélévitch on forgiveness, has played a central role in subsequent discussions of the nature and conditions of forgiveness. For example, Jacques Derrida's influential essay on forgiveness is built in part around *L'Imprescriptible* and a subsequent article Jankélévitch published in the magazine the *Nouvel Obs* on 25 March 1965. Citing especially the latter text, Derrida challenges what he sees as the "exchange" component of Jankélevitch's argument as well as the notion that certain crimes like the Holocaust are inexpiable, or, as Jankélévitch is quoted here, "infinite." See Jacques Derida, *Cosmopolitanism and Forgiveness*, 33–8. For all of Jankélévitch's brief contributions on the topic, see *L'Esprit de Résistance: Textes inédits, 1943–83*.
11 See Paul Arrighi, "L'Imprescriptibilité," *Le Monde*, 29 March 1965.
12 One of those who agreed with Jankélévich argued that if the Nazi criminals were not punished in perpetuity, this would give them the freedom to propagate their dangerous doctrines all over again.

13 These perspectives, solicited from jurists and scholars, were gathered and reported in an essay published in *Le monde* on 15 January 1965 entitled "Faut-il oublier?"

14 See Ledoux, 53–5.

15 See chapter one here for a discussion of post-war perceptions of Nazi and German "aberrations," sexual and otherwise. See also the chapter "Mapping the West" in Kim Christian Priemel's *The Betrayal: The Nuremberg Trials and German Divergence.*

16 Marguerite Duras, *La Douleur*, 60–1.

17 For a much more detailed account of the evolution of the memory of the Dark Years in France in the 1970s, see *The Vichy Syndrome*, 98–218.

18 In a second article appearing in *Le Monde* (29 May 1979) at the time of the Leguay Affair entitled "Sur qui pleurer?" Comte argued that launching procedures against Leguay and other collaborators with the Nazis might well be having the opposite of the effect intended. These procedures, in Comte's view, could be encouraging, rather than discouraging, new acts of anti-Semitic violence. In February 1983, at the time of Barbie's arrest, Comte published another polemical essay, "La Justice de qui?" (Whose Justice?) in which he sharpened his attacks, this time against the French people as a whole. They were cowardly and complacent in indicting a "harmless old man," and they had shown a new "failure to resist" in indulging in the "unhealthy vertigo caused by striking a despicable but defenseless beast while selling arms to Irak [*sic*] and other countries," and ignoring the crimes of Stalinism.

19 Rabl's superior in Munich apparently, although Beate Klarsfeld does not confirm this.

20 In a subsequent correspondence with Steiner dated 16 December 1971, Geissmann reiterated his belief that when they arrested Jews and deported them, Barbie and other Gestapo members knew the fate of these Jews full well. The Jews were being sent "coldly and knowingly to their deaths" (K: P1/381). Interrogated by magistrate Riss on 19 December 1983, Barbie claimed that he did not remember meeting Geissmann. Barbie then claimed that there was a contraction in Geismann's statement. According to Barbie, the fact Geissmann came to the offices of the Gestapo on many occasions without "anything bad" happening to him was in contradiction with his claim that Barbie was demonstrative in his hatred of the Jews (K: P1/49). Barbie's logic here is obviously not particularly rigorous.

21 See Hammerschmidt 166–7. Hammerschmidt quotes Barbie as stating that he understood that in becoming a Bolivian citizen he would have to give up his German citizenship. Thanks to friends in La Paz, Barbie's path to citizenship was accelerated beyond the norm. Earlier, to secure a more legitimate legal status for himself and his family (they had left Europe with only Red Cross certificates of identification), Barbie had applied for

a German passport at the Embassy in La Paz but had been turned down. Sensing danger, he decided to pursue Bolivian citizenship.

22 Nahmias was deported to Auschwitz in late July 1944. He also claimed to have seen and taken care of the children of Izieu vey briefly. Barbie noted that the date of the telex announcing the arrest of the children was from April. Nahmias clarified his statement, noting he had not cared for them in Lyon but at Drancy later on.

23 In her audition with Christian Riss, Irène Clair-Fémion, a Resistance member who had been deported to Ravensbrück, was shown photos of Barbie and announced that she would be *bouleversé*, or deeply disturbed or upset, to be confronted with Barbie in person. She stated nevertheless that she would confront him in court if it was necessary to the prosecution. She was later a witness in the trial. Clair-Frémion testified first during the tenth hearing of the trial on 22 May 1987.

24 The text of the Paris Court of Cassation December 1985 decision can be found at https://www.legifrance.gouv.fr.

25 Without stating explicitly that some individuals would be just as happy if Barbie died in prison, in an interview in *Le Monde* on 24 December 1985, Simone Veil did observe that "one can well ask oneself if for a certain number of people it will not be very convenient for the trial to be delayed."

26 According to Pierre Mérindol, the December 1985 decision by the Paris Court of Cassation marked the final outcome of a disagreement that had existed from the outset of the Barbie affair between that body and the Lyon Court of Appeals concerning the nature of crimes against humanity. Mérindol writes that the president of the Lyon court and a former resister himself, Hubert Ogier, preferred a "restrictive definition" of crimes against humanity, in line with the views of Riss and Badinter. The judges of the Court of Cassation, as noted, preferred a more inclusive definition. One of Ogier's supporters was the Lyon prosecutor Pierre Truche, who publicly expressed his belief at the time that crimes against *Résistants*, unlike those committed against Jews, should not be considered crimes against humanity because they had chosen to fight the occupant. Ogier, who retired in June 1986, stated in retirement that the Barbie trial would be "unjudgeable," as noted, because of its "composite" nature. See Mérindol 12–15.

4 The Barbie Trial Begins: Opening Rituals and the Departure of the Accused

1 Although eight weeks would be considered relatively short by American standards for a trial of the magnitude of the Barbie trial, it was lengthy by Assize court standards. Usually an Assize trial lasts no more than two weeks.

2 In *Le salaud lumineux*, Vergès explained that he needed the suite because he received numerous visitors. He added that he also reserved a room for his secretary there because it would have been "inelegant" to have her stay in a cheap hotel (317–18).

3 Barbie's statement from prison accusing the Aubracs of treason is included as an appendix to Gérard Chauvy's *Aubrac: Lyon 1949*, 371–422.

4 On 15 May, four days after the trial began, the weekly magazine *L'Express* devoted an article to Vergès's past and his connections with the Swiss financier François Genoud entitled "The Metamorphoses of M. Vergès."

5 For an excellent documentary film on the life and career of Jacques Vergès, see Barbet Shroeder's *Terror's Advocate*.

6 For speculations about where Vergès actually was, and his artful dodging on the subject, see Barbet Schroeder's 2007 documentary on Vergès, *Terror's Advocate*.

7 Jacques Vergès's literary affectations were well known. In this instance, he seemed to be referring to New Novel made famous by the likes of Alain Robbe-Grillet and Claude Simon, among others. The New Novel challenged traditional literary conventions, including straightforward chronological narration. It also championed the notion that fiction does not reflect reality but creates its own reality. Given that, in his defence of Barbie, Vergès was intent on writing *an alternate reality* to the one championed by the prosecution, *another history* in which Barbie was a scapegoat and the real culprits were white Europeans, America, and Israel, Vergès was writing a kind of "new novel." Moroever, during his questioning of Raymond Aubrac during the trial, Vergès made a point of touting his familiarity with Robbe-Grillet's work in suggesting that Aubrac was having *glissements* or "slippages" of memory, noting that he, Vergès, had borrowed that term from Robbe-Grillet. I am grateful to my colleague Lynn Higgins for her insights into the New Novel, and how its aesthetic ideas might apply to Vergès's defence of Klaus Barbie.

8 On 30 April, *Le Monde* reported that a similarly anti-Semitic tract had been received by President Cerdini and leading members of Lyon's Jewish community.

9 For a discussion of the Roques Affair, see Henry Rousso, *Le dossier Lyon III*, 121–34.

10 The village of Nantua had experienced its own horror during Nazi assaults on the Resistance in the region. In the materials gathered during the investigation for Barbie's 1954 trial, an entry for an attack on the village on 14 December 1943 reads: "In Nantua, notably, the town was surrounded and then raids on individual residences were carried out. One hundred and twenty healthy men were taken as hostages and then led off towards Compiègne [a deportation staging point.] The Captain of the Gendarmerie

[and another man] were sent to the Montluc Prison in Lyon. Doctor Mercier, a local celebrity, was led away and executed near the village of MEILLAT" (K: EP 5/2P).

11 Literally "room for lost steps," or "room for pacing."

12 According to Annette Kahn, the cost of the transformation of the entry hall of the *Palais de Justice* into the Assize courtroom was 1 million francs (*Why My Father Died*, 14).

13 See Vergès, *Le salaud lumineux*, 283. According to Vergès, most prisoners with diagnosed illnesses like this are not obliged to remain in prison during their trial. This was in fact the case of Maurice Papon who, ten years later, stayed in a comfortable, not to say luxury, hotel during his own trial for crimes against humanity.

14 The current French *code pénal* took effect in 1994. Previously, the *code pénal* in effect was the code established in 1810.

15 See *Justice.fr* for the current composition of the court in an Assize trial (https://www.justice.fr). If the judgment of an Assize court is successfully appealed, the new trial constituted includes nine jurors, rather than six.

16 *Klaus Barbie 1987: Mémoires d'un procès* (A publication of *Le Mémorial National de la Prison de Montluc*, 2017) 57.

17 It is also the chief prosecutor's role to explain the procedures involved in the trial to non-jurists. As will be discussed, Truche would take several opportunities during the course of the trial to explain the legal and historical complexities of the Barbie case to the jurors.

18 See Damon C. Woods, "The French Court of Assizes," *Journal of Criminal Law and Criminology*, vol. 22, no. 3, 1931, 329.

19 The chief prosecutor is not, however, present during the jury's deliberations, but the president and his or her assessors are, as stated.

20 It is also the case that in the French Assize system the president, her or his assessors, and the chief prosecutor all form part of the magistrature and often work together in the same court. They are therefore more familiar with each other than any of them are with defence counsel.

21 Cerdini only briefly challenged Barbie's account of his life in challenging his statement in court concerning the cause of death of his father, which was ultimately a matter of little consequence to the trial. Cerdini also showed himself to be attentive to Barbie's age (and decrepitude), at one point referring to the defendant's advanced age and inviting him to be seated.

22 As Henry Rousso observed in a conversation with the author, Serge Klarsfeld considers himself a militant in the cause of justice, especially where the crimes of former Nazis are concerned. As a civil parties lawyer in the Barbie trial, he clearly did not feel obliged to observe every aspect of the etiquette of an Assize trial. The same could of course be said of Jacques Vergès.

23 See the comments on the confrontation between Elie Nahmias and Barbie in the previous chapter.

24 Vergès also called five other witnesses to testify at the Barbie trial. Eddine Lakhdar-Toumi's father had fought in the French Resistance and then disappeared, fighting for the cause of Algerian liberation. Lackhdar-Toumi had filed a complaint charging French troops with crimes against humanity for his father's murder. The complaint had been rejected, proof for Vergès of the profound inequity of the French justice system. Another witness, Paul Guiochon, a former military nurse, affirmed that Barbie's crimes were no worse than the ones he, Guiochon, had seen in Algeria and Indochina. A soldier in the latter combat, Jacques Fastré, testified to the same end. As for the defence witnesses more directly concerned with the matters at hand, Yves Danion, a French volunteer in the Waffen SS at seventeen had little to offer other than affirming that it was "possible" in the SD to sign a report for an action without having ordered it. The last witness was the historian Jacques Forment de Launay, who testified to having been the first to publish the Izieu telex signed by Barbie in 1974.Without referring directly to de Launay's testimony, Vergès tried to exploit its implications in once again claiming the the telex was a fraud, fabricated by Klarsfeld and his allies.

25 The procedure is explained in https://www.justice.fr in the section entitled "Déroulement d'un procès devant la cour d'assizes."

26 Shortly after Barbie's arrest and return to France, a number of prominent lawyers were asked if they would defend Barbie. The far-right lawyer and politician, Jean-Louis Tixier-Vignancourt, who had earlier defended Louis-Ferdinand Céline and the French rebel general and OAS leader Georges Salan, stated that "The last remaining freedom a lawyer possesses is to choose his cause. I have absolutely no taste for defending Klaus Barbie" On the other end of the political spectrum, Jean-Paul Lévy, a member of the League of the Rights of Man, stated "Absolutely not. Barbie has the right to a lawyer that is certain. But it won't be me." Jacques Vergès responded more cagily: "A lawyer does not have the right to answer a question like that. Either he says he will, and he is client-hunting, or he refuses and in that case he doesn't have the right to say so, because this would be to betray the interests of the defense." See *Le Monde*, 8 February 1983.

27 In *Le salaud lumineux*, Vergès offers yet another account of his arrival and Servette's departure. He states that before meeting with Barbie, the two men met in a Lyon brasserie and Servette laid out for Vergès the reasons he was leaving Barbie's defence team. The two men then went to visit Barbie in prison. When Servette announced his resignation, Barbie pleaded with him to stay, but Servette refused. Vergès does not state the reasons Servette supposedly resigned. Whichever version of the story of the changing of the

guard is accurate, Vergès's account here conforms to the "two men against the world" version of his defence of Barbie he enjoyed reiterating inside the courtroom and out.

28 As was the case with jury members, replacements for the judges were present should a judge become incapacitated during the trial itself.

29 As if acknowledging the historic nature of the trial and its photographic record, Cerdini told the photographers it was time to cease *graver sur la pellicule*, "engraving on film."

30 Of the jurors, Christiane Levrat spoke at the fiftieth anniversary of the Barbie trial of the intensity of the experience, of the testimony, etc. She did not, of course, speak of the jury's secret deliberations. See *Le Progès*, 9 October 2017. To the best of my knowledge, the other jurors have remained silent about the trial, at least recently.

31 In his account of the jury selection for *Libération*, Sorj Chalandon insists that the defence in fact rejected two jurors, the first because she had been born in Lyon in 1928 and was old enough to remember the horrors of the Occupation. The second person rejected was born in Algeria and was apparently a *pied noir*. Chalandon speculated that she might have had sympathy for "the generals," the notorious leaders of the revolt to keep Algeria French. The Holocaust Memorial Museum transcript of the trial shows that each side rejected one member of the jury, and in addition the defence rejected one of the alternates. It does not identify the individuals in question, however.

32 Two of the civil parties lawyers in question were François Le Phuong and Paul Lombard.

33 The next day, a group of civil parties lawyers, including François Le Phuong and Paul Lombard announced that they were petitioning for a second procedure against Barbie for crimes against humanity for Larat and others tortured and murdered following their arrest at Caluire. This procedure, should it be undertaken, would not be linked to the current trial. Lombard stated to the court that he also did not believe that the Caluire affair could be "erased from history," but that he also did not wish to see it treated incidentally in the "brouhaha of an Assize court." Later, on 12 June, Moulin and the Caluire affair made another surreptitious entry into the trial, when Pierre Meunier, one of Moulin's trusted assistants brought up the subject of Jean Moulin in denying Barbie's claims that Moulin had died of self-inflicted wounds in trying to kill himself. When Cerdini sought to interrupt the testimony, Ugo Iannucci, a civil parties lawyer who insisted that the testimony was interesting "from the standpoint of history" and that this was not an ordinary Assize court trial. Nevertheless, Cerdini insisted to Meunier that Moulin was not the issue at stake and that he was not to refer to him.

34 The DVDs of the trial shown on *Arte* simultaneously show the scribe reading the indictment and Barbie's face in the corner of the screen.

35 See Sorj Chalandon and Pascale Nivelle, *Crimes contre l'humanité: Barbie, Touvier, Bousquet, Papon* (1998). An abridged version of the *Acte d'Accusation* is included in the volume. The discussion of Izieu is on pp. 19–24.

36 Available on *Légifrance*, the *Ordonnance* in question in fact says nothing about the inclusion of children as victims of the crimes in question. It does, however, allow that these victims are not restricted to French citizens but can include "foreigners" and refugees from other countries.

37 Pinkus Chmilenicky was a Jew deported from France to Auschwitz in 1942. Collaborating with the SS, he was known to have beaten, murdered, and robbed Jewish inmates. When he returned to France after the war, he was recognized by other returned deportees. He was condemned to death in France in 1950.

38 As discussed earlier, the 1954 indictment, the evidence gathered, and the final judgment of the 1954 military tribunal are included in Klarsfeld's dossiers. In the indictment itself, the general charges against Barbie *and five of his colleagues* are presented in broad terms, without specifics, generally covering the Lyon (and Grenoble) regions between 1942 and 1944. However, in the judgment of the tribunal, precise questions related to *specific crimes committed* (date, place, etc.) *by Barbie alone* are raised and answered, as are questions related to extenuating circumstances. Presumably, Vergès was attempting to play on the language of the *indictment* and not the judgment of the tribunal.

39 For a discussion of Bousquet's 1949 trial, see chapter one of my *Vichy's Afterlife*: "Memory and Justice Abused: The 1949 Trial of René Bousquet," 24–42.

40 Paul Vuillard was eighty years old at the time of the Barbie trial. He had been in the Resistance during the war. Prone to longwindedness, Vuillard surprised the court at the end of his closing statent by suggesting that crimes against humanity should be judged only in international courts, and if this were the case, Barbie could be executed for his crimes. As Vuillard gave his statement on 18 June, the day of general de Gaulle's famous plea to resist to the French by radio form London, he waxed sentimental and nostalgic on the Resistance as well. See chapter six here.

41 It is interesting to note that the counterarguments presented by the civil parties to Vergès's arguments for dismissal are not included in the television version of the trial presented on the *Arte* channel. While perhaps overly legalistic in nature, they nevertheless help explain why Pierre Truche, fearing the trial was getting off course, decided to intervene and address the jury at length and straightforwardly about what the facts and issues at hand really were.

42 In his account of the exchange at the time, Pierre Mérindol certainly sensed the necessity (indeed urgency) and effectiveness of Truche's intervention. He notes the Vergès's argument, seemingly "rigorous" in its logic and conclusions, proved "troubling" to the court and jury. This was why "the Prosecutor General Truche, fearing that the jurors would be too impressed by this apparent rigor, rose to deliver a master course in the vulgarization of the law, reducing its amalgamations to what they were. Implicitly, Truche's intervention was a shot across the bow of Barbie's defense lawyer: no one will manipulate this jury, and every time it is useful to intervene and clarify the litigious aspects of a juridical debate, the prosecution will intervene" (29–30).

43 The fact that Vergès handed Barbie a note just before his announced departure is clear in the video recording of the trial.

44 Recall Judith Miller's criticisms of the trial discussed in the introduction here.

45 One of the civil parties lawyers, Roger Souchal, made his response to Barbie more personal. Noting that he, Souchal, had been tortured by the SD and deported from Strasbourg during the war, Souchal stated "You disappoint me, you are a coward."

46 The comparison of Barbie to the Duke of Enghien was clearly outrageous. But as planned, it drew the ire of civil parties, prompting several of them to engage in Vergès's ploy by denouncing the comparison. But in the end, civil parties lawyer Paul Vuillard decided not to play along, calling Vergès's strategy for what it was: "Please! Your fable of one man standing alone, of a man illegally hounded and pursued, this fable has the odor of derision and cynicism."

47 Following Barbie's exit on the third day, the court heard the testimony of the psychiatric team that had examined Barbie, discussed in a previous chapter.

48 According to Article 320 of the French penal code in force at the time, President Cerdini had the authority to force the accused to remain in court. However, as many of those present were aware, and as some of the lawyers, including chief prosecutor Truche observed, to *constrain* Barbie to appear regardless of how legitimate the idea that he must face his accusers would recall unhappily earlier political trials, including those conducted by the Nazis themselves. In those trials, the defendant *had no rights* before the court. In a democracy, by contrast, the rights of the defendant must be protected if the political power in question is to appear legitimately democratic. On the other hand, justice dictates that the victims also have their rights, including the right to face the accused in court. This is also a fundamental legal principle that democratic courts must observe. Faced with this dilemma, Cerdini came up with an equitable solution. While Barbie would be allowed

to remain absent from the courtroom while victims who had had the opportunity to face him during the investigation testified, for those victims who had *not* had that opportunity, the accused would be forced to appear in court and face them. They, at least, would not be confronted with an empty box instead of their tormentor. As subsequent hearings of the trial would reveal, this would also occasionally provoke fireworks with which the court and President Cerdini would have to contend.

5 The Witnesses

1 See Susan Sontag, "Reflections on *The Deputy*," in Eric Bentley, ed., *The Storm over* The Deputy (1964), 117.

2 See Hanna Arendt, *Eichmann in Jerusalem*, especially chapter fourteen, "Evidence and Witnesses," 220–33.

3 Fourcade responded to Cerdini's explanations by interjecting "C'est un comble!" ("This is an outrage!") and "Quelle horreur!" tolerated by Cerdini perhaps because the witness was visibly impaired by her age.

4 In his confrontation with Barbie during the investigation which took place on 5 February 1983, Kroskof-Thomas was not nearly as melodramatic in his description of his meeting with Barbie in wartime Lyon. There was no talk of an "angel of death," nor did he describe himself as being traumatized in any way by his encounter with Barbie. While Kroskof-Thomas referred to Barbie's pinkie finger as separated from the others when Babie made gestures, there was no reference to the gesture's effeminacy (K: P1/51).

5 For a discussion of this phenomenon in a post-Holocaust world, see Carolyn J. Dean's excellent study *The Failure of Empathy after the Holocaust* (2004).

6 As noted in the introduction, Blardone was attacked by the negationist André Chelain in his book on the trial, attributing Blardone's supposedly perverse tastes to his Italian name and origins. When questioned during the investigation on 23 February 1983, Blardone stated that he was born in Vagognia, Italy, in 1923 (K: P2/III, 96). During this questioning, Blardone observed that Barbie and the other SS seemed to take particular pleasure in abusing and torturing women.

7 In his testimony, Srul Kaplon also testified that Barbie sicced his dog on his victims. Kaplon testified that the order he heard Barbie give to the dog once was "Wulf, eat the Jew!"

8 Reported in Ted Morgan, "The Barbie File," *New York Times Magazine*, 10 May 1987.

9 In an interview with Lesèvre during the investigation datet 23 February 1983, Lesèvre offered these comments about Barbie while imprisoned at the *Ecole de santé*: "During my stay [there] full of sad memories I remember the

special joy Barbie took in throwing himself at prisoners lying on the floor and turning them over with the toe of his boot. If the prisoner in question was a Jew, Barbie never failed to crush the prisoner's face with a kick while saying: "it's a Jew!" (K: P2/III, 11).

10 On 20 July 1983, Kadosche-Lagrange and Barbie faced off in the presence of their lawyers and investigating magistrate Riss. Barbie responded to Kadosche-Lagrange's claim that he was holding a cat. "I never owned a cat," he explained. He continued: "I belonged to a very disciplined unit of the SS and it is nonsense to say that I owned a cat" (K: P1/36). *In La loi du sang,* Johann Chapoutot notes that, according to Nazi ideology, cats are sinister, oriental creatures, and so to be avoided (203).

11 It is worth noting that Kadosche-Lagrange's account of what transpired during her confrontation with Barbie in 1983 corresponds exactly with what she testified in court (K: P1/36). This is significant because Vergès would later maintain that the entire episode was a fantasy of her own perverted sexuality.

12 De Gaulle-Anthonioz's evocation of "human rags" in Nazi camps, of these living creatures who no longer seem alive has been echoed in the works of camp survivors and writers like Jorge Semprun. See in particular Semprun's 2002 novel, *Le mort qu'il faut.*

13 In this instance in particular, a camera behind the raised podium where judges and jury sat panned the crowd and then zoomed in, first on Blardone and then Kadosche-Lagrange.

14 In the *procès-verbal de confrontation,* or document recording the encounter between Barbie and Kadosche-Lagrange occurring on 20 July 1983, contained in Klarsfeld's files (K: P1/36) and cited above, the document notes that Jacques Vergès was present throughout the encounter.

15 In accordance with the French Penal Code in effect at the time, the civil parties have the right to a response, or "*réplique*" after the closing argument made by the defence is completed. In this instance, Vergès decided to pause in his argument to allow the civil parties to speak. He stated that he detected their desire to do so. De Bigault then asked if his *plaidoire* was completed and said that the *réplique* would only be given then. Cerdini pointed out that the civil parties lawyers were correct in this instance. While the exchange, although heated, seemed trivial, it was also suggestive of a desire on Vergès's part to assume command of the courtroom, the more to disrupt it by breaking the rules.

16 Chief prosecutor Truche had gone on record as opposing the inclusion of resisters along with Jews among the victims of such crimes, and although he faithfully prosecuted the case in accordance with the new definition, reporters and others were aware of Truche's ambivalent attitude. To a certain degree, Truche was arguing the case à *contrecoeur.*

17 As Pierre Mérindol points out in *Barbie, le Procès*, the link between Vergès and Frossard was more personal than their shared denunciations of French crimes in Algeria. Frossard, Mérindol notes, led the campaign at the newspaper *L'Aurore* protesting France's intended execution of the convicted Algerian militant Djamila Bouhired. Bouhired was spared. She eventually became Vergès's wife, although they later divorced.

18 I have here translated the original French of Césaire's statement that Vergès quoted in court. For a more recent translation of the *Discourse in Colonialism* itself, see Joan Pinkman's translation in the bibliography here.

19 Truche would later underscore the faulty calculations Vergès had indulged in to arrive at this figure. See the conclusion here.

20 Wiesel's comment here is from a brief account of his experience and reaction to Vergès's questions during his testimony, included in Bernard-Henry Lévy's collection of documents related to the trial, *Archive d'un Procès: Klaus Barbie*, 90. The *New York Times* reported in its coverage of the trial on 3 June that, following his testimony, Wiesel angrily stated on the courthouse steps that Jacques Vergès was "full of hatred, hatred for me personally, hatred for the Jewish people, and hatred for the victims."

21 Charles S. Maier, *The Unmasterable Past: History, Holocaust, and German National Identity*, 3.

22 Nolte's essay is included in *Forever in the Shadow of Hitler?* The passage cited here is on page 22.

23 For those interested in the *Historikerstreit*, Maier's *The Unmasterable Past* remains an excellent guide. For the question of the uniqueness of the Holocaust, there are of course numerous arguments made for and against. One of the best presentations of the case *for* the uniqueness of the disaster, see Yehuda Bauer's *Rethinking the Holocaust*, chapters 2 and 3 in particular. For the question as to whether Nazi Germany can be considered a variant of totalitarianism or fascism, and whether it can be "normalized" in historical terms or remains in fact an aberration, see especially chapter nine in Ian Kershaw's *The Nazi Dictatorship: Problems and Perspectives of Interpretation*.

24 In an interrogation of Barbie by investigating magistrate Riss dated 19 December 1983, Barbie was categorical that Jewish matters were handled not by him but by Eichmann and directly from Berlin. He stated: "I would like to make clear once and for all certain matters for which I am indicted, and that concern Jewish matters. It is stated in the minutes of the Eichmann trial that all actions concerning Jews were centralized through Berlin in Office IV. This office was called 'Office IV Eichmann' for good reason. Thus, all action against Jews in occupied territories occurred as a result of orders coming from Berlin via Paris" (K: P1/49).

6 The Civil Parties and Prosecution Make Their Case

1 The issue is covered in Article 132–3 of the *Nouvel Code Pénal.* It is referred to as the *non-cumul des peines,* or non-accumulation of sentences. According to *Maître* Sabine Haddad, the expression *non-cumul* is normally applied to a single sentence when multiple crimes and sanctions are involved, whereas *confusion* is applied in a case like Barbie's, where there have been multiple condemnations and therefore sentences.

2 Depending on one's perspective, there were other awkward moments in the trial when, in striving for a powerful image, the civil parties lawyers proposed similarly incongruous visions to the court. At the end of his closing statement, Roland Dumas, a lawyer for Lise Lesèvre, proposed that the court leave behind as its judgment and legacy, a "single white page." When inevitably someone would ask what it symbolized, they should be told "it is the shroud of the children of Izieu."

3 According to Roland Dumas, the other civil parties lawyers accorded the honour of being the first to address the court to Klarsfeld.

4 *Hunting the Truth* 344–5.

5 The civil parties lawyer Alain Lévy also expressed the desire to see French criminals against humanity brought to trial as well. Curiously, as noted in the introduction, subsequent critics of the trial failed to acknowledge these calls for French criminals to be punished.

6 In his closing statement before the court, Bernard de Bigault du Granrut also spoke movingly of his Resistance past and the loss of some of his family members. His statement will be discussed shortly.

7 In a 2002 essay entitled "La signature du crime contre l'humanité," Michel Zaoui stated that the fate of the Izieu children also made it possible to comprehend the true meaning of crimes against humanity. Zaoui wrote: "The tragedy of the children of Izieu, for which Klaus Barbie was responsible, made it truly possible to understand what a crime against humanity was, even when Barbie was also being prosecuted for other crimes of the same ilk" (53). The essay is included in Jean-Paul Jean, *Barbie, Touvier, Papon: Des Procès pour la mémoire.*

8 See *La Vérité aura le dernier mot* (1985).

9 Barbie's affirmation of his German nationality was made in his interrogation while in French Guyana (K: P1/6).

10 De Bigault would later sum up these arguments and reflect on crimes against humanity in general terms in a 1998 essay entitled simply "*Le crime contre l'humanite.*" The essay is included in *Le Crime contre l'humanité: Mesure de la responsabilité?* See bibliography.

11 Admittedly, de Bigault's statement veered towards the overly didactic and pedantic at times.

12 Presumably here Jakubowicz is referring to de Launay's *Le monde en guerre 1939–1945*, published in 1945.

13 Maurice Szafran, "Pierre Truche, procureur général," in *Archives d'un procès: Klaus Barbie* (1986), 198.

14 The interview in question was published in the 10–16 July 1987 issue of the magazine.

15 Vansteenberghe also stated to the court that while she fully understood the risks she took in joining the Resistance, she did not want the price she paid overlooked. For this reason, she stated, she had brought her X-rays to court to demonstrate that while being tortured by Barbie and his men, five of her vertebrae had been fractured. She gave her testimony seated.

16 The translation into French of the 15 February report is included in *Klaus Barbie 1987: Mémoires d'un procès* (43).

17 This separation is visible in photographic reproductions of the telex in, for example, *Klaus Barbie 1987: Mémoire d'un procès*, 46. Additionally, where the letter "B" followed by the letter "A" is at the beginning of the word, there is also a strange compression of letters following these letters. So BARBIE is written as B A RB I E, and in the text, BARGELD is written as B A RG E L D.

7 Barbie's Defence Takes Centre Stage

1 In her role as an FLN militant, Bouhared had been brutally tortured by French authorities.

2 In his closing statement, Mbemba did evoke Barbie's basic "humanity," an episode to be discussed shortly.

3 In his memoir of the trial, *L'autre mémoire du crime contre l'humanité*, Mbemba offered a different reason for Barbie's "invisibility." He stated that Barbie was essentially "evacuated" from the trial because the trial was actually the "trial of Nazism" (57) rather than that of the accused.

4 For an excellent discussion of Hannah Arendt's insights as well as her blindspots in assessing the connections between European colonialism and the subsequent genocidal crimes of totalitarianism and Nazism in particular, see Michael Rothberg's chapter on the topic, "At the Limits of Eurocentrism: Hannah Arendt's *The Origins of Totalitarianism*," in *Multidirectional Memory: Remembering the Holocaust in the Age of Decolonization*.

5 In his memoir of the Barbie trial, *L'autre mémoire du crime contre l'humanité*, Mbemba was more precise about the crime to which he was referring, except that the number of those killed in this account is "89,000 to 200,000 dead" as opposed to the figure of 30,000 he mentioned in court. Comparing the crime to the Nazi destruction of the French village of Oradour, in the town of Moramanga, the "Madagascan Oradour," colonial troups arriving by

night enacted scenes of "indescribable carnage," shooting peoples in piles "indiscriminately." Mbemba had borrowed the term "Madagascan Oradour" from the author of an earlier account of the massacre, written by Pierre Boiteau in 1954 (*L'autre mémoire* 121).

6 In *Le Salaud lumineux* Vergès told his interviewer that in their dealings with Barbie neither he nor Mbemba nor Bouaïta ever detected the slightest trace of racial prejudice in Barbie (285).

7 In his statement before the court Mbemba went on to explain that in his own country he had seen political fanatics renounce their fanaticism and anti-religious individuals return to their faith at the end of their lives. Although he did not state explicitly that Barbie had renounced his Nazism, this was certainly a legitimate conclusion one could draw from Mbemba's words.

8 Bouaïta was referring to Pascal Bruckner's controversial book *Tears of the White Man*. The book is hardly a denial of colonialism's crimes, but rather an indictment of some of those French intellectuals who explain the woes of post-colonial regimes exclusively in terms of their history of being colonized.

9 The Nazi massacre of 34,000 Ukranian Jews outside Kiev in 1941.

10 In court Vergès never explained what he meant by this. Presumably, this meant that no French policing authority could intervene in the activities of the Gestapo. In fact, as the Barbie case as well as the Touvier trial seven years later demonstrated, French police and paramilitary organizations like the *Milice* were completely subordinate to their German counterparts.

11 Although Vergès did not cite it in his statement, Article Eight of the *Declaration of the Rights of Man and the Citizen* states that "Only strictly and obviously necessary punishments may be established by the law, and no one may be punished except by virtue of a law established and promulgated before the time of the offense, and legally applied."

12 For a detailed discussion of the controversy over Arendt's book, see the introduction to Golsan and Misemer, *The Trial That Never Ends*, 3–21.

13 Along these lines, see Claude Chabrol's excellent 1993 documentary, *Eye of Vichy*.

14 Never one to miss a literary reference or allusion, Vergès was referring to Sartre's 1944 play, in which hell is portrayed as three people torturing each other eternally in a sitting room from which they cannot escape.

15 On this point Vergès proved prescient. In the 1997 controversy involving the Aubrac's claims concerning their Resistance activities, the issue of Lucie Aubrac's account of her efforts to free her husband who was in Barbie's hands was central. The controversy will be discussed in the conclusion here.

16 See Antoine Spire, *Ces enfants qui nous manquent*, 118–20.

17 See Antoine Spire, *Ces enfants qui nous manquent*, 122. In his book, Spire expresses his disagreement with the two civil parties lawyers in question, Serge Klarsfeld and Roland Rappaport, on the grounds that it was important to underscore as much as possible, through figures like Bourdon, the shameful compromises made by the French during the Occupation.

Conclusion

1 This, of course, is not the position taken here concerning the performances of the civil parties lawyers, nor did many journalists cited here share this view.

2 Alain Delon was a major star of French films for fifty years. Known for his good looks and piercing blue eyes, Delon also co-starred in some American films as well.

3 The film in question is part of the Arte DVD collection of selections from the official video recording of the trial shown on French television.

4 Jean-Martin Mbemba summarizes some of the favourable press reviews for the defence's arguments in *L'autre mémoire du crime contre l'humanité* 155–63.

5 The most thorough discussion of scapegoating and sacrificial violence, and their expression in myths, literary works, and other cultural artefacts can be found in *Violence and the Sacred*, originally published in French in 1972.

6 Paul Bénichou, *Morales du grand siècle*, 378.

7 For a discussion of the "Mitterrand Affair," see my *Vichy's Afterlife* 103–23.

8 For a discussion of the Bousquet affair and the trial of Paul Touvier, see my *Memory, the Holocaust, and French Justice*.

9 To this day, the exact figure remains unknown.

10 For the history of the Papon Affair and the trial itself, see my *The Papon Affair*.

11 Bancel and Blanchard's essay is included in Blanchard and Veyrat-Masson, *Les Guerres de mémoires*.

12 In 2001 the publication of Colonel Paul Aussarresses' *Services Spéciaux: Algérie 1955–1957*, an unapologetic account of the brutal actions of French special forces in dealing with suspected Algerian terrorists provoked considerable controversy. Aussarresses spoke at length of the torture, rape, and murder of insurgents and claimed that his actions and those of his men were well known by French authorities in Paris. President Jacques Chirac eventually stripped Aussarresses of his rank and his Legion of Honor. He was also ordered never to wear his uniform again. Chirac's actions against Aussarresses were later overturned by the European court as a violation of Aussarresses' right to free speech.

13 The *harkis* were Arabs who fought alongside the French during the Algerian War. Many were abandoned in Algeria after the liberation of the country

and massacred by the new regime. Others immigrated to France, where their situations were often deplorable.

14 The historian Donald Reid argues convincingly that, certainly at the time of the Barbie trial, figures like Lucie Aubrac were revered in France as *rebels*, in her case, in her role as a leader of the Resistance. By the time of the Aubrac Affair, however, it was *victims* who were revered in French culture, not rebels. This made figures like Lucie Aubrac more "vulnerable" to criticism in the new millennium. Arguably, at least, this transition occurred, as Stéphane Ledoux has suggested (and as discussed in the introduction here), during the Barbie trial itself, with its shift in focus from Resistance victims and heroes to Jewish victims of the Nazis and their Vichy minions. The shift is also evident in the phenomenon of the "competition of victims," so much a cornerstone and legacy of the Barbie trial itself.

15 For excellent discussions of the Aubrac Affair, its implications, and consequences, see Susan Rubin Suleiman, *Crises of Memory and the Second World War*, 36–61, and Leah Hewitt, "Identity Wars in 'L'Affaire Aubrac': History, Fiction, Film," 264–84.

16 For an authoritative discussion of France's "memory laws," see Marc Olivier Baruch, *Des lois indignes? Les historiens, la politique, et le droit*. For a briefer account in English, see my chapter "France's Crooked Legal Vector of Memory" in *The Vichy Past in France Today*.

Bibliography

Accoyer, Bernard. *Questions mémorielles: Rassembler la nation autour d'une mémoire Partagée: Rapport de la Mission Parlementaire D'information.* Assemblée nationale, 2009.

Anders, Günther. *Nous, Fils d'Eichmann: Lettre ouverte à Klaus Eichmann.* Translated by Sabine Cornille and Philippe Ivernel [Nouv. éd.], Rivages Poche, Petite Bibliothèque, Payot & Rivages, 2003.

Arbour, Louise. *War Crimes and the Culture of Peace* (The Senator Keith Davey Lecture). Published in association with Victoria University by U of Toronto P, 2002.

Arendt, Hannah. *Eichmann in Jerusalem: A Report on the Banality of Evil.* Penguin, 1992.

Arendt, Hannah. *Responsibility and Judgement.* Edited by Jerome Kohn, Schocken Books, 2003.

Arendt, Hannah. *Thinking without a Banister: Essays in Understanding 1953–1975.* Edited by Jerome Kohn, Schocken Books, 2018.

Aussarresses, Paul. *Services Spéciaux: Algérie 1955–1957.* Perrin, 2001.

Baruch, Marc-Olivier. *Des Lois indignes? Les historiens, la politique et le droit.* Tallandier, 2013.

Bass, Gary Jonathan. *Stay the Hand of Vengeance: The Politics of War Crimes Tribunals.* Princeton Studies in International History and Politics, Project Muse, 2019.

Bauer, Yehuda. *Rethinking the Holocaust.* Yale UP, 2001.

Benhabib, Seyla. *Exile, Statelessness, and Migration: Playing Chess with History from Hannah Arendt to Isaiah Berlin.* Book Collections on Project Muse, Princeton UP, 2018.

Bentley, Eric, ed. *The Storm Over the Deputy.* Grove Press, 1964.

Bevernage, Berber, and Nico Wouters, eds. *The Palgrave Handbook of State-Sponsored History After 1945.* Palgrave Macmillan, 2018.

Bilsky, Leora. *Transformative Justice: Israeli Identity on Trial*. Law, Meaning, and Violence, U of Michigan P, 2004.

Binder, Guyora. 1989. "Representing Nazism: Advocacy and Identity at the Third Trial of Klaus Barbie." *The Yale Law Journal*, vol. 98, no. 7, 1989, http://www.jstor.org/stable/796747. Accessed 27 February 2018.

Blanchard, Pascal, and Isabelle Veyrat-Masson, eds. *Les Guerres de mémoires: la France et son histoire*. La Découverte, 2008.

Boulanger, Gérard. *Les Secrets du procès Papon: Souvenirs sur l'affaire*. Documents, Cherche midi, 2018.

Bower, Tom. *Klaus Barbie: The Butcher of Lyon*. Pantheon, 1984.

Bower, Tom. "They Were Just Following Orders." *The Washington Post*, 21 October 1979, https://www.washingtonpost.com/archive/opinions /1979/10/21. Accessed 13 June 2019.

Bredin, Jean-Denis. *L'infamie: Le Procès De Riom, février-avril 1942*. B. Grasset, 2012.

Butler, Judith. *Parting Ways: Jewishness and the Critique of Zionism*. New Directions in Critical Theory, Columbia UP, 2012.

Césaire, Aimé. *Discourse on Colonialism*. Monthly Review Press, 2000.

Chalandon, Sorj, and Nivelle Pascale. *Crimes contre l'humanité: Barbie, Touvier, Bousquet, Papon*. Plon, 1998.

Chaney, Kevin R. "Pitfalls and Imperatives: Applying the Lessons of Nuremberg to the Yugoslav War Crimes Trials." *Penn State International Law Review*, vol. 14, no. 1, Article 4, 1995. http://elibrary.law.psu.edu/psilr /vol14/iss1/4.

Chapoutot, Johann. *La Loi du sang: Penser et agir en Nazi*. Bibliothèque Des Histoires, Gallimard, 2014.

Chauvy, Gérard. *Aubrac: Lyon, 1943*. A. Michel, 1997.

Conan Éric, and Henry Rousso. *Vichy, un passé qui ne passe pas*. Nouvelle édition mise à jour, Pluriel, 2013.

Courtois, Stéphane, et al. *The Black Book of Communism: Crimes, Terror, and Repression*. Translated by Jonathan Murphey and Mark Kramer, consulting editor Mark Kramer, Harvard UP, 1999.

Dean, Carolyn. *The Fragility of Empathy after the Holocaust*. Cornell UP, 2004.

Derrida, Jacques. *Cosmopolitanism and Forgiveness*. Routledge, 2001.

Dimsdale, Joel E. *Anatomy of Malice: The Enigma of the Nazi War Criminals*. Yale UP, 2016.

Doman, Nicholas. "Aftermath of Nuremberg: The Trial of Klaus Barbie." *University of Colorado Law Review*, vol. 60, no. 3, 449–70, 1989.

Douglas, Lawrence. *The Memory of Judgment: Making Law and History in the Trials of the Holocaust*. Yale UP, 2001.

Ferrari, Robert. "The Procedure in the 'Cour d'Assises' of Paris." *Columbia Law Review*, vol. 18, no. 1, 1918, pp. 43–62, https://www.jstor.org/stable/1111063. Accessed 10 April 2020.

Ferro, Marc, and Serge de Sampigny. *Pétain en vérité*. Tallandier, 2013.

Finkielkraut, Alain. *Remembering in Vain: The Klaus Barbie Trial and Crimes against Humanity*. European Perspectives, Columbia UP, 1992.

Frossard, André. *Le Crime contre l'humanité*. R. Laffont, 1997.

Gide, André, et al. *Souvenirs et voyages*. Edited by Pierre Masson [Reimpression], Bibliothèque De La Pléiade, 473, Gallimard, 2012.

Gildea, Robert. *Fighters in the Shadows: A New History of the French Resistance*. The Belknap Press of Harvard UP, 2015.

Girard, René. *Violence and the Sacred*. Translated by Patrick Gregory, Johns Hopkins UP, 1972.

Golsan, Richard Joseph. *Memory, the Holocaust, and French Justice: The Bousquet and Touvier Affairs*. Edited by Richard Joseph Golsan, Contemporary French Culture and Society, Dartmouth College/UPNE, 1996.

Golsan, Richard Joseph. *The Papon Affair: Memory and Justice on Trial*. Routledge, 2000.

Golsan, Richard Joseph. *The Vichy Past in France Today: Corruptions of Memory*. Lexington Books, 2017.

Golsan, Richard Joseph, et al. *Literature and History: Around Suite Française and Les Bienveillantes*. Yale French Studies, no. 121, Yale UP, 2012.

Gordon, Bertram M. *Collaborationism in France During the Second World War*. Cornell UP, 1980.

Hammerschmidt, Peter. *Klaus Barbie, nom de code Adler*. Broché, 2016.

Hausner, Gideon. *Justice in Jerusalem*. Holocaust Library, 1966.

Herbert, Ulrich. *Werner Best, un nazi dans l'ombre*. Tallandier, 2010.

Hirsch, Francine. *Soviet Judgment at Nuremberg: A New History of the International Military Tribunal after World War II*. Oxford UP, 2020.

Igounet, Valérie. *Le Négationnisme en France*. Que sais-je? 2020.

Ingrao, Christian. *Believe and Destroy: Intellectuals in the SS War Machine*. Translated by Andrew Brown, Polity Press, 2010.

Ingrao, Christian. *The SS Dirlewanger Brigade: The History of the Black Hunters*. Translated by Phoebe Green, Skyhorse Publishing, 2011.

Jankélévitch, Vladimir. *Forgiveness*. Translated by Andrew Kelley, U of Chicago P, 2005.

Jankélévitch, Vladimir, et al. *L'Esprit de Résistance: textes inédits, 1943–1983*. Edited by Françoise Schwab, Albin Michel, 2015.

Kahn, Annette. *Why My Father Died: A Daughter Confronts Her Family's Past at the Trial of Klaus Barbie*. Summit Books, 1991.

Kershaw, Ian. 1993. *The Nazi Dictatorship: Problems and Perspectives of Interpretation*. Arnold, 1993.

Kessel, Joseph, and Francis Lacassin. *Jugements derniers: Les procès Pétain, de Nuremberg et Eichmann*. Texto, Le Goût De L'histoire, Éditions Tallandier, 2018.

Klarsfeld, Beate, and Serge Klarsfeld. *Mémoires*. Flammarion, Librairie Arthème Fayard, 2015.

Klarsfeld, Serge. *Chronique de l'affaire Papon: Une nécessaire contribution documentaire: Extraits des bulletins de liaison de 1981 à 2002 de L'association Les Fils Et Filles Des Déportés Juifs De France rédigés par Serge Klarsfeld*. Fils et filles des déportés juifs de France, 2002.

Klarsfeld, Serge. *La Chronique Des Fils Et Filles: 25 Années de militantisme de l'association: Les Fils Et Filles De Déportés Juifs De France, 1979–2004: Extraits des bulletins de liaison de L'association précédés par la chronique de l'action des Klarsfeld de 1968 à 1978*. FFDJF, 2004.

Klaus Barbie: 1987 Mémoires d'un procès. Le Mémorial National de la Prison de Montluc, 2017.

Knowlton, James, and Truett Cates. *Forever in the Shadow of the Holocaust?* Humanities Press, 1993.

Koonz, Claudia. *The Nazi Conscience*. The Belknap Press of Harvard UP, 2003.

Koposov, N.E. *Memory Laws, Memory Wars: The Politics of the Past in Europe and Russia*. New Studies in European History, Cambridge UP, 2018.

Lampert, Tom, translator. *An Uncompromising Generation: The Nazi Leadership of the Reich Security Main Office*. By Michael Wildt, George L. Mosse Series in Modern European Cultural and Intellectual History, U of Wisconsin P, 2009.

Lang, Jochen von, ed. *Eichmann Interrogated: Transcripts from the Archives of the Israeli Police*. The Bodley Head, 1983.

Laughland, John. *The Death of Politics: France Under Mitterrand*. Michael Joseph, 1995.

Ledoux, Sébastien. "The Barbie Trial (1987): Narrator of the Holocaust in France." *Revue GenObs*, vol. 1, no. 2, 2017, https://ojs.trentu.ca/ojs/index.php/genobs/article/view/148/112. Accessed 21 December 2021.

Lewy, Guenter. *Perpetrators: The World of the Holocaust Killers*. Oxford UP, 2017.

Linklater, Magnus, et al. *The Nazi Legacy: Klaus Barbie and the International Fascist Connection*. Holt, Rinehart, and Winston, 1984.

Lottman, Herbert R. *The Purge*. 1st ed., Morrow, 1986.

Maier, Charles S. *The Unmasterable Past: History, Holocaust, and German National Identity*. Harvard UP, 1997.

Mann, Thomas. "Brother Hitler: Journey to Perplexity." *Esquire Magazine*, 1939, https://iamyouasheisme.wordpress.com/2016/11/05/brother-hitler/. Accessed 21 December 2021.

Marrus, Michael R., and Robert O. Paxton. *Vichy France and the Jews*. Schocken Books, 1983.

Mbemba, Jean-Martin. *L'Autre Mémoire du crime contre l'humanité*. Présence africaine, 1990.

Mérindol, Pierre. *Barbie: Le Procès*. La Manufacture, 1987.

Michel, Johann. *Le Devoir de mémoire*. Que Sais-Je? Histoire, 4125, Presses universitaires de France, 2018.

Miller, Arthur. *Echoes Down the Corridor: Collected Essays 1944–2000*. Edited by Steven Centola, Viking Penguin, 2000.

Miller, Judith. *One, by One, by One: Facing the Holocaust*. Simon and Schuster, 1990.

Morgan, Ted. *An Uncertain Hour: The French, the Germans, the Jews, the Klaus Barbie Trial, and the City of Lyon. 1940–1945*. William Morrow and Company Inc., 1990.

Nicolaïdis, Dimitri. *Oublier nos crimes: L'amnésie nationale, une spécificité française?* Collection Mémoires, 1184, Autrement, 2002.

Noguères, Henri. *La Vérité aura le dernier mot*. Seuil, 1985.

Nordmann, Joë, and Anne Brunel. *Aux Vents de l'histoire: Mémoires*. 1st ed., Actes sud, 1996.

Paris, Erna. *Unhealed Wounds: France and the Klaus Barbie Affair*. Grove Press, 1985.

Pendas, David. *The Frankfurt Auschwitz Trial, 1963–1965: Genocide, History, and the Limits of Law*. Cambridge UP, 2006.

Poirot-Delpech, Bertrand. *Monsieur Barbie n'a rien à dire*. Gallimard, 1987.

Pratt, Valéry. "Nuremberg, les droits de l'homme, le cosmopolitisme: Pour une philosophie du droit international." Dissertation, Édition Le Bord de l'eau, 2018.

Priemel, Kim Christian, and Alexa Stiller, eds. *Reassessing the Nuremberg Military Tribunals: Transitional Justice, Trial Narratives, and Historiography*. Studies on War and Genocide, vol. 16, Berghahn Books, 2014.

Rassat, Michèle-Laure. *La Justice en France*. 2nd ed., Que Sais-Je: Collection Encyclopedique, 612, Presses Universitaires de France, 1987.

Ricœur, Paul. *Le Crime contre l'humanité: Mesure de la responsabilité? Actes du cycle des conférences "Droit, Liberté Et Foi", juin 1997*. Cahiers De L'école Cathédrale, 33, CERP, 1998.

Ricœur, Paul. *The Just*. U of Chicago P, 2000.

Reid, Donald. *Germaine Tillion, Lucie Aubrac, and the Politics of Memories of the French Resistance*. Cambridge Scholars Publishing, 2007.

Reisman, W. Michael, and Chris T Antoniou. *The Laws of War: A Comprehensive Collection of Primary Documents on International Laws Governing Armed Conflict*. 1st ed., A Vintage Original, Vintage Books, 1994.

Rémond, René. *Quand l'état se mêle de l'histoire*. Les Essais, Stock, 2006.

Rothberg, Michael. *Multidirectional Memory: Remembering the Holocaust in the Age of Colonization*. Stanford UP, 2009.

Rousso, Henry, and Richard Joseph Golsan. *Stalinism and Nazism: History and Memory Compared*. European Horizons, U of Nebraska P, 2004.

Ryan, Allan A. *Quiet Neighbors: Prosecuting Nazi War Criminals in America*. 1st ed., Harcourt Brace Jovanovich, 1984.

Scheffer, David. *All the Missing Souls: A Personal History of the War Crimes Tribunals*. Human Rights and Crimes against Humanity, Princeton UP, 2013.

Segev, Tom. "Moment of Truth for Michel Thomas." *Haaretz.com*, 13 September 2002, https://www.haaretz.com/misc/article-print-page/1.5121859. Accessed 22 June 2020.

Shklar, Judith N. *American Citizenship: The Quest for Inclusion*. (The Tanner Lectures on Human Values), Harvard UP, 2001.

Shklar, Judith N. *The Faces of Injustice*. Storrs Lectures on Jurisprudence, Yale Law School, Yale UP, 1990 [1988].

Shklar, Judith N. *Legalism: Law, Morals, and Political Trials*. Harvard UP, 1964.

Short, Philip. *A Taste for Intrigue: The Multiple Lives of François Mitterrand*. 1st US ed., Henry Holt and Company, 2014.

Simonin, Anne. *Le Droit de désobéissance: Les Éditions De Minuit en guerre d'Algérie*. Documents, Les Éditions de Minuit, 2012.

Simpson, Gerry J. "Didactic and Dissident Histories in War Crimes Trials," Dee J. Kelly Law Library, 1997, https://www.thefreelibrary.com/Didactic +and+dissident+histories+in+war+crimes+trials-a019491001. Accessed 25 January 2022.

Stangneth, Bettina. *Eichmann before Jerusalem: The Unexamined Life of a Mass Murderer*. Translated by Ruth Martin, Alfred A. Knopf, 2014.

Suleiman, Susan-Rubin. *Crises of Memory and the Second World War*. Harvard UP, 2006.

Théolleyre, Jean-Marc. *Procès d'après-guerre: "Je Suis Partout", René Hardy, Oradour-Sur-Glane, Oberg et Knochen*. La Découverte, 1986.

Tillion, Germaine, and Tzvetan Todorov. *Combats de guerre et de paix*. Opus, Éditions du Seuil, 2007.

Todorov, Tzvetan. *La Signature humaine: Essais 1983–2008*. Seuil, 2009.

Todorov, Tzvetan, et al. *Torture and the War on Terror*. The French List, Seagull Books, 2009.

Truche, Pierre. *Juger, être jugé: Le magistrat face aux autres et à lui-même*. Fayard, 2001.

Truche, Pierre. *Juger les crimes contre l'humanité: 20 ans après le procès Barbie: Actes du colloque des 10, 11, Et 12 Octobre 2007, École Normale Supérieure Lettres et Sciences Humaines*. ENS éd, 2009.

Varaut, J. Marc. *Procès Petain*. Perrin, 1995.

Vergès, Françoise. *L'Homme prédateur: Ce que nous enseigne l'esclavage sur notre temps*. Albin Michel, 2011.

Vergès, Jacques. *De la stratégie judiciaire*. Documents (Editions De Minuit), Editions de minuit, 1992.

Vergès, Jacques. *De mon propre aveu: Souvenirs et rêveries.* P.-G. de Roux, 2013.

Vergès, Jacques. 2011. *Justice et littérature.* Questions Judiciaires. Paris: Presses universitaires de France.

Vergès, Jacques. *Lettre ouverte à des amis algériens devenus tortionnaires.* Lettre Ouverte, A. Michel, 1993.

Vergès, Jacques. *Pour en finir avec Ponce Pilate.* Le Pré aux clercs, 1983.

Vergès, Jacques, and Bloch Étienne. *La Face cachée du procès Barbie: Compte-rendu des débats de Ligoure.* Formule Rompue, S. Tastet, 1983.

Vergès, Jacques, and Jean-Louis Remilleux. *Le Salaud lumineux: Conversations avec Jean-Louis Remilleux.* M. Lafont, 1994.

Viout, Jean-Oliver. "The Klaus Barbie Trial and Crimes Against Humanity." *Hofstra Law and Policy Symposium,* vol. 3, Article 14, 1997, https://scholarly commons.law.hofstra.edu/hlps/vol3/iss1/14. Accessed 21 December 2021.

Welzer, Harald. *Les Exécuteurs: Des hommes normaux aux meurtriers de masse.* Translated by Bernard Lortholary, Nrf Essais, Gallimard, 2007.

Wieviorka, Olivier, et al. *Nous entrerons dans la carrière: De la Résistance à l'exercice du pouvoir.* Xxe Siècle, Éd. du Seuil, 1994.

Wilson, Robert. *The Confessions of Klaus Barbie, the Butcher of Lyon.* Pulp Press Publication: Arsenal Edition, 1984.

Wittmann, Rebecca. *Beyond Justice: The Auschwitz Trial.* Harvard UP, 2005.

Zaoui, Michel, et al. *Mémoires de justice: Les procès Barbie, Touvier, Papon.* Seuil, 2009.

Index

Page numbers in *italics* indicate figures.

Abdallah, Georges Ibrahim, protesting own trial, 137
Abendroth, Kurt, on Barbie, 32–3
absolute morality, 46
Académie Française, 88
Adenauer, Konrad, de Gaulle and, 68
Algeria: French crimes in, 48, 54; French in, 88, 89; French victims of, 193–4
Algerian War, 290–1n13
Allen, Woody, Kroskof-Thomas and, 148
Alliance Resistance network, 147
Altmann, Klaus, Barbie's name choice, 49, 119, 124, 129, 260
Altmann, Rabbi Adolph, 49
American Counter Intelligence Corps (CIC), 9, 33, 47, 80, 81, 259
Amin Dada, Idi, 193
Amnesty Law, 99
Andean Fourth Reich, 47
André, Francis, 150, 214; Barbie and, 197
Andréani-Jungblut, Elfrun, closing argument of, 197, 206
Annuls of Revisionist History (journal), 113

Antigone (Sophocles), 217–18
anti-Semitism, 13, 20, 44, 273n30; Barbie's, 48–50; Hausner on, 56
Arabs, violence against, 114
Arafat, Yassar, 211
Ardies, Tom, Bolivian interview, 47–8
Arendt, Hannah, 17, 145; on defendants of Auschwitz trial, 61–2; on demonizing someone, 36; description of Eichmann, 180; Eichmann and banality of evil, 9, 36; Eichmann as desk killer, 64; *Eichmann in Jerusalem*, 9, 12, 20, 36, 144, 229; Fest and, 36; Holocaust from modern totalitarianism, 56; insights of, 288n4; *The Origins of Totalitarianism*, 220
Arpaillanage, Pierre, 102
Arrighi, Paul, on statutes of limitations, 88
Aschenbach, Ernst, Hagen and, 72
Ascherson, Neal: on Barbie trial, 19; disgust for "modern world," 10; radio interview of, 13–14
Assize Court (Lyon), 3–4, 13–15, 19, 24, 42, 46, 56, 59, 79; defence lawyer and, 119; evidence

Assize Court (Lyon) (*continued*)
   presentation, 121–2; indictment
   in Barbie trial, 131–2; jury in,
   118, 120, 129; jury selection, 120;
   Maier on Barbie trial, 171; power
   of president in, 120–1; pre-trial
   investigation of case, 269–70n26;
   reading of oath, 128–9; witnesses
   and oaths in, 118–19; workings of
   French, 117–18
Aubrac, Lucie, 230, 291n14; testimony
   of, 124, 289n15; Vergès defaming,
   112, 253
Aubrac, Raymond, 253; on Barbie,
   32; testimony of, 124–5, 186; Vergès
   defaming, 112; Vergès questioning,
   278n7
Aubrac Affair (1997), 27, 291n14
Auschwitz: children of Izieu, 191;
   Kadosche-Lagrange and, 162;
   Lischka, Hagen and Heinrichson
   knowing about, 77; trials, 61–4;
   Wiesel on, 167
Auschwitz-Birkenau, 74, 100
Aussaresses, Paul, French dealing with
   Algerian terrorists, 290n12
Azouvi, François, 88

Badinter, Robert, 98, 263; Eichmann
   trial and, 56; filming of Barbie trial, 7;
   Truche for Barbie prosecution, 200
Bal, Claude, 253; *Que la vérité est amère*,
   112
Bancel, Nicolas, 251
Banchard, Pascal, 251
"Baraque aux juifs" memorial,
   Montluc Prison, *236*
Barbie (Mérindol), 269n14
Barbie, Klaus: admiration for
   Israelis, 48, 49–50; "afterlives" of,
   24; announcement to not attend
   trial, 15, 25–6, 29; anti-Semitism

of, 48–50; arrest and return to
   France, 91–3; behaviour in court,
   29–30; brutality of, 84–5; as
   "Butcher of Lyon" label, 5, 33, 55;
   Cerdini describing crimes of, 4;
   characterization of, 9; choosing
   "Klaus Altmann" as identity, 49,
   119, 124, 129; chronology of,
   257–61; death of, 261; death of son,
   39; description of crimes by, 84;
   documents showing responsibility
   in Nazi hierarchy, 205–6; escape
   along "Rat Line" to South America,
   49, 80, 137, 260; extradition from
   Bolivia, 55–6, 93, 94, 126, 137;
   filming of trial, 7; interest in, 10; IQ
   test of, 39; Knab and, in 1952 trial,
   81, 82; Knochen as direct superior,
   209; linguistic manipulations of,
   61; living in Bolivia, 43, 44, 190,
   276–7n21; morality and, 46; as Nazi
   idealist, 30, 30–1, 45–50; Nazi SS
   and Gestapo experience, 45–6, 50;
   on number of victims, 126; painting
   self as victim, 136; on Palestinian-
   Israel conflict, 48–9; photograph
   of, *28*; protesting own trial, 137;
   psychoanalysis of, 37–45; refusing to
   testify, 59; role in Holocaust, 6; self-
   exoneration of, 137; trial in Lyon
   Assize Court, 3–5; trial of 1952, 185,
   201; trial of 1954, 82–4, 185, 201;
   Vergès on, 227, 234–5; witnesses,
   victims and others on, 31–6
Barbie trial, 22–3; Auschwitz trials
   and, 61–4; Barbie's behavior
   during testimony, 62; besmirching
   Nuremberg, 52–3; civil parties and
   lawyers, 125–6; closing arguments
   of civil parties lawyers, 188–98;
   closing arguments of prosecution,
   181, 199–209; co-counsel defence

closing statements, 219–26;
courtroom preparations, 116–17;
defence (Vergès) closing statement,
226–35; defence counsel, 117,
122–5; Eichmann trial and, 55–8,
60–1; instruction leading up to, 62,
63; International Military Tribunal
(IMT) and, 54–5; investigation
of case, 8; legacies of, 245–56;
Oberg-Knochen trial significance
for, 68–71; opening of, 111–27;
opening rituals and salvoes, 127–39;
performative dimension, 7–8;
psychoanalysing accused in, 37–45;
resources for, 7–8; role of Klarsfelds
in, 8, 23, 43; transcript of, 265–6;
Truche summation, 181, 199–209;
verdict of, 4, 237–45. *See also*
defence; trial witnesses
Bardèche, Maurice, *Nuremberg ou la
terre promise*, 12
Bartelmus, Erich; on brutality of
Barbie, 84–5; sentence of, 275n7;
trial of 1952, 82
Bastian, Gert: expert testimony of,
178–9; Vergès and, 179–80
Bauer, Fritz, Auschwitz trial
prosecutor, 61
Beaticle, Odette, witness to
Heinrichson's actions, 74
Begin, Menachim, 223
Believe and Destroy (Ingrao), 50
Benguigui, Fortunée, Izieu mother, 114
Ben Gurion, David, 20
Bénichou, Paul, 245
Berman, Charles, Mbemba on, 221
Berman, Gustave, negationist
materials of, 113
Best, Werner, on confession
strategies, 43
Beuve-Méry, Hubert, Frossard on,
165–6

Beyond Justice (Wittmann), 61, 64
Bilsky, Leora: on plurality of voices,
189; *Transformative Justice*, 20–1, 56
Binder, Guyora: on crimes against
humanity, 15, 16; on London
Agreement, 54
Black Book of Communism (1997), 27,
170, 252
Blardone, Mario, 12, 237; death of,
158; testimony of, 150–1, 156, 157,
284n6; Vergès and, 159–61, 175,
244, 265
Blume, Walter, case of, 43
Bolivia, 260; authorities, 95; Barbie's
role in 1980 coup, 47–8; extradition
of Barbie from, 55–6
Bouaïta, Nabil: closing statement of,
221–6; co-counsel to Vergès, 21,
123, 125, 166, 181, 215, 218, 267n3;
crimes against humanity, 240
Bouhared, Djamila, 288n1; Vergès
defending, 211, 286n17
Bourdon, Lucien, 231; trial of, 231
Bousquet, René, 73, 90, 133, 134, 247;
assassination of, 64; Oberg and, 66;
Vergès label for, 214; Vergès on, 122
Bower, Tom: on Cologne trial, 76;
on Hagen, 73; *Klaus Barbie*, 81; on
Lishka, 72
Boyer, Robert, for fair trial, 126
Brecht, Berthold, 37
Browning, Christopher, 272n19
Browning, Earl, on Barbie, 33
Bruckner, Pascal, 222; *Tears of the White
Man*, 289n8
Bruller, Jean, 106. *See also* Vercors
Brunner, Aloïs, deporting Jewish
children, 190
Butcher of Lyon, Barbie label, 5, 33, 55

Caldéron, Yolanda, on Barbie, 33
Calley, William, My Lai massacre and, 48

Camus, Albert, 8

CDJC. See *Centre de Documentation Juive Contemporaine* (CDJC)

Céline, Louis-Ferdinand, 230; Barbie and, 280n26

Central Justice Service, Streim, 173

Centre de Documentation Juive Contemporaine (CDJC), 229, 234

Cerdini, André, 263; on Barbie's age, 279n21; on Barbie's attendance in trial, 15, 16; calling witnesses to order, 157; describing Barbie's crimes against humanity, 4; French penal code and accused, 283–4n48; Kadosche-Lagrange and, 154; leading trial, 3–4, 19, 31, 44, 50, 111, 116–17, 127–30, 136–8; on photograph with associate judges, *110*; power of president in trial, 120–1; power to call witnesses, 145; questioning Holfort and Streim, 173; reading of oath, 128–9; verdict of jury, 4; Wiesel testimony and, 169

Césaire, Aimé, 166

Chaban-Delmas, Jacques, testimony of, 146

Chalandon, Sorj, 3; on crowd's reaction to Vergès, 5; on jury selection, 281n31; on Klarsfeld's closing argument, 189–90; on Vergès behavior, 161

Chapoutot, Johann, Nazism analysis, 47, 285n10

Charlie Hebdo (journal), 255; trial of, 255–6

Chelain, André, 13; as Holocaust denier, 12, 284n6; *Le procès Barbie, ou la Shoah-Business à Lyon* (*The Barbie Trial, or Shoah Business in Lyon*), 11–12

Chirac, Jacques, Aussaresses and, 290n12

Chmilenicky, Pinkus, Auschwitz and, 282n37

Chomsky, Noam, on Faurisson, 13

chronology, 257–61

CIC. See American Counter Intelligence Corps (CIC)

civil parties lawyers, closing arguments of, 188–98. See also closing arguments

Clair-Frémion, Irène, testimony of, 151–2, 277n23

Clor, Robert, testimony of, 157

closing arguments: civil parties lawyers, 188–98; defence co-counsel, 219–26; defence Vergès, 226–35; prosecutor Truche, 77, 181, 199–209, 242–5

Cochet, Georges, account of 1954 trial, 82–4

Cohen, Robert, Ravaz representing, 131

Cold War, 9, 69, 71

Cologne trial (1980), Lischka, Hagen and Heinrichson, 71–7

Comte, Gilbert, on statute of limitations, 90–1

conflation of sentences: argument by Vergès, 184–8; *confusion des peines*, 184, 185

confusion des peines: principle, 184, 185. See also conflation of sentences

Cordier, Daniel, 253

Coste-Floret, Paul, on war crimes, 86

Coty, René, 211; commuting Oberg and Knochen's sentences, 68; commuting of sentences, 83–4

Coulibaly, Amédy, 255

Court of Cassation (1980), decision on conflation of sentences, 188

Court of Cassation (1985), 14, 15, 21, 23, 25, 26, 52–4, 98; crimes against humanity, 215; decision of, 130, 201–2; decision of, and its impact, 102–8; Vergès arguing based on decision of, 185–6

Courtois, Stéphane, on Communist crimes, 252

Courvoisier, André, testimony of, 157

crimes against humanity, 141; Barbie's arrest and return to France, 91–3; Barbie trial, 253–4; bloated definition of, 64; case of Jean Leguay, 89, 90–1; defined by Allies, 147; Donnedieu de Vabres on, 201; French National Assembly (1964) on, 85; Frossard and, 163–7; global conception of, 239–40; international scope of, 188, 195; Jackson on definition of, 58; making imprescriptible, 85–9; Nuremberg definition, 101; Poliakov testimony, 170–1; Schwartz and, 172–3; Truche on, 200–1, 204; Vuillard on, 282n40; Wiesel's definition, 170

crimes against peace, 103

Croatian National Congress, 94

Croire et Détruire (Ingrao), 43

Cros, Jules, arrest and torture of, 99, 101

Dabringhaus, Erhard, witness, 145

Damned, The (Visconti), 38

Danion, Yves, witness at Barbie trial, 280n24

Dannecker, Theodore: aid to Heinrichson, 74–5; Lischka and, 75; on trip reports to camps, 76

Dark Years, 6, 69, 85, 233, 246

Darquier de Pellepoix, Louis, 134

Dean, Carolyn, The Fragility of Empathy after the Holocaust, 37

death marches, 108

de Bénouville, Pierre Gullain, Vergès defaming, 112

de Bigault du Granrut, Bernard, 125, 161; closing statement by, 194–6, 285n15, 287n6

Debray, Régis, 139; advisor to Mitterand, 11; defence witness, 124

de Brinon, Fernand, Lischka and, 75

de Castro, Alvaro, on Barbie, 35

Declaration of the Rights of Man and the Citizen, 289n11

Decourtray, Albert: on Barbie defence, 127, 230; Izieu ceremony, 114

defence: closing statement of co-counsels, 219–26; closing statement of Vergès, 226–35; Vergès for Barbie trial, 211–19; Vergès on role of lawyer for, 215–19. See also closing arguments

de Gaulle, Charles, 60; freeing Oberg and Knochen, 68, 86

de Gaulle-Anthonioz, Geneviève, 20, 60; Lesèvre memoir and, 152; Ravensbrück, 162; testimony of, 100, 146–7, 156–8, 193, 196, 285n12

Delarue, Jacques, testimony of, 177–8

De la stratégie judiciare (Vergès), 217–18, 238

de Launay, Jacques Forment, witness at Barbie trial, 196–7, 280n24

Delon, Alain, 238, 290n2

Delpech, Bertrand Poirot-, trial novel by, 11

Demjanuk, John, trial of, 7

De mon proper aveu (Vergès), 212–15, 219

Derrida, Jacques, essay on forgiveness, 275n10

Der Spiegel (magazine), 136
de Sainte Marie, Anne-Marie,
  testimony of, 230
Devaquet, Alain, Roques'
  committee, 114
Dimsdale, Joel, on psychologists at
  Nuremberg, 31
Doenitz, Karl, Nuremburg trial, 51
Doman, Nicholas R., on Barbie
  trial, 255
Donnedieu de Vabres, crimes against
  humanity, 201
Doublet, Maître, Oberg lawyer, 70
Douglas, Lawrence: on crimes against
  humanity, 53–4; *The Memory of
  Judgment*, 53
Douzon, Laurent, on anniversary of
  Barbie trial, 162–3
Douzon, Pierre, lessons of trial,
  270–1n35
Dubost, Charles, on crimes against
  humanity, 54
Duke of Enghien, 139, 283n46
Dumas, Roland, 223; Lesèvre's lawyer,
  178, 287n2
Duras, Marguerite: declining to
  appear, 130; *La Douleur*, 89, 123
Durkheim, Émile, 240

Eden, Anthony, in Suez crisis, 48
Eichmann, Adolph, 30, 43; acting
  on orders from, 95; Arendt
  on demonizing, 36; Arendt's
  description of, 180; Barbie and,
  208; comparing Barbie trial to,
  55–8, 60–1; as a desk killer, 64; trial
  of, 6, 7, 18, 22, 25, 29, 51,
  141, 272n15; Vergès on trial
  of, 217
Eichmann in Jerusalem (Arendt), 9, 12,
  20, 36, 144, 229
Einsatzcommando, function of, 43

Epuration, trials occurring during,
  65–6, 69
Era of the Witness, The (Wieviorka), 141
expert testimony, 141; Bastian, 178–9;
  Delarue, 177–8; Holfort, 173–6;
  Lainé, 177; Streim, 173–6; validity
  of evidence, 173–80. *See also* trial
  witnesses

Face à Barbie (Lesèvre), 152
Fastré, Jacques, witness at Barbie trial,
  280n24
Faure, Edgar, on telex by Barbie,
  206–7
Faurisson, Robert: Bouaïta on,
  222; negationist, 12–13; Roques'
  committee, 114; theses of, 113
Favet, Julien: testimony of, 204; Vergès
  on testimony of, 231, 232–3
Feder, Alain, Frossard and, 165
Federal Republic of Germany, 9, 86,
  92, 93, 132, 136, 176, 243
Fest, Joachim, Arendt and, 36
Final Solution, 43, 53; Hitler's, 144;
  Nazi, 6, 55, 246
Finkielkraut, Alain: on Barbie's trial,
  16–17, 52–3, 169, 222; on defence
  arguments, 239; *La mémoire vaine
  (Remembering in Vain)*, 16, 17, 53;
  Nazism and Nazi crimes, 21–2; on
  Noguères, 225–6
Flicoteaux, Commandant, specificity
  of Nazi crimes, 71
Floreck, Ernest, on brutality of
  Barbie, 84
Fourcade, Marie-Madeleine: Bouaïta
  on, 222; witness, 147–8
Fourth Reich, Andes, 47
*Fragility of Empathy after the Holocaust,
  The* (Dean), 37
France Inter (radio), 115; Wiesel
  interview, 168, 169

Frankfurter, Felix, Karski and, 150
French Communist Party, 11
French Delegation, Occupied Paris, 75
French Huguenots, 39
French National Assembly, 23, 25; on crimes against humanity, 85–7
French occupation, shaping Barbie's political outlook, 34–5
French Penal Code, 125, 135; Article Five of, 184, 185; authority over accused, 283–4n48; response after closing argument, 285n15
French Resistance. *See* Resistance
Freud, anal phase of human development, 41
Front de Libération Nationale (FLN), 113, 126, 166, 213, 288n1
Frossard, André: Beuve-Méry and, 165–6; definition of crimes against humanity, 164; Feder's questioning of, 165; Gompel and, 163–4; Mbemba on, 221; testimony of, 151, 163–7, 170, 171, 191, 195, 205; Vergès and, 166–7, 219, 286n17

Garapon, Antoine, 123, 255
Garçon, Maurice, on statute of limitations, 88
Gayssot Law (1990), 254
Geissmann, Raymond, 93; on Barbie, 273n4; Klarsfelds and, 93; testimony of, 57, 229
Genet, Jean, on Vergès defending Barbie, 113
genocide, 254; Rwandan, 256
Genoud, François, 211; on Vergès fees, 126–7
German Occupation of France, 3
Gestapo and SS, on Barbie in, 31–2, 45–50
Gestapo Memoir, 35
Gide, André, 8

Girard, René, on violence, 240–1
Goering, Hermann, 30, 209; Nuremburg trial, 51; testimony of, 59
Gompel, Marcel: *Collège de France*, 108; Frossard and, 163–4; torture and death of, 108
Gompel, Sophie, 163
Gonin, Daniel: analysis of Barbie, 39, 41, 42; on predilection for "cat and mouse games," 97
Gourion, Alain, on hypocrisy of defence, 196
Great War, 39
Groupement d'intervention de la police nationale (GIPN), 112
Gudefin, Francine: testimony of, 150, 197; Vergès and, 158
Guevara, Ché, 11, 124
Guiochon, Paul, witness at Barbie trial, 280n24
Gustmann, Wolfgang, on Barbie, 31
Guyon-Belot, Raymonde, testimony of, 157, 180

Hagen, Herbert, 25, 94, 176, 274n14; Cologne trial of, 51, 71–2, 73–4, 76–7; sentences for, 274nn20–1
Hague Convention (1907), 67
Halaunbrenner, Ita, Izieu mother, 114, 207
Halter, Marek, sculptor of monument, 115
Haltoz, Guy, death of, 202
Hamlet (Shakespeare), 14
Hammerschmidt, Peter: Barbie's brutality, 45; Barbie's extradition from Bolivia, 55–6; biographer of Barbie, 34; *Klaus Barbie*, 9
Hardy, René: death of, 112; Garçon on, 88; Moulin's betrayer, 35; second trial of, 80–1

Harrower, Molly, on analysis of Nazi
leaders, 38
Hausner, Gideon, 57; on anti-
Semitism, 56; screening witnesses,
144, 145; on six million accusers
without voices, 57, 60; trial's
meaning and significance, 20
Heinrichson, Ernst, 25, 94, 176;
Cologne trial of, 52, 71–2, 74–5,
76–7; Dannecker as aid to, 74–5;
sentences for, 274nn20–1
Herrenschmidt, Noëlle, 123, 255
Hewitt, Leah, 253
Heydrich, Reinhard, 43, 66;
assassination of, 68; Oberg and, 66
Hiding in Plain Sight (Stover, Perskin
and Koenig), 71
Himmler, Heinrich, 66, 209, 271n3;
decency and, 272n24; morality
and, 46
Hitler, Adolf, 209; Berlin Olympics
(1936), 221; Final Solution, 6, 144;
Hitler Youth, 37; loyalty to, 47;
Nazism and, 37; Third Reich,
20, 179
Hofmeyer, Hans, on Auschwitz trial, 62
Holfort, Rodolf, expert testimony of,
173–6
Holocaust, 11, 17, 55; Barbie's role
in, 6; denialism in France, 12, 13;
denying of, 113–14; Nazi crimes
during, 71; presentation of, 15–16;
uniqueness of, 286n23; victims of,
193; Wiesel on, 167–8
Holocaust Memorial Museum, 281n31
Holtzman, Elizabeth, on Nazi war
criminals, 10
homosexual, psychological condition
of, 37–8
homosexuality, 38
Hôtel Terminus (film), 9, 24, 29, 30,
31–3, 40, 47, 153

humanism, 21, 245
Hunting the Truth (Klarsfeld), 91, 122,
267n5
Hussein, Saddam, Vergès consulting,
211

Iannucci, Ugo, 281n33; closing
statement of, 197; on defence
arguments, 224, 226; on Vergès
argument, 187–8
ideological hegemony, 15
Indictments Chamber of the Lyon
Court of Appeals, 131
Ingrao, Christian: Believe and Destroy,
50; Croire et Détruire, 43
instruction: crimes against humanity
adjustments in 1964 law, 85–93;
impact of 1985 Paris Court
of Cassation decision, 102–8;
investigation commences in 1983,
93–8; investigation phase of Barbie
case, 79–80; last convoy of August
1944, 96, 100, 108–9, 208; legal
developments (1983–5), 98–102;
trials of 1952 and 1954, 80–5;
Vergès on last convoy (1944), 230;
victims and witnesses during, 96–8
International Association of Jurists, 86
International Criminal Tribunal for
the former Yugoslavia, 18
International Military Tribunal
(IMT), 51–3, 273n25; Barbie trial
and, 54–5; Jackson as justice on, 58;
Nuremberg, 55, 99
Israeli League of the Rights of Man,
223, 280n26
Izieu: Auschwitz and children of,
191; authenticity of telex, 132, 152,
173–4, 197, 207–8; commemoration
day, 114–15; deportation of Jewish
children of, 48–9, 57, 99, 114–15,
121, 168, 192, 204, 206; Faurisson's

theses to citizens of, 113; Klarsfeld
on children of, 190; round-up at,
36, 147–8, 172; telegram, 78; Vergès
on chronological order of round-
up, 227; Vergès on round-up of
children, 230–1; Vergès on telex of,
233–4; Zlatin as director of
school, 107

Jackson, Robert H., 274n6; on
function of Nuremberg Tribunal,
58–9; legacy of Nuremburg, 58;
on meaning of crimes against
humanity, 58; testimony of key
defendants, 59
Jacob, Gilberte, 226
Jakubowicz, Alain: closing statement
of, 193, 196, 198; on hypocrisy of
defence, 196; on memory of victims,
57, 60; on Vergès argument, 187–8
Jankélévitch, Vladimir, 8; on anti-
Semitism, 49; on law on crimes
against humanity, 87–8
Japanese war criminals, 9, 201
Jeunes Arabes de Lyon, 114
Jewish Question, Final Solution of,
6, 55
Jews and Resistance fighters and, 4, 5,
15; last convoy of August 1944, 96,
100, 108–9
Joan of Arc Day, 111
John Paul II (Pope), 164
Justice in Lyon (Golsan), 5–6, 19, 24

Kadosche-Lagrange, Simone, 32, 237;
Auschwitz, 162; Barbie striking,
191; confronting Barbie, 97–8;
Jakubowicz on Jewish victims, 193;
photograph of, 143; testimony
of, 60, 146, 153–5, 285nn10–11,
285nn13–14; Vergès and, 160–1,
175, 244, 265

Kaduk, Oswald, Miller on courtroom
behavior of, 62–3
Kahn, Annette: on Blardone, 158;
memoir of the trial, 151
Kansas City Police Department, 38
Kaplon, Srul, testimony of, 284n7
Karski, Jan, testimony to American
leaders, 149–50
Kelley, Douglas, on Nuremberg
tribunal, 38
Kelly, Grace, Kroskof-Thomas and, 148
Khomeini, Ayatollah, 193
Klarsfeld, Arno, Touvier trial and, 248
Klarsfeld, Beate, 8, 43; on existence of
telex, 207; Hunting the Truth, 91–2;
on Nazi war criminals, 92; tracking
Barbie, 93
Klarsfeld, Serge, 8, 43, 139, 211, 229,
237, 246, 263, 290n17; closing
argument by, 155, 189–92, 194;
debate with Noguères and Vercors,
168; on decision of Court of
Cassation, 104–7; Hunting the Truth,
91, 122; Kadosche-Lagrange and,
98; on Leguay, 90–1; on Lishka, 72;
locating original telex, 121–2; on
Nazi war criminals, 92; on Oberg
and Knochen's death sentence,
68; photograph of, 182; Rousso
and, 279n22; tracking Barbie, 93;
on Truche and Vergès, 245; Vergès
and, 115–16, 122, 133, 134
Klaus Barbie (Bower), 81
Klaus Barbie (Hammerschmidt), 9
Knab, Werner: Barbie and, 136;
Barbie and, in 1952 trial, 81, 82;
sentence of, 275n7
Knochen, Helmut, 25; Barbie's direct
superior, 209; death sentence, 68;
de Gaulle release of, 86; as desk
killer, 68; Hagen and, 73, 74; telex
from Barbie, 205; trial of, 61, 65–71

Koenig, Alexa, 71
Kolb, Eugene, on Barbie, 33
Korman, Charles, on Barbie as proud
    soldier of Reich, 198
Kouachi brothers, *Charlie Hebdo*
    (journal), 255
Kovner, Abba, testimony of, 60
Kroskof-Thomas, Michel: testimony
    of, 196, 204, 205, 284n4; Vergès
    and, 158; Vergès on, 229–30;
    witness, 148–9
K-Zetnik, testimony of, 60, 144

Lacombe Lucien (Malle's film), 38,
    89–90, 214
La Douleur (Duras), 89, 123
Lafforgue, François, Riss and, 94, 98
Lainé, Tony, testimony of, 177, 204
Lakhdar-Toumi, Eddine, witness at
    Barbie trial, 280n24
La Maison des otages (Frossard), 164
La malade imaginaire (Molière), 41
La mémoire vaine (Finkielkraut), 16,
    17, 18
Lanfranchi, Fortuné, testimony of, 156
Langer, Walter, 37
Lanzmann, Claude, *Shoah*, 221
La Phuong, François, protesting
    defence closing statement,
    224–6
Lapin Blanc, Barbie frequenting, 32
Larat, Bruno, 130
Laval, Pierre, 65, 73, 90
Lévy, Alain, 226, 264, 287n5; on
    Barbie's trial absence, 20
Lévy, Jean-Paul, Barbie and, 280n26
League of the Rights of Man, 223,
    280n26
Le Chagrin et la pitié (Ophuls), 89
Ledoux, Sébastien, on Court of
    Cassation, 102–3

Ledoux, Stéphane, 291n14
Legalism (Shklar), 18
Leguay, Jean, 133, 134, 191; case of,
    89, 90–1; death of, 192
Leguay Affair, 276n18
Le Monde (newspaper), 66–70, 90–1,
    104–6, 108, 112–13, 115–17, 141,
    165, 252
Lenoir, Anne-Marie de Sainte-Marie,
    witness, 96
Léotard, François, moment of truth
    for French, 115
Le Pen, Jean-Marie, 13, 115
Le Phuong, François, civil parties
    lawyers, 281nn32–3
*Le procès Barbie, ou la Shoah-Business à
    Lyon* (Chelain), 11–12
Leroy-Ladurie, Emmanuel, on Barbie'
    conviction, 5
Le salaud lumineux ("The Luminous
    Bastard") (Vergès), 11, 44, 227,
    278n2, 280n27, 289n6
Lesèvre, George, 108
Lesèvre, Jean-Pierre, 108
Lesèvre, Lise: on Barbie, 32;
    death of husband and son, 108;
    Dumas as lawyer, 178, 287n2;
    Nordmann for, 197–8; photograph
    of, *142*; testimony of, 60, 116,
    146, 193, 196, 284–5n9;
    torture of, 203
Les Exécuteurs (Welzer), 38
Levi, Primo, 244; suicide of, 112
Levrat, Christaine, Barbie trial juror,
    281n30
Lévy, Alain: on Barbie trial, 138;
    closing argument, 6
Lévy-Willard, Annette, 246
L'Express (magazine), 79
L'Extrémiste (Péan), 126–7
Libération (newspaper), 3, 253

Libman, Charles: Barbie as "Klaus
Altmann," 119, 129; on Izieu
children, 135
Linklater, Magnus: Barbie and
telegrams from Himmler, 66; *The
Nazi Legacy*, 47
Lischka, Kurt, 25, 94, 176; Cologne
trial of, 51, 71–3, 75–7; Oberg
and Dannecker, 75; sentences for,
274nn20–1
Lombard, Paul: on Barbie as proud
soldier of Reich, 198; civil parties
lawyers, 281nn32–3
London Agreement, Binder on, 54
Ludolph, Manfred, on Barbie
investigation, 93
Lyon: *Chambre d'accusation*, 101, 102;
Court of Appeals and Ogier,
271n41; last convoy of 11 August
1944, 96, 100, 108–9; opening of
Barbie trial, 111–12. *See also* Assize
Court (Lyon)

Macdonald, Kevin, *Mon meilleur ennemi*
(film), 10, 29, 30, 33–5
Macias, Enrico, Bouaïta on, 222
Macron, Emmanuel, opening court
records, 7
Maier, Charles S., on Holocaust, 171
Malle, Louis, *Lacombe Lucien* (film),
38, 89–90, 214
Mann, Thomas, "Brother Hitler," 37
Mao Zedong, 216
Marrus, Michael, on Oberg/Bousquet
agreements, 66
Mattogno, Carlo, Holocaust denier, 113
Mauroy, Pierre, on trial informing
French, 115
Mbemba, Jean-Martin: co-counsel
to Vergès, 21, 123, 125, 166, 181,
196, 215, 218; closing statement of,

219–26, 288n2; on fanaticism,
289n7; memoir of Barbie trial,
288–9n5
Mechachera Law, 254
Mémoires de Justice (Zaoui,
Herrenschmidt, and
Garapon), 123
Mémorial de la Shoah, 7, 12, 264
Memory of Judgment (Douglas), 53
Meridian (BBC radio program), 13
Mérindol, Pierre: on Barbie's attitude,
127–8; on Barbie trial, 10; on
Barbie's victims, 126; on defence
closing, 224, 228; Paris Court of
Cassation (1985) decision, 277n26;
on Truche's role, 199, 201, 203;
true opening of trial, 129; on
Vergès and Truche in trial, 283n42;
on witnesses called, 130
Messner, Ute: Barbie's daughter, 33,
63; Genoud and, 126
Meunier, Pierre, 281n33
Miller, Arthur: on Auschwitz trial, 62;
describing defendant Kaduk, 62–3;
on German people and Auschwitz,
89; on German spectators at
Auschwitz trial, 63
Miller, Judith, 20; *One, by One, by One*, 16
Milosevic, Slobodan, Vergès
defending, 211
Minn, Peter, 31
Mitterrand, François, 139; Barbie's
extradition from Bolivia, 55–6;
Bousquet and, 247; Debray
advising, 11; Papon and, 249;
Vergès label for, 214
Mon meilleur ennemi (film), 10, 24, 29,
30, 33–5
Monsieur Barbie n'a rien à dire ("Mister
Barbie Has Nothing to Say")
(Poirot-Delpech), 11

Montluc Prison, *28*, 79, 84, 96, 108–9, 151, 154, 204, 230; memorial of "Baraque aux juifs," *236*

morality, Barbie on absolute, 46

Morgan, Ted, trial as necessary travesty, 60

Morgan, Tom, *An Uncertain Hour*, 8

Moulin, Jean, 27; arrest of, 130, 259; Barbie claim on, 271n5; Barbie comparing self to, 45–6; Barbie victim, 35; betrayal of, 124, 253; ceremony of transferring ashes of, 86; death of, 259; Frossard on, 165; martyrdom of, 112; Oberg on death of, 67; Resistance hero, 6; torture of, 107, 139, 193; wife of, on Barbie, 52

Murillo, Mirna, on Barbie, 33

My Lai massacre, 48, 169, 222

Nahmias, Elie, confronting Barbie, 96–7

Nantua, village of, 278n10

National Front, 251; Le Pen's, 13

national sovereignty, Nuremberg as protecting principle of, 53

Nazi crimes: Final Solution, 6, 246; French complicity in, 89; specificity of, 71; last convoy of August 1944 to, 96, 100, 108–9

Nazi idealism, Barbie's, 30–1, 45–50

Nazi ideology, 15, 24; Barbie and, 40

Nazi Legacy, The (Linklater), 47

Nazism, 6, 8, 24, 29, 35, 44; Barbie and, 44–5; Barbie's, 45–50, 48; crimes of, 89; Hitler and, 37; inequality of races, 45–6; Mbemba describing advent of, 220; Schwartz on, 172; victims of, 140, 193; Wiesel on, 167; witnesses speaking of, 147

negationism, 13, 17, 113, 254

New York Bar Association, 58, 274n6

New York Times (newspaper), 62

Night Porter, The (Wertmuller), 38

Noguères, Henri: debate with Klarsfeld and Vercors, 168; denouncing Vergès, 193–4; Finkielkraut on, 225–6; on hypocrisy of defence, 196; Klarsfeld and Court of Cassation's decision, 105–7, 108; on sparing court "certain lies," 138; term "innocents," 105

Nolte, Ernst, on Holocaust, 171

non-accumulation of sentences, 287n1

Nora, Pierre, Barbie trial as place of memory, 6

Nordmann, Joe, closing argument of, 197–8

Nouvel Observateur (magazine), 88

Nuremberg, 6, 7, 12, 18; Barbie's disdain for, 48; Blume case at, 43; Charter, 106; International Tribunal, 99; Jackson on function of tribunal, 58–9; Jackson on legacy of, 58; legal and historical legacies of, 52; principle of national sovereignty, 53; restrictive judicial moor of, 53; specialists on trials, 37; tribunals, 200–1

Nuremberg ou la terre promise (Bardèche), 12

Oberg, Karl, 25; Barbie and, 247; Bousquet as star witness, 67–8; death sentence, 68; de Gaulle release of, 86; as desk killer, 68; Hagen and, 73, 74; Lischka and, 75; trial of, 65–71

Oberg/Bousquet accords of 1942, 66, 67

Occupied Lyon, 23–4, 45, 265

October Revolution, 252

Oedipus the King (Sophocles), 241

Ogier, Hubert, crimes against humanity, 271n41, 277n26

Ogre, The (Tournier), 38
One, by One, by One (Miller), 16
Operation Spring Wind, 66
Ophuls, Marcel, 9, 29; *Hôtel Terminus,* 9, 29, 30, 31–3, 40, 153; *Le Chagrin et la pitié,* 89
Ordinary Men (Browning), 272n19
Origins of Totalitarianism, The (Arendt), 220
Ory, Pascal, 38
Otten, Johann, on Barbie, 31, 40
Oullins round-up, 100–1
Owens, Jesse, Hitler and, 221

Palais de Justice, 3–5, 13, 14, 90, 111, 116, 127
Palestinian-Israel conflict, 48, 49
Palk, Ferdinance, on Barbie, 32, 35
Panthéon, 158; Moulin's ashes to, 86; Moulin's remains interred in, 6
Papon, Maurice, 191, 247; prosecution of, 58; trial of, 6, 7, 27, 64, 86, 102, 192, 249–52, 255, 269n25
Paris Court of Appeals, 104, 131, 248
Paxton, Robert, on Oberg/Bousquet agreements, 66
Péan, Pierre, 126
Pétain, Philippe, 65, 158
pedophilia, 37, 38
Penthouse (magazine), 215
Permanent Military Tribunal: Armed Forces of Lyon, 133; Lyon (1952 and 1954), 80–5
Perraud, Antoine, on Truche and Vergès, 238
Perskin, Victor, 71
Perticoz, Eusèbe, 232
Poirot-Delpech, Bertrand, trial novel by, 11
Poliakov, Léon, testimony of, 170–1
Pol Pot, 193, 211

Pompidou, Georges, 247
prosecution, closing arguments of, 181, 199–209. *See also* closing arguments; trial witnesses; Truche, Pierre
Purge, first or original, 65

Que la vérité est amère (film), 112, 253

Rabl, Wolfgang, on retrying Nazi criminals, 92
Rappaport, Roland, 290n17; closing argument of, 192–3; Court of Cassation decision, 107–8; on Nazi oppression, 172; questioning Streim, 175
Rat Line, Barbie's escape along, 49, 80, 137, 260
Ravaz, Bruno, representing Cohen, 131
Ravensbrück: Clair-Frémion on, 151–2; de Gaulle-Anthonioz, 162; horror at, 100; Lesèvre on, 152–3; Resistance victims at, 192
Reid, Donald, 291n14
Remembering in Vain (Finkielkraut), 16, 17, 18, 53
Remilleux, Jean-Louis, Vergès and *Le salaud lumineux,* 44
Resistance, 4, 5, 11, 15, 27; Court of Cassation on, 103–4; crimes against members of, 14, 102–8; French, 55; Jews and, 4, 5, 15; Vergès on, 10; as victims, 108–9
Riss, Christian, 263; Barbie invoking Eichmann trial to, 57; Clair-Frémion and, 277n23; Cologne trial of 1980, 52, 76; Court of Cassation and, 103–4, 108; final arraignment of Barbie, 100–2; instruction of Barbie case, 89, 94–5; Lafforgue and, 98; magistrate, 7–8, 23, 25; photocopy of Izieu telex, 175; pre-trial questioning of witnesses, 145

Ritzler, Barry: on lack of empathy, 46; Rorschach tests at Nuremberg, 38–9

Rivière, Jean-Claude, 114

Robert H. Jackson Center, 274nn6–7

Rocard, Michel, French detention camp report, 169

Roosevelt, Franklin D., Karski and, 150

Roques, Henry, negationist themes, 114

Rorschach tests, Nuremberg tribunal and, 38–9, 46

Rossinot, André, on trial's meaning, 115

Rousso, Henry: on disallowance of copy of telex, 121; Klarsfeld and, 279n22; on Oberg-Knochen trial, 69–70; The Vichy Syndrome, 68, 85, 89–90, 235, 246

Rumsfeld, Donald, Vergès label for, 214

Rwandan genocide, 256

Ryan, Allan, on shielding Barbie, 9

sadism, 38

Salan, Georges, Barbie and, 280n26

Salas, Denis, 293

Sánchez-Salazar, Gustavo, witness, 145

Schendel, Kurt, Klarsfelds and, 92

Schneider-Merck, Johannes: on Barbie, 33; on Barbie's Nazism, 47

Schwartz, Laurent, testimony of, 172–3

Second Purge, Nazis and French collaborators, 64

Semprun, Jorge, 285n12

Serbat, Guy, witness, 147

Servette, Alain de la: as Barbie's defence counsel, 126, 280–1n27; Cochet and, 83; lawyer for Barbie, 100; war crimes, 101

sexual perversion, Nazism and, 38

Sharon, Ariel, 223

Shklar, Judith, Legalism, 18

Shoah (film), 221

Shoah Business, 11

Silence of the Sea, The (Vercors), 106

Simbikangwa, Pascal, 256

Simpson, O.J., 14

Six, Franz: function of Einsantzcommando, 43; on liberation of Knochen, 68

SNCF, 100, 101

Sontag, Susan, Eichmann trial, 141

Sophocles' Antigone, 217–18; Oedipus the King, 241

Souchal, Roger, response to Barbie, 283n45

South America, 268n9

Speer, Albert, 272n17; Vergès label for, 214

Spire, Antoine, 232, 290n17

Splendors and Miseries of the Courtesans (Balzac), 214

Stangneth, Bettina, on Barbie and Eichmann, 36

Story of a Secret State (Karski), 149–50

Stourdzé, Marcel, testimony of, 155–6

Stover, Eric, 71

Strasser, Otto, 37

Streicher, Julius, Nuremburg trial, 51

Streim, Alfred, expert testimony of, 173–6

Streisand, Barbra, Kroskof-Thomas and, 148

Suez crisis, Eden in, 48

Sulieman, Susan, 253

Szafran, Maurice, on Truche, 200

Taubira Law, 254

Taylor, Robert, Barbie as Nazi idealist, 30, 33, 47, 273n26

Théolleyre, Jean-Marc: Barbie's
    departure from trial, 137; on
    Knochen-Oberg trial, 66–7, 69;
    testimony of, 162; trial as Barbie's
    last act of war, 116; on trial
    witnesses, 141
Third Reich, 20, 179
Third World, 17, 22, 193, 212, 227
Thousand Year Reich, idea of, 47
Tillion, Germaine, Panthéon and, 158
Time (magazine), 148
Tixier-Vignancourt, Jean-Louis,
    Barbie and, 280n26
Todorov, Tzvetan, on Barbie's
    trial, 18
Tournier, Michel, *The Ogre*, 38
Touvier, Paul, 6, 247; alias "Paul
    Lacroix," 247; crimes against
    humanity, 247; prosecution of, 58;
    trial of, 6, 7, 27, 64, 102, 192, 248–9,
    255, 269n25
Transformative Justice (Bilsky), 20–1, 56
trial witnesses: Blardone, 150–1, 156,
    157, 159–61; Chaban-Delmas, 146;
    Clair-Frémion, 151–2; Clor, 157;
    Courvoisie, 157; Dabringhaus, 145;
    de Gaulle-Anthonioz, 146–7, 156–8;
    Fourcade, 147–8; Frossard, 151;
    Gudefin, 150, 158; Guyon-Belot,
    157, 180; Kadosche-Lagrange, *143*,
    153–5, 160–1; Kroskof-Thomas,
    148–9; Lanfranchi, 156; Lesèvre,
    142, 152–3; Sánchez-Salazar, 145;
    Serbat, 147; Stourdzé, 155–6;
    Tillion, 158; Vaillant-Couturier, 145,
    156; Vitte-Léger, 153; Zlatin, 155,
    156, 158–9
Tribunal Permanent des Forces Armées, 82
Truche, Pierre, 13, 113, 211;
    addressing jury, 118; on Barbie
    motivations, 41–3, 50; on Barbie's

name, 129–30; coping with
    witnesses, 157; defence by diversion,
    139; describing witnesses, 146–7;
    on extenuating circumstances, 209;
    opposition to resister inclusion,
    285n16; photograph of, *183*;
    prosecutor, 14, 21, 26–7, 113;
    strength of arguments, 135–6; trial
    summation, 77, 181, 199–209,
    242–5, 270n28; on trial witnesses,
    140; on Vergès argument on
    "conflation of sentences," 185–7; on
    Vergès arguments, 282n41, 283n42

Uncertain Hour, An (Morgan), 8
Uncompromising Generation, An
    (Wildt), 50
Union Générale des Israélites de
    France (UGIF), 4, 57, 92–3, 95,
    99, 146, 147–8, 149, 172, 204–5,
    228–9
United States, Central Intelligence
    Agency (CIA), 47
United States Holocaust Memorial
    Museum, 7, 263
University of Colorado Law Review, 255
Un Salaud lumineux (Vergès), 231

Vaillant-Couturier, Marie-Claude:
    testimony of, 100, 156, 193, 196;
    witness, 145, 146
Vansteenberghe, Alice Joly: testimony
    of, 202, 230; witness, 96, 288n15
Védrinne, Jacques, analysis of Barbie,
    39, 40
Vel d'Hiv roundup, 90, 91
Vercors: debate with Klarsfeld and
    Noguères, 168; decision of Court of
    Cassation, 106–7; *The Silence of the
    Sea*, 106
verdict, Barbie trial, 237–45

Vergès, Jacques, 181; autobiography *De mon proper aveu*, 212–15, 219; background and upbringing, 212–13; Barbie's lawyer, 4–5, 26–7; Blardone and, 159–61; case for double jeopardy, 132, 134–5; closing statement for defence, 226–35; closing statements of co-counsel, 219–26; conflation of sentences argument, 184–8; conviction for character defamation, 112–13; defence strategies, 23, 39, 41, 44, 56–7, 127, 271–2n10; denouncing French nation, 133; denouncing Lévy, 138–9; description of client, 9; difficult straits by witness testimony, 181, 184; Frossard and, 166–7; Gudefin and, 158; interview, 11; Kadosche-Lagrange and, 160–1; Klarsfeld and, 115–16, 122; Kroskof-Thomas and, 158; literary affectations of, 278n7; on *Monsieurs les donneurs d'ordre* (gentlemen who give the orders), 214–15; on Nazi crimes, 17; photograph of, *210*; pleading case, 14; reputation of, 211–13; on Resistance, 10; on role of defence lawyer, 215–19; on Sophocles' *Antigone*, 217–18; trial as legal lynching, 115–16; trial by rupture, 22, 169–70, 217–19, 272n18; on trial of Adolph Eichmann, 217; Wiesel and, 168–70; Zlatin and, 158–9

Vichy Syndrome, The (Rousso), 68, 85, 89, 246

Vidal-Naquet, Pierre, 229; on Faurisson, 13; on Papon, 251

Vietnam: Americans in, 48, 54; My Lai massacre, 48, 169, 222

Visconti, Lucino, *The Damned*, 38

Vitte-Léger, Ennatt, testimony of, 153

Vuillard, Paul: closing argument of, 189; on crimes against humanity, 282n40; on double jeopardy, 134; on Vergès argument, 186

war crimes, defining, 103

Washington Post (newspaper), 76

Weber, Didier, analysis of Barbie, 39, 40–1

Welzer, Gérard, civil parties lawyer, 184

Welzer, Harald, *Les Exécuteurs*, 38, 272n23

Wertmuller, Lina, *The Night Porter*, 38

Wiesel, Elie: on Holocaust, 167–8; Nobel Peace Prize laureate, 146; testimony of, 167–70, 170, 171, 195; Vergès and, 168–70, 219, 243, 286n20

Wieviorka, Annette: on era of the witness, 60; *The Era of the Witness*, 141

Wildt, Michael: Nazi Generation, 273n31; *An Uncompromising Generation*, 50

Wilson, Robert: Bolivian interview, 47–8; on lack of empathy, 46

witnesses, 140–1; on Barbie, 31–6; experts validating evidence, 173–80; testimonies of key, on war crimes and crimes against humanity, 163–73; those encountering accused directly, 141, 144–63. *See also* crimes against humanity; expert testimony; trial witnesses

Wittmann, Rebecca, *Beyond Justice*, 61, 64

Woods, Damon, on defence lawyer in Assize court, 119

World War I, 34, 50, 70

World War II, 3, 13, 31, 39, 48, 50, 52, 86; crimes against the Resistance, 215; crimes by Resistance during, 70

Yad Veshem museum, 115

Yale Law Review, 15

Zaoui, Michel, 123, 255; on Barbie trial, 169–70; closing statement of, 196–8; on fate of Izieu children, 287n7; protesting Bouaïta closing statement, 223–4, 226; on Vergès' defence, 239

Zlatin, Sabine, 107; closing statement by, 155; testimony of, 155, 156, 158–9

Marga Minco (Sara Menco)
1) Bitter herbs
2) An empty house
3) The other side
4) The address

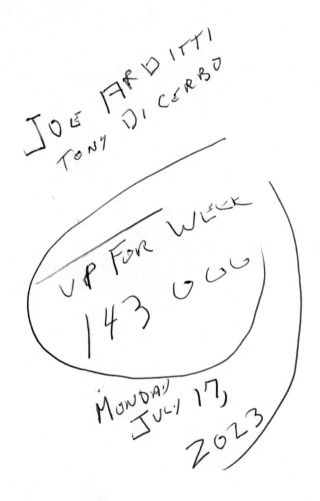

JOE ARDITTI
TONY DI CERBO

UP FOR WEEK
143 000

MONDAY
JULY 17,
2023